CINEMA CIVIL RIGHTS

CINEMA
CIVIL RIGHTS

Regulation, Repression, and Race in the Classical Hollywood Era

ELLEN C. SCOTT

RUTGERS UNIVERSITY PRESS
New Brunswick, New Jersey and London

Library of Congress Cataloging-in-Publication Data
Scott, Ellen C., 1978–
   Cinema civil rights : regulation, repression, and race in the classical Hollywood era /
Ellen C. Scott.
      pages   cm
   Includes bibliographical references and index.
   ISBN 978–0–8135–7136–2 (hardcover : alk. paper) — ISBN 978–0–8135–7135–5
(pbk. : alk. paper) — ISBN 978–0–8135–7137–9 (e-book)
   1. African Americans in motion pictures.   2. Racism in motion pictures.
3. Stereotypes (Social psychology) in motion pictures.   4. African Americans
in the motion picture industry x History—20th century.   5. African American
political activists—History—20th century.   6. African Americans—Civil rights—
History—20th century.   7. Motion pictures—United States—History—20th
century.   8. Motion picture industry—United States—History—20th century.
9. Motion pictures—Censorship—United States—History—20th century.   I. Title.
   PN1995.9.N4S35 2014
   791.43'652996073—dc23
   2014014281

A British Cataloging-in-Publication record for this book is available from the
British Library.

Visit our website: http://rutgerspress.rutgers.edu

Manufactured in the United States of America

This book is dedicated to my grandmother,
Rachel Evangeline Scott
(May 23, 1933–December 1, 2012)

CONTENTS

ACKNOWLEDGMENTS

Writing a book is supposed to be a lonely, solitary proposition. But everything about this process has convinced me that the very best things happen only when people work together. My gratitude goes to Gaylyn Studlar, for her brilliant early direction of this project, and to Matthew Bernstein, Matthew Countryman, and Catherine Benamou, for their supportive and nuanced readings and advice. I was supported, as well, by a really wonderful community of scholars at the University of Michigan, for which I am very thankful. I would also like to thank the Mellon and Ford Foundations for generous pre- and post-doctoral support, the PSC CUNY Research Foundation, and Leslie Mitchner of Rutgers University Press for seeing promise in this project.

Archives and their enthusiastic staffs were vital to this project. I am so grateful to everyone at the Academy of Motion Picture Arts and Sciences, especially Barbara Hall, Val Almendarez, Jenny Romero, Kristine Krueger, and Janet Lorenz for inspiration, friendship, direction and, occasionally, housing. I also would like to thank the staff members at the state archives of Maryland, Ohio, and Virginia, especially William Markley at the Ohio Historical Society and Joanne Porter, a gifted archivist at the Virginia State Archives, who went out of her way to give me support and aid my research. Many thanks also to Jonathon Auxier at the Warner Bros. Archive, Ned Comstock at the University of Southern California, and Mark Quigley at UCLA, as well as Zoran Sinobad at the Library of Congress and Bill Gorman at the New York State Archives.

I am also indebted in countless ways to the intellectual community at the University of Pennsylvania, especially Herman Beavers, John L. Jackson, Camille Charles, Timothy Corrigan, Karen Beckman, Peter DeCherney, Meta Mezaj, Barbara Savage, Tukufu Zuberi, and Doug Massey, who have always supported me as a scholar and believed that I had a contribution to make. Valerie Swain-Cade McCoullum, Pat Ravenell, Brian Kirk, Carol Davis, Onyx Finney, Deborah Porter, Deborah Broadnax, and Gale Garrison and the staff of the University of Pennsylvania Library always helped me, cheered me on (and up when I needed it), and made Penn a home for me again.

Thanks also to those members of the academic community who provided collegial support to me in this process: Jacqueline Stewart, Tamara Walker, Bambi Haggins, Chris Cagle, Iliana Teitelbaum, Frances Gateward, Lea Rosenberg, Sonia Peterson Lewis, Ines Casillas, Lesa Lapeyrouse, Karen Bowdre, Nicole Turner, Eric Schaefer, Daniel Barrett, Ling-Ling Zhao, Charles Gentry, Kristen Whissel, and the Penn Cinema Studies and Philadelphia Cinema Studies Colloquia. I also owe a great debt to my colleagues at Queens College, who have generously welcomed and supported me: Amy Herzog, Jonathan Buchsbaum, Roopali Mukherjee, Anu Kapse, Susan McMillan, Leslie McCleave, Joy Fuqua, Zoe Beloff, Michael Lacy, Julian Cornell, Noah Tsika, Dean Bill McClure, Dean Tamara Evans, Karen Mandoukous, and my mentors, Mara Einstein and Rick Maxwell. Thanks to Jose Ruiz who helped with many technical woes. My gratitude also extends to Eric Schramm, whose thoughtful comments went a long way toward clarifying and tightening the writing in this book. I also want to thank Eric McDuffie, Joe Barbarese, Ilina Singh, Almitra David, Ms. Rachel and Mr. Roland Wilson, and all my teachers and the staff at Friends Select School who educated me in innumerable ways. There are also those whose extraordinary acts of provision made this project possible, like Kevin Delaney, David Berger and Holly Maxon, Dick Easterlin and Eileen Crimmins, Magali Safardi Larsen, and Drew Faust and Charles Rosenberg.

Thanks to my friends Lori Dean, Rachel Anglade, Rasool Berry, Misty Felton, Josina Guess, Charles and Isabel Barkley, Charlie and Helen Potter, Erica Haviv, Danielle Herbert, David Noble, Dustin Kidd, and Josh Klugman. To my students, especially the Ethnic Media Collective, thank you for your inspiration. Lastly, I owe an inexpressible debt to my family, the Scotts and Grosses, especially Diane Morris, Pat Waddy, David Scott, Frederick Scott, and Norma Scott and her cousin, Henry Sampson. I want to reserve my deepest gratitude for my mother, Gretchen Condran, my grandmother, Rachel Scott, my sister, Margaret Scott, and my father, Barry Scott, for their support. I want to thank my son, Kenji Thomas Johnson, because his wisdom and energy reminds me of what really matters. Thanks also to Seymour, Buddy, and April for keeping me company. And to my husband, Doug Johnson, who read countless drafts and still managed to take care of all of us, there are not words enough to say how much you have done; this would not have been possible without you.

CINEMA CIVIL RIGHTS

INTRODUCTION

The idea of American freedom has in practice consistently relied upon a pathological denial of the rights of African Americans to equal citizenship—and a simultaneous denial that these rights are being withheld. Accordingly, classical Hollywood, in its role as America's dream factory, largely maintained the myth of Black inferiority while minimizing America's long history of racial injustice. Countless films reinforced Black stereotypes, normalized economic and social segregation, and systematically avoided admitting the unjustness of racial inequality, often through the dissemination of the mammy, mulatto, buck, and Uncle Tom characters. As Donald Bogle has compellingly argued, the tradition of stereotypy, one that transcended the plantation chronotope and infiltrated various urban locales, became a direct expression of Hollywood racism.[1] Studies of exceptions to Hollywood's patterned racial mythology have predominantly focused on how African American talent, either directorial or onscreen, exceeded the imposed limitations.[2] However, the structure of limitation itself requires investigation.

Alongside stereotyping in classical Hollywood cinema lies a quizzical pattern of images both strange and attenuated from the actual, lived narratives of civil rights, distanced and alienated from their roots in history and Black experience. Take, for instance, *Storm Warning*, a 1950 Warner Bros. film about the Ku Klux Klan with no Black people in major roles; the Klan's victims are played by Ginger Rogers and Doris Day, both platinum blondes. Another example is *The Foxes of Harrow* (1948), where an enslaved woman's attempt to kill her newborn child to save him from slavery is a brutal footnote in a white plantation story.

Another film exemplifies this pattern of repressed civil rights representations. *The Ox-Bow Incident*, an anti-lynching film made in 1943, does not feature a Black protagonist (although Black actor Leigh Whipper appears as a bystander who condemns the mob action). It is set in the Old West rather than the contemporary South, where lynching was still practiced during the Second World War. Lynching, while discussed obsessively in the drama, is shown at a distance and expressionistically—as hanging bodies casting a shadow. Lost in the film's chiaroscuro white guilt is any feeling of the racial brutality of lynching. Despite these omissions, Walter White, head of the National Association for the Advancement of Colored People (NAACP), praised the film for its bold forthrightness. It reminded him, he wrote to Twentieth Century–Fox, of the recent Mississippi lynching of Black fourteen-year-olds Ernest Green and Charles Lang, who allegedly assaulted a white girl later found to be their frequent playmate. The girl was never assaulted; a single unreliable witness made the accusation. "But the mob, as in the 'Ox-Bow Incident' refused to search for the truth," wrote White. "With pliers they pulled pieces of flesh out of the still living bodies of the youngsters. One member of the mob drove a screwdriver down the throat of one of the boys as he cried out for mercy. . . . So you can see, therefore, that the film 'The Ox-Bow Incident' is most opportune."[3] Though ostensibly a letter of congratulation, White's overlay of the vivid description of the actual lynching onto the mild *Ox-Bow Incident* brings to mind the silences—the ominous tameness and lingering triviality—of Fox's film, which failed to show lynching's place in a brutal racialized regime of white supremacy. It is this tameness—and warped indirection—in the appearance of questions of Black equality on the American screen that is the central focus of this book.

REPRESSION AND REPRESENTABILITY

Storm Warning, *The Foxes of Harrow*, and *The Ox-Bow Incident* suggest that civil rights abuses were not absent entirely from the classical Hollywood screen. And yet they leave us with the question of how to make sense of cinematic narratives that touch on Black civil rights but where racial taboos have strangely chased race itself out of the text's center. How do these narratives speak to Black freedom struggles? How do we more systematically account for the structures behind what Ed Guerrero calls "racial fragments" and what Thomas Cripps calls the "absent presence" of Black people and anti-Black racism in American cinema?[4] This book takes the position that we can best account for these representations (and their haunting absences) by understanding three things: the system of cinematic repression, the pattern of representability that emerged as a result, and the responses of Black activists to these latent, stuttering manifestations.

What follows, then, is a history of the repression of civil rights on the American screen and the struggle of African American activists to find civil rights among a jumbled cache of images that most often ignored the Black need for freedom. While it highlights moments of screen revelation, this book pushes beyond the films themselves to account systematically for the decision-making processes that yielded them. The institutions that regulated cinema—the Production Code Administration, state censorship boards, and the studios themselves—combined to create what I term a "system of vetting," a repressive apparatus that worked across various texts to create the warped image of Black life we often associate with classical Hollywood. This book's institutional focus reveals how each element of this system (rather than any individual director or film) contributed to the behind-the-scenes discussion of acceptable Black images and how race crucially marked these discussions. Simultaneous with and parallel to the narrative of Hollywood's Black representations is the story of race and independent filmmakers, who, as J. Ronald Green, Jane Gaines, and others have articulated, struggled against great odds to develop a meaningful representation of the Black condition in America.[5] Although many race filmmakers also repressed interracial discourse according to Hollywood norms, it is true that these films provide something closer to an interior Black perspective on civil rights abuses.[6] As I show, the system of vetting stifled race filmmakers significantly. My focus in the book, however, is on Hollywood films—which unduly shaped the standards to which all other films (race, foreign, and independent) would be held.

The system of vetting created an imposing wall of repression. Yet repression is an unpredictable and unstable instrument—one prone to revealing perversities. Repression has a dominating force. Even when it is resisted, the tension created by the uttered prohibition remains a center of gravity, a focal point, and the most stable ground on which representation is based. According to Michel Foucault, repression leads to a counterintuitive and unruly "incitement" around the taboo.[7] Christian Metz likewise insists that censorship is never complete or linear but rather sets in motion the mechanisms of circumlocution. It is a technology of "refractions" that deflects the repressed material into other realms.[8] Despite, or even because of, the hysterical efforts to repress the much-evidenced truth of America's racial wrongs, Hollywood obliquely revealed these wrongs quite frequently in its films. Furthermore, the documentable reality and historical fact of Black suffering sometimes impelled even racist film producers to admit certain injustices, especially when the wrong could be diffused by an air of pastness and without an in-depth exploration of racism's dynamics (as in the social problem film's formula). Notwithstanding the repressive logic of these films that tentatively engaged civil rights, they frequently circumnavigated the terrain of Black oppression. And they ultimately failed to avoid the civil rights questions they repressed.

But as the above examples show, these moments were by no means direct or satisfying expressions of the pain and struggle of African Americans—or of the subjective experiences of oppression Black people really shared. Nor did these Hollywood films typically have a direct impact on freedom struggles. But the persistent appearance of civil rights issues in mainstream films demands deeper consideration, especially given the structuring importance of the taboo of admitting America's racial wrongs to the preservation of whiteness as we know it. How, why, and under what pressures of sublimation civil rights issues were allowed to surface in American cinema is a story that can only be told with great attention to the policies and politics of the institutions charged with repressing American cinema—the Motion Picture Producers and Distributors of America (MPPDA) (later known as the Motion Picture Association of America [MPAA]), state censors, and indeed the Hollywood studios themselves. In the light of these policies, the repressed, compressed screen renditions take on a clearer logic.

Thus, rather than discussing civil rights' appearance in the cinema solely in terms of repression, I address it in terms of "representability." As Patricia White provocatively asks in her study of lesbian representability under a Hollywood system that prohibited homosexuality: "When representation is forbidden, where do we look?" The result of repression is not absence but rather diffused, oblique, indirect, deniable presence—a presence that can be made recognizable through intertextuality, extratextual discourse, and through visual coding.[9] White's notion differs from the idea of "reading against the grain," which is unbound by the structures and "realities" of the text; it seeks the evidences of repressed material that are ironically entwined in the very sinews—the narrative structures and signifiers—that seal their prohibition. Prohibition itself, in this way, is generative. When it comes to civil rights, the notion of representability allows us to examine both representation and repression, and more exactly how representation emerges through a veil of domination and in spite of the intent of the censor and even the author. That is, it allows us to examine not only the policies of various censors—that is, what was prohibited—but also how repressed material manifested itself, if in strange and errant ways. In this case, it reveals how even in racist texts (or texts where Black people are absent or where racial politics are reversed and white people are the physical or psychic victims of violence broadly known to be racialized), the obsessive return to narratives of racial violation is often the centering force and a symptom of an underlying, often ideologically misguided concern about civil rights.

Each of the first three chapters examines a different repressive institution that restrained the cinematic civil rights imagination. Chapter 1 explores the MPPDA, which oversaw the Production Code Administration (PCA), the most centralized and consistent censor of the American cinema during the classical era. Drawing on earlier studies of the MPPDA, which indicate the importance of industry policy, this chapter delineates the PCA's hand in repressing racial lynching, miscegenation, and social equality and in rerouting this racial imaginary into other realms. Chapter 2 investigates the racial policies of state censorship boards. It shows that race was a structuring anxiety in film regulation beyond the Progressive Era where Lee Grieveson, Dan Streible, J. Douglas Smith, and Charlene Regester, among others, have noted its prevalence.[10] Chapter 3 gives a case study of studio production itself. The chapter gleans (from close analysis of archival evidence of internal negotiations) the role of the studio—and the studio head specifically—in spurring and repressively "managing" representations of civil rights issues by focusing on Twentieth Century–Fox's Darryl F. Zanuck. The final chapter explores how African Americans turned Hollywood's repressions into their own expression, critiquing Hollywood's silences and amplifying the muted images Hollywood did present. What I provide in chapter 4 is a textually engaged analysis of Black film protests. It includes not only the NAACP but also those unofficial actions organized or improvised by those with less institutional power or clout in the years leading up to the mass movement for civil rights.[11] It is crucial that this book ends not with the films themselves but with how activist publics used them to reveal what they repressed—and explained their negative or positive value to American civil rights issues.

Together these chapters reveal that understanding the process of adaptation, creative development, and censorship that most American films endured is crucial to understanding Black representations. Screenplays from which racial angles were removed reveal that the reach of civil rights censorship was far greater than can be seen on the surface of the films themselves. Although exploring the history of any one film is helpful, systematic analysis of policy and representation reveals more about the patterns of repression that limited civil rights images.

I turn now to defining the term "civil rights" as I use it in this book. I define the term, following Martha Biondi, as "the right to due process and equality before the law."[12] The concept of "the law" has both legal and imaginary components, however. Civil rights issues were made visible through three main guises during the classical Hollywood era: lynching, social equality, and miscegenation. I focus on these three structuring concerns. However, I occasionally include other issues—onscreen Black militancy, white racism within the criminal justice system, or racial brutality during slavery, for example—when they raise questions of civil rights among activists or industry officials. Each of the three core civil rights themes on which I focus has an important relationship to the American narrative of race and to the symbolic system of racial oppression. In the United States, lynching was a racialized form of violence and punishment that was much more frequently visited upon Blacks than whites.[13] But one wouldn't know this from watching American films, where lynching was most frequently seen in the western—and there as an outmoded form of justice on the lawless frontier. During the 1920s and 1930s, it is little surprise that the anti-lynching movement was the least common denominator of civil rights activism. Lynching was perhaps the greatest violation of civil rights, one that not only stamped out Black life with a demeaning, gruesome force but also with a clear symbolism of white corporeal control meant to facilitate the enforcement of segregation. Southern whites used the term "social equality between the races" when African Americans dispensed with the deference and groveling that segregation required—and especially when they seemed to have a camaraderie with white women. For them, "social equality" was communicated by various screen signifiers that spanned the gamut from sassy Black maids to interracial cabaret numbers to slave revolts. The underlying threat was integration and violation of the social ordering of the color line. Social equality's broken racial boundaries not only threatened to bring about miscegenation but further threatened to undermine the racial hierarchy.

While lynching and equality have a clearer relationship to movement goals, miscegenation has had an important, if indirect relationship to civil rights. Of course, Black civil rights activists never fought for the right to miscegenate. However, Black activists had to fight against the myth of the Black male rapist that formed the basis for white conceptions of miscegenation. Miscegenation is, perhaps, the most historically consistent excuse for the denial of civil rights and equality—the white race card that has undergirded centuries of Black subjugation, motivating segregation and the denial of rights. Denying Black men and women the right to marry with other races was also itself a curtailment of Black civil rights, one that implicitly argued Black inferiority. Further, miscegenation stood at the epicenter of other American race problems. Though for many whites "miscegenation" was synonymous with the Black rape of white women and the weakening of the white race, this narrative repressed a host of realities that America could not accept: that white men had historically raped Black women, that white women desired Black men, and that miscegenation's contingent myth of the Black rapist was designed to excuse lynching as a form of social violence and control.[14] For many African Americans, the word "miscegenation" signified something bigger—and uglier—than Black rape. It was a justification for segregation, white violence, torture, and railroading—a fearsome illusion cast, like a dark shadow, across the color line. From a cinematic perspective, miscegenation helped to enshrine white womanhood as the center of the scopic regime in which Black being—let alone desire—was most often visible only as symptom, wound, rupture, mistake, and blemish. The history of denial accompanying miscegenation made repression of cinematic images of interracial desire necessary—and linked these representations to the quest for civil rights. Although activists highlighted many other important civil rights issues, these issues were essential to the onscreen color line. Their cinematic repression helped to maintain their repression in the broader American imaginary.

CRITICAL CULTURAL HISTORY
BEHIND SCREEN REPRESSION

Behind the textual and institutional history that this book relates is a broader cultural history that vitally informed it. The thirty years under consideration were some of the most eventful in African American history and held a crucial, formative place in what Jacquelyn Dowd Hall has called "the Long Civil Rights Movement." This movement had antebellum moorings and was vitally braided into a broader set of cultural activities and shifts.[15] The narrative of civil rights in the period was neither one of progress nor decline but rather a patchwork of racial ambiguity and ambivalence. The present book begins in 1926, when the film industry created a centralized agency, the Studio Relations Committee (SRC), whose purpose was the review and censorship of the studios' films. This was just before tumultuous changes brought about in Hollywood by the widespread adoption of synchronized sound and in the country at large by the stock market crash of 1929. The Great Depression was a desperate time for all racial groups. In some instances, fallen fortunes united the races, as the less regulated early 1930s cinema often conveyed. But as Harvard Sitkoff and others have argued, the Depression had a disproportionate effect on African Americans.[16] They were not only the last hired and first fired, but, as Robin Kelley has shown, were often told they were ineligible for relief, since there was still demand for domestic and unskilled labor.[17]

In the midst of this crisis, in 1931, nine African American teenagers were framed as having raped two white girls on a train in Scottsboro, Alabama. Weeks after the accusation, they were tried by an all-white jury and all but one sentenced to death. With the help of various outsiders, including the NAACP, civil rights activists such as Ida B. Wells, and the Communist Party, the "Scottsboro Boys," as they came to be known, avoided a quick death sentence and each was granted a retrial. Alabama prosecutors continued to doggedly pursue the young men, however, even after Ruby Bates, one of the accusers, recanted her testimony, revealing that Scottsboro police had threatened to prosecute her for sexual activity with white boys on the train if she did not accuse the nine defendants of rape. The case is exceptional not for its violation of Black civil rights: the railroading of Black Americans was nothing new. Scottsboro was remarkable, instead, because progressives and civil rights activists managed to raise national consciousness about the unfair condition of southern racial justice. The trials also have an important link to both the long civil rights movement and its cinematic representation. Not only did the cases against the Scottsboro Boys go to the Supreme Court twice, producing precedent-setting opinions on the need for adequate legal representation and leading to bans against all-white juries, but the national press coverage of the racial injustices within the American judicial system prompted protests across the nation. But while filmmakers might have been expected to compete with each other to screen the Scottsboro story, movies, unlike newspapers, were not protected by the First Amendment and thus were subject to censorship. Indeed, a 1915 Supreme Court ruling (*Mutual v. Biograph*) pronounced film "a business pure and simple." Thus the fear of censorship, and the system of vetting I describe in these pages, arose to block the screening of a central event in civil rights discourse in the 1930s, making it a structuring absence in the cinema of the 1930s—and beyond.

Part of the success at raising consciousness about the Scottsboro tragedy stemmed from the rising "Cultural Front," a nebulous, loosely coordinated body of progressives of many races who were working to democratize American culture during the 1930s. A number of Franklin Delano Roosevelt's New

Deal programs, such as the Federal Theater and Federal Writers Projects, gave place and momentum to Cultural Front activities by facilitating collaborations between artists, writers, and intellectuals on the Left. As Michael Denning describes it, "Just as the radical movements of abolition, utopian socialism, and women's rights sparked the antebellum American Renaissance, so the communisms of the depression triggered a deep and lasting transformation of American modernism and mass culture."[18] The Cultural Front's progressive racial vision and creative intellectual labor made popular an ethnically conscious definition of democracy and accelerated the cultural component of the 1930s anti-lynching agenda. Beyond the anti-lynching movement, the Cultural Front had other effects relevant to this study. Not only did it include film writers, as Denning argues, but the specific localized politico-creative movements such as the Chicago Renaissance provided the foundation for the tradition of Black film criticism based on not only "positive" Black representation alone, but on aesthetic representations of justice, history, and humanity that I outline in these pages.

Many of the most important shifts in Black history and Black representation between 1930 and 1960 were brought about by World War II. The war not only changed the national agenda to war mobilization, but it prompted massive migration and semi-official federal adoption of the rhetoric of racial democracy advocated by the Cultural Front. The story of the wartime civil rights struggle begins in January 1941, nearly a year before Pearl Harbor, when A. Philip Randolph, leader of the Brotherhood of Sleeping Car Porters, organized a massive March on Washington for civil rights and the end of discrimination in national defense industries. Randolph ultimately postponed the march only after he convinced President Franklin Roosevelt to issue a groundbreaking promise to Black Americans—Executive Order 8802—which ended discrimination in defense industries and formed the Fair Employment Practices Committee (FEPC).[19] Though the president stopped short of enforcing desegregation, he had crossed a threshold in admitting the Constitutional guarantee of racial equality that could not be uncrossed. His action and, crucially, the racial rhetoric he adopted prompted U.S. wartime language and imagery to become more inclusive of Black Americans. Randolph's explicitly all-Black march was not a southern movement but pointed out American racial injustice on a national, institutional, and indeed governmental level.[20] Further, it is significant that Randolph enacted what was then the century's largest and most nationally resonant civil rights protest by first mobilizing his own union, the Brotherhood of Sleeping Car Porters, a class of men assumed to be subservient. This altered the national discourse on civil rights by revising the image of Black American servility so comforting to many whites.[21] The wartime shift in rhetoric and image, however, did not mean that America had actually arrived at a more thoroughgoing racial equality. Not only did military segregation and brutal racism continue but, according to the *Negro Yearbook*, there were fifteen documented lynchings and forty-three documented attempted lynchings during the war: all those lynched in this period were African Americans.[22]

In the midst of America's war for democracy in Europe and the Pacific, there also occurred what were arguably the nation's worst cluster of race riots, in Harlem and Detroit, in 1943. Part of this violence was clearly backlash against the changing image—and physical movement—of Black people. Nearly one million African Americans were serving in the segregated armed forces, many "remigrating" temporarily to the South for training and thereupon receiving the brunt of the South's racist backlash against the Black soldier in uniform. In addition, according to Henry Louis Gates, so many southern Blacks moved north and from rural locales to southern cities to gain employment in the defense plants that this movement became the most substantial internal migration in American history.[23] How did these events influence film productions? The answer comes through films that were at once restrained and forthcoming on the question of Black equality, such as *Bataan* (1943), *Sahara* (1943), and *Crash Dive* (1943); *Stage Door Canteen* (1943), which included Black soldiers in an integrated milieu; and *Stormy Weather* (1943), *Thank Your Lucky Stars* (1943), *This Is the Army* (1943), and *Follow the Boys* (1944), which included Black soldiers but avoided obvious integration so as not to offend the South. But the wartime concerns about civil rights are also visible in the struggle over other minor Black characters and in films where Black characters and themes were entirely suppressed through censorship.

Following World War II, the United States entered a strange and often paradoxical moment in racial discourse and ideology. Absent the wartime imperative, the image of Black inclusion was no longer a national priority. Pro-integration government films like *The Negro Sailor* (1945), a follow-up to the wartime *Negro Soldier* (1944), were delayed. And America's postwar track record on lynching and riots indicates how incomplete American wartime integration was, with its pockets of freedom amidst vast seas of intolerance. Another twenty-eight lynching attempts, some outside the South, took place in 1946.[24] Doubt and uncertainty—and sometimes plain-faced reversal and backlash—engulfed the unfulfilled racial promises of the war years. The failures of these promises are perhaps best exemplified in the Columbia, Tennessee, riot of 1946, in which Black veteran James Stephenson struck a white shopkeeper who had threatened his mother. A decorated and uniformed Black veteran was blinded and beaten by whites in South Carolina in the same month.[25] And yet despite this backpedaling many Americans, even some Hollywood producers and screenwriters, felt the nation should honor its democratic promise. Hollywood studios made racial problem films, with their often incomplete, ideologically fractured messages about race relations and integration.[26] The postwar uncertainty produced some of the most hesitant but also revealing films about racial equality, like *Pinky* (1949), *No Way Out* (1950), and *The Well* (1951), which I examine here.

Black cinematic representation in the 1950s was influenced not only by the postwar racial concerns, but also by important shifts in the film industry. First was the Supreme Court's Paramount Decrees of 1948, which challenged the vertical integration of the film industry, forcing the studios to divest of their theater holdings (and thus dismantling the studio system). The effects of this movement were not immediate and developed gradually over the course of the 1950s and 1960s. But the long-term effect of these decrees would be to allow a more significant place for independent cinema—a cinema that could potentially break Hollywood taboos about race and racial controversy. Second, the Supreme Court's 1952 Miracle Decision extended First Amendment protections to the film industry, meaning that state censorship was largely unconstitutional and the system of vetting on which the repression of sex, race, and violence had developed would be gradually changed. Finally, the coming of television pushed the film industry, which was competing with the new medium in the era of the baby boom, toward greater revelation, controversy, and maturity, including in the realm of race.

Also, vitally shaping 1950s cinematic representations of race was the beginning of the mass movement phase of the long civil rights struggle itself, which took place in the wake of transnational anticolonial independence struggles and amid a Cold War clampdown on racial progressivism.[27] Three events—the Supreme Court's *Brown v. Board of Education* decisions of 1954–1955, the lynching of Emmett Till in 1955, and the Montgomery bus boycott of 1955–1956—helped to put the civil rights movement on a national stage through television and, to a lesser extent, cinema. These events also signaled a shift of national proportions in both the legislation of civil rights issues and Black activism. Though activists shared an aim through the many stages of development of the long civil rights struggle, the strategies, intermediate goals, and even the theory of freedom that guided them shifted significantly. One example was the shift in civil rights leaders' strategies from the diplomatic to the legislative. The first major southern NAACP court victory in school desegregation was in 1938, but in general the late 1930s civil rights struggle was marked by negotiation with existing white power structures rather than direct action. This legislative campaign for full desegregation would continue, with concentrated victories in the 1950s and 1960s. With the shift to legislative tactics came a greater militancy and a retreat from what Martha Biondi has described as a diplomacy-based civil rights agenda.[28] I trace this shift not only with regard to its impact on Black civil rights representability, but also in its effect on Black film activism. These real-life racial issues and social problems, both residual and spectacular in nature, shaped African American experience in a structural way during the period under study. Film representation may have avoided the real facts of America's racial history in favor of ideologically bound fantasies, but at important moments and in strange, affecting images, these repressed images came forcefully to light.

1 · REGULATING RACE, STRUCTURING ABSENCE

Industry Self-Censorship and
African American Representability

The Motion Picture Producers and Distributors of America (MPPDA) was the most consistent and powerful censor of American films in the classical era.[1] Headed initially by Will Hays, former postmaster general and a representative of the Midwestern sensibilities key to securing the industry's moral image, the MPPDA worked for the common interests of the major Hollywood studios. Its role, from the late 1920s until 1968, was to suggest changes to Hollywood film scripts to avoid outside censure and censorship by local, state, and international boards. From 1934 to 1968, it seriously undertook the task of reviewing all the major studios' screenplays. Sensational stories from the headlines, stage, and history might have appealed to individual producers, but the MPPDA was there to weigh each plot and script against what it considered the industry's collective moral responsibilities and its larger financial interests. This soft censorship was carried out through two successive subunits: the Studio Relations Committee (SRC) (1926–1934) and the Production Code Administration (PCA) (1934–1968).

The MPPDA is most famous for the Production Code, a document devised by industry leaders and two prominent Catholic consultants that largely curtailed screen depictions of sex and crime. For much of its history, the Production Code only contained one explicit reference to race—a prohibition on showing miscegenation, which it defined as "sex relationships between the black and white races."[2] But beyond the Code, the PCA censored films according to "Industry Policy," an unwritten constellation of MPPDA-designated prohibitions outside the Code that governed delicate subjects as varied as Communism, the presentation of American businesses, and race relations.[3] At times, Industry Policy caused greater concern to the industry than the Code itself. Industry

Policy vitally affected African American representation—and the representation of civil rights abuses. In different ways and using different methods, film scholars Ruth Vasey, Lea Jacobs, Stephen Prince, and Stanley Cavell have suggested that when it came to white sex and violence the PCA's censorship was, in Foucauldian terms, "productive."[4] More specifically, the PCA forced producers to be creative, which led to the repressed material appearing symptomatically and diffusely throughout the texts. Vasey and Jacobs have demonstrated that the advice of MPPDA censors gradually trained Hollywood screenwriters in representing controversy through subtle allusion rather than direct revelation. Thus, they were more than censors; they helped to author a system of representational aversion that allowed indirect, deniable representations to pass beneath the radar. But to what extent did the PCA's incitation to allusion extend to the representation of African Americans?

The movie industry's self-regulation of civil rights issues can be divided into five eras: the SRC era (1926–1934), in which this self-censorship was governed by the MPPDA's Studio Relations Committee under the leadership of Jason Joy and, later, James Wingate; the early Code era (1934–1941), in which the far sterner PCA headed by Joseph Breen governed the process; World War II (1941–1945), during which the Office of War Information's campaign to improve Black representations drew attention to racism in Hollywood; the postwar era (1946–1955), during which Breen continued his leadership; and the Shurlock era (1955–1961), when Geoffrey Shurlock headed the PCA during the early years of the civil rights movement. During this thirty-two-year span, the MPAA helped to devise a formula for representing civil rights issues onscreen, but to do so while veiling any racial resonance and even omitting direct signifiers to race relations. Over the course of this history, however, based on various cultural shifts—including the Cultural Front, white southern backlash, the democratic discourse of World War II, and the civil rights movement—the PCA gradually shifted its policies on the treatment of racial issues to allow for more nuanced and direct representation.

CIVIL RIGHTS IN HOLLYWOOD IMAGES
UNDER THE SRC, 1926–1934

The term "pre-Code" is a widely accepted misnomer: the Code was written in 1930 but it was not until 1934 that it was fully enforced. Thus, the term "pre-Code" designates not the era before the Code's existence but rather an era of weak enforcement from 1930 to 1934. This section covers not only the pre-Code era as designated by scholars such as Thomas Doherty, but also the four years prior in which Jason Joy was actively developing the industry censorship standards that would govern the next three decades. Some scholars have suggested the pre-Code era featured greater onscreen racial freedom.[5] This is only partly true. Black and white extras mingle in crowd scenes, prisons, and breadlines in the hardboiled, unsentimental, pre-Code cinema of the Great Depression. SRC head Jason Joy generally did not cut from finished films these scenes of naturalized integration where the poor, Black and white, intermix without differentiation (but with a wealth of racial wisecracks and insults). This may have been because Joy saw himself as an ally of producers, and these unscripted moments of racial equality were largely backdrop. But when he learned that a script called for racial mixing—especially in pictures set in regions where segregation reigned— he consistently fought hard to have it removed, at least partly out of fear of white backlash. Thus Joy, who is known for having been liberal in his censorship of sexuality and who aided producers in indirectly representing the erotic, sought on the other hand to establish a firm color line and called for the elimination of racial integration, miscegenation, and the racial abuses of the criminal justice system in film.[6]

Race and Punishment in the SRC Era

The abusive penal system became the basis for a film cycle in the early 1930s. Under MPPDA scrutiny, it was almost impossible for producers to show the criminal justice system's endemic evils or weaknesses, though several tried to reveal the corruption and brutality that produced fatal injustices. Films like *The Last Mile* (1932), *20,000 Years in Sing-Sing* (1932), and *Ann Vickers* (1933), which raised social questions about the morality of state punishment and depicted prisoner discontentment and revolt, were a tough sell in the face of Depression-era censors, even the more lenient SRC.[7] But films that used Black characters to pose challenges to the criminal justice system were subject to even greater scrutiny.

Joy restricted the racial implications of the anti-penal film cycle of the early 1930s. Initial treatments for *I Am a Fugitive from a Chain Gang* (1932), *Hell's Highway* (1932), and *Laughter in Hell* (1933), all chain-gang films, criticized the criminal justice system's brutality and boldly showed that it gave (southern) states the power to lynch. All these films even showed Black multitudes and bit players, sometimes in speaking or singing roles, obliquely revealing state punishment's disproportionate racial impact. But Joy censored each film for its depiction of race relations. Joy's persistent concern about offending the South may be explained by the fact that his right-hand man was white Southerner Lamar Trotti, who consistently defended southern segregation, to the point of suggesting the industry avoid alienating even those who supported the Ku Klux Klan.[8] In the case of *I Am a Fugitive from a Chain Gang*, Joy warned producers not to include too many Black extras so that the southern locale would be less obvious, an instruction that the film's producer, Darryl F. Zanuck, refused to heed.[9] Nervously employing a double negative, Joy asked David O. Selznick, the producer of RKO's *Hell's Highway*, "Would it not be a good idea not to show the negroes and whites chained together?"[10] Selznick avoided these shots. But in other

sequences the racial separation was less firmly policed. Black and white prisoners communicate with each other across the segregated cellblocks, work together
on gangs, and, most importantly, escape together, an act that shows allegiance
and coordination. Though Joy wanted to avoid offending the South, the film
indicted southern race prejudice obliquely. Not only does the head guard call a
Black mule-tender a baboon, but Selznick shot scenes in which only Black men
are lynched by an all-white posse after a mass escape. Joy twice railed against this
sequence and, though Selznick ignored him, RKO official B. B. Kahane removed
this and other scenes of "the capture and slaughter of convicts."[11]

In terms of race, an important film of the chain-gang cycle was Universal's
bitterly gritty *Laughter in Hell*, a film that also featured the only onscreen Black
lynching of the decade. In the original synopsis, *Laughter in Hell*'s Barney was a
sympathetic, slow-witted white man who, catching his wife in an act of infidel-
ity, murders her and her lover. Sentenced to a prison chain gang, he develops
a friendship with a Black inmate named Jackson, eventually escaping but not
before suffering whip-wounds that fester without treatment and witnessing four
Black inmates being lynched by prison officials.

Joy's initial concern was less brutality than the film's Alabama setting, given
"the South's dislike of criticism."[12] Showcasing his characteristic alignment with
producers, Joy told his supervisor, Will Hays, that the studio should be allowed
to be honest, because "if brutality persists on in these days and systems are
wrong, I see no reason why we should not be permitted to say so."[13] Trotti, ever
concerned about a white southern backlash, pressed Joy to defend whiteness;
southern blame should be alleviated by establishing the "justice" of Barney's
imprisonment, contrasting "the brutal head guard with more humane officials,"
"soft-peddling . . . flogging [and] hanging," and setting the film in the 1880s to
diminish its commentary on present conditions.[14]

As the film moved from treatment to first draft, Joy's racial concerns mounted,
and he worried specifically about the lynching of Black men and a scene where
Jackson and Barney are whipped. "Perhaps you want to consider having one of
the hanged men a white man to avoid a note of racial prejudice," Joy suggested.[15]
The studio, however, maintained these elements. A week later, Joy took a sterner
tone in defending the racist South. It would violate "policy," he said, for Universal to contrast a drooping American flag in the prison with a Confederate flag
proudly hung in the courtroom or to name any particular southern states. Even
the "suggestion that negroes and whites are placed in the same cages" was anathema, although they could be shown "in the same camp together, provided they
are not shown to occupy the same quarters." Integrated quarters could not "be
possible in any Southern state and I'm quite sure that it would add a note that
Southern audiences would resent."[16] Joy desperately wanted Universal to cut the
hanging of Black men by the chain gang official. "Personally," he wrote, "I wonder if you are going to get out of this scene on the screen all that you hope to

get. . . . It is difficult for me to believe a chain-gang boss would have the right to execute State prisoners."[17] Joy also recommended visual techniques to downplay the lynching, describing with considerable detail how to achieve the effect of lynching without directly showing it. If Universal insisted on keeping the scene, he said, censorable details like the shadows of the hanging figures, shots of the noose around a man's neck, and other "gruesome" details should be removed and the whole thing played as much as possible by suggestion.

But Universal Studios boss Carl Laemmle refused to cut the lynching scene, arguing that the director would handle it "with discrimination."[18] In the end, Laemmle and director Edward Cahn persisted in shooting the scenes graphically. Despite interventions from the MPPDA's James Wingate (a former New York state censor), state censorship took its toll: New York, Ohio, Massachusetts, and Pennsylvania (as well as Chicago) cut almost all of the lynching sequence, allowing only shots establishing that a hanging is about to take place. However, each state modified the scene in a different way, indicating its own state-level approach to the art of indirection and regulatory editing. Pennsylvania permitted the most, a "view . . . of guard bringing noose toward him, of wagon moving and of rope stretching."[19] Ohio allowed only a "view of rope hanging from tree as prisoners approach place of execution."[20] New York permitted "scenes where prisoners get on cart and cart drives away."[21] These states also cut a scene where Barney and Jackson are whipped together. Thus the SRC learned a valuable lesson from municipal, state, and even international rejection of these sequences: racial lynching would be taboo on the Hollywood screen for the remainder of the 1930s.

Pre-Code Miscegenation

SRC concerns about racialized violence in the penal system were largely limited to this cycle. But concern about miscegenation—and its suggestion of Black equality—predated the Code itself. A document entitled the "Don'ts and Be Carefuls" that Joy used to guide producers before the Code forbade miscegenation. But in industry discourse and in practice, miscegenation meant more than just implied interracial sex. As early as 1927, Hays had pronounced it "inadvisable always to show white women in scenes with negroes where there is any inference of miscegenation or *social relationship*," a very broad standard that could keep any adjacent social mixing off the screen.[22] Though Joy sought to remove miscegenation from the screen, he did not always succeed. For example, Joy never reviewed First National's *Golden Dawn* (1930), based on Oscar Hammerstein's operetta set in British East Africa during World War I, a film with mulatto characters and direct representation of interracial desire. Mooda (Alice Gentle) openly states that she is half white and half Black, and has an illicit relationship with a white man. Further, a white colonialist blithely explains in song how to woo a "dusky jungle queen" and get her to "share a jungle bungalow with you."[23]

Nor did the SRC try to eliminate the provocative dance sequence in *Flying Down to Rio* (1932), in which dark Brazilians dance closely with blondes wearing very little. Later, white men, gawking at the Black Brazilian dancers, even quip, "No wonder it never gets cold in this country." Although set abroad, this sequence's American implications are heightened through its star—Etta Moten, an African American singer and actress. Joy, however, raised no objections, perhaps because the race of the characters was not specified in the script. Joy also limited his enforcement of the studio's ban on miscegenation to Black-white couples, stating that white marriage to dark-skinned Pacific islanders, Asians, or Native Americans was permissible.[24] Not only did Joy's liberalism make tangential miscegenation more visible, but in several films, such as *Isle of Escape* (1930), the use of African American extras as South Sea Islanders, Brazilians, or Africans in romantic scenes with white American actors furthered the film's connotation of American, Black-white miscegenation.[25]

But Joy counseled against script elements that showed Black-white miscegenation on the narrative surface, especially when these films bore connections to the real-life Rhinelander court case of 1925, in which white socialite Kip Rhinelander claimed he was tricked into marrying Alice Jones, a woman he thought was white but was actually a Black domestic. In *Five Star Final* (1931), newspapermen reveal that white Nancy Townsend (Frances Starr) is really Nancy Vorhees, who ten years earlier killed her unfaithful husband. The film not only focuses on revealing hidden identities but openly mentions the Rhinelander case as a point of comparison, a fact that prompted censors' attention to the film's "public opinion angle."[26] The script hinted at miscegenation when a newspaper man quipped, "I'll go in your contest, Ziggie, if you'll get me a girl with ten thousand dollars . . . *and she don't even have to be white,*" a line absent in the finished film after Joy asked producer Hal Wallis to remove it. In RKO's newspaper yarn *Is My Face Red?* (1932), initial treatments had "a white man . . . having an affair with a mulatto." Joy asked producers to "forego" this element, citing offense to "race-conscious people" and the Code's "clause regarding miscegenation."[27] The producers acquiesced.

But the SRC's removal of miscegenation was often incomplete, as we can see in the MPPDA's file on *Morocco* (1930). In Paramount's original treatment, the French Foreign Legion commander, a Corsican, was to have a Moorish wife who flirts with an American in a café where "blacks and whites mingle, wealth being the only distinction." This café and its style of integration were problematic for Joy who, after correspondence from French consultant Valentin Mandelstamm, warned that the script was not specific enough about whether "they are black women and white men or vice versa."[28] Joy wrote Paramount that the "Café scene in which you have black sitting with white, etc. etc. wealth being the only distinction should be modified so that blacks and whites are not shown together. In this connection Madame Caesar ought to be a French lady rather than a Moor. This is more logical and avoids the danger that otherwise would develop," a vague reference to the ban on miscegenation.[29] Paramount did avoid any direct inference of miscegenation, but Madame Caesar (Eve Southern) is consistently associated with the Moors. She speaks their language, wears their garb, and consorts with them by night when she has them attack Tom Brown (Gary Cooper). The film also connotes racial mixing in another way, one more pertinent to American race relations. Several Los Angeles "black beauties" play African entertainers and lovers of the Legionaries, as Black press reviewers noted.[30] Thus the film gives the aura of miscegenation without any case in point. And the racially controversial aspects of the story that Joy sought to remove were only dulled.

We can also see Joy's concern about miscegenation in the file on the all-Black film *Hallelujah!* (1929). Joy urged MGM to omit shots of Zeke (Daniel Haynes) passionately kissing his fiancée, Missy Rose (Victoria Spivey), because "white people will object to a strong negro exhibiting passion."[31] This indicates that the concern about miscegenation was limited not only to the narrative, but to the spectator's gaze at the screen. Strong Black men who exhibited sexuality threatened white scopic regimes even when their sexuality was directed toward Black women—in part perhaps because censors knew white women were also watching. This suggests that the SRC was concerned not only about onscreen signifiers of miscegenation but also about audience titillation that might give rise to imaginary miscegenation.

Perhaps the greatest pre-Code concern about miscegenation was occasioned by a film that was not made until 1948, with objections coming from not only Joy but also his MPPDA superiors. *Lulu Belle* was a well-known contemporary play, supposedly based on the life of singers Florence Mills or Josephine Baker, about a hardboiled Black woman who vamps a white barber and then a white boxer. The title character threatens whiteness and respectability with her undeterred, interracial social climbing, her humiliation of white men, and her defiance of the law.[32] She drives all her white lovers to madness until one of them kills her in rage. Co-written by Edward Sheldon and Charles MacArthur and staged for 461 Broadway performances in 1926, the play was reprised multiple times over the next several years and was coveted as a property by nearly every studio. Studio fascination with *Lulu Belle* (a property often discussed alongside *Shanghai Gesture* and *Harem*) seems to have been an extension of Hollywood's fixation with the "exotic mode" Gaylyn Studlar has described. This mode "exploited the display value of a heightened cultural exoticism" even if the exotic subject was actually white.[33] In the case of *Lulu Belle*, however, the pleasurable "otherness" did not have the deniability of carnivalesque alterity that Studlar describes, as the play was based on a purportedly true contemporary scandal.[34] Harry Warner wanted to adapt the play himself, but he wrote to Hays that he understood its danger from a personal angle: "All I can say is, when I saw the play with my wife, I was ashamed to look at her, and at that time I was married to her for 23 years."[35] In seeking MPPDA approval, studios sought to remedy the film's violations of the miscegenation clause in several ways. In 1930, one producer from Fox sought to make the film with a white woman playing Lulu Belle in blackface. Universal sent in multiple treatments in 1930 and 1932 that made Lulu Belle French, French-Creole, or just "white."[36] But to Hays, these modifications still left the implication of justified adultery and, worse, let audiences make connections to the scandalous play in which the protagonist was undeniably Black.[37] While the SRC allowed many pre-Code films showing adultery, it was the stain of miscegenation that led to the MPPDA's rejection of the play under the Formula of 1924, which discouraged "studios from picturizing a book or play containing 'salacious or otherwise harmful' subject matter for fear that it might have 'a deleterious effect on the industry in general.' "[38] Despite proposals from MGM, Warner Bros., and Universal (as well as director Howard Hawks) to make the story without miscegenation, the SRC and PCA rejected all requests until 1948 — and even then Lulu Belle, played by white actress Dorothy Lamour, was portrayed as French rather than a light-skinned Black woman. The threat of aggressive Black sexuality loomed over both the *Lulu Belle* and *Hallelujah!* film projects and suggests that the fear of visualizing interracial desire greatly influenced the SRC, whether or not it took place onscreen.

Joy not only acquiesced to the white racist view of miscegenation, but also was indifferent to Black activists and civil rights groups.[39] He consistently heeded Trotti's advice to ignore the NAACP. For example, with *Hallelujah!* Trotti counseled that Joy should only consider approaching "negro advancement groups" if he wanted to obviate their "rais[ing] a holler." But, he continued, "I don't think it matters whether the negroes like the picture or not, but I do wonder whether whites are amenable to such realism."[40] Two years later, in 1930, when NAACP executive secretary Walter White protested against a proposed sound version of *The Birth of a Nation,* Trotti took a similarly hard line against appeasing African Americans. He could not "see how we can be expected to say it cannot be shown. . . . The picture is semi-historical and the negro villain is shown as an individual, not as a representative of a class. It was certainly no more unfair to the negro than *Uncle Tom's Cabin* was unfair to the whites of the South."[41]

While southern interests motivated screen treatment of African Americans, MPPDA files reveal the complex, contradictory mechanisms of this repression. Trotti's figuration of the South stood behind Joy's constant vigilance in the protection of southern interest, even in scripts where there was no southern angle or setting.[42] And we can see Trotti's imprint on Joy's decision to censor integration, miscegenation, and lynching. Thus, it mattered that it was a racial conservative like Trotti who voiced the South to the MPPDA. But producers also were devising strategic signification to surmount the MPPDA's objections.

Interracial Intimacies and Deniable Racial Mixing

In this atmosphere of rising repression, cinematic miscegenation and racial equality began to take an altered form. Same-sex interracial intimacy—and sometimes integrated co-habitation—could be shown without offending the miscegenation clause or disturbing racial hierarchies. Studios often protected themselves by confining these bonds to an official employer-servant relationship and by surrounding social equality with Black stereotype. Studios also used non-Black figures to argue for racial civil rights in a way that would have been too threatening from a Black character, often using visual and narrative parity to link the onscreen civil rights advocate to its Black characters.

An example of the latter phenomenon is *Massacre* (1934), in which Joe Crazy Horse (Richard Barthelmess) comes to identify with his Native people, championing their civil rights, leading an armed revolt, and addressing the Indian Affairs office in Washington. Of particular interest is Joe's relationship to Sam (Clarence Muse), his sidekick. Sam and Joe share a knowingness about the burden and benefits of playing to racial stereotypes. When their racist boss asks Sam about Joe's trip to the reservation, Sam responds, "Chief's going down to the old plantation to see his old pappy," satirically mocking the association of African Americans with the plantation, and linking the plantation to the reservation, both spaces of white racial oppression. Sam and Joe ride together through the night to the reservation; upon seeing it, Sam remarks: "The white folks didn't give the Indians much of a break." Later, after having visited stoic, sad tribesmen, Sam honks at a horse, making it bolt, then quips, "That's the first sign of life I've seen since we come on the plantation," again employing a comic slippage between the plantation and the reservation that verbally links Black and Native oppressions. Later, after his war against the white man begins, Joe escapes police custody by having Sam pretend to be him, echoing the film's earliest sequences when we see Sam's face superimposed on Joe's body with the aid of a hand-held mirror. By linking Joe and Sam through their bodies and their common oppression, the film uses Native American oppression to reference Black oppression it dare not speak.

Some producers went so far as to represent Black-white friendships that blossomed in the urban milieu, though they made these deniable through the guise of servitude. In *Baby Face* (1933), career hussy Lily Powers (Barbara Stanwyck) and her African American comrade, Chico (Theresa Harris), are inseparable, with the latter supporting Lily as she suffers abuse at the hand of her father in his speakeasy. While Lily raises herself from the soot-drenched steel town where she grew up to a New York penthouse, using the Nietzschean axiom "Crush out all sentiment" to exploit a succession of men, Chico is her only constant. In the story outline Chico is described as her "friend" and "only confidant," the person to whom the dissembling Lily reveals her true motivations.[43] And as Lily rises to

FIGURE 1. Equality of costume was an important way of surreptitiously arguing for social equality in 1930s Hollywood film. Publicity still from *Baby Face* (1933). Courtesy of Warner Bros. Archive.

power, Chico becomes her maid. But script drafts explain that Chico is a maid in name only.[44] A strange ambiguity haunts this relationship. Is this service relationship a cover for an equal friendship? Or are Chico and Lily romantically— miscegenetically—linked? The two are first united by their shared sexual exploitation, and later Chico's musical rendition of "St. Louis Woman" becomes a crucial signifier of Lily's empowered sexual exploits.[45] Here, as in other pre-Code films, Black singing voices become surrogates for white sexuality, and in the process they publicize the sexual stains, impurity, and unwhiteness of their class-passing white mistresses. Black voices perform a kind of miscegenetic intrusion on white sexual intimacy. While the precise nature of Chico and Lily's bond remains diegetically amorphous, the sexual signifiers linking the two play on the tension around miscegenation, though it renders these in an utterly deniable way. Further, the unexplained contingency of their peculiarly strong attachment highlights moments where (gendered) similarity eclipses racial hierarchy and the two live together as equals. Perhaps the strongest argument for the parity of these two women in the finished film is the costuming, which places the actresses on equal footing (see figure 1).

The SRC strongly recommended toning down overt sexuality in *Baby Face* in a lengthy exchange of letters with Warner Bros.[46] But nowhere did it even mention the deep, profoundly intense, same-sex interracial relationship. Since their concern was about Lily's relationship with men, the protective guise of the master-servant relationship may have distracted censors from the social equality and vital relationship Lily and Chico share. While *Baby Face* obscured Black women's autonomous humanity and the real oppression of servitude, on another register the lingering intimacy, shared sexual knowledge, and physical proximity of Black and white women suggested social equality and even, perhaps, the miscegenation the screen disallowed.

MISCEGENATION IN THE EARLY CODE ERA

In 1934, Joseph Breen's arrival in Hollywood meant films such as *Golden Dawn* and *Flying Down to Rio* could no longer pass MPPDA scrutiny. Breen not only reviewed all Hollywood scripts, but his Production Code Administration had the sanctions Joy lacked: Code violators would be slapped with a $25,000 fine and be denied the PCA seal that unlocked national distribution to lucrative first-run theaters.

Even interracial desire expressed in song failed to pass muster under this new regime. In an early script of *Belle of the Nineties* (1934), a song called "Creole Man" revealed Mae West's character's desire for "a creole man—warm, high-brown skin; the kind of face to share your bread and gin with; the kind of guy it's heavenly to sin with . . . black, shiny hair—hair you wanna see upon a pillow; sleepy eyes that give me such a thrill—Oh, I'm talkin' 'bout my creole man."[47] With Breen's more restrictive approach, these lines would never make it to the screen. Still, in a provocative musical exchange in the film between Mae West and an all-Black band led by Duke Ellington, West employs her famous double entendre in describing the Black musicians' skill with their instruments—a fiddler who "sure do pull some bow" and a "hot cornet that you could never forget." Editing and reaction shots get across some of the desire Breen sought to remove.

But Breen did allow some visible signs of miscegenation onscreen. Breen generally accepted interracial romance between whites and non-Black racial groups, as Joy had before him. Films could skirt the Code's anti-miscegenation clause when the nonwhite love interest was a Native American, as in *Behold, My Wife* (1934), or a South Seas islander, as in *White Heat* (1934). Not only did Othello (whom Breen called a "Moor" rather than a Negro) pass PCA muster in three screen adaptations (*Men Are Not Gods* [1936], Orson Welles's *The Tragedy of Othello* [1953], and Sergei Yutkovich's 1955 Russian adaptation), but, in the early Code era, he approved at least one American Black-white interracial relationship onscreen. With the stage-proven *Show Boat* (1935), Breen saw "no serious objection" to casting Paul Robeson, "the negro, to play the part he played on the stage," even though a white woman in blackface would play his wife. Breen cautioned, however, against "any physical contact between the white woman and the negro man for the reason that many people know Aunt Jemima is a white woman and might be repulsed by the sight of her being fondled by a man who is a negro."[48] In the finished film, Hattie McDaniel plays Robeson's wife. But Breen's combined allowance and disgust indicates that though *Show Boat,* a proven stage hit, could stretch the miscegenation ban's boundaries, interracial touch still had to be avoided.

Imitation of Life and "The Negro Question"

John Stahl's *Imitation of Life* (1934) was never primarily a miscegenation narrative.[49] But Joseph Breen emphasized the implicit miscegenation angle, which was censorable under the Code, in order to curtail a number of other racial issues that did not come under the Code's purview. "The main theme," Breen defensively argued, "is founded upon the result of sex association between the white and black race (miscegenation), and as such, in our opinion, it not only violates the Production Code, but is very dangerous from the standpoint both of industry and public policy."[50] Although Breen praised "the beautiful mother-daughter love," even "as it applies to the colored woman with her white child," what he found censorable as miscegenation was Peola—whom he called miscegenation's "result." As a signifier of said transgression, her very existence violated the Code and emerging industry policy.[51] Breen argued that the problem with Peola was that she suggested the "possibility of miscegenation," one that went unpunished and was latent, omnipresent, and free-floating in the film because it had no "active portrayal" therein.[52]

Breen's official argument that the film was about miscegenation hid numerous deeper racial concerns—most prominently that it pointed to the problem of American racism. Breen enumerated "the serious racial problems" presented by Peola's "passing for white."[53] "Prejudice against the black race," which the film "brought into sharp relief," frightened PCA consultant J. B. Lewis, as did the use of the word "nigger . . . in derision." In the script, the impoverished Bea Pullman (Claudette Colbert) makes a fortune on a pancake recipe that Delilah (Louise Beavers) has devised. Lewis worried that the Pullmans appear to exploit Delilah, never giving her "proper credit" for their fortune and leaving the two Black women "somewhat downtrodden throughout the plot."[54] These factors made Lewis believe that "this picture would incite new racial prejudices and might lead in some instances, to open hostility."[55] Nor was the MPPDA concerned only about the South. Hays wrote to Universal's Robert Cochrane that the depiction of lynching and miscegenation would "prevent exhibition in Southern states . . . English colonies . . . [and] large northern cities which have substantial percentage of negro population," a concern that suggests a desire to avoid being associated with any potential northern Black dissent. This concern was significant enough that the MPPDA successfully stalled the film's production for several months, hoping to avoid its production entirely.[56]

But the clearest indication that the MPPDA was concerned with more than simply miscegenation came from the New York office—the place where industry policy was often decided. Maurice McKenzie, executive assistant to Hays, explicitly told Breen that "the big problem . . . is not, as we see it, a problem of miscegenation—that is, the act of miscegenation has occurred so remotely in the ancestry of the characters that it need not concern us." What was a "policy" concern—and one "fraught with the gravest danger," McKenzie stated—was the film's "racial problem," most dangerously revealed in "the lynching scene."[57] Hays found Breen's report of the film's "persons and situations (lynching scene, pretending to be white when black, etc.)" so dangerous that he told its producer that he hoped the picture would not be made.[58]

Preeminent among the industry's policy concerns was that "the big dramatic punch of the picture describes the lust of a young negro boy who believes that a white girl has given him a 'come on' signal and who nearly gets lynched as a result."[59] According to the Chicago Defender's Harry Levette (who was also an extra in many Hollywood films), the near-lynching scene occurred when "Peola, pretending to be white, accused a young colored man of attempting to flirt with her. Just as they have strung him up, she breaks down with remorse and screams, 'Don't, don't do it, I'm a n—r too.'"[60] Citing experts, the MPPDA impressed upon the studio "the troubles such a picture will encounter. . . . The lynching scene would appear to be especially dangerous."[61] Breen's resolve against the lynching scene only strengthened.

So, too, did Universal's resolve to shoot the scene.[62] Breen predictably discouraged this, because including it would "undoubtedly aggravate and emphasize" the film's "dangerous element." With Hays, Breen was even more absolute: "The danger point in this story is the handling of the 'negro question.' . . . They are going ahead with its production. . . . We have advised them definitely, however, that the element of lynching would, we believe, be entirely unsuitable for screen presentation, and that we would not pass the picture if it were in."[63] Universal eventually dropped this plot line. Though in many cases self-regulation was softer than outside censorship, the clear, unambiguous push for omission of racially motivated lynching can genuinely be called censorship.

Breen used the idea of miscegenation to argue against a film whose actual threat lay in a much broader set of racial problems (including, prominently, racism), as the PCA internal memo's invocation of "the Negro question," "prejudice," "inflammatory racial questions," "exploitation," and, most clearly, "lynching" indicates. Universal's self-censorship strategy followed the implications of Breen's initial letter, removing the harshest racial elements. None of the film's characters uttered the word "nigger."[64] Black men—the biggest threat with regards to miscegenation—were entirely written out save a single line of dialogue about Peola's father. Mother love—between Bea and Delilah—would flow broadly, replacing heterosexual romance as a representation of interracial intimacy.

Visually, however, the film would challenge Hays's 1927 stipulation that "white women" should not be shown in scenes indicating "social relationship" with Black people. Peola is, in fact, distanced from other Black people. Her connection to the Black community is limited to verbal allusions to her eventual happiness at a Negro college. Conversely, the film strongly suggests Peola's link to whiteness throughout the film, in what we might call "comparison blocking"— that is, shots that would cause audiences to compare Peola to the film's white characters, demonstrating her similarity. For example, on the night of Bea's party, Bea herself and several party guests bear a striking resemblance to Peola, in terms of skin tone and dress (see figure 2). Using the film's details and margins against censorship's proscriptions, Stahl employed dress, hairstyle, and clothing, all mise-en-scène intangibles that had been used to subvert censorship in the fallen women's film, to suggest Peola's equality with white people—perhaps even suggesting to some her presence and integration into a white world—that the narrative denied and that the PCA wanted audiences to overlook.[65]

The film's final sequences visually confirm the messiness of racial categorization that the film's narrative instructs us to ignore. The incredible variation in phenotype and skin tone among the crowds at Bea's funeral undermines audiences' visual assurance of the distinguishability of Black and white and, by extension, the severability of the races. Breen would privately praise *Imitation of Life* to Universal's Harry Zehner, calling it, despite its "spotty" box office numbers in the South and throughout the country, "a very fine picture . . . that has real merit."[66] This indicates that despite—and perhaps even because of—its relegation of transgressions of the color line to the visual minutiae of mise-en-scène, the film had avoided the industry policy concerns about racial violence, prejudice, and miscegenation Breen so toiled over. But the result was a film where latency and surrogacy replaced direct imagining of the racial injustice to which the original book—and industry self-censors—made reference.

Crafting Deniable Lynching: Breen and Mob Violence in the Late 1930s

Breen's concern about screening the lynching of African Americans, evident in the file on *Imitation of Life,* continued into the late 1930s. Between 1936 and 1938, in the midst of a heightened national struggle for a federal anti-lynching bill, studios proposed many films opposing mob violence.[67] The emergent national discussion on lynching was partially crystalized in films like *Fury* (1936), *They Won't Forget* (1937), *It Could Happen to You* (1937), and *Outcast* (1937), as Black press reviewers noted.[68] Warner Bros.' *Black Legion* (1937), Columbia's *Legion of Terror* (1936), and the Halperin brothers' *Nation Aflame* (1937), all of which came on the heels of sensational trials of Black Legion members in 1935 and 1936,

FIGURE 2. Scenes with Peola (Fredi Washington) lookalikes at the party (*top*), intercut with actual images of marginalized Peola (*bottom*), graphically assert her presence among whites, where the narrative insists on her absence—and highlight the impossibility of enforcing segregation. Frame captures from *Imitation of Life* (1934).

revealed that white supremacist terrorism could be found in the North as well as the South.

Lynching represented a trio of offenses to the industry censors: it suggested the weakness of law and order in keeping the peace; it was brutal; and it had racial implications. Industry policy on racial discrimination was honed early in the PCA's existence. In the file on *The Prisoner of Shark Island* (1936), for example, Breen stated clearly: "It is our policy to suggest that any picture prepared for general distribution should avoid the use of any material which tends to bring up the racial differences and prejudices between the black and white races. We suggest, therefore, that all such material be deleted or changed."[69] This policy on screen depictions of racism would affect all representations of civil rights abuses but would become particularly important for the screen regulation of lynching. Indications that government officials condoned lynching were generally unacceptable to Breen.[70] State censor boards disliked lynching to the point of removing the word from dialogue. Films suggesting that officers of the law were racist also concerned Breen.[71] So with the 1930s anti-lynching film cycle, Breen set parameters on how lynching and racial terror could be pictured. He counseled filmmakers that the mob's sadistic incitements to maim had to be omitted, and warned that censors would cut shots of a rope hanging over a tree limb.[72] But as had been true under Joy's SRC, Breen was concerned about lynching not just because of law enforcement or brutality but also because of its revelation of white racism.

Lest we think that Breen's concern about lynching was merely about brutality, it is useful to compare his reactions to *Imitation of Life* and *Fury*. While Breen disallowed *Imitation of Life*'s lynching, he allowed—and even helped to get across—a far more graphic lynching sequence in the prestige film *Fury* only two years later when the mob's victim was not Black—and survived the attack.[73] Still, Breen let pass the inclusion of minor Black characters in both *Fury* and *They Won't Forget*. And though directors Fritz Lang and Mervyn LeRoy had never intended to make films about Black lynching, they used these bit roles to indicate indirectly the racial terror their films elided, symptomatically revealing its structuring absences.[74] In *Fury*, the first figure we see after the lynch party is formed is a Black shoeshine man, who has been watching the mob's formation from behind the door of the bar. He is elevated on the shoeshine stand, invisible to the determined mob in plain sight (see figure 3).

Elevation was key to lynching's spectacular logic, as the Black body, strung at a height, dangled as an uplifted banner of white supremacy. Here the elevated Black figure looms above the crowd, reminding viewers of Black lynching. Having Black extras and bit actors circulate on the margins of these lynching scenes was a seemingly unsophisticated way to signify the racial history of lynching, especially by contrast with the complex representations of sexuality in the Code era. But it was also one that could be utterly denied because these figures were

FIGURE 3. The Black shoeshine escapes from the mob but to a raised position not dissimilar from that of the lynching victim. Here he directly addresses the camera. Frame captures from *Fury* (1936).

entirely divorced from the questions of justice in the mainstage narrative, and their role in the scene hidden in plain sight.

They Won't Forget references the Scottsboro incident and the railroading of Black suspects, as Matthew Bernstein notes.[75] Not only do police officers initially accuse Black janitor Tump Redwine (Clinton Rosemond) of the murder of Mary Clay (Lana Turner), but they keep Redwine incarcerated after another man, Robert Hale (Edward Norris), has been charged, using racial terror to encourage his false testimony. The consistent visual framing of Redwine behind bars in the elevator and the prison and among encroaching white bodies is enhanced by the camera's own gaze, which, like that of the press, surrounds him on all sides and zeroes in with narrowing precision (see figure 4). This, along with his bullied testimony in court, cinematically renders the sense of his being railroaded, while the repeated use of the tune "Dixie" in these scenes associates this entrapment with the white South.

The PCA's repression of lynching's racial history is confirmed most clearly in its prohibition on *Stevedore*, a leftist, anti-capitalist play written by George Sklar and Paul Peters and produced first by the Federal Theater Project but eventually at Broadway's Civic Repertory Theater. The play is about a Black dockworker framed for raping a white woman because he organizes Black and white workers against capitalism. The play finishes with Black workers barricading their neighborhood against a white lynch mob, a Black woman shooting dead her white would-be assaulters, and white dockworkers joining the Black defense in solidarity. In 1937, Universal's Carl Laemmle, intending to make the film, submitted a thirty-six-page treatment to the PCA. The script was co-written by Hollywood portrait artist Roman Freulich, a Polish-born Jew, and Rena M. Vale, a scriptwriter for Universal who was, at the time, a communist and friend of Paul Robeson (though she would later become very active in California's anticommunist movement). Freulich and Vale's treatment promised to broaden the scope of the original play with an opening documentary montage revealing segregation in neighborhoods and on trains and contrasting Black poverty with white wealth. Freulich had made two earlier films: *Prisoner* (1934), an avant-garde, dialogueless sound film, and *The Broken Earth* (1936), a meditative film starring Clarence Muse as a Black sharecropper praying for his sick son. The latter film Freulich intended as the first of a trilogy films centering on Black life. However, neither this trilogy nor *Stevedore* would come to the screen. First, Joseph Breen pronounced the play unfilmable:

> This story seems to us to be exceedingly dangerous from the standpoint of the Production Code, because it deals with such an inflammatory subject. Portraying as it does the unfair treatment of the blacks by the whites, and touching upon the subject of an alleged attack by a black man on a white woman, an attempted lynching of a negro, etc., it suggests to us the kind of story which, if made into a

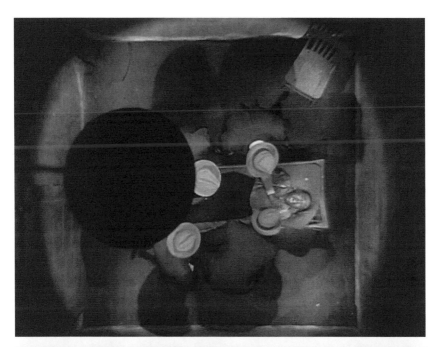

FIGURE 4. The cinematography communicates the white state surveillance that entraps Tump Redwine (Clinton Rosemond) in these frame captures from *They Won't Forget* (1937).

picture, we would have to reject, in the dispensation of our duties in connection with the Production Code.[76]

Breen summed up his rejection of *Stevedore* with reference neither to miscegenation nor lynching, but rather to an "inflammatory racial question," the same reason he had given to opposing *Imitation of Life*.[77] A 1938 MPPDA internal report on Industry Policy, which praises Breen's *Stevedore* decision as a "public service," reveals the industry policy against racial lynching. Breen was to be lauded for insisting "that screen material involving racial conflicts between white and blacks be handed in such a way as to avoid fanning the flame of race prejudice. The film *Fury* proves conclusively that there is a way to handle satisfactorily and with tremendous dramatic power the heinous crime of lynching without including the racial angle."[78]

An exception from 1939 suggests the shape of the PCA's policy on racial lynching. In MGM's *The Adventures of Huckleberry Finn*, Jim (Rex Ingram), a runaway slave, is nearly lynched because townsfolk think he has murdered Huck (Mickey Rooney). What makes the timid PCA's acceptance of this storyline strange is the film's discourse on freedom. Unlike in the novel, in the film Jim's wife and son are free—and Jim talks about meeting them in a free state. Further, when Huck first discovers Jim's escape and says he has to return him to his owner, Jim neither shrinks nor acquiesces but rather, as the 1940s sociologist and Black film scholar Lawrence Reddick notes, shows "the passionate wish for freedom on the part of the runaway slave."[79] Throughout the film Jim is perpetually one misstep away from lynching. A white mob searches for Jim and when asked whether they plan to arrest him, they say, "We don't arrest that kind," revealing a racism that never graced the screen in the 1936–1937 lynching film cycle. Jim eludes lynchers until Huck's wounds force him to either take him to a doctor or watch him die. The doctor turns Jim in, ironically for the murder of the boy he just saved. A mob storms the jail and overcomes the sheriff. "Why doesn't someone come help me?" Jim says as he shrinks from the madding throng. Several close-up subjective shots from Jim's perspective reveal lynching's terror, as the mob congeals and breaks into the jail. But by the end of the scene, Jim stops cowering and stands to meet his would-be killers. Huck's appearance halts the lynch party. At the end of the film, Huck, who has become an abolitionist, convinces the widow to free Jim. The final image is of Huck waving goodbye to Jim, who has boarded an abolitionist's steamboat to travel North to his family. How did such a strong scene of lynching, linked to anti-slavery sentiment, make it to the screen if the PCA had effectively barred racialized lynching?

Though Breen had creatively helped *Fury*'s makers—and despite the similarities in the setting and sadism of the two lynching scenes, he strongly warned Louis B. Mayer about the scene's racial lynching and insisted that the word "nigger" be "dropped":

The entire sequence showing the mob of whites attempting to lynch a negro is questionable and open to some danger, because of the possibility of inciting racial and sectional animosities. The fact that the negro is saved after he is proved innocent at the last moment is, of course, a mitigating factor. It is our feeling, however, that certain Southern political censor boards may delete the entire sequence or reject the whole picture. We therefore suggest that you assure yourself with regard to this possibility. In any case, these scenes should be handled with the greatest care.[80]

Breen did pass the film with the scenes of the near lynching of Blacks intact. But this case, like *Show Boat,* indicates that "pre-tested," historical, venerated literary and stage fare could achieve a exceptional status in the eyes of the PCA.

Breen worried about lynching films, whether the setting was southern or northern. The Black Legion was a white supremacist group making headlines in the mid-1930s. But Breen argued, in response to Warner Bros.' initial *Black Legion* treatment, which showed Blacks and whites living together, that "it has been our policy not to approve stories which raise and deal with the provocative and inflammatory subjects of racial and religious prejudice."[81] Warner Bros. insisted that prejudice was "truth necessary to make the film a valuable document," and the Breen Office, in a memo, reported that they would relent, allowing the studio to "treat the subject as broadly and strongly" as they wished and to "test out the limit of . . . acceptability." No Black people appear in the finished film, however.[82]

Breen insisted even more strongly that the racial angle be omitted with *Nation Aflame,* an independent film produced by the Halperin brothers, who were best known for their zombie films. In an early synopsis, the film showed "a Negro's house . . . burned down because of some charge that has been trumped up against him" and "a Jew made victim of the clan [*sic*]."[83] The company indicated indirection by stating, "We do not, necessarily, show what is actually done, only the results. But the Jew has been killed."[84] Breen, however, suggested the story would be approved only if "organizations, such as the American Legion, Knights of Columbus, Elks, etc. would not be indicated . . . and also that the victims of the avenging angels would not be definitely characterized as Jews, Catholics, or negroes."[85] Once they had secured an initial okay, however, the Halperins boldly inserted race and religion into later drafts, keeping in racial brutality until June 1936 and a Black speaking character until November, despite Breen's warnings. Breen was steadfast, however, requiring that Negroes, Jews, Greeks, and varying "others" be assiduously avoided in the script:

It will be necessary for you to delete from your story any suggestion that the "angels" are organized to combat "race and religion." It is our suggestion that you confine your motives in this regard to "foreigners" and that you do not raise any racial or religious questions. That is because such a discussion is highly inflammatory and likely to promote and inspire very definite and unfavorable audience reaction.[86]

Later Breen removed race not only from those at the story's center but even from marginal montage sequences, stating that "shots which definitely indicate specific races are very objectionable, and should be changed not only to avoid characterizing any particular nationality but also to get away from the gruesomeness that appears in them."[87] Breen's dogged caution may be partly explained by the fact that Marie Presstman, head of the Maryland board of censors, had written to Breen with concern about the cumulative effects of films about "Ku Klux organizations" on young boys. But nowhere did Presstman indicate race as a concern.[88]

Ultimately, *Legion of Terror, Nation Aflame,* and *Black Legion* all failed to show the Legion's Black victims. Instead, each film relegated treatment of race to speeches: white judges, law enforcement, or elected officials verbally condemn "racial and religious" prejudice or the Legion's attack on American values like "equality and religious freedom." Instead of being marked by race or religion, the victims of the Legion are "foreign." These substitutions and speeches distance us from the corporeal realities of Black lynching. The case of the Black Legion cycle suggests that the problem with lynching and racial terror was not the South or brutality but that it made visible "inflammatory" racial and religious tensions.

In sum, as the issue of lynching became the subject of a studio cycle, Breen pushed filmmakers to make lynching deniable, portraying it through indirect signifiers. The effects of the presentation of lynching as always deferred, never occurring—that is, as a narrative of relief and rescue—contributed to a broader denial of lynching's real social effects and significant social consequences. More importantly, for the purposes of industry policy, Breen attempted to keep racial lynching off the screen altogether, only allowing the idea of racialized lynching to surface in established "classic" narratives and where the lynching is averted. While these domesticated views of lynching caused viewers to imagine lynching's horror, they also allowed them to experience catharsis and relief from its the most dire racial realities.

Social Equality in the Early Breen Era

In the late 1930s, the loudest southern protests against the MPPDA concerned not lynching or miscegenation but depictions of "social equality." And the PCA responded by tightening its restrictions on these elements, as the cases of *Artists and Models* (1937), *One Mile from Heaven* (1937), *The Spirit of Youth* (1937), and *Of Mice and Men* (1939) suggest. In the SRC and early PCA era, an emerging but inconsistent policy on integrated scenes can be discerned: generally scenes indicating professional equality got away without even a warning, in films like *Arrowsmith* (1931) (where a Black doctor works alongside a white one) or *Daniel Boone* (1936), where Clarence Muse plays the well-dressed, articulate Black servant Pompey, who is portrayed as a soliloquizing, gun-toting hero of the settlement. Even integrated public schools (in *Three on a Match* [1933]) or jails (in *Ladies of the Big House* [1933], *Hold Your Man* [1934], and *The Mayor of Hell* [1933]) escaped regulatory commentary on their interracial camraderie. However, as early as 1934, Breen warned Columbia Pictures that in the zombie film *Black Moon* (1934), starring Fay Wray, "care will be needed with this scene of Lane [Jack Holt] and his wife [Dorothy Burgess] dancing to the accompaniment of the Negro orchestra."[89] Here, as elsewhere, Black-white musical sequences bothered the budding PCA, probably because they posed the threat of physical intimacy. As Atlanta censor Mrs. Alonzo Richardson told *Variety*, the "injection of Negro cabaret scenes" were particularly offensive, since in the South, "half-naked negro women dancers do not appeal."[90] Nevertheless, the PCA files on films with interracial musical sequences in the 1930s indicate only inconsistent regulation of racial mixing. For example, there is no visible concern about race in the file on *The Big Broadcast of 1936* (1935), even though Black radio personalities "Dot" and "Dash" (the Nicholas brothers, in one of their most developed, integral roles) cross the color line when they stand in for white radio crooner the Great Lochenvar, proclaiming their love for swooning (and unsuspecting) white ladies on the other end of the wireless.

Self-appointed guardians of the white southern order sent several scathing letters that ricocheted through Hollywood's upper echelons in the late 1930s, most concerning interracial musical sequences. Among the most pointed, detailed, and sustained set of critiques was in regard to "Public Melody Number One," a musical sequence in the Jack Benny comedy *Artists and Models* in which Martha Raye in blackface plays moll to Louis Armstrong's gangster (see figure 5). At first glance, it is not clear why this scene offended the white South. The settings announce it as a stage-bound fantasy. And Raye is in blackface, hardly a mode associated with social equality. However, some contextualization and close reading make clearer how this scene offended the southern system of segregation. The Irish Raye already threatened the color line because her stage persona—especially her scat singing—linked her with blackness and jazz.[91] She never touches Armstrong, but her excited proclamations about his "hot cornet" and exaggerated hip-thrusts to his music are suggestive. Her slightly exaggerated, campy dance holds both parody and homage. Where, as Michael Rogin has argued, blackface minstrelsy typically exaggerates racial color with burnt cork in order to reify, by contrast, the whiteness of the performer underneath, Raye's light-skinned blackface—combined with her playful mixing with Black people—points disconcertingly to the limits of race's visibility.[92] Armstrong's horn, though only a symbolic weapon standing in place of a gun, literally blows away the scene's only white men (four machine gun-toting G-men and a police officer). Although the conceit of music and comedy soften undertones of Black aggression, Armstrong nevertheless plays one of the Code era's only Black gangsters, and his mulatto moll (played by a white woman) musically celebrates his triumph over white authority.

Threats of a "movement" of exhibitors, the press, and the city censors of the South reached MPPDA officials at the end of 1937 and hinged specifically on two musical numbers: "Public Melody Number One" and "Turn on that Red Hot Heat," a Technicolor night-club sequence from *Vogues of 1938* (1937), in which white spectators beheld the Black body in ways that Will Hays worried about. Describing in detail the camera's treatment of the moving Black body, Hays lamented *Vogues'* "body exposures, particularly the breasts; the close ups and the extravagant motions, horizontal positions, etc.—all accentuated by the color (Technicolor and racial)." New Orleans theater manager E. V. Richards forwarded a letter from Dolph Frantz, editor of Louisiana's *Shreveport Journal*, to a long list of Hollywood elite, worrying that the industry would face "far reaching attacks" by "a mass formation of the Southern Press."[93] Frantz described "an increasing feeling of protest as the producers seem to becoming bolder and more thoughtless about placing whites and negroes together in pictures."[94] Atlanta city censor Mrs. Alonzo Richardson also cut the scene from *Artists and Models* and described to Breen the problem with Martha Raye's performance, using, in part, words from preview audiences:

> "She out-niggers the niggers." Her postures, her dancing, her whole presentation of this scene is altogether disgusting. . . . In the South, white women can't act with negroes themselves on the same plane. There is a place for both in the pictures, and each in his proper place makes for real art . . . but a lady must be a lady. . . . One wiggle of Miss Raye's stomach condemned her.[95]

Frantz's, Richards's, and Richardson's statements indicate the hold of a southern segregationist logic on the southern censors and press—the very mechanisms of dissemination upon which the studios would rely for exhibition and advertising.

Breen's response accommodated southern racism: "We have repeatedly warned the studios about the shooting of such scenes. Unfortunately, it is not usually set forth in the script that certain of the dancers are to be negroes. . . . I shall take this opportunity of again reminding the studios of the inherent difficulties in the shooting of such scenes."[96] Thereafter Breen more carefully scrutinized social equality, calling on Paramount not to shoot "Martha Raye dancing with a colored chorus" in *The Big Broadcast of 1938* (1938).[97] Breen asked David O. Selznick to avoid "social equality" between Black servant and white employer in

FIGURE 5. *Facing page:* Parallel editing joins Martha Raye's leggy descent with shadows magnifying Louis Armstrong's horn. In the frame at the bottom, Armstrong and his Harlem dancers angrily chase off the white, gun-toting G-men, saying, "Get out of here, you rhythm rascals you!" Frame captures from *Artists and Models* (1937).

Nothing Sacred (1937), set in New York.[98] After the wife of Georgia senator Richard Russell complained of a "repulsive . . . negro dance sequence" where there was racial mixing and jitterbug dancing in RKO's *Radio City Revels* (1938), Breen asked RKO to omit a scene from *The Story of Vernon and Irene Castle* (1939) where the Castles dance to a Black orchestra, because he was "certain" southern audiences would object and "deluge" the studio "with letters of protest."[99] Even the "characterization of Hilda the colored maid" in *The Mad Miss Manton* (1938), set in the modern, urban North, bothered Breen because her "impertinent, familiar attitude toward her employer" might "be found objectionable in the South, where the showing of Negros on terms of familiarity and social equality is resented."[100] These letters reveal that Breen's restrictive vigilance encroached on national film fare. Indeed, even on the cusp of the war for democracy in October 1941, the PCA instructed RKO's William Gordon that *Syncopation* (1942), which the PCA saw as a story dealing "with a mixture of white and negro characters," had to be watched "so handling of the scenes where mixed characters come together" would bear "no offensive flavor . . . in those states where any undue mixing or familiarity between whites and the negroes, especially where a white girl is concerned, would be regarded as highly offensive."[101] Here, as in other places, Breen's stated concern about integration adopted language associated with miscegenation. These examples, together, signal the wide range of screen material—from maids talking back to interracial dancing—that counted as offensive social equality between the races.

But the PCA did not eliminate all signs of racial equality and social mixing as the South wanted. In the midst of the uproar, the PCA approved the Fredi Washington vehicle *One Mile from Heaven,* a film that would be touted by Will Hays's National Previewing Committee.[102] As I discuss below, North Carolina exhibitors both avoided and protested the film, indicating the PCA's failure to contain or completely understand what "social equality" meant. Though *One Mile from Heaven* steered clear of miscegenation, it angered Southerners because it raised the specter of integration.

The film was based on a true story from the juvenile court of Judge Benjamin Lindsey. Lucy "Tex" Warren (Claire Trevor), a tomboyish newspaper reporter, finds a striking human-interest story: Flora Jackson (Fredi Washington), a widowed Black seamstress, is raising a blonde, Shirley Temple–like child, Sunny (Joan Carroll), as her own in a predominantly Black neighborhood. When a local store clerk hints that Sunny is white, Lucy seeks to return Sunny to the white world. But when she learns that Sunny is barely legitimate—the daughter of a rich heiress and an imprisoned gangster—Lucy relinquishes the case to a judge who awards the child to "its rightful mother," Barbara Harrison (Sally Blane). The logic of legal divorcement of Black from white is undone, however, when Harrison and her new husband (like the real figures in Lindsey's court) invite Flora to live with them. In the film's final sequences, the Harrisons host a party for Sunny and her Black friends from the neighborhood. Warren ultimately decides that publishing Sunny's story would do too much damage to the child and refuses to bring it to her editor.

One Mile from Heaven represents Washington's figurative reprisal of her *Imitation of Life* role. But it also demonstrates the maturation of studio handling of the PCA's miscegenation policy. Flora, despite her lightness, does not desire to be white. Instead, the racial problem is that she loves—and desires to mother—an abandoned white child. Thus the interracial connection is packaged in a much safer form—the same tender, melodramatic mother-love Breen had called "beautiful" in *Imitation of Life*.

But even as the film tempers its miscegenetic edge, it subtly challenges the logic of segregation. First, it deliberately confuses viewers about Sunny's racial heritage. We believe that Sunny is Black, at first, because Flora, whom we trust, tells everyone that she is Sunny's biological mother.[103] It is only at the end that we discover that Flora has been lying about Sunny's biological parentage. Second, the film is decidedly Black-centered. The loveless Lucy, who frames the story, is never its emotional center. The film's only established romantic pairing is Flora and her boyfriend, Officer Joe (Bill Robinson). Third, through subplots, visual coding, and emotional bonds, the narrative integrates its Black and white characters. Joe, the narrative reveals, is a well-paid police officer, working on an apparently integrated force, who wields his authority against white reporters and gangsters who illegally trespass on Flora's property. Additionally, the film's strongest emotional bond is between Sunny and Flora. Even after it is determined that Sunny is white, so firm is Sunny's insistence that she belongs to Flora, and so sympathetic is Flora's own plea for her rights to the child she has reared since infancy ("You can take her away from me but you'll never take her love"), that the idea that the two belong together is far more compelling than the judge's legal solution: that Flora is a mammy who must return Sunny to the white world. Besides, Fredi Washington is no mammy. She is dressed in a manner that mirrors—or even upstages—white star Claire Trevor (see figures 6 and 7). Sunny's distraught face underscores that, although she may be white, Flora is her mother. The film's visual coding unites Flora and Sunny where the narrative divides them. In the very courtroom where the two will be legally "divorced," Sunny and Flora's black hats frame their equally white faces. Later portions of the scene repeatedly obfuscate both of their faces, showing mother and daughter fused behind a veil of blackness, symbolized by their matching black hats.

The film also offered Washington her least tragic film ending. The film's final scene shows Flora satisfied with her continued connection to her white daughter. Even scenes where Flora personifies the tragic mulatta associate her torture with white wrongs—white intrusion on Black domestic life (literal and figurative), white legal inconsistency about the definitions of race and motherhood,

Wonder How Dixie Likes This Type of Social Equality

Bill Robinson and Fredi Washington seem to be on perfectly equal terms in their latest film, "One Mile from Heaven," along with Claire Trevor and Douglass Towley. In left group, Fredi (seated, extreme right) is dressed as swell as star, Claire Trevor; and how about this happy party at the right?

FIGURE 6. Frame capture of *One Mile from Heaven* (1937) (*top*) and a clipping of a story on the film from the *Baltimore Afro-American* (*bottom*). Clipping courtesy of *Baltimore Afro-American*.

FIGURE 7. Production still from *One Mile from Heaven*. Author's personal collection.

and white media exploitation of Flora's visual image (a facet that makes a significant if unwitting intertextual point about Washington herself).

Most upsetting to the segregationist logic was the film's unresolved ending. The promise of Joe and Flora's impending marriage seemed both to solve the industry's problem with Fredi Washington's racial indeterminacy and to reassure white audiences that Washington's sexual desire, unlike her motherly yen, stayed within the race. But upon closer examination, these closing sequences highlight the untidiness of any sort of interracial attachments in a society divided along the color line. We learn that Joe will be assigned to the beat where the Harrisons live, allowing him to be close to Flora. But does this mean that he will police a white neighborhood? Not only does Joe's state-endowed authority challenge the racial order of things, but the screen presentation of Robinson departs slightly but significantly from his typical role. Bill Robinson's first dance sequences are not performed primarily for white onscreen audiences but for and with Black children. The film closes as Sunny and all of her Black friends from Maple Hill sit around the Harrisons' swimming pool, eating cake that Flora serves. Bill Robinson, dressed as a bandleader, does a tap dance for the party, which cheers riotously. This utopian ending deserves comparison to *The Jazz Singer* (1927), in which time and space elastically and impossibly expand, erasing the pressure of the suspense narrative, to create room across cultural difference.[104] Robinson's costumed tap performance at the celebration is, like Jakie Rabinowitz's black-face finale, the triumph of entertainment over narrative resolution—designed to avert audience questions and conceal rather than resolve the film's racial prob-lems. Nevertheless, the ending also implicitly endorses integration, as it sutures an impossible spatial and emotional divide—promising that Sunny will con-tinue to be connected to her (former?) Black mother and community.[105]

The film represents the triumph of melodrama over sex (in connection with Fredi Washington) and of racial spectacle (Bill Robinson's tapping) over racial problems. But the southern bloc still had problems with the racially entwined images themselves. The assimilation of Washington into Hollywood's norma-tive melodramatic representation not as mammy but as a resplendent, hurting mother, the fact that Washington's "hurt" is caused quite directly by whites, and the narrative centrality and prominent billing of Black players made the film ripe for claims of social equality across the color line, despite the juridical restora-tion of racial boundaries. The film's visual and dialogical intangibles—the verbal exchange during the trial and in the finale, the fashionable costuming of Fredi Washington, and the northern setting—subtly transmitted equality and under-mined the implicit racial hierarchy of the judge's decision.

As *One Mile from Heaven* and *Artists and Models* reveal, the South sensed equality in just the ambiguous, deniable interracial moments that the industry thought would appease both Southerners and African Americans. Following white southern protests of 1937, the MPPDA revised its racial industry policy with the help of a new Southerner-in-residence, Francis Harmon. Though Har-mon's suggested policies were mild by contrast with Trotti's, Breen was increas-ingly vigilant in policing displays of social equality even outside the musical realm, as the PCA files on *The Spirit of Youth* and *Of Mice and Men* illustrate.[106]

Alongside images of women troubling race and gender roles in the late 1930s with implied social equality came a pair of films that invoked Black masculinity. *The Spirit of Youth* (1937) was a film about Joe Louis—and starring the Brown Bomber himself. Breen queried Will Hays about whether it was acceptable "*from the standpoint of policy,* because it shows . . . several scenes of a black man, vic-torious in a number of fistic encounters with white men," the same issue that prompted a federal ban on interstate commerce of Jack Johnson fight films.[107] After seeing the picture and consulting prominent African Americans, Hays, according to Breen's paraphrase, decided there was "no way in which this picture could be denied our certificate of approval on the basis of the suggestion of the black-white phase of the story."[108] But Breen still attached to the certificate of approval a request that producers avoid southern distribution.[109] Although he mandated no cuts, Breen noted the unfortunateness of the film's use of "a white man to play the part of the punch drunk pugilist, who begs and received money from the negro manager. This is the kind of incident which causes wide-spread protest in all parts of the country."[110] In contemporary prints, this sequence is absent and Louis only fights white opponents in montage sequences or those dampened in intensity by parallel editing.

While the South was focused on dancing, it gave little attention to a film that strongly challenged racial segregation: *Of Mice and Men* (1939), based on a New York stage adaptation of John Steinbeck's novel. Crooks (Leigh Whipper), a field hand maligned, beaten down, and segregated, plainly states that he is kept out of the bunkhouse where white hands live because he is Black. When a white field hand, Candy (Roman Bohnen), says to Crooks: "Must be nice to have a room all to yourself this way," Crooks sarcastically replies without looking up from his book: "Sure: and a dung heap under my window all to myself." In this, Crooks points to segregation's unspoken degradations, showing separate-but-equal to be a myth. Throughout the film, Crooks's articulate bitterness on the stigma of blackness in America voiced a critique rarely heard in Hollywood films. Breen was too distracted by the script's white mercy killing, sex pervert, and loose woman to give much attention to its racial angle, a fact that may have spared the film this racial commentary. Besides, before Breen's initial censorship letter, producer Hal Roach removed what MPPDA officials described as the play's major racial worry—that Crooks and white ranchers discussed their experiences at bawdy houses.

But Breen did sense strong stuff in Crooks's monologue and attempted to alter it. However, perhaps unable to pinpoint the source or feeling a lack of will or authority to cut the bitter commentary on segregation wholesale, Breen hemmed his concerns by snipping the film's racial language, since the script's obscene phrases ("guts," "nuts," "rat," and "butt") were already being clipped: "To avoid offense, we advise that the three uses of the word 'black' be changed to 'colored.'" This change, one designed perhaps to avoid Black spectators' offense, by no means removed segregation but it did soften the scene's racial severity. Breen also wanted the line about the dung pile removed—"to avoid objection or offense."[111] But in the case of this literary best seller, Breen did not put the power of the Code behind these suggestions, and producers maintained these lines as originally written. Breen had moderated Hollywood's racial discourse in the midst of battles between Cultural Front leftists and staunch racist holdouts. However, his concern was not only about the South but, as *Black Legion* suggests, about any films that touched on America's "inflammatory" racial questions. Increasingly this moderation meant a marginalization of stories revealing racial prejudice, animus, and social equality between Black and white.

THE PCA AND RACE IN WARTIME

The coming of war disrupted not only PCA praxis but the staff itself. Breen went on hiatus between 1940 and 1941. More broadly, the coming of war thrust America—and American films—into an international discourse on the meanings of democracy that meant a sudden reconsideration of the PCA's most racist policies—such as barring social equality.

OWI and Regulating Blackness in the War Era

World War II brought the industry new outside pressures greatly affecting the representation of Black civil rights on screen. According to Clayton Koppes and Gregory Black, in July 1942 the U.S. Office of War Information (OWI), a government censorship agency, opened up its Motion Picture Bureau and asked all Hollywood studios to submit scripts.[112] In addition, the OWI instituted a Los Angeles Branch to monitor Hollywood film activity more closely. Unlike the PCA, the OWI could not compel changes. But the pressure of patriotism meant film companies often followed the OWI's recommendations, and projects that presented acute problems for the OWI were often scrapped. What is more, because a film's foreign distribution was contingent upon a federal license during World War II, the OWI used the threat of denying this license to encourage studios to accept their dictates during the process of production. Therefore, by fall 1943, all major studios with one exception (Paramount) were submitting all their scripts—and often multiple drafts—to the OWI for approval.[113]

The OWI's philosophy was markedly different than the PCA's. The PCA had been formed in the fire of religious protest with the Catholic morality of the Production Code as its constitution. By contrast, the OWI was guided by a progressive political interest in the international reputation of the United States, and its leaders had been influential New Dealers.[114] Thus, OWI sought to eradicate misinformation about various racial groups, national and international.

With an eye toward broad international diplomacy, OWI staffers censored Hollywood's racial and national stereotypes.[115] For example, OWI reviewer Eleanor Bernais could not recommend overseas distribution of *Charlie Chan in the Secret Service* (1944) due to the film's racist depiction of Chinese people. Although Chan filled "a responsible position competently," the script made him "a bland and inscrutable Oriental, whose quaintness is emphasized by his frequent use of cryptic proverbs, delivered in pidgin English. This portrayal might well appear to the Chinese as an American caricature of their race."[116] Neither did the OWI support Hollywood's attempts to racially villainize the Axis. They coached Hollywood studios out of screening racist hate in *Land of the Free* (unproduced), *Joe Navy* (unproduced), *God Is My Co-Pilot* (1945), and *Little Tokio, USA* (1942).[117] With *Joe Navy*, OWI reviewers told Hollywood scriptwriters how to tell their story, prescribing a character arc in the protagonist, Ollie. They also saw "an opportunity for more specifically characterizing our Japanese enemy." But they cautioned the studio against employing the term "sneaky-eyed little monkey" and references to "yellow-stained fangs." "These references are made in a name calling spirit, which attacks the enemy on the basis of racial characteristics rather than his Fascist ideology. Such an attack is particularly unfortunate since millions of our allies (including the Chinese) have colored skins and slanted eyes."[118]

African Americans were a particular concern for the OWI. As Koppes and Black have noted, in a 1942 Office of Facts and Figures survey, 49 percent of Black respondents opined that they would be at least as well off if the Japanese were to win the war because the Japanese were people of color and less likely than whites to discriminate.[119] The OWI therefore attended carefully to Black characterization and to any lines of dialogue suggesting American belief in racial superiority. OWI reviewers made it standard policy to ask for modifications of the ubiquitous Black menial to reduce stereotypes of American workers.[120] For example, the OWI's response to *Sing a Jingle* (1944) called attention

> to the characterization of a Negro valet (pp. 3 and 4) as an eye-rolling comic, who trembles with fear at mention of the war. He says he has a weak heart which "comes on me every time I think of them bullets poppin' around." Couldn't the Negro valet be played straight? American Negroes constitute the largest minority group in this country. They are proud of the members of their race who are distinguishing themselves on the battle fronts, many of whom have courageously given their lives, and could resent this presentation of the Negro as a coward.[121]

The OWI drew attention to the ridiculousness—and the damage—of Hollywood presentations of dark-skinned people. In many instances, the studios responded by omitting racial material the OWI found problematic, an effect that decreased the number of Black representations in Hollywood film, but nevertheless projected abroad an America more in line with New Dealers' idealized racial democracy.

The OWI went beyond condemnation of comic stereotypes. For example, they incisively critiqued *Cabin in the Sky* (1943) and *Stormy Weather* (1943), arguably Hollywood's flagship wartime celebrations of Black Americans designed to appease the OWI mandate to improve Black representation. Here the OWI criticized not only characterization but the films' overall racial "feeling." They claimed that *Cabin in the Sky*'s all-Black cast contributed "to the feeling of segregation of Negroes. . . . At the present moment Negroes are contributing their full share to the war effort working not only in factories and fields . . . but also as doctors, nurses, scientists . . . dying side by side with other Americans." This portrayal of them as "simple, ignorant, superstitious folk incapable of anything but the most menial of labour . . . [and] for the most part unfit for the responsibilities of citizenship . . . can only be resented by Negroes themselves and in addition, serves to stimulate already existing prejudices on the part of other Americans— thus weakening developing unity."[122] The pervasive ideological scope of the

OWI's racial argument went beyond cosmetic changes. They saw stereotypes as instruments of dissent, undermining national unity, the war effort, and America's international reputation.

The OWI was also instrumental, in certain cases, in designing improved Black characterizations. For example, they complained of the portrayal of Tambul, the heroic Sudanese soldier in early script drafts for *Sahara* (1943).[123] "For all the good intentions of the script, Tambul remains apart from the others, a sort of Gunga Din," the OWI reviewer argued. He "is made unnecessarily heroic, and a little simple, thus failing fully to convince us. For example, his ability to guide the tank through the blinding sandstorm while he clings unprotected to its prow (p. 59). While water is portioned out to others at the run, we never see Tambul take so much as a drop. Yet he is able to sing for hours as he collects the dripping water in the well (p. 68, p. 79)."[124] By the next script review, with the addition of goggles for his sandstorm ride and a sequence showing him satisfying his own thirst, the OWI reviewer happily noted "the Sudanese Negro character" appeared "on equal footing . . . no longer a faithful Gunga Din but a convincing brother in arms."[125] The modification of *Sahara* suggests that the OWI criticized inhumanity not only in the portrayal of weak, scared Black menials but also of strong Black heroes.

However, the OWI was lax in its mandate against racial superiority in several areas. Blackface was a key example. In response to *Dixie* (1943), Paramount's Technicolor story of pioneering minstrel Dan Emmett, starring Bing Crosby, OWI reviewers complained about uncritical presentation of blackface with "its unfortunate connotation of Negro inferiority," the term "darkies," and "Rastus-Sambo type of jokes," which might undermine national unity; but they ultimately adjudged these "not serious enough" to inhibit international distribution. Similarly, though they worried that, in *The Adventures of Mark Twain* (1944), Twain himself used the term "darky" and told racist jokes, the OWI liked the film as "Americana" and recommended its approval for foreign distribution.

But in their quest to image an idealized American democracy, the OWI censored depictions of American racism. Indeed, OWI's Motion Picture Bureau represented a dubious culmination of New Deal philosophies, compelled, as they were, to make their mark on history in the censors' red ink. The desire to erase signs of discrimination from the screen is demonstrated in the file on *Dark Waters* (1944), starring Merle Oberon and featuring Rex Ingram. While OWI reviewers praised producers for stereotype-free Black characterization, they asked them to remove "white and colored" signs indicating bayou segregation, which "corroborat[ed] enemy propaganda on racial inequalities," a request the producer obliged. In response to the unproduced *Liberty Ship*, the OWI asked the producers to remove a sequence showing housing discrimination.[126] "The problem is real, the challenge deserves statement, but it is a challenge to which there should be an answer. . . . It is questionable whether, at this time, it is wise to raise an issue that cannot be satisfactorily solved."[127] And although they critiqued *Stormy Weather* for its depiction of a segregated world, they also worried that the film would too strongly depict white racism. In one sequence, Bill Robinson is shown riding a boxcar but becomes frightened when he hears guards. "Are these guards to be white?" OWI reviewers asked. "Brutality of railroad guards towards all hoboes and especially Negroes, has been the cause of many controversial and unpleasant incidents between white and Negroes. Perhaps this short incident could be eliminated."[128] And though they lambasted the subtle servility of the Black character Joe (Canada Lee) in the script for Alfred Hitchcock's *Lifeboat* (1944), they denied it foreign distribution for another reason: because it showed American mob violence, presenting a poor view of American democracy.[129] OWI patriotism sanitized screen representations of the problem of mob violence that was the greatest evidence of the need for victory against racism at home.

Most troubling was the government repression of *In This Our Life* (1942), a film that clearly depicted the railroading of Black men. Based on the Pulitzer Prize–winning novel by white Southerner Ellen Glasgow, the film had a significant racial subplot. Parry Clay (Ernest Anderson) is the son of Minerva (Hattie McDaniel), a maid for the white southern Timberlake family. He is studying to be a lawyer while working in the Timberlake's hardware store and doing odd jobs for them. While driving home from a bar, Stanley (Bette Davis), the eldest Timberlake daughter, kills an eight-year-old child in a hit-and-run accident. When police question her, she claims that Parry was washing her car that evening, thus framing him. Parry is arrested. When Roy (Olivia de Havilland), Stanley's younger sister, visits Minerva to console her, the Black mother professes Parry's innocence. "But why didn't Parry tell police?" Roy pleads. "They just came and took him off," responds Minerva. "He tried to tell them but they don't listen to no colored boy." Later, when visiting Parry in jail, Stanley pressures him to corroborate her story, saying that she will help to get him off if he does. Parry, however, refuses to condemn himself with her lies. When told that it is his word against a white woman, Parry's beleaguered response ("It ain't no use. Ain't no use in this world. . . . My telling the truth ain't gonna help me. There ain't nothing gonna help me") sharply marks the unfairness of America's justice system toward Black men. Despite Stanley's eventual confession and Parry's implied release, the film's dismal portrayal of American race relations and Parry and Minerva's resounding disbelief in the possibility of justice for Black Southerners led the OWI to recommend against its foreign distribution. "So strong is the race feeling in [the film's] Virginia community," they explained, "that the young Negro was practically condemned in advance. It is made abundantly clear that a Negro's testimony in court is almost certain to be disregarded if in conflict with the testimony of a white person."[130] So while government pressure worked to improve African American characterization and to encourage images of an integrated America, it impaired the international circulation of images of segregation and mob violence in the United States.

Wartime Racial Policy: Comparing the PCA and the OWI

Although the MPPDA discussed the OWI's agenda, it affected their praxis little.[131] While the PCA actively protected the "Good Neighbor" policy, forwarding anything offensive to Latin Americans to Hays appointee Addison Durland, the organization largely left the government to enforce its African American anti-stereotype agenda on its own. But in light of these new pressures, the MPPDA launched two successive self-studies of African Americans in Hollywood film (one in 1944 and the other in 1945) to defend itself against racial critique. The reports touted the absence of Black villains in Hollywood films. Indeed, only one Hollywood film of 1944—*Zombies on Broadway*—showed a Black villain, a Caribbean zombie. But though designed to show studios' racial progress, the reports revealed that only three Code-sanctioned films offered African Americans major roles between October 1944 and September 1945: *I Love a Bandleader*, with Eddie "Rochester" Anderson, and two Charlie Chan films, *The Scarlet Clue* and *The Jade Mask*, featuring Mantan Moreland.[132] Whether these films truly starred Black men, however, is debatable, and in all cases the reported stars were playing menials. The MPPDA acknowledged that of the films showing Black people in 1944, the majority were porters or bootblacks and that "negroes are seldom shown as educated and professional characters or in roles which give them cultural equality." But professional roles, the MPPDA argued, were not true to life and "might not really be the service to them which is desired. . . . For example, it is doubtful whether the general public will remember Paul Robeson any better or more enthusiastically as 'Othello' than it will remember him as the field-hand in 'Show Boat.' "[133] This report operated more as a justification for continued racism than an opportunity for self-analysis and change.

The PCA's lack of commentary on the issues that troubled the OWI—like racial servility, blackface, or American racism—indicates Breen's desire to seem impervious to the OWI's concern about African Americans. Breen said nothing of the blackface in *Dixie* or the repudiation of Black suffrage in *Tennessee Johnson* (1942). He even allowed sung references to "darkies" in *The Vanishing Virginian* (1942) and defended anti-Black jokes in *The Adventures of Mark Twain*. Nor did he critique wartime Black subservience in *Lifeboat* or *Sahara* as did the OWI. Breen deferred the entire soldier angle in *Follow the Boys* (1944) to the army's own censors. The film divided its Black representation between ridiculous, clowning Black soldiers in a dance sequence and the Delta Rhythm Boys as soldiers solemnly singing, "All races all religions / That's America to me," a refrain from the Popular Front standard "The House I Live in." What did concern Breen regarding Black representations were the breasts of Lena Horne and Hazel Scott. In *Stormy Weather* (1942) and *Broadway Rhythm* (1945), Breen required reduced breast exposure.[134] Despite Black protest of, for example, the excision of Black soldiers from newsreels and Walter White's threat of a Hollywood Negro Bureau by war's end, the MPPDA opted against affirmative steps to regulate Black representation in a manner paralleling the OWI.[135]

In reality, Breen's policies were gradually shifting. For example, in *The Ox-Bow Incident*, the Black preacher tries to halt a lynching by telling about his brother who was lynched, which gave more exposure to the subject than in any film since *Laughter in Hell*. Though Breen dampened its brutality, he did not, as with *Stevedore*, bar the film or its racial angle (one accentuated by the film's Mexican lynching victim). But thoroughgoing treatment of Black lynching victims would still be a structuring absence into the early 1940s. Rex Ingram, Leigh Whipper, and later Joel Fluellen (who were frequently cast onstage and onscreen as victims of white brutality) all circulated around the idea of lynching and racial injustice without directly revealing it. Through their symptomatic roles (most often as witnesses rather than victims of violence), they intertextually gesture toward what the screen does not show.[136] Several films included both Black men and hangings in the same narrative but did not combine them. For example, in *Among the Living* (1940), directed by Stuart Heisler and written by leftist Lester Cole, a white man is nearly lynched for killing Pompey (Ernest Whitman), a Black servant—a bizarre, symptomatic reversal. In George Stevens's *The Talk of the Town* (1942), Dilg (Cary Grant), a labor leader falsely accused of setting fire to a local mill, is nearly lynched. Hovering around the story is Tilney (Rex Ingram), a servant of the law professor who stops the lynch mob. Though Breen squelched references to lynching out of deference to political censors, a mob does enter the courtroom with a rope. Similarly, Frank Borzage's *Moonrise* (1947), though it focuses on white Danny Hawkins (Dane Clark), repeatedly mobilizes the iconography of hanging in a southern town and gives Rex Ingram a near-starring role as Mose, the only friend and confidant of the man whose father is executed by hanging in the film's first frames, and whose life is haunted by the fear of gallows. *The Talk of the Town* and *Moonrise* were at least legible as pertinent to Black life to members of the Black press.[137]

Evidence of marginal PCA progress with integration can be seen in Breen's passage of *Bataan* (1943), *Sahara* (1943), and *Crash Dive* (1943), which came through the Code office without a complaint from Breen about "social equality" offending the South. Likely because of Black protest, Breen also took new interest in Black characterization and in the depiction of the plantation. He admonished William Gordon of RKO, producer of *I Walked with a Zombie* (1941), to "give some thought to the possible reaction of negroes in this country to a story of this sort dealing with voodoo practices by colored people."[138] By the end of the war, Breen had even come to critique the Birmingham Jones character

(Mantan Moreland) in the Charlie Chan films. In his letter regarding *The Scarlet Clue,* Breen asked that Birmingham "be played so as not to offend Negroes" and insisted that "Negroes prefer references to 'Negro boy' rather than 'colored boy.'"[139] Nevertheless, the film's early sequence of Birmingham flipping through police mug shots, encountering many members of his family and ultimately himself, undercuts this dignity.

Several memos, however, indicate that despite marginal progress, Breen sought to maintain the industry's staunch conservatism on "racial equality"—especially during World War II when racial ideology was in flux. Breen stated unequivocally that leftist screenwriter Emmet Lavery's 1943 screenplay adaptation of Pearl Buck's *China Sky,* with its "potent, sympathetic" Black aviator, interracial blood transfusion, and Sino-European romance, was "frankly . . . a plea for complete racial equality."[140] Breen was alarmed that "the action . . . and numerous lines of dialogue . . . seem to argue that all men are and should be completely equal in all things irrespective of origin, of race, color . . . or previous condition of servitude." The passage of such a film would imply, he thought, PCA approval for a thesis that more Americans would revile than support. Breen classified the screenwriter as a "special pleader," a term he regularly used to denote those with leftist sensibilities on race. In a dig at the egalitarian screen image the OWI so often supported, Breen said, "The point to be considered . . . is that here again, under the guise of entertainment, it would appear we are engaging in propaganda for one side of a controversial question"—by which he meant the question of "complete racial equality."[141] Breen attempted to cultivate support for his position directly from Hays, who upon Breen's recommendation agreed that the story should be halted. Breen even told Hays that the film (and others like it) showcased the need for the industry to "formally" address limiting racial equality "as a policy matter."[142] The script disappeared for over a year, and when it eventually reached the screen, the racially provocative equality and all Black characters were removed.

In 1941 and 1942, the PCA approved two films with surprisingly direct representations of Black-white interracial desire. Both films were passed during Breen's hiatus as chief of the Production Code Administration, when he worked as general manager for RKO. Breen's departure was reported in the trade press as early as April 25, 1941, but his resignation was not official until June 1941.[143] He returned as PCA chairman in May 1942. During this time, Breen continued to act as a PCA consultant on a number of important or controversial films.

In 1941, the PCA approved René Clair's *The Flame of New Orleans,* despite the fact that in the script and press material the studio referred to Marlene Dietrich's maid, Clementine (Theresa Harris), as "a quadroon." Breen, before his departure, warned that a shot of a white man throwing coins into Clementine's bosom was "unacceptable" and "must be omitted."[144] Despite Breen's protests, the finished film included this scene.

Even more surprising is the PCA approval of *The Love Wanga*, a film originally produced 1935 but not officially released in the U.S. until 1941. Breen's signature is not present on any of the correspondence for *The Love Wanga*, which suggests his limited involvement with the film (which the PCA's New York office likely handled since it was technically "foreign"). The film was a "quota quickie" made by Paramount in Haiti but abandoned.[145] In it, Clelie (Fredi Washington), a light-skinned Black Haitian plantation owner, performs voodoo revenge on her lover, white plantation owner Adam Maynard, who has spurned her for a white woman. Not only is the film consistently focalized through Clelie, but Washington's performance builds sympathy for Clelie's racialized revenge. Though Black rage is only revealed through the horror film's codes of voodoo and zombies, it is still remarkably palpable. *The Love Wanga*'s characters—and its filmmakers—approach voodoo with a reverent credulity as a racialized, if supernatural, equalizing force exacting racial vengeance where there is no justice. It is an underground, cosmic recourse for abuses of civil rights and inhumanity.

The Love Wanga exposes what censors carefully kept out of *Imitation of Life*. In *Imitation of Life*, Peola's fractured racial identity makes her a fragile, hysterical, broken woman. In *The Love Wanga*, Clelie's racial liminality gives her the power of multiplicity—making her queen and "master" of both races—a Black voodoo goddess by night and a wealthy plantation owner among whites by day. Although Clelie initially calls herself "white," after being told repeatedly that she is Black she states, "All right. I'm black. I'll show him what a black girl can do!"[146] Early sequences of the film gave audiences what they had been denied in *Imitation of Life*, an erotic, empowered view of Washington—the actress they had come to know as Peola (see figure 8).

While in *Imitation of Life*, the implication of miscegenation was reduced to a distant ancestor or a "rare but scientific skin condition," in *The Love Wanga* Washington kisses one white actor and wants to make another hers. The PCA had stopped *Imitation of Life* from showing lynching, and there was little discussion of Black men. In *The Love Wanga*, by contrast, not only does lynching surface, if in indirect ways through the hanged Black body, but the fantasy of Black revenge is indulged through the voodoo capture of the white maiden.

Distributor Willis Kent sought a PCA seal, claiming it was a "south sea island film" and that he would release it "without credits," thus hiding the cast's racial identities.[147] The PCA required the elimination of "a close up navel shot . . . of Fredi Washington" at the beginning of the film, which boldly revealed the white epidermis of the Black body (see figure 8), and sequences of Blacks dancing "illicitly" at a voodoo ceremony.[148] The PCA also pushed Kent to cut shots of a Black woman's corpse hanging from a tree (one that represents and mirrors Clelie's spiritual demise and impending death) and the sequence of the zombie "carrying white girl away—showing his arm around her waist" and over her mouth "in close up"[149] (see figure 9). But though kisses on the neck and chest

FIGURE 8. *Above*: These shots depict the interracial desire and the body of Fredi Washington that *Imitation of Life* (1934) effaced. Frame captures from *The Love Wanga* (1935/1941).

FIGURE 9. *Facing page*: Black hands, first superimposed over the white woman's bodice through dissolve and then physically grabbing her face and waist. Frame captures from *The Love Wanga*.

had to be omitted, Washington's lengthy kiss and embrace with her white co-star Sheldon Leonard remained intact, according to the PCA documentation. *The Love Wanga* received PCA approval on September 10, 1941, despite the Code's miscegenation ban.

Meanwhile, Breen, consulting from his desk at RKO, censored miscegenation in major studios' films more firmly than ever. Original scripts for the Asian/white interracial love films *The Moon and Sixpence* (1942) and *Shanghai Gesture*

(1942) both included scenes where Blacks and whites intermingled. Breen asked the studio to cut moments where Black men were desirable to or desiring of non-Black women from both films and to cut Black women from a dive barroom in *The Moon and Sixpence*. These cuts ensured that Asian-white desire would not bleed over into Black-white desire and that the Black male sexuality that motivated the ban on miscegenation was firmly excised.[150] The studios complied. Less than a month after *The Love Wanga*'s passage, Breen found "unacceptable" the mere "flavor of miscegenation" in MGM's *White Cargo*, starring white actress Hedy Lamarr as Tondelayo, a jungle waif in British colonial Africa, who appears to be half-Black and marries a white man. Though the film reveals twenty minutes before its conclusion that she is not Black but the child of Arab and Egyptian traders, this was too much miscegenation for Breen. "The trick of holding back to the end of the film the fact that Tondelayo is not a Negress," Breen stated, "is in violation of at least the spirit of the Code clause covering miscegenation, and hence would make the finished picture unacceptable."[151] But despite repeated warnings, and given Breen's dubious authority, the studio did not listen.

The PCA's uneven treatment of miscegenation during the early 1940s was due largely to Breen's absence. Still, why did the PCA, sans Breen, loosen the miscegenation restriction? The PCA's strange acceptance of *The Love Wanga*'s bold representation of miscegenation was likely due to the film's age and low profile, in contrast with new major studio offerings like *White Cargo, The Moon and Sixpence,* and *Shanghai Gesture.* But we can also see the PCA's allowance of miscegenation during Breen's absence as a reflection of a change in the regulation of sensitive issues related to civil rights. As a broadening spectrum of issues confronted the PCA in light of America's involvement in the war, even standard Code issues pertinent to civil rights could be treated with greater fluidity.

As noted, during the pre-Code era the MPPDA avoided engaging with the NAACP. This changed in the late war years, however. Seeing in *Song of the South* (1946) a perfect storm of Black indignation and white ignorance, in 1944 Breen counseled Walt Disney to consult a qualified Black representative. Having queried the NAACP about whether "darky" was an offensive word, Breen advised Disney "it might be well from the standpoint of our negro patrons" to avoid using the expression at all. Indeed, the file indicates Breen's growing awareness of African American spectators and their response to stereotypes during the war era. "These good people," Breen wrote Disney, referring to African Americans, "in recent months, have become most critical regarding the portrayal on the motion picture screen of the members of their race, and it will be well for you to take counsel with some responsible leaders among the negroes concerning this particular story."[152]

In particular, Breen worried about Black leaders' responses to the "scenes [that] show Negro groups singing happily":

It is the characterization of the individuals in these groups to which certain types of Negro leaders are most likely to take exception. It is recommended therefore that these groups not be played for comedy, that their clothes be plain and reasonably clean, rather than having them dressed in rags, and that the scenes depend upon the singing of the groups to hold audience interest, rather than funny business which is certain to be resented by some negroes.[153]

Clear in this quotation is Breen's awareness of the kinds—and nuances—of representation likely to produce offense. The PCA's modifications play down, but do not entirely omit, the film's racist characterizations. To the PCA staff, the only way to get across *Song of the South,* a film in which broken English, strong dialect, and the motif of the "happy darky" predominated, in a postwar society marked by rising African American esteem and militant social activism, was to present the film as historical, thereby justifying the stereotype by displacing it in the past (and implicitly suggesting that there was an era when African Americans behaved thus). This was the strategy and public relations advice that PCA offered Disney, telling him to make sure that he took pains to "establish the fact that [Uncle Remus] and his kind belong to a bygone day."[154] Disney, however, ignored this advice and instead failed to establish clearly when the story was set—and though the film received a PCA seal, it was widely criticized for backward depictions of Black folks.[155] Breen disavowed his ability to make racial changes to scripts (claiming to be a "moral" censor only) when corresponding with Black activists about projects such as *Uncle Tom's Cabin* in 1944 and *The Adventures of Mark Twain,* but by the end of the war years he no longer utterly dismissed Black activists' claims, as discussed in later chapters.

In sum, several of the first hesitant and incomplete acknowledgments of Black equality by a more mature film industry came during the war and immediate postwar era. Miscegenation was more directly represented in several instances due to Breen's absence. Though there were no major shifts with lynching and integration, Breen showed his hallmark gradualism (permitting, for example, the racial aura surrounding *The Ox-Bow Incident*'s lynching and the direct, if marginalized, revelation of segregation's impact in *Of Mice and Men*). He avoided the appearance of policy change while subtly modifying his advice to the studios to consider the complaints of Black leaders and the federal government's shifting racial ideology. But while making subtle accommodations, he kept the screen from depicting "complete racial equality," seeing it as a matter of industry welfare.

RACIAL PROBLEM FILMS AND POSTWAR MPAA POLICY

The subtle shifts in the wartime MPPDA foretold a more substantial postwar shift. On June 15, 1945, amid increasing direct protest of the industry's depiction of minorities, the MPPDA (renamed the Motion Picture Association of America in 1946) passed a resolution changing the Production Code. No longer would it read that "the history, institutions and prominent people of *foreign* nations shall be represented fairly." Now it would read "*all* nations shall be represented fairly"—and the MPPDA president was given authority to appoint a committee to study this issue.[156] Several months later, George Houser, the white co-founder of the Congress of Racial Equality (CORE), one of the first civil rights groups involved in direct-action nonviolent protest, wrote to new MPAA chairman Eric Johnston that he was "glad" that Johnston, whose "liberal views on racial issues are well known," had assumed the post. Believing the end of Black caricatures to be essential for "complete racial democracy," Houser opined, "Potentially the movies could do more for the cause of racial justice than almost any other public institution. . . . We would appreciate some assurance from you that you will not continue to allow the movie industry to misinform the public on the true facts of racial equality."[157]

Johnston consulted with Francis Harmon before responding. Harmon assured him that CORE was not an important Black organization and encouraged him to send a dated 1937 memo about onscreen race relations and the 1944 report on Negro performers.[158] Johnston, however, broke with Harmon's advice and made CORE an unprecedented promise: "We are in agreement, of course, in wanting to see the motion picture industry live up to the standards of American democracy, and there will be a continuing effort by me in [*sic*] behalf of racial justice and inter-racial cooperation."[159] This promise was important because the industry had for so long avoided going on record with civil rights organizations, let alone admitting America's problems with racial justice in a letter that could be quoted in the press.

Around the same time, Johnston again went on record in oblique support of civil rights: when Memphis censors banned *Curley* (1947), an "Our Gang" comedy showing an interracial classroom, Johnston argued against such censorship and sent lawyers to the South to defend his position. Johnston showcased the industry's bold new racial rhetoric in his speech condemning Memphis censorship: "Here is conclusive evidence that political censorship of any medium of expression . . . cannot be tolerated if we expect American democracy to last. . . . The Memphis Board's action is outrageous. It is un-American. Surely the Board does not speak the mind of the millions of fair-minded citizens of the South who believe in freedom of speech. We count on their support."[160]

Under Johnston, bold and socially relevant images became crucial to the industry's argument that film was not a "business pure and simple" but rather, as the Supreme Court would later opine, "a significant medium for the communication of ideas" that deserved and needed First Amendment protections.[161] Thus between 1945 and 1951, many of the very social problems that the industry had sought to hide in *Imitation of Life*—discrimination and prejudice—would become regular screen fare. Indeed, the concern evident in late 1930s PCA files about depicting "social equality" was not present in the postwar era, even though films like *The Jackie Robinson Story* (1950) directly confronted the wrongs of segregation and argued for assimilative integration. This, however, did not mean that Hollywood's racism was suddenly cured or that the MPAA's censorship of lynching, miscegenation, and social equality ceased. Instead, there was a gradual modification process. As filmmakers developed a rhetorical framework for dealing with racism and discrimination as aberrations that were corrected and punished by tolerant white men, the PCA could sanction these themes. In what Peter Roffman and Jim Purdy have called the "Social Problem film" genre, films finally began to showcase American problems such as poverty and discrimination. But the formula was to "arouse indignation over some facet of contemporary life, carefully qualify any criticism so that it can in the end be reduced to simple causes, to a villain whose removal rectifies the situation."[162] The MPAA was vital to the development of this new paradigm for racial representation but also for the containment and continued repression of the civil rights imaginary.

Regulating Miscegenation in the Postwar Era

Miscegenation had been the PCA's issue of record in regulating interracial relations on screen. By the late 1940s, with Eric Johnston's ascendancy, the fire behind the regulation of miscegenation at the MPAA had gone out. Two films best exemplify the nuances of the MPAA's postwar policy on miscegenation: Twentieth Century–Fox's *Pinky* (1949) and Ealing Studios' *Pool of London* (1950).

Pinky featured Hollywood's first Black/white interracial kiss and depicted the degradations of segregation (though without actually arguing for a movement against it). Thus it raised profound concern both about miscegenation and "industry policy."[163] The allowance of the film's controversial racial content resulted from a power struggle in the MPAA leadership. In 1948, Breen took another hiatus from his chairmanship of the PCA.[164] In consultation with Eric Johnston, Judge Stephen Jackson, Breen's replacement, gave approval to the film's miscegenation angle. Harmon, fearing negative results for the industry from Jackson's naiveté and finding himself the sole voice of restraint in the absence of Breen and Hays, warned Jackson of *Pinky*'s potential calamities for the association (though Harmon himself supported the film). He worried that Southerners would claim the industry supported President Truman's civil rights program.[165] In his role as MPAA executive he warned Fox of the recent legal battles over *Curley* in Memphis, the southern backlash against civil rights programs, and the racial tensions invoked by Huey Long and Eugene Talmadge. And he predicted that southern politicians would create new censorship boards and laws, either to spite the industry generally or to prevent the film being shown (this would actually happen in Marshall, Texas).[166] Harmon also referred to "the coming to the fore of Ku-Klux activity," as a backlash against the release of the film in this pivotal moment.[167] However, he firmly advised that the MPAA "should not state that the picture should not be made or even discourage it being made": that decision should rest with the studio.

Joseph Breen returned to leadership of the PCA before the film was shot. He did not argue against the film's style of engagement with civil rights as an industry policy matter. But he was by no means going to allow miscegenation in a film without a fight. Breen wrote Jason Joy, who was now working as the head of public relations at Twentieth Century–Fox, requesting that "physical contact between Negroes and whites" be eliminated from the picture. But, curiously, Breen did not discuss this question as a matter of the Code but rather of "general good and welfare . . . with the idea of avoiding offense to audiences in a number of sections of the country."[168] As was the case with *Show Boat,* Breen was most worried about interracial touch and, in this case, a planned kiss. But neither would Joy, an experienced industry censor, easily relinquish ground he had already won under Jackson's leadership. Beginning his letter colloquially with "Dear Joe," Joy, emboldened perhaps both by his prior relationship with Breen and by the fact that Breen's letter indicated a change in enforcement of miscegenation, signaled that the studio was going to go ahead and make a film where there was not only Black/white physical contact but a Black/white love story:

> I think you were not as active as you are now when the book *Quality* was presented to the Production Code Administration. I know that my conversations were mostly with Judge Jackson. However we did present the book before we purchased it and, as you know, were urged by Judge Jackson, who, I think, had consulted Eric Johnston's office, to make the picture. At that time there was no suggestion that there should be no physical contact between various characters in the picture.[169]

Joy also gave a reading of the miscegenation angle that rendered it tragic, perhaps to appease Breen and avoid adhering to his suggested omission of interracial physical contact. Joy wrote:

> I note that you suggest that there should be no physical contact between whites and negroes in the picture, but that you do not make it a Code matter. . . . It is our intention, as indicated in the script, to have many instances of physical contact between Dr. Chester [who would become Tom Adams in the film] and Pinky. We believe these contacts to be absolutely necessary to the power of the story, as it relates to these two unhappy people. But these contacts will be as tender and restrained as any that we've ever put on screen. . . . Incidentally, you know of course that the actress who will play the part of Pinky will in fact be a white girl.[170]

This quote is quite typical of Joy: he manages to be placating even while arguing that he will do precisely what he wants. In emphasizing the unhappiness of the interracial couple, Joy suggests that this interracial contact is doomed and implicitly punished. This hails back to a formula for depicting Asian-white romance that had been developed earlier, in films such as *The Bitter Tea of General Yen* (1933) and *Madame Butterfly* (1935). Joy also noted that casting would, in any event, dispel the realism of these "interracial" love scenes. His comments suggest also that tenderness, as opposed to sensuality, was a representational strategy designed to lessen offense and produce multiple readings. *Pinky's* plot does not end in tragedy, however, and despite the casting, the interracial kissing scenes contain direct reference to blackness.

Harmon gave a divided response to *Pinky*, which exemplifies the confused state of industry regulation at this time and the MPAA's overall befuddlement about how to represent race in light of cultural flux and dissonance in the nation's racial politics. When the film was first submitted, Harmon had responded more like Breen, providing an official perspective that was virulently alarmist. A year later—after Truman's election—Harmon supported the production of *Pinky* and boldly prescribed bucking white southern convention. He pushed producer Darryl Zanuck to take a more controversial miscegenation angle: "To be true to life in the South," Pinky would be the offspring of "one of Miss Em's male relatives" and thus the old woman's blood relative and rightful heir. The goal of such a representation would be, Harmon stated, to reveal an essential "conflict in Southern life and thought": "Southern white people condone or tolerate 'social equality' on the level of vice while shouting to high heaven their opposition to 'social equality' on the level of virtue."[171] Zanuck backed away from Harmon's suggestions, telling Harmon that the picture should deal with "tolerances" rather than the *"illicit* miscegenation angle."[172] The MPAA's acceptance of the film shows a noteworthy shift in their policy: they were not prohibiting miscegenation as a Code matter and even allowing an interracial kiss.

Indeed, Breen had largely stopped discussing miscegenation as a Code issue by 1947, as the PCA files on *The Foxes of Harrow* (1947), *Show Boat* (1950), *Pool of London, Angelo* (1951), *The President's Lady* (1952), *Lydia Bailey* (1952), *The View from Pompey's Head* (1955), and *Baby Doll* (1956) indicate. Breen still removed signifiers of interracial sex from some of these films, but he discussed it only in terms of "illicit" (i.e., extramarital) sexuality. By contrast with the constant discussion of miscegenation and careful consideration of what constituted it in the 1934 *Imitation of Life* correspondence, the complete absence of the word "miscegenation" in these files suggests that after Eric Johnston's ascendancy, the PCA no longer considered miscegenation a part of the Production Code.

Breen, however, continued to bar acts signifying miscegenation, forbidding an interracial sexual proposition from *Baby Doll* in 1952 and meticulously removing "illicit" interracial mingling from *Lydia Bailey* (1952).[173] In *Angelo* (or *Il Mulatto*)

(1951), an Italian "brown-baby" film, Breen wasn't bothered by miscegenation's "result," as he had been with *Imitation of Life*. But he insisted that Angelo's white, adulterous mother not be described as "blameless."[174] From Fox's *The President's Lady* (1952), one of the first films to admit that white men slept with their slaves, Breen wanted the clearest revelations of this practice removed, as when a Black slave woman (Vera Francis) says to her white lover (Whitfield Connor), " 'You come out to see me tonight?' and his reply, 'If I can.' "[175]

The most egregious example of Breen's insistent anti-miscegenation policy (in spite of the shifting views of his superiors) is Basil Dearden's 1950 production *Pool of London*. Although its narrative principally concerned Dan McDonald (Bonar Colleano), a white sailor on leave who unwittingly involves himself in a robbery, McDonald's Black friend, Johnny (Earl Cameron), meets and shares an immediate mutual attraction with Pat (Susan Shaw), a white ticket taker at a London vaudeville house. Though the two never even discuss their affection, the night they spend walking the streets contains a palpable, tender, innocent, and utterly realistic romantic tension. When Pat asks Johnny out to dinner, he responds, "Are you sure?" Her reply, "Why not?" shows a carefree attitude that questions miscegenation's taboo.

From the second shooting draft, Breen called on Ealing to eliminate this mutual attraction. Though he had allowed Pinky, played by the white actress Jeanne Crain, to kiss her white lover, he indicated that "in this whole relationship between Pat and Johnny, it will be important that you carry out the present intent . . . and avoid any physical intimacies such as kissing or embracing between the two."[176] He eliminated a "silent scene of Johnny climbing upstairs to Pat's room," which he found contained "unacceptable sex-suggestive implication." What is more, Breen mandated the exclusion of scripted scenes showing dance partners of different races at a dance hall. Scenes of white women propositioning Johnny—both Pat and later a white prostitute—were unacceptable. "There must be no suggestion that Pat is asking Johnny to stay with her, in connection with her line, 'I know what it is . . . but . . . don't you understand . . . it doesn't matter.' "[177] In addressing the British producers, less accustomed than Hollywood producers to American censorship standards, Breen was resolute. Despite Breen's mandated changes, the public nature of Pat and Johnny's relationship lends it legitimacy and innocence. And the striking noir cinematography that captures their first scenes together holds out the promise of their mutual romantic energy. The same year, the PCA passed MGM's *Show Boat*, without mention of miscegenation in any written correspondence despite its tragic mulatta (who would be played by Ava Gardner rather than Lena Horne, who keenly desired the role). The PCA's decisions to allow agonized, blackface miscegenation in *Show Boat* and *Pinky*, and to disallow the mere suggestion of wholesome interracial attraction in *Pool of London*, indicate Breen's resistance to modern, normalized interracial relationships pairing white actors with Black ones.

The Near-Lynching That Saved Us All:
Racialized Lynching on Screen at Mid-Century

In the late 1940s, the PCA responses to three films, *The Burning Cross* (1947), *Intruder in the Dust* (1949), and *The Lawless* (1950), demonstrate the industry's subtle modification of its constraint on representing racialized lynching. Not only did these films feature nonwhite lynching victims, they revealed lynching as a part of a broader system of racial discrimination.

In the mid-1940s, as the number of lynchings decreased, lynching's iconographic importance for the depiction of racial problems heightened. *The Burning Cross* (1947) broke the taboo against picturing lynching's Black (political) victims. The protagonist is Johnny (Hank Daniels), a white GI, who returns from the war to find himself distinctly disadvantaged compared to those not drafted. Jobless and disillusioned with postwar America, Johnny turns to the Ku Klux Klan. When Black veteran Charlie West (Joel Fluellen) votes in defiance of Klan orders, the night riders not only burn a cross on his lawn, but burn Charlie, his wife (Madie Norman), and father (Clinton Rosemond) alive in their newly purchased home. The event is witnessed by Charlie's eight-year-old son, Bubby (Glenn Allen), from a nearby field, where his father had instructed him to wait until the Klansmen leave. A federal agent tries to avert the lynching by warning the sheriff. But the sheriff is a Klansman, too.

Breen's most important changes to the film were applied to the scenes of Klan violence against Black people. "Grandpa should not be shown in the burning house with his arms outstretched 'the flame enveloping him in a burning human cross,'" Breen wrote, changing the iconography of the film's the most highly symbolic sequence. And the entire burning of the house with its inhabitants was so gruesome that it should "be merely suggested rather than photographed."[178] Still, the PCA's passage of the film is surprising and probably explained by the fact that the PCA anticipated minimal distribution for this low-budget film, produced and financed by white leftists.

In stark contrast to the PCA's response to *The Burning Cross* is their reaction to *Intruder in the Dust,* based on the novel by prominent white Southerner William Faulkner. Nowhere in the written correspondence does the PCA discuss the film's racial angle or its treatment of lynch mobs. Perhaps this was in part because there is no actual lynching in the film, although the prospect of lynching is the major source of tension. In the film, Lucas Beauchamp (Juano Hernandez) is an African American landowner accused of killing a poor white man on the damning accusation of the man's brother. A fair-minded, multiracial team, made up of white Southern lawyer Gavin Stevens (David Brian), his teenage nephew, Chick Malison (Claude Jarman), African American teenager Aleck (Elzie Emanuel), and dainty old white woman Eunice Habersham (Elizabeth Patterson), join forces both to prove that Lucas is not responsible for the killing and to prevent his lynching. Audiences are positioned to sympathize with Lucas because they know he is innocent of any crime. The poor, downtrodden white Southerners who form the lynch mob are easily convinced of the Black man's innocence when the dead man's father confirms it. The sheriff shows some complicity with the lynching by leaving the jail to a deputy. But ultimately he sees to it that the jail is protected and he listens to the town's lawyer. Although both cinematographically and figuratively, the film presented the shadow of lynching, it is resolutely the story of white liberals and the psychology of conversion from racism. All these aspects likely made *Intruder in the Dust* the kind of lynching story the PCA could approve—especially since it eschewed actual violence in favor of symbolic hate that could be taught away by appeals to conscience. According to the PCA records, Breen didn't comment on the lynching angle. Still, the film's suggestion of the white lynch mob's racism solidified the break with the industry policy of avoiding the subject of racial lynching.[179]

Joseph Losey's *The Lawless* did not manage to avoid PCA censure. *The Lawless*'s Paul (Lalo Rios), a Mexican American youth, is drawn by a web of discrimination into a trap that nearly leads to his lynching. Like Rios's later film *The Ring* (1952), *The Lawless* squarely admitted the prevalence of American bigotry against Latinos much to the PCA's chagrin. The problem for Breen with this story was not the racist lynch mob per se, but its linkage to the broader fabric of American society.

> The story itself is a shocking indictment of America and its people . . . which the enemies of our system of government like to point to. The shocking manner in which several gross injustices are heaped upon the head of the confused, but innocent, young American of Mexican extraction, and the willingness of so many of the people in your story to be a part of, and to endorse, these injustices is, we think, a damning portrayal of our American social system.[180]

As the reference to "enemies of our system of government" suggests, both the film's racial angle and its connection to the Left in the Cold War era worried Breen—and the entire PCA staff—which collectively professed that their misgivings about it were "very, very grave indeed."[181] Interracial violence would be acceptable only if indirectly represented—and represented in ways that distanced the film from the communist racial rhetoric that was now unacceptable.

As late as 1954, Breen called for the omission of the word lynching from the official synopsis for *Bad Day at Black Rock* (1954). Though it was his last year at the PCA, Breen snipped this reference from the industry's official synopsis of the film, thus decreasing the association of racial hate with lynching's violence. While Breen occasionally offered studios representational strategies, his insistence on indirection—and deracialization—minimized lynching's brutality.

It also systematically disconnected lynching from the bodies and lives of African Americans who were its perpetual physical and psychic victims. In the late 1940s, Breen allowed greater evidence of racial lynching but still preferred stories where no racial brutality was visible.

REGULATING CIVIL RIGHTS IN THE SHURLOCK ERA

In 1954, Breen retired as PCA chairman. His successor, Geoffrey Shurlock, never managed to control producers as Breen had, though his lapses are perhaps explained by the changing status of industry self-regulation after the Miracle Decision, when the Supreme Court ruled that most state censorship violated the First Amendment.[182] In the same year Breen retired, the MPAA officially removed the ban on miscegenation, placing it in a new category called "Special Subjects," to be "handled with care." In 1956, the organization removed miscegenation from the Code entirely, making it, theoretically, allowable.[183] Rather than barring certain racial subjects from the screen, Shurlock sought to restrain the graphicness of an emerging group of brazen 1950s directors. Although a number of film scripts in the mid- to late 1950s featured African Americans—often with strong interracial theme—Shurlock weighed in on the racial angle of these films on surprisingly few occasions, choosing instead to view these films in terms of Christian morality, and suggesting eliminations to the depiction of adultery in particular, as the files on *Carmen Jones* (1954) and *Band of Angels* (1957) suggest. Shurlock instructed producers to minimize use of the word "nigger" but did not make this a condition for approval. Shurlock passed *Edge of the City* (1957), *The Defiant Ones* (1958), and *Odds Against Tomorrow* (1959) with epithets and interracial fight sequences. He made no mention of the realistic attempt to lynch a Mexican boy in *Trial* (1955). Shurlock did not censor, or even mention, the revelation that "white" southern writer Garvin Wales (Sidney Blackmer) is part Black in his letter appraising *The View from Pompey's Head* (1955). He also made no alteration to scenes of mulattas with white male love objects in *Kings Go Forth* (1958), *Band of Angels* (1957), or *Imitation of Life* (1959).[184] In *Imitation of Life* the sexuality of the mulatta did bother Shurlock, but only in its most extreme sequences, where she dances, scantily clad, in a nightclub. On the MPAA's official analysis chart for *Malaga* (1960), Shurlock even described Dorothy Dandridge's character as a "mulatta," suggesting the increased acceptability of this category in official MPAA documents.

Though the racial boundaries of the PCA had changed, they had not disappeared. The defining concern during Shurlock's reign was racial violence that might touch a nerve with the unfolding civil rights struggles. Shurlock's tenure coincided with the beginnings of the mass movement for civil rights. As the racial problem cycle petered out with the rise of the mass movement, onscreen civil rights questions were remixed, with a seemingly brutal and incautious abruptness, with other stories. Some filmmakers, like Samuel Fuller and Nicholas Ray, even irreverently mocked the social problem film's on-the-nose gravity, pointing out the genre's improbability and staginess through their own affected, off-kilter presentational style.

Shurlock allowed slow, tense, staged fight scenes between Black and white individuals in *The Defiant Ones*. He even allowed an attempted lynching scene in the film. With Columbia's 1956 film *Reprisal!*, producer Harry Cohn replaced the Black lynching victims with Native Americans. But Shurlock still warned him about "excessive gruesomeness" in the opening shots where "two bodies drop to the ground . . . and lie in two grotesque heaps."[185] Accordingly, Cohn removed this sequence so we never see the lynching victims. But later returns to the "scene" of the lynching, where the ropes still dangle, to reinforce its psychic effects. Shurlock also warned the studio against Black riot violence in *Island in the Sun* (1957), a film set on a fictional Caribbean island on the cusp of independence. In a letter that seemed to rest on industry policy more than the Code, Shurlock told Cohn that the film's end, when a planter's son commits suicide by inciting a newly enfranchised Black crowd to violence with racist slurs, violated the Production Code's prohibition on suicide as means to avoid punishment for a crime. But he also made his objection racial: "There also comes to mind," Shurlock wrote, "the more subtle and difficult question of whether or not this story constitutes an unfair portrayal of the Negro race, and whether or not the story is told in such a way that it could reasonably inflame Negro people."[186] Shurlock here worried not only about violence but about mass racial violence and how this onscreen Black mob, anxious for their rights, might affect Black American spectators.

The semi-documentary *Phenix City Story* (1955) principally treated gangsterism, prostitution, and gambling in a southern town. But the most provocative sequence showed the brutalized corpse of the daughter of a Black janitor (James Edwards) being thrown out of a moving car onto the lawn of protagonist John Patterson (Richard Kiley). Medium shots of her corpse with the neck twisted around and blood running down into her gaping eyes troubled Shurlock (see figure 10). Patterson's father sadly identifies the corpse as "Zeke's baby," and when his son asks whether they killed her just for this, his response, "They've killed for less," indicts a broader racism. So too does the following scene, when Patterson calls the police. The racist policeman's mundane dispatch—"Somebody just threw a dead nigger kid on the Patterson lawn, go check it out"—is uttered without urgency, between bites of his sandwich. Though narratively the dead child is framed as only one more problem in the white politician's struggle against southern corruption, the sequence does evoke the absolute lack of regard for Black life in the South. This sequence, in the year of Emmett Till's lynching (though before the occurrence), revealed, in a minor key, an emerging civil rights narrative that

FIGURE 10. In the year of Emmett Till, Black children appear as victims of white masculine aggression in the exploitation film *The Phenix City Story* (1955). Frame captures.

the film—despite its use of the same televisual, reportorial documentary style used in Edward R. Murrow's "A Study of Two Cities" (1954)—never explicitly addresses.[187] Accordingly, it was Shurlock's most overriding concern, one he and other MPAA officials repeated in numerous letters: "In addition to the overall problem of brutality, there was the specific item of the murder of the Negro child, which we thought was unacceptable."[188] Perhaps since the girl is replaced by what is obviously a doll in the sequence where she is thrown from a car, Shurlock's weakened PCA authorized the completed film with the aforementioned brutality to the Black body intact.

Further evincing Shurlock's intense regulation of civil rights iconography was his response to Roger Corman's *The Intruder* (1962), based on Charles Beaumont's novel where a racist, rabble-rousing stranger comes to town on the eve of court-ordered school desegregation. Shurlock linked his concern about the film's forty-three uses of the word "nigger" to its "excessive violence" between whites and Blacks.[189] Shurlock worried that the story, which included the iconography of the Little Rock Nine, hooded Klansmen dynamiting a Black church, and a Black boy nearly lynched on a school swing set by an epithet-spewing white mob, was inflammatory and "could incite hatred toward white people on the part of negroes in the audience" (see figure 11). This concern was "based on a realization of the profound and highly explosive problem of integration which is seething in this country. There are so many imponderables in this situation involving friction between the law, inherited emotional patterns and justice, that we feel our industry should be prudent in the sense that we do not unwittingly complicate the problem."[190] Corman fought Shurlock's ban, claiming that the violence and epithets were essential to the film's "documentary validity" and that he had "shot the picture on location in the South and this is the way the people down there would refer to negroes under the circumstances portrayed."[191] Corman strategically muted the book's violence, eventually receiving a Code seal. But he deliberately included active icons of the unfolding civil rights struggle—embattled children walking to school, Black boys talking to white girls, racial violence outside the school house, and angry, everyday faces of the mob. Though the film's style is semi-documentary, through lighting, iconography, and the centering narrative device of the "stranger," Corman imbued the southern civil rights settings with a sense of the bizarre, eerie, and otherworldly, perhaps as an expressionistic indictment of the zombiesque white southern racists. But Shurlock's memos to Corman clearly indicate that he wanted to avoid civil rights polemics as a matter of industry policy. Here, as with *Island in the Sun* and *The Phenix City Story,* though he allowed the representation of small-scale interracial violence and invectives, even this timid censor's permissiveness drew the line at extremely brutal or large-scale violence whose iconography gestured toward the mass movement.

FIGURE 11. The combination of lynching iconography with the schoolyard reframed the rabid racism of the school integration struggle in *The Intruder* (1962). Frame captures.

CONCLUSION

Between 1930 and 1960, the industry self-regulation of civil rights imagery underwent gradual shifts. Love or romance between Blacks and whites was routinely barred during the pre-Code and Breen era, though it sometimes slipped past Joy's notice or appeared indirectly in the form of Black-white same-sex intimacies and "miscegenation" between whites and dark people of other races. The PCA's anti-miscegenation policy shifted in moments of Breen's absence and finally began to lose its hold in the late 1940s, as the industry increasingly relied upon the appearance of being "socially minded" to argue for First Amendment protections. Joy and Breen enforced what amounted to a ban on screening racialized lynching, a move that siphoned off these representations to non-Black lynching victims. But again, in the late 1940s, Breen broke with this policy in the interest of exploring social issues. On other policies, like the ban on social equality, the PCA shifted more markedly over the course of their tenure. For instance, social equality was repressed onscreen in certain pre-Code and late 1930s films and surprisingly into the war years when the Federal government pushed Hollywood to represent Blacks and whites with greater equality. But with the rise of integrationist discourse, the PCA seemingly liberalized its policy but only as the industry simultaneously limited the terms of Black social inclusion to something other than "complete racial equality." Similarly, the PCA would gradually come to recognize Black activists' positions on racial representation as relevant to industry policy but only in limited terms.

In terms of the development of MPPDA policy, who was in charge at various MPPDA offices mattered greatly to the style of enforcement and to what was possible in representing civil rights. Just as Joy differed from Breen, Francis Harmon embodied and represented the "Southern spectator" quite differently than did Lamar Trotti and altered industry policy on racial issues. Similarly, the shifts in enforcement under Eric Johnston in contrast with Will Hays suggest his impact on the politics of how to represent Black injustices.

Rarely did self-regulators simply ban a theme or subject. Instead they muted and dampened them. Self-regulators used a number of factors to determine the permissibility of various plots: the relative stature of the source material, the prestige, national origin, and reputation of the company involved, how directly racial issues were imagined or broached, how many racial issues were presented, and whether other moral issues were of greater importance. Pre-tested properties had the advantage of offering the studio accepted cultural narratives of race and could sometimes be the vehicles for breaking new ground, as the cases of *Show Boat, The Adventures of Huckleberry Finn,* and *Of Mice and Men* confirm. The PCA's process of script doctoring and vetting often encouraged elliptical, indirect representations of Black-white love, lynching, and integration, representations where there was a vague sense of tension around interracial relationships but where there was no racial case-in-point.

But it is also true that the MPPDA repressed race more violently and completely than sex. The substitution of white victims, for example, in the case of lynching removed lynching's racial dimensions and failed to raise questions about Black humanity and racial justice. What is more, though force was the hallmark of American interracial relationships—the touchstone on which oppression hinged—it was just this force that was repressed in the cinematic depiction of lynching. Likewise, "undue" tenderness, as in *Pool of London,* also evoked PCA censure. "Social equality"—in the form of Black backtalk and indiscriminate intermixing—was, during the 1930s, dampened in certain films, which accordingly lost a sense of the friction and hope of interracial encounters; and the repression of Black/white miscegenation contributed immeasurably to its continued stigmatization. When it came to racism, the MPPDA both perpetuated it and disavowed its existence onscreen. In sum, industry self-regulators helped produce a cinema haunted by Black absence, but they also, in more limited ways, aided producers in a momentary and oblique revelation of American racial politics.

2 · STATE CENSORSHIP AND THE COLOR LINE

The Production Code gave rise to film texts in which emblems of racial controversy were legible but deniable—repressed but still palpable. State censors went beyond the PCA in their repression, cutting films to conform to their state's de jure or de facto racial politics and vitally shaping America's system of film vetting. They created a regionally accented cinema, often controlling images throughout their entire distribution area. State censorship also influenced the SRC and PCA.[1] The PCA kept careful records of states' decisions on all studio films as well as many independent, exploitation, and foreign films, and they made sure PCA-approved films generally conformed to state censors' standards.[2] Because these state censors had such great influence, the question of their impact on images of civil rights—especially in contrast with the PCA—is an important one.

Though both state censors and the PCA vetted films, state censors reviewed independent, race, and foreign films the PCA never even saw. Edna Carroll, head of the Pennsylvania Board of Censors, challenged a March 1953 *Box Office* article claiming that state censorship was no longer needed. As she argued: "The so called 'self-discipline' of the industry covers only those organizations participating in the Motion Picture Association. By actual statistics, some 30 percent of the product reaching us has no previous censorship," referring to the foreign and independent films the board analyzed.[3]

States regularly censored films on the grounds of miscegenation, social equality, and racial strife. They also censored race films as a segregated cinematic genre.[4] Most states passed Hollywood racial problem films like *Imitation of Life* (1934 and 1959), *Pinky* (1949), *Intruder in the Dust* (1949), and *Island in the Sun* (1957) without cuts, focusing attention instead on marginal films that were available to African American audiences and less confined by Hollywood's taboos. While these films were not always liberating, historically accurate, or dignified, they revealed aspects of American race relations that Hollywood routinely effaced.

State censorship was strongest between 1915 and 1952. In 1915, the Supreme

Court's Mutual Decision determined that motion pictures were not protected by the First Amendment. In 1952, the Supreme Court's Miracle Decision reversed Mutual, and state censorship went into decline. But because state boards were active before the SRC was formed, their standards and policies influenced industry self-regulation criteria.

Ten state boards were legally empowered to censor films during most of the period from 1930 to 1960, but only seven of these were active: the Pennsylvania State Board of Censors (established in 1913), the Ohio Division of Film Censorship (1913), the Kansas Board of Review (1913), the Maryland State Board of Motion Picture Censors (1916), the New York Motion Picture Division (1921), the Virginia Division of Motion Picture Censorship (1922), and the censor board governing Massachusetts' Lord's Day Observance Statute (1922).[5] This chapter relies on the extant records of film elimination and rejection materials in three states (New York, Maryland, and Virginia), which cover most of the period from 1930 to 1960, and a selective analysis of Ohio's and Kansas's eliminations and rejections.[6] Pennsylvania destroyed 300 cubic feet of its materials, rendering sustained analysis of their policies impossible, and Massachusetts appears not to have retained any of its state censorship files.[7] Nevertheless, existing state censorship records reveal the limiting effect of racial politics on screen content in several large American metropolises of the North and Southeast, regions where race relations have historically been extremely contentious. In this chapter, I privilege discussion of films and state censors' policy over analysis of individual censors and bureaucrats. My research has shown that state censors were far less public or vocal about their decisions than municipal censors, preferring the institutional veil of state bureaucracy to any bluenose public persona. This veil made it difficult to discover relevant background information on these censors that might have influenced their racial decisions. Instead of focusing on the individual censors, I focus on the effect of censorship on spectatorship—that is, how the censors systematically and gradually, through censored shots and banned scenes, worked to bend the racial trajectory of the cinema on important local American screens and in specific communities.

DEFINING "MISCEGENATION": STATE CENSORSHIP AND THE CONTROL OF "FOREIGN" DESIRES

The PCA restrained onscreen miscegenation, which the Code defined as "sex relations between the black and white races." Breen worried particularly about touch and about the actor's race in regulating miscegenation. But what were state censors' policies on miscegenation and what screen action did they stifle? And did their definition extend beyond the PCA's?

No censor cut every film scene suggesting interracial desire, but two overarching commonalities prevailed. The first was the rampant censorship of forced love scenes, especially when these sequences revealed white men's lecherous desire for dark women. It is true that states often censored signifiers of rape, regardless of race. But their broad censorship of even quite indirect references to sexual force between the races muted an emerging discourse that pictured miscegenetic force and desire as emanating from white men. Second, the boards consistently censored interracial desire in non-Hollywood films—especially those that dismantled the miscegenation-lynching matrix, calling attention to the destructive consequences of the "white male archetype" of the Black male rapist or presenting miscegenation in a way that naturalized interracial desire and threatened racial boundaries.[8] To indicate how sensitive state censors were to miscegenation in contrast with the PCA, it is useful to explore how they censored even Hollywood's quite tame representations of unforced miscegenation.

State Censorship of Hollywood Miscegenation

States went further than film industry self-regulators in censoring miscegenation, for example, excising even joking Hollywood references to interracial love and white/Asian love scenes. Because American miscegenation was often linked with sexual and social problems—prostitution, sexual frustration, illegitimacy, rape, and adultery—interracial desire consistently appeared pathological and was easier to censor. State censorship of miscegenation was frequent enough that it was likely one of the causes for the MPPDA's ban. Kansas frequently censored illegitimate mulattos in the 1910s.[9] Beginning in the 1920s, the Virginia board claimed interracial love scenes would "incite to crime" by prompting violation of the state's miscegenation laws.[10] But, surprisingly, cinematic miscegenation was censored even in states where the legal apparatus was designed to protect equal civil rights, such as Ohio and New York.

Studio films that confounded their presentation of miscegenation through elaborate and serious disavowals—*Imitation of Life* (1934), for example—passed in Ohio and New York without cuts to their scenes of interracial desire. However, the New York censor in the 1930s surprisingly cut comedic visual and verbal allusions to interracial longing from several films. For example, in Warner Bros.' *I've Got Your Number* (1934), where in the first ten minutes a white woman expresses her desire for a "Filipino House Boy" and an effeminate character claims to be a "man's man," the board's only change was to a scene suggesting Black-white sexual desire. When Chrystal (Louise Beavers), sitting alone in the dark with Johnny (Alan Jenkins) while reading his palm, predicts calamity, Johnny says, "Aww, Chrystal—ain't my luck ever gonna change?" The board eliminated another white man's disgusted reply—"What do you think?"—specifically stating, "(Chrystal is a colored girl)."[11] In New York even this minor allusion to a white man getting "lucky" with a Black woman prompted censorship. Similarly, at the end of *Three Cheers for the Irish* (1940), Casey (Thomas Mitchell), an Irishman whose anxiety about his daughter's love for a Scotsman is the film's theme,

FIGURE 12. Omar nuzzles Chinese gambling-house women that the censors dubbed "Black." Frame capture from *Shanghai Gesture* (1942).

asks a nurse passing through a hospital waiting room to show him his grand-child. When the nurse opens the blanket to reveal a Black baby, Ohio required elimination of Casey's question of his son-in-law: "You are Scotch, aren't you?" and his reply, "Aye."[12] The patterned excision of Black-white interracial attraction or parentage shows southern and northern censors' sensitivity to miscegenation and their desire to guard against even Hollywood's occasional and marginal references to it.

State censors also regularly eliminated scenes of desire between whites and Asians or Pacific Islanders. With an eye toward film's mechanics, they analyzed and removed shots, editing, framing, or dialogue that might incite spectators toward interracial sex or violence. In several instances, the imputed blackness of desirable orientalized women seems to have motivated censorship. Among the four pages of material Ohio cut from *Shanghai Gesture* was a scene in a brothel-like Chinese gambling house where Omar asks "two colored girls" for a cigarette (see figure 12).[13] Although the two women appear actually to be Asian, in an atmosphere of racial ambiguity the board assigned them a censorable blackness.

As Breen had feared, Ohio censors saw too much miscegenetic blackness in *White Cargo* (1942) and removed several erotic scenes, including when Tonde-layo whips her own body while lying on the couch.[14] Beyond fearing public sanction for interracial relationships, these films threatened destabilization of racial categories. Even joking or deliberately elusive cinematic references to racial mixing that generated doubt about racial heredity and identity were subject to cuts.

State Censorship of Coercive Miscegenation

More consistently, state censors removed scenes connecting violence to cross-racial sexual desire. Even elliptical representation of such coercion was censorable—and especially when such sequences exposed white men's oppressive desire for dark women.[15] This practice began before the classical Hollywood era. For instance, in Ohio the violent, incestuous rape scene from *Within Our Gates* (1919), which Jane Gaines has described as "protest against all of the master's sexual encounters with his own slave women," never made it to the screen.[16] New York removed a similar fierce sexual struggle from *Siren of the Tropics* (1927), where Papitou (Josephine Baker) repeatedly fights off the unwanted sexual advances of a white trader.[17] *Siren* is particularly agonizing because jovial comedy quickly devolves into rape, underscoring how the threat of rape crucially shaped Black women's subjectivities, as Valerie Smith and Darlene Clark Hine note.[18] The film's structure of spectatorial identification is bifurcated. While on the one hand, the camerawork in *Siren* titillates spectators with eroticized views of the struggling Black nude, the scene as a whole denies the cultural myth that Black women were "willing participants" in miscegenetic rape by showcasing the intensity of their fight against white domination and by celebrating moments of evasion.

Films registering dark women's disgust, bitterness, and resignation at their victimhood under (often habitual) white attackers particularly bothered censors. The chairman of New York's censorship board, Irwin Esmond, banned MGM's 1934 *Laughing Boy*, where poverty on the reservation forces Slim Girl/Lily (Lupe Velez) to resume prostituting herself to white men after marriage to a native man (Ramon Navarro). Esmond felt the film traded the novel's focus on "the Indian problem" for "very raw sex."[19] Esmond's cuts, however, were more racial than sexual. He retained prostitution but reduced white men's culpability for Lily's sex slavery, an element that had worried the SRC.[20] He cut the phrase "white men" from Lily's line "You are as bad as the white men," as well as from her later line, "They'll pay, those white men, for what they done to me." He also removed a white john brutally coercing Lily into sex. Thus New York censored lines calling out whiteness in derision but also indicating white men's miscegenetic lechery. Similar racial censorship of *Massacre* (1934), where a white Indian agent rapes a Native girl at her father's funeral, indicates that this kind of censorship was more than an anomaly in New York.[21] Though these films were not without stereotype, they admitted the psychological conditions of Black and Brown women's (sexual) slavery that the white slave film effaced.

Even cryptic dialogue referring to forced miscegenation ended up on the states' cutting room floor. From Oscar Micheaux's *Birthright* (1939), New York,

Pennsylvania, and Maryland cut elliptical lines denoting that a young white Southerner has used his knowledge that the family's Black maid has stolen a brooch to coerce her into sexual relations.[22] Never does this sequence sensationalize or even visually represent this attempted rape. However, it does make Black women's suffering under the pressure of white desire the melodramatic center. Thus, state censors cut white male rape not only when physical struggle was directly shown but also when they thought it was visually signified or elliptically referenced in dialogue.

Lost records make Pennsylvania's general policy on miscegenation hard to determine, but Pennsylvania was the only state to require cuts from *Pinky*. Though the film featured a muted front-stage Black-white interracial romance between Pinky (Jeanne Crain) and white doctor Thomas Adams (William Lundigan), crucially, the scene Pennsylvania removed was one of white-on-Black sexual assault. Thinking she is white, two white men offer Pinky a ride in their car as she walks through a Black section of town at night. When she reveals her race, the two men attack her in the middle of the road. One holds her arms and forces alcohol down her throat as the other examines her body and face, pronouncing her "real pretty" and "the whitest dinge I ever saw." Though Pinky eventually escapes, it is not before she has been "manhandled." Pennsylvania Board chairwoman Edna Carroll cut this scene and issued the film a permit "with reluctance—not because of the theme but because of the inflammatory direction. We . . . advise that if this film causes real distress at any place or for any people in the state, we will feel privileged to the right to revoke the license."[23]

Coercive Miscegenation, Virginia, and the Image of the Old South

The civil rights implications of states' policies on coercive miscegenation is clearest in its postwar examples. *Pinky*'s censorship indicates coerced sex could be the difference between an interracial film's censorship or its passage without eliminations. In the summer of 1957 in Virginia, two mainstream Hollywood films tested censors' longstanding opposition to miscegenation. These films came in the midst of "Massive Resistance," when Virginia governor Thomas Stanley led an attack on school desegregation designed to derail *Brown v. Board of Education* using a state's rights argument and the tactic of "Interposition" (which paid homage to the secessionist logic of the Civil War).[24] While individually the Virginia censors supported "Massive Resistance," the *Miracle* decision of 1952 had ostensibly reduced their power significantly (though they would go on censoring films into the 1960s).[25]

In *Band of Angels* (1957), Amantha (Yvonne DeCarlo), a plantation heiress, finds upon her father's death that she is part Black and is sold into slavery. Hamish Bond (Clark Gable), an older, urbane slave master from New Orleans, who has several light-skinned Black mistresses, buys her and treats her with some respect. They eventually fall in love. When the Civil War begins, they flee the South with the help of Hamish's educated former slave Ra-Ru (Sidney Poitier), whose fiery rebellion softens in light of his old master's shifting fortunes. Letters flooded in before the film's release and focused on a scene where Ra-Ru slaps Amantha.[26] But the board cut neither this interracial slap nor scenes suggesting white men's love affairs with mulattos.[27] Instead, it struck two lengthy soliloquies from a scene in which white slave handler Calloway (Ray Teal) sexually attacks Amantha on a boat headed south to a slave auction. When Amantha resists Calloway's advances, he says: "Any more shenanigans an' I'm gonna chain you to a post down there with them hot-natured blacks; . . .—an' ain't gonna care what happens to yuh. Just so they don't bruise yuh too bad, yuh hear? . . . I rather let them wear a couple o'hundred dollars worth off yuh than t' get a lot o'worriment."[28] This line provoked audiences to imagine Black men brutally raping a (liminally) Black woman played by a white actress. On the level of the diegesis, the scene also suggests the coercive lust of the white slave handler for the enslaved Black woman. The direct indication of the horror of white male rape of Black women under slavery seems to be at the heart of the reason for excision here, as the board cut similar lines of dialogue spoken by Budge (Juanita Moore), another female slave, whose adornments mark her Jezebel status. Budge's cut lines confirm the degrading conditions of life as a Black slave/mistress:

> Some fella buy you. An' what he do? What he den do? Maybe it won't be so bad. Maybe you git something you like outta it. One o' them Frenchy fellas in New Orleans. Maybe he buy you. You know what he'll do? He'll (whispering not distinct). (Laughing:) Den yuh get old and it don't matter. Don't matter whatcha done had. Sure can't take it away. (laughing)

The reference to the American South's history of racialized sex slavery is oblique. But the provocative question the soliloquy repeatedly raises and leaves dangling—"what he den do?"—destroys the portrait of "old southern" racial morality.

The same summer, by contrast, the board did not censor Darryl Zanuck's *Island in the Sun* (1957), despite over thirty letters of protest, including six petitions (some with over forty names).[29] Virginia attorney general J. Lindsay Almond, who spearheaded the Interposition fight, intervened in *Island's* censorship, requiring a special screening for Richmond's Circuit Court judge and three officers of an aggressive segregationist organization calling itself Defenders of State Sovereignty and Individual Rights. But committee members could find no legal objection that would hold up in court. Though all agreed that the film "portray[ed] principles of which they did not approve," it also, in their opinion, "illustrated great social problems which are created by integrated society and further strengthened the official position of the Commonwealth of Virginia disapproving the creation or existence of such a society in this state."[30]

So in 1957, arguably the year that Virginia fought most vociferously against civil rights, the state picked its screen miscegenation battles, cutting *Band of Angels*, a film that might hurt the image of the Old South on which the state was basing its Interposition fight, but maintaining conspicuous silence on the multiply miscegenetic *Island in the Sun*, set on a contemporary tropical island. While *Island in the Sun* depicted unforced miscegenation, *Band of Angels* indicts the brutality of slave-era miscegenation and reveals it as most horrific for Black women condemned to sexual servitude and rape by white men. From 1930 to 1960, state censors regularly cut films that challenged dominant narratives of miscegenation in their suggestion of the plausibility of white men's desire for Black women, but also the historical truth that white men consistently used rape as an extension of white privilege and a form of domination.

Interracial Attraction in Foreign and Race Films

The films that incurred the most censorship for their depictions of miscegenation were not Hollywood films but foreign and race films. One striking early example is New York's elimination of a Black man stating, "'Of course, Chong Lee and I are going to be married.' (Chinese girl and Negro)," from Yiddish filmmaker Harry Lynn's *The Youth of Russia* (1934), which suggests the board's willingness to censor Black masculine desire, even when it was directed toward an Asian rather than a white woman and even when it was morally anchored in a promise of marriage.[31] Although the context cannot be verified because the film is no longer extant, perhaps the New York board considered such forceful articulation of desire disturbing to racial norms.

Throughout the classical Hollywood era, state censors—and particularly Ohio—repeatedly cut non-Hollywood films that muddled the inviolate category of "white woman," and in doing so revealed the instability of racial genus.[32] Ohio banned as "harmful" the exploitation film *Chloe: Love Is Calling You* (1934). White actress Olive Borden plays Chloe, who is trying to avenge her Black father's lynching but along the way falls in love with a white man who works for Col. Gordon (Frank Joyner), the rich factory owner who orchestrated the killing. Later she discovers that Gordon is her biological father and that she is white. The lynching, though not shown in the film, may have factored into *Chloe's* censorship. But the narrative twists trick audiences into believing she is Black and then insist (on a string of unstable evidence—most notably, the dress she wore as a child) that she is white and can marry a white man. The instability of these signifiers creates a strange, unintended uncertainty about Chloe's racial identity and frays the material basis for racial categorization. *Chloe* was released without a PCA seal. It was unlike *Imitation of Life* in that it admitted interracial desire and sex: it accepted (perhaps because of its New Orleans setting) the premise of a half-caste, "creole" Negro and allowed both Black and white suitors to pursue Chloe. Another film challenging the category of "white woman" was British

Lion's *Big Fella* (1937), in which interracial camaraderie is the unstigmatized norm but censors focused instead on miscegenation. After Joe (Paul Robeson) goes on a drinking spree with white floozy Marietta (Marcelle Rogez), his girlfriend, Manda (Elizabeth Welch), resentfully suggests that Joe and Marietta had an affair. The board cut this conversation, finding illicit such "dialog between them concerning white woman" (though the board allowed Marietta to flirt with a visibly unresponsive Joe, and her winking claim that he "can get anything he wants").[33] For Ohio, perhaps the idea of Black folks resentfully discussing a white woman's (interracial) sexual exploits seemed inappropriate for the screen. Though Joe denies that there was any affair between him and Marietta, the mere mention of its possibility brought the idea of interracial sex between a Black man and woman to a question, while its removal left the idea unacknowledged among a host of deniable, if strong, signifiers. So such censorship heightened the ambiguity of this scene, causing the expression of white/Black romance to rest entirely on a visible semiology without confirmation.

In the 1930s, Ohio censors had a documented policy of banning all miscegenation scenes, as its file on *Czarna Perla* (*Black Pearl*) (1934) confirms. The film, a Polish retooling of Josephine Baker's films, features a white sailor (Eugeniusz Bodo) who marries (and brings back west) a dark-skinned Tahitian woman, Moana (Anne Chevalier), whom the film calls "Black." With an endearing awkwardness, she assimilates, ultimately becoming a dancing sensation on the stage. However, as was true with Josephine Baker, her mutable identity—highlighted by the many roles she ably assumes and her dramatic costume shifts from high Western fashion to sarong and back again—bleed the lines between East and West, native and white, and savage and civilized (see figure 13). Despite their licit marital status, the board gave as its sole reason for rejection the "relationship between the white man and the black woman," stating plainly, "Miscegenation is contrary to our code of censorship as well as . . . the code of the Motion Picture Producers and Distributors of America," words suggesting that the categories "Black" and "white" extended not only to the South Seas but to foreign films made in foreign contexts. This policy explains why, in 1941, Ohio also banned Black distributor Sack Amusement's planned run of the Josephine Baker vehicle *Princess Tam Tam* (1935), an adaptation of *Pygmalion* where not only is the African American starlet accepted into white society (she passes as royalty) but a white aristocrat "pretends" to be in love with her. Though only presenting the idea of white desire for miscegenation, it was likely banned for bending the color line.[34]

In light of this policy, it is little surprise that Ohio banned the multiply miscegenetic film *The Love Wanga* (1935/1941), set in Haiti but with a largely American cast. The figure of the (transnational) mulatta in *Chloe: Love Is Calling You*, *The Love Wanga*, and *Czarna Perla*, and the fallen white woman in *Big Fella*, made race—and the color line—seem malleable, undermining the stability of

FIGURE 13. Not only did *Czarna Perla* (1934) show a white man and native woman kissing, but Reri's easy adaptability to a variety of contexts—and perhaps most affectingly to cinematic glamour norms—troubled racial binaries. Frame captures from *Czarna Perla*.

racial—and sometimes national—categories. For Ohio censors, these films seemed to violate regional norms and practices—and their banning and lack of negotiation indicates the strength of censors' response to miscegenation.

In the late 1940s and early 1950s, as racial representation got bolder, states continued to cut miscegenation, regardless of their declining power. State censors had a pattern of censoring foreign views of miscegenation—particularly those in neorealist films or which featured touch between Blacks and whites. From *Angelo (Il Mulatto)* (1951), where the Church impels a white man to care for his dead wife's brown baby when he is released from prison, the board removed lines of dialogue mocking the illegitimate mulatto.[35] Even decades-old mixed scenes in a jazz club seemed dangerous to Maryland board chairman Sydney Traub in 1951. From *Ave Maria* (1936), he cut "all shots including flashback of colored man seated next to white woman at table in cafe as he leans against her and puts his face practically against her face, while lighting another white girl's cigarette."[36] Though Traub was, on balance, a racially progressive censor and cut the word "nigger" from this and all other films during this period, Maryland was still the South. The film's multiracial nightclub setting and the white woman's look of pleasure—and also the repetition of this image—probably contributed to Traub's disapproval. In the 1950s, Virginia cut interracial dance sequences from Jean Gabin's *Razzia sur la Chnouf* (1955) and the German exploitation film *The Nature Girl and the Slaver* (1957), both of which palpably represented white women's unembarrassed, highly sexualized dance performance for Black men.[37] In the 1960s, Virginia outlasted all other state boards in its censorship of consensual interracial relationships. Virginia censors were especially bothered when it occurred in European, independent, and exploitation films such as *Black Like Me* (1964), *The Cool World* (1964), and *My Baby Is Black* (1961).[38]

But the cuts most germane to civil rights were those made to foreign films that addressed racism and showcased naturalized interracial desire. In Ealing's *Pool of London*, as I have discussed, the romantic interest between the handsome Jamaican sailor and the kind and beautiful white cashier develops innocently and casually as the two spend several evenings together (see figure 14).[39] Breen had already cut interracial touch and removed a scene of Johnny going up to Pat's room. Still, Ohio initially banned this film—and, upon appeal, required the excision of a very mild "scene on tram where Johnny and Pat are jostled toward each other, showing their romantic attraction to each other" and a scene in which a racist bar owner expels Johnny.[40]

Senza Pietà (1948): A Case Study in Naturalized Miscegenation

Senza Pietà, Alberto Lattuada and Federico Fellini's neorealist tale of postwar Livorno, epitomizes state censors' responses to the more naturalistic, unmoralized treatment of Black masculinity in postwar foreign films on interracial desire. *Ebony*, a publication which often preferred foreign, independent, and B-films

FIGURE 14. Johnny (Earl Cameron) and Pat (Susan Shaw) share an earnest, romantic night on the streets of London. Publicity still from *Pool of London* (1950).

to Hollywood's big-ticket fare, praised the film for "striking realism in picturing squalor, decadence, and depravity" and its "sincere approach . . . to sex politics and race." But the film was banned in Ohio, Pennsylvania, and Maryland.[41] It sensitively explores the intimate connection between Black soldier Jerry (John Kitzmiller) and poor Italian woman Angela (Carla De Poggio).[42] As Angela descends into poverty and prostitution, her pure and genuine connection with Jerry is her only relief from the tortures of sex slavery. Unlike the film's white men (who use her), Jerry values Angela for her "goodness," and the two share a moral code.

The lack of racial condemnation during the couple's public courting—as they enjoy the innocent pleasures of amusement parks and cafés—marks a sharp departure from Hollywood's contemporaneous treatment (in *Pinky*, for example) of interracial love as producing narrative-halting social and psychological stigma (see figure 15). The film's soundscape mixes and mingles the fates of Angela and Jerry and amplifies the idea of Jerry as the film's center by grafting Black spirituals (such as "Nobody Knows the Troubles I've Seen") onto Italian prostitutes' sexual enslavement.

The link between supposed social "opposites"—white prostitute and Black American soldier—illuminates the transnational forces that oppress them both.

FIGURE 15. Jerry (John Kitzmiller) and Angela (Carla De Poggio) are soulmates and friends in *Senza Pietà* (1948), Lattuada and Fellini's grim neorealist tale that shifted the iconography of interracial romance. Frame captures.

FIGURE 16. The white under-world threatens their union and cuts short their lives. But the film restores Angela and Jerry's connection in death. There is more interracial touch in this shot of their death than in most Hollywood films. Frame captures from *Senza Pietà*.

Though neither wants to be reduced to "do[ing] anything for money," Jerry, in order to keep Angela from prostitution, essentially prostitutes himself, going from being a Black soldier to a near black-marketeer. Though Jerry never accepts the bribe that would make him a traitor, the U.S. Army holds him in a prison camp—one filled with Black soldiers. Jerry plans to escape with a man who has only barely escaped lynching in the South and whose poetic comparison of these two incarcerations is sealed when he is killed by the MPs' bullets. As Jerry flees the prison camp of the army he once served, the sound of machine guns, which will be repeated as a sonic marker of his fugitive status, announce that the country for which Jerry fought just a year earlier has unjustly turned on him, an argument that symbolically projected the postwar disappointments of Black Americans.[43] The couple ends in tragedy: after Jerry holds him up at gunpoint, local crime lord and pimp Pier Luigi (Pierre Claude) kills Angela. In a final sequence marked by Jerry's subjective perspective (his thoughts borne in voiceover, spirituals, and subjective shots), he drives a truck bearing Angela's body off a cliff, uniting with her in death (see figure 16).

Despite *Variety*'s facile (and hostile) claim that the film was "about miscegenation," the film is more an experiment in using racial blackness as an analogy for postwar European "downtroddeness."[44] It is not interracial love but mutual desperation that forms the film's strongest bonds. The film resists even the appearance of miscegenetic rape: it is Angela who makes the first move. When Jerry professes love and proposes they stay "together always" (kissing her hand and saying "we could live and be so happy together"), Angela admits that she is not in love with Jerry but then assents to go away with him (like her best friend who escaped Italy with her Black boyfriend). Jerry plans to treat her as a sister, thus ostensibly defusing any sexual tension. Nevertheless, not only are the two continually linked by "fate," but their close physical contact—which culminates in a symbolic moment of union in a church—is left unmoralized by camera or narrative and solidifies the idea of the two as soul mates, which had been established earlier when a palm reader claims Angela and Jerry's palms have the same "lines."

In 1950, when *Senza Pietà* was set for an engagement at Cleveland's African American Esquire Theater, the Ohio censor board assembled a committee to gauge public response. This committee unanimously called for a ban and, after consulting with the Maryland and Pennsylvania boards and finding Maryland had banned the film, the board complied. The film, which veered from the pristine, sexless Black soldier enshrined in Hollywood's social problem films, was judged by one viewer to "incite and irritate adjustments of race relations."[45] The board claimed the ban was due to "low moral living" and "prostitution," and that the film's insinuation that the U.S. military (i.e., Jerry) was involved in "black market" trades would hinder foreign relations. But E. J. Stutz, of the distribution company Realarts, suspected the ban was about race and fought back. He conducted his own test screening, provided statements from local civil rights leaders supporting the film, and sent the board the Chicago censor's report—that it should be shown to adults without cuts.[46] Stutz exemplified a class of distributors who commandeered civil rights leaders' righteous zeal to achieve civil liberties for racially oriented foreign, independent, and exploitation films. Board chairman and longtime Ohio film censor Susannah Warfield was unmoved. Finally, Stutz offered to cut racial scenes, but the board maintained its rejection.[47] The earliest Cleveland showing I could find was in 1954, four years after Stutz first tried to distribute it and six years after it was made. If foreign films like *Senza Pietà* and *Pool of London* offered African Americans the imaginatively stirring option of seeing themselves "in translation" as social equals, their censorship shut off access to these foreign channels and limited Black internationalist cinematic spectatorship.

It is clear that state censors in various locales sought to repress miscegenation from the screen, though their efforts did not extend to all films. But their focus on white-coerced miscegenation and international, race, and foreign film images indicates the ideological scope of their project. States censored films that varied from Hollywood's standard treatment. They limited the cinema's projection of white-on-Black interracial rape. And they severely curtailed the image of interracial attraction as natural, common, and easy.

WHITE MORAL PROPRIETY AND MOVING BLACK BODIES

Censors' primary racial concern during the period under study could be reduced to a single figure: the dark temptress. Through year after year of censorship records, this figure is a recurring obsession. Censors' fear of the dark woman was equally strong in films that imagined miscegenation and those that strongly displayed Black desire or desirability within the race. Black-cast race films and quasi-anthropological jungle films that tended to feature this figure were disproportionately censored, usually for nudity and what censors called "indecent dances."

Savage Lusts: Controlling the Miscegenetic Gaze

As I argued in my chapter on the MPPDA, Jason Joy was concerned not only about miscegenation onscreen but titillation that might incite desiring looks from spectator to screen and across the color line. State censors, too, cut both onscreen miscegenation and film material stirring the miscegenetic gaze. Censors believed that avoiding the direct gaze at the bodies of primitive "others"—especially in films whose scientific or expeditionary purpose made moral positioning unclear—would help preserve the whiteness of morality. Native nudity, but also the groping of "native" women (or children), prompted Maryland to censor sixty-six films between 1945 and 1960.

Censors also sought to remove onscreen miscegenetic spectatorship—white characters looking lustfully at Black characters—from interracial burlesque scenes in films such as *The Rage of Burlesque* (1954) and *Hurly Burly* (1954) and Hollywood films such as Walter Wanger's *Vogues of 1938* (1937) and the Nina Mae McKinney films *What Price Jazz* (1934) and *They Learned about Women* (1933).[48] Black dancers were too alluring. New York explicitly mentioned the race of the dancers in *What Price Jazz*, calling for removal of "all views of negro girls dancing in ensemble in indecent manner."[49] From *Vogues* (which the MPPDA also worried about), Virginia removed a dance sequence where Black women "drop their evening wraps" and shimmy in close-ups before the camera. Crucially, censors explicitly tagged "that part of negro woman's dance with two men where men look at her in a salacious manner."[50] In *The Rage of Burlesque*, censored in New York, a white man patronizes various international burlesque shows in New York and seems equally thrilled by Harlem dancer Miss Inferno as with the film's star Lillian White.[51] Interracial burlesque shows (and even their cleaned-up Hollywood correlates) fed the miscegenetic gaze by featuring racially and morally mixed spaces. In its press book, *Hurly Burly*, which was banned in Ohio, openly publicized mixing, joining via collage Black and white performers. New York censors worried about illicit Black dancing in the Spanish-language version of Fox's *Only a Woman* (1934) and called attention to a troubling "mulatto" dancer in *Pasiones Tormentosas* (1947). Black dancing women were also excised from *Weegee's New York* (1948), *Negra Consentida* (1949), and *Verlorenes Rennen* (1948).[52] Collectively, the boards more readily deleted sequences with a carnivalesque, burlesque, or otherwise free atmosphere where spectators were hailed into a space where both racial and sexual boundaries seemed loosened.

Race Films

Oscar Micheaux is essential to understanding the logic of state censorship of race films. State censors often grossly cut his subtle and embedded critiques of American civil rights. Though scholarly work on Micheaux is extensive, it is important for understanding state censorship of civil rights to note that Micheaux's films were regularly censored in Maryland, Ohio, Virginia, Kansas, and New York.[53] Of Micheaux's forty-two films made between 1919 and 1948 (when he ceased production), at least eighteen incurred state censorship. Every single one of the censor boards (including Pennsylvania, whose records are incomplete) censored at least one Micheaux film—and most boards censored many of them.

Of Micheaux's nineteen productions between 1930 and 1948, at least ten were censored at the state level, and several of these were banned. Censors made many dialogue deletions, which, though they seem minor, maimed Micheaux's complex—often satirically bitter—language and his deft communication of Black social milieu. For example, from Micheaux's first talkie, *Daughter of the Congo* (1930), New York cut references to passing in lines between a Black woman and her banker brother: "You should be ashamed, passing yourself off as a white man!" and his race-troubling retort: "There are thousands of Negroes doing the same thing."[54] New York cut from *Harlem after Midnight* (1934) the repeated line "Is she is or is she ain't?"—a line used to question the race of a prostitute being delivered to a white man.[55] Ohio, too, cut these lines—and three full pages of dialogue from the film. In Micheaux's work, even this suggestion of miscegenation, embedded in vernacular dialogue, was not able to get past censors. We can begin to sense the social—and artistic—consequences of this censorship when we consider how removing a line such as "We got a good customer—a rich old bird on Riverside drive who likes 'em young and tender—and the word 'Creole' will tickle him and make him anxious," altered the lexicon of Micheaux's ironic critique of the American color line when it was cut from *Harlem after Midnight*.[56] In cutting this and over three pages of dialogue from the film, Ohio reauthored the film. The widespread censorship of his work diminished his screen presentation of racial critique, especially as it occurred in the everyday vernacular speech Micheaux rendered so carefully.

Race Films in the 1940s

Micheaux would only make one film in the 1940s, and it would receive special censorship by the state's attorney general in Maryland. Board chairman Sydney Traub invited the state attorney general to help him censor *The Betrayal* (1948), since it was a "negro picture in which reference to miscegenation occurred several times," and he wanted "an interpretation of [the board's] powers in regard to the elimination of exploitation of [the] sociological problem [of miscegenation] upon the screen."[57] But the rigorous state censorship of race films—even those approved by the PCA—continued, with Maryland cutting as many as seventeen new and rereleased Black feature films in a single year. In the 1940s, recurrently appearing in the elimination files were the films of Black director Spencer Williams and those made by All-American Productions, known for its Black newsreels. Of Spencer Williams's ten feature-length films, half underwent censorship, usually in multiple states.

Censors suppressed sexuality more than any other aspect of the race films.[58] Concern about sexuality was not, of course, limited to race films. With race films, however, censors gave little consideration to the film's overall narrative logic and moral outcome: Black religious films were repeatedly expurgated because white censors thought them insufficiently moral. For example, from Spencer Williams's religious film *Go Down Death!* (1944), which told of a preacher wrongfully slandered for sexual sin by several disloyal parishioners, Maryland and Ohio removed the shot of the ringleader, Mabel, sitting on the preacher's desk with her thigh exposed through a split in her dress, even though her action was clearly moralized by the narrative.[59] *The Blood of Jesus* (1941), with its scriptural voiceovers and authentic representation of the temporal structures of gospel music and prayer, was clearly a religious film. Nevertheless, New York and Ohio cut a dream sequence of tame dancing set in what Ohio censors called a "dive" where Sister Jackson engages in "sinful" behavior. These nightlife scenes are squarely condemned within the narrative structure: indeed, the connection between the nightlife and prostitution so frightens Sister Jackson (Cathryn Caviness) that she calls on God for mercy. But Maryland censors were so unhappy with the moral resolution of Williams's *Juke Joint* (1947) that they tampered with the film's final image, shown through a keyhole, of a mother who has lifted her grown daughter's dress to whip her bottom.[60] While censors had allowed shots of ladies' undergarments in other films, Williams seemed to combine moral punishment and sexual scopic pleasure in the same shot, casting doubt on the film's ultimate moral positioning. Jacqueline Stewart has astutely suggested that Williams's films call into question the moral center by highlighting the questionable morals of the moralizers, an ambiguity censors intuited.[61] But robbing Williams of his final shot fundamentally changed the film's meaning, denying it closure. So during the 1940s, when Hollywood films were increasingly winning favor with state censors, censors mistrusted Black religious filmmakers' moral framework around sin. Similarly, despite its strong political themes, touching on rarely broached issues such as Black immigration, racial equality, and class struggles within Black communities, Ohio reduced *Murder on Lenox Avenue* (1941) to sex and initially banned it, though they later reversed their decision.[62] In barring this film for over three months during its initial run, they deterred audiences from experiencing both its putatively immoral and expressly political elements.

In addition to disciplining the sexuality of the Black subject in front of the camera, censors seem to have desired to discipline the camera itself. Out of *Hi-De-Ho* (1947), the Maryland board cut the "scene showing Cab Calloway looking down front of Minnie the Moocher's dress and accompanying remark: 'Sure I see something.'"[63] It was onscreen Black male looking—especially when the camera followed this look—that the board found dangerous. With *The Dreamer* (1948) (which starred Mantan Moreland and Mabel Lee), censors were again concerned about the camera's Black male gaze and cut "entire sequence of dancers coming from the beautifier machine where camera pans dancer's thighs and breasts."[64] While the male gaze certainly dominated the cinema, the African American male gaze troubled those censors who imagined it.

The vast majority of the scenes censored from race films were nightlife scenes of song and dance. These eliminations, at first glance, seem unimportant to civil rights—or, perhaps, to the films themselves. But Black song and dance contained powerful (if abstract) signifiers of (bodily) rebellion. Though censors may have felt that they were only helping the race by eliminating scenes that exploited them, their cuts removed the modern trickster—and the modern, sophisticated Black woman—from the screen. As Robin Kelley has argued, for Black working-class people, dance halls were places to "recuperate, take back their bodies" that during daylight hours had been set to the master's time, discovering in the dynamic interplay of motion and rhythm a new logic of self-formation.[65] And as Paul Gilroy has noted, when political discourses of freedom are impossibly repressed in the Black public sphere, "racialized sex" can become "an ephemeral residue of political rebellion," hosting "erotic allegories of political desire."[66] Though race films were generally focalized through Black middle-class characters and sensibilities, they contained (in many senses of the word) a broader set of discourses that reflected a range of class perspectives. Nowhere, perhaps, was the broader Black world more evident than in the nightclub sequences censors so often cut, where classes mixed and mingled and where performance was explicitly discursivized. As Jacqueline Stewart argues, the race films' textured blend of performance styles sometimes came to complicate the elitist notions of authentic blackness by attuning audiences to variable registers of everyday performance within Black communities.[67] Though many race films moralized these working-class dance halls and dives, they nevertheless also presented their collective dynamism, the approachable, call-and-response amateur performances, and their pleasures (though these were typically presented through the guise of uplift and morality). Many race films showcase a kind of public freedom of movement and body, a self-possessed power of decision making, an almost poetic vernacular wisdom woven into dialogue, dance, and song that fundamentally offended censors because its twists and turns disrupted dominant racial ideology as embodied in Hollywood's comparatively fixed and static Black images.

SOCIAL EQUALITY, INTEGRATION, AND STATE CENSORSHIP

By contrast with miscegenation, state censors rarely removed "social equality" (as in *Imitation of Life* and *Artists and Models*, where races intermix socially).[68] Before and during the classical era, Kansas, Ohio, and Virginia eliminated several sequences because they challenged segregation.[69] When Virginia banned *Veiled Aristocrats* (1932), in which a white man proposes to a Black woman passing for white, the board cited not miscegenation but social "association" between the races, an ambiguous term that could mean social intermingling or interracial desire.[70] Since this censor's ruling came as the Virginia legislature was recodifying racial legislation, including segregation of all "public halls and public places" and of schools, it was probably tinged with a segregationist impulse.[71]

During the classical era, the communist cinema's "social equality" repeatedly led to banning. In 1935, Ohio banned *Harlem Sketches*, a documentary distributed by the communist Film and Photo League because, the board stated, it "advocate[d] equal social rights for Negroes" and showed "Negroes of Harlem banded together in groups carrying banners displaying communistic ideas."[72] According to the *Defender*, *Harlem Sketches* showed "a real cross-section of Harlem life" during the Depression. The film, which was presented to the Mayor's Investigating Committee as evidence for conditions precipitating the Harlem riots, revealed "tenements and gathering places . . . , vacant lots . . . the lines before the relief headquarters, religious revivals and dance halls" and demonstrations led by Black communist organizer James N. Ford.[73] Ohio also banned *A Greater Promise* (1936), a narrative film about an interracial farming collective in Soviet Birobidzhan not only for "anti-religious propaganda" and glorification of "regimentation and collective farming" over and against "private ownership and inheritance," but because it "portrays social and racial equality of widely differing races and social events."[74] The board customarily cut communist messages from films and banned at least six films as "communist propaganda."[75] But in cases such as those I describe above, Ohio feared not only the spread of communism but also the liberalizing effects of the communist interracial imaginary.

Leftist racial critique again came under fire when Pennsylvania banned Leo Hurwitz's leftist poetic documentary *Strange Victory* (1948) because it was too "inflammatory" in its anti-racism. This film, which begins and ends with images of a newsstand atop a busy subway staircase, aims to pierce the veneer of postwar normalcy and prosperity with memories—here automatic and even abstract— of World War II's violence. The voiceover narration is thick with the veteran's sharp doubts and battle-induced stupor. It questions the so-called American victory: "But why does yesterday wander through today like a ghost? Why is the news still bad? And if we won, why do we look like we lost. And if Hitler died, then why does his voice still spread through America . . . ?" The film applies these questions to race relations directly. What does victory against Hitler mean in a country where, the film points out, Black fighter pilots coming home from the war are refused employment by racist American commercial airlines? With images of the stamping of birth certificates with racial tags and the office niceties that cover up the "gentleman's agreement" against hiring Black people outside service work, the film highlights the subtle institutionalization—even Hitler-esque mechanization—of racism.[76] Because the board found the film's jaded, critical narration "inflammatory," they banned the film in toto.[77]

However, films such as *One Mile from Heaven* and *Artists and Models*, which bore the PCA's seal of approval and in which integration was indirect and deni-able, fared much better at the state level, never making it to any state's controver-sial film files. Scenes of interracial teamwork, in films like *Bataan, Sahara,* and *Home of the Brave*, were also left untouched by state censors. This was even true of the 1940s racial problem film cycle. The independent film *The Jackie Robinson Story* (1950), one of the era's most clear-eyed portrayals of segregation, passed the New York, Massachusetts, Kansas, Maryland, and Ohio boards without eliminations. This semi-documentary not only starred Robinson himself, but frankly demonstrated white racism's everyday ugliness through sequences where the Negro League team is denied dining room service at a roadside restaurant and Robinson isn't even allowed to sit down to wait for the takeout food the manager begrudgingly supplies. Social equality, though an issue for the PCA, appears not to have been consistently regulated at the state level.

ELIMINATING RACIAL STRIFE

States generally accepted screen social equality (such as it was). However, they more frequently censored interracial strife— accomplishing this in two central ways: cutting racial offense (epithets and other kinds of racial insults) and inter-racial violence. While both kinds of cuts aimed to minimize racial disturbances resulting from the cinema, the racial ideology undergirding these two types of censorship seems quite different. On the one hand, expurgating racial offense sometimes endeared censors to local civil rights activists. On the other, remov-ing onscreen racial conflict shortcircuited the era's most urgent cinematic sig-nifiers of white injustice and Black resistance. State censors wanted to aid state officials in maintaining social control. But their written policies against offense to races suggest that they were sometimes guided by racial liberalism—or even the bidding of local civil rights leaders who sought to define the freedom from racial defamation as a civil right. New York, for example, removed scenes of semi-nude bodies of women of color (and scenes where white men claim ownership over them) because, in their words, these scenes were "exploiting" these women.[78] Similarly, New York censored as "inhuman" brutality against Black natives from Hollywood's jungle films.[79] Many state boards also regularly eliminated epithets, regardless of whether the film morally condemned these offensive words. Epithets were embattled signifiers and states' only consistent concession to non-white viewers. But such "liberal" state censorship to please non-white audiences was inconsistent, sporadic. And because censors lacked attention to context, their changes often decreased the films' potential for anti-racist social commentary.

STATE CENSORS AND THE CINEMATIC REPRESENTATION OF INTERRACIAL VIOLENCE

All states cut onscreen Black-white interracial violence, though this regulation fell into distinct eras and there was a surprising array of opinions on what kinds of scenes might incite to violence. The Kansas censors frequently purged shots of interracial violence in the 1920s.[80] But there is scant evidence that the board continued this censorship after 1930 (though it cut a fight scene between "Jack Johnson and a white man" from the MGM two-reeler *Flying Gloves* [1933]).[81] Interracial boxing was also occasionally a problem for the Virginia board, which banned a 1935 fight film showing Joe Louis not only triumphing over Max Baer but knocking him down several times along the way, because it might "incite to crime."[82] The Virginia board also mentioned a race riot with "far too much realism and race hatred" and the film's tendency to be "irritating" to Black people as reasons for rejecting Micheaux's *A Son of Satan* (1924).[83]

During the Depression, New York came down hard on modern cinematic images showing or "inciting" revolt against authority (whether racial or not)— particularly when onscreen resisters fought with police or when police were brutal or repressive.[84] Few films dared to show Black revolt. But New York did soften at least one scene of Black-white racial conflict, including all "close views" in a sequence from *Trader Horn* (1931) where "natives are choking whites (by sound or expression) showing extreme cruelty."[85] New York also cut brutal scenes where racial injustice was unmistakable, as when a "white settler deliberately" shoots Alessandro (Don Ameche) in *Ramona* (1936).[86]

State censors varied in their policies on lynching: New York almost never censored lynching except in Mexican films of the 1950s; Kansas cut hanging scenes from the 1910s through the 1930s but then seems to have abruptly abated this policy in the 1940s; Pennsylvania so strongly opposed lynching in *The Ox-Bow Incident* (1942) that they cut not only the film but disallowed images from the pressbook.

Ohio provides a nice case study of the effects of stern state censorship of lynching. By the 1930s, Ohio cut most lynching scenes and lines of dialogue promoting lynching, rejecting into the 1950s both pro- and anti-lynching films like *The Birth of a Nation* and *Within Our Gates*.[87] Ohio was concerned about lynching's brutality even when the victims were white. In 1936, Ohio censors left intact *Fury's* sadistic (though largely inert) mob, but removed long sequences where spectators are uncomfortably positioned to feel the mental anguish of a white lynching victim, Joe (Spencer Tracy), deleting views of him "looking out of the bars through the flames" and "struggling to break the [window] bars" of the prison in which he will eventually burn.[88] The board also severely amended *The Ox-Bow Incident*, removing dialogue that proffered lynching as an alternative to courtroom justice. As in Pennsylvania, these deletions eviscerated *Ox-Bow's* final scenes, removing all shots of "tightening loop in rope"; "rope hanging from tree"; "three men being dragged in rope by mob to be hung"; "throwing the rope over the tree"; and all "scenes of lifting men up to the nooses—whipping horses from under victims and all showing shadows of men hanging from tree."[89] If the political edge of lynching films of the late 1930s and early 1940s was that they allowed audiences to feel the terror and injustice of lynching through the staging of the victim's brutal suspense, state censorship purposely stemmed these spectatorial effects.

State Censors and the Battle over Lynching in the Late 1940s and 1950s

The greatest deliberation on screening mob violence came in the late 1940s and early 1950s, when social problem films rather than westerns broached the subject. Though the number of lynchings in the United States declined, in the rising Cold War atmosphere the idea of lynching became crucial in this era to critiquing of American systems of race—and class—marginality.[90] Censorship battles attended a cycle of visually dark mob violence films. Each adopted noir's bleakness and grit in depicting mob fury. The cinematic alterity of these foreign, B, and independent films—with their attendant ideological difference—provided an alternative to Hollywood's rendition of racial violence that broadened the definition of oppression. All these films called contemporary America to account for the history of white-on-Black violence in response to the trumped-up excuse of miscegenation. In this section, in light of the preceding analysis of state censors' efforts to stem racial strife, I give more sustained consideration to each film's textual politics and social struggles.

The Burning Cross (1947), the first—and in many ways most daring—of the late-1940s racial problem films, was initially banned in Ohio and Virginia. I have already discussed the film in chapter 1. But closer examination helps explain how state censorship altered the film's meanings. Produced by leftist Selvyn Levinson, the film embodied the Left's more strident approach to depicting race relations. The film begins with a lengthy voiceover accompanying a shadowy montage of Klan hangings: "The South, defeated, poverty-stricken, its traditions shattered, was desperate. Out of this desperation came the Ku Klux Klan."[91] Black World War II navy veteran Charlie West (Joel Fluellen) is the film's most memorable Klan victim. The Klan doesn't want Black people exercising their franchise. So it sends our protagonist, Johnny, an out of work, mentally unstable white veteran, to stop Charlie from registering. But Charlie, quoting Lincoln, stands up for his rights—and the Klan burns a cross on his lawn, sticks a knife in his door, and beats him. Though Charlie is not the center of the narrative, he holds the privileged status in the film's economy as bearer of the look (though watching violence also makes him its psychic victim): perched on the limb of a tree, Charlie, unseen, witnesses the Klan's murder of an Italian man —and it is his gaze we share through the Klan's lengthy secret rites. Charlie is thus crucial to the film's exposure of the Klan. He defies the Klan and tells a policeman what he saw. But the police are in cahoots with the Klan, which then comes to Charlie's home to silence him. While on this mission, Johnny finally realizes the Klan is wrong. He fights to keep his hooded brethren from lynching Charlie until he himself is knocked unconscious. Charlie, meanwhile, meets the Klan with armed resistance. But the Klan overpowers him and burns Charlie and most of his family alive. The only survivor is Charlie's seven-year-old son, Bubby (Glenn Allen), who harrowingly relates over the radio how he watched his family's home go up in flames and that he will never see his family again. In the end, we learn that Johnny's voiceover, which has guided us through the narrative, is his testimony to the special prosecutor. Johnny is now working against the Klan.

In *The Burning Cross*, Klan racism and white supremacy are directly implicated rather than buried in subplots and indirect signifiers.[92] There is no last-minute rescue as there would be in censor-sanctioned films like *Intruder in the Dust*; long shots of the Black family through windows, enveloped in flames, accompanied by the screams of Charlie's wife, Ginny (Madie Norman), force audiences to feel the social and melodramatic weight of the Klan's unswerving brutality. Charlie also tries to defend himself using a gun. And the irony that he is a veteran is emphasized in the mise-en-scène (see figure 17). Further, Charlie's strong belief in the right to vote frames the film's racial conflict not as a racial gang war (as in films like *No Way Out* [1950] and *Blackboard Jungle* [1955]) but as a quest for citizenship. Charlie says: "President Lincoln said 'Government of the people, by the people and for the people.' I was born in America, my father was born in America, his father was born in America so I figure what Mr. Lincoln said includes me too." When Johnny protests that he "just doesn't want to see [him] get hurt," Charlie replies, "But who is going to hurt me for doing my

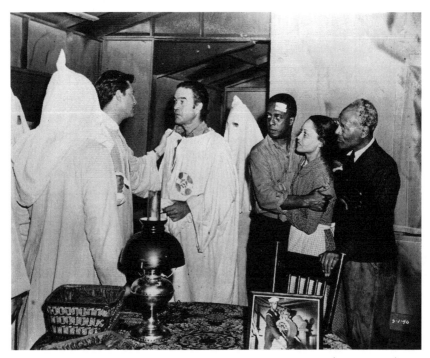

FIGURE 17. The Klan threatens Black World War II veteran Charlie (Joel Fluellen) and eventually burns him and his family alive. Publicity still from *The Burning Cross*.

duty as a citizen, like the government says?"—a question that looms over the film's conclusion.

The Ohio board objected not only to the film's violence but suggested it might inspire racial revolt. Concluding that the film might inflame what it called "Militant Minorities" or their adversaries, it issued this statement:

> Minority groups ... must see [*The Burning Cross*] in terms of their historical backgrounds, past experiences and present problems. [They] are undoubtedly feeling the pressure of invisible control [and] ... might find in the picture a pattern for militant leadership. ... There is a possibility of militant minority group members of an audience harboring such an idea and wanting to put it into effect rather than to trust to somewhat slower but more peaceful methods of change through education. This picture will be shown, conceivably, in communities where a minority group leader may now be waiting for psychological stimulus to move aggressively "for the new day for his minority group" with consequent violence.[93]

The board saw the film as challenging the very gradualism that it, as a part of the state's educational apparatus, championed. Instead, the film seemed to argue for "aggressive," "militant" tactics and had the potential to radicalize Black spectators. This was the first film of its kind—a racial problem film with a bitter, bloody confrontation between the Klan and Black Americans and that advocated for a radically immediate intervention rather than gradual tolerance. It was the kind of film that *Stevedore* or *Nation Aflame* might have been had Breen allowed racial lynchings in contemporary settings in the 1930s. When the film got an Ohio permit (upon appeal), the board still eliminated "the close-up brutality scene as the negro goes to the door of the cabin" and wanted "softening of brutality in close-up scenes of the raid on the negro and his family."[94]

In Virginia, the unpredictable effects of this new kind of film moved censors to screen the film for local civic groups. Virginia, which only occasionally censored lynching, rejected *The Burning Cross* in September and, after an appeal, again in October, opining that the film would tend

> to excite prejudices and intense emotions thereby reviving controversies and disputes which the Board believes presently to be quiet and not occupying public attention. . . . The general theme and design of this picture is of such inflammatory nature that it . . . would be promotive of the revival of animosities, dislikes and enmities which may cause quarrels and breaches of the peace and consequently corrupt morals or incite to crime.[95]

In this twisted logic, exposing racism might prompt a breach of the "peace," bringing too much "public attention" to racial violence.

Virginia civil rights activists struck back. The Virginia Conference of the NAACP, B'nai B'rith, white civil rights activist Virginia Durr, labor activist Brownie Lee Jones, and the American Veterans Committee—all individuals and groups that were working to bring the white South to conscience—condemned Virginia's banning as "undemocratic." In their straining to see cinematic acknowledgment of the "changing," leftist South, they may have seen things in the film that were not there. Nevertheless, both Durr and Clark Foreman of the Southern Council on Human Welfare publicly called on HUAC to investigate the Virginia board as a subversive group for banning a film exposing the "un-Americanism of the Ku Klux Klan and the danger to freedom in this country resulting from organized prejudice." According to the *Los Angeles Sentinel*, the nineteen unfriendly witnesses before HUAC also invoked *The Burning Cross* before the committee— to point out the committee's twisted definition of un-Americanism. They offered to show HUAC the film as an example of the real threat to America. HUAC predictably declined.[96] When the Virginia NAACP attempted to appeal the ban, the state censorship board ignored them. Virginia Conference NAACP president J. M. Tinsley rebuked the board for disregarding "a public trust and an opportunity to educate the people with facts that will promote better understanding between racial groups."[97] So loud was the furor from prominent Virginia civil rights activists that Walter White, who didn't often support branches' film activism, also intervened, writing to Screen Guild Productions, the film's distributor, to offer legal help.[98]

Screen Guild appealed the board's decision. The company billed the film as righteous social truth that revealed the KKK—and America's "frightful social conditions"—and, through the reformed Johnny, "a fair picture of the 'changing south'" "hard on the heels of a lynching in South Carolina and a near lynching in North Carolina."[99] When the Richmond City Court assigned a former Klan member, Judge Julien Gunn, to hear the appeal, it seemed the film's fate was sealed. But, after screening the film for Black and white spectators, he surprisingly reversed the censor's ban, condemning the modern Klan as a distortion—an organization that had gone "too far."[100] Nevertheless, Gunn gave state censors full discretion to make eliminations. But the board, perhaps fearing bad press or future court action, conspicuously avoided racial deletions, cutting hanging from the prologue (which linked Klan brutality to the Confederacy), tarring and feathering, a drunken woman dancing for beer, and the shooting of a white character.[101]

Though no Black militants arose to overthrow Ohio or Virginia state governments, Black Virginians did use the film to call for aggressive voting rights reform.[102] In a unique distribution arrangement, the Norfolk NAACP sponsored the showing of The Burning Cross, sharing proceeds from ticket sales with Jewish liberal theater owner Abe Lichtman's Booker T. Theater.[103] In his antigradualist "Freedom Now!" campaign, Norfolk NAACP leader Jerry O. Gilliam urged civil rights workers to promote The Burning Cross, which he described as "depicting the courage of a southern negro who dared defend his home and family against attack."[104]

On the heels of The Burning Cross, Ohio censored several other mob films, banning Monogram's Violence (1947), eliminating mob scenes from Try and Get Me (1949), and recalling Crossfire (1947) after a spectator protested that the film "provokes race hatred" (the board ultimately rereleased the film without changes). The most symptomatic and obviously repressed of these texts was Warner Bros.' anti-Klan film Storm Warning (1950), which was censored in Maryland, Pennsylvania, and Ohio.[105] In it, Ginger Rogers plays Marsha Mitchell, a cosmopolitan New York model, who, while on a business trip, stops overnight to visit her small-town southern sister, Lucy (Doris Day). While alone on the town's dark streets, Marsha witnesses the Klan seizing a white man (whom we later learn is northern reporter Walter Adams [Dale Van Sickle]) from the courthouse and preparing a rope to hang him. He is shot in the back while trying to escape, only feet away from where Marsha is hiding. Remaining undetected, she sees the faces of several culprits who have removed their hoods.

When Marsha meets Lucy's husband, Hank (Steve Cochran), she recognizes him as one of the Klansmen. When the honest district attorney, Burt Rainey (Ronald Reagan), subpoenas Marsha, she appears in court but falsely testifies that she saw nothing. Later, after she confronts Hank and he nearly rapes her, she decides to testify and the Klan kidnaps her. In the climactic final scene, and under the banner of a fiery cross, the Klansmen whip Marsha on the head and face and accuse her of being an "outsider," "busy-body," and for "defying the Klan." Hank, aiming for Marsha, accidentally shoots his wife. The film ends with Marsha kneeling with the wounded Lucy in her arms and the amorous D.A. at her side. The camera pulls back to reveal the burning cross, whose embers are fading as its top half dramatically falls to the ground.

Though posing as a Klan exposé, the film contains three glaring historical inaccuracies that *The Burning Cross* avoided. First, in *Storm Warning* the Klan is primarily a "racket"—a money-making scheme run by gangsters—rather than a racist terrorist organization designed to enforce segregation. Second, because the defenseless victim is killed by gunshot, the narrative neglects to render the torture of lynching, although the (unused) lyncher's rope becomes a key piece of evidence in convicting the Klan leader. Third, the film doesn't connect the Klan to "the race problem" in the foreground, showing only white victims of the Klan.

Despite the narrative omission of African Americans, they nevertheless become a marginal presence etched indelibly into the text's shadows.[106] The script explicitly called for African American extras to be present at the scene of the lynching—a fact that the PCA notes in its file on the film. In addition, the film indicates the racism it can't directly name by including a constellation of indirect signifiers—for instance, the Ku Klux Klan (which is mentioned by name), the southern setting, and the numerous Black extras. Marsha even turns to look at these extras as she enters the bus station, and they also look toward her. In addition, the sound system in the recreation center plays jazz, which the owner disparagingly refers to as "jungle music."

Further, though the film avoids picturing lynching, it tensely reveals the mob's fury. The film is haunted by its own repressions and those of the southern town it represents. The mix of noir's chiaroscuro in the nighttime lynching scene and "live" televisual aesthetics to capture the day's seething southern masses point to the visual iconography of the budding civil rights movement in ways beyond narrative. Outside the courthouse, a radio reporter broadcasts live from amid a crowd of hundreds: "There are very angry people here, sullen and hostile. [Member of the crowd: You're a great speechmaker, mister. Why don't you go home!] Indeed your radio reporter won't be surprised if someone comes up from behind and bops him on the head. If this microphone suddenly goes dead on you, you will know why." Here, as in the scene of Adams's killing, a white reporter replaces the Klan's usual Black victims. But African American extras are present in almost every frame in this scene, visually testifying to the Black connection to the Klan that the narrative elides. On a narrative level, Black interest in the trial indirectly indicates the Klan's racial villainy. In shots of the crowd after the inquest, Black extras are even visibly disappointed that the judge's ruling has left the Klan unscathed. On an extra-narrative level, as had been true in *Fury* and *They Won't Forget*, the Black extras act as a reminder of the story the text doesn't tell, abstractly symbolizing the repressed connection between race and lynching.

In lieu of African Americans, in *Storm Warning* it is white women the Klan victimizes, an important narrative twist that operates as both substitution and reversal. It is important that the film's heroine is a strong-willed, wily, and righteous woman—but also a blonde with a small, frail frame—one who is employed as a model constantly subject to male looking. Rogers's physical form performs two subversions: first, her knowledge and strength seems to contradict her physical frailty, and second, her frailty transports the iconography of the "Little Sister" scenario from *The Birth of a Nation* into a film narrative that condemns the Klan for harming those very people the organization was purportedly intended to help: white women. The film's most tragic "peripheral" victim of the Klan is also a white blond woman, cast as the quintessential 1950s white female domestic ideal: the innocent Doris Day, whose accidental death at the hands of her own husband in the film points out the Klan's threat to the family and to "their own kind," that is, other white folk. Rather than the victims of the Klan being the dark and alien, it is the Klan members themselves who bear the mark of "darkness." Hank, Lucy's husband, is the darkest named character in the film, with black hair and darker skin tone.

As was true of Charlie in *The Burning Cross*, Marsha's status as looker—onlooker—gestures beyond her own victimization. A woman who had spent her career giving men "knowing" looks, Marsha's knowingness points toward the African Americans the film marginalizes, taking on new depth and social purpose. In numerous sequences where she looks brazenly offscreen with rancor toward the Klan, her eyes tell us that she knows something about who the Klan's real victims are. In fact, her performance nearly derails the film's narrative. It is difficult for us to maintain a sense of suspense, because she is not afraid and we can therefore not be afraid for her. Her steely, righteous, condemning eyes convince us that nothing will happen to her because she is the vital witness and the film's ocular center.

The PCA passed *Storm Warning* after Warner Bros. cut Hank's brutality both in the mob scene and when he punches his wife.[107] Ohio censors, who were tracking local Klan incidents in their files, found unacceptable Hank's sexual advances toward Marsha, but also the film's direct depiction of the Klan. Warfield telegrammed A. S. Howson of Warner Bros., indicating her "deep" concern over the "Klan picture."[108] Despite the film's "*anti*-Klan" treatment, Warfield worried that it was "very violent and emotionally stirring in some of its sequences. We feel doubt as to the timeliness of this picture and our chief concern is what public reaction will be."[109] The board approved only a "trial showing" of *Storm Warning*—with a threat of "recall at any time for re-screening if we become in any way doubtful of our decision."[110] Utilizing a "provisional seal," a regular practice that kept distributors under constant threat, the Ohio board reminded Warner Bros. of its power and reiterated its strongly held, vaguely racial concerns over its content.

From the film, Warfield finally minimized Hank's attempted seduction/rape of Marsha and reduced the film's climactic Klan flogging to a single "flash" of the final whip stroke (see figure 18).[111] Pennsylvania and Maryland made similar deletions to the flogging, suggesting but not dwelling on the action.[112] As we see from *Storm Warning*, even the suggestion of strong Klan violence, when removed from racial implications, was troubling to censors in the late 1950s.

In the 1950s, an era in which, as Susan Courtney shows, cinematic narratives often disparaged white women because they tended "only to exacerbate crises of white masculinity with emergent identities of their own," *Storm Warning* seems to have taken the sophisticated white woman's side, revealing repressive, small-town white men (and their repressed wives) as "the problem" and centralizing the white woman's look.[113] Even though the film studiously avoided censorship by displacing lynching from its Black victims, state censors still cut it in ways that diminished the impact of its violence and by extension the strength of its statement about the Klan.

While Ohio's censorship of *Storm Warning* seems egregious and strange, more broadly censored were three foreign lynching films that directly referenced race and critiqued America: *Native Son* (1951), *La Putain Respectueuse* (*The Respectful Prostitute* hereafter) (1952), and *J'irai Cracher sur Vos Tombes* (*I Spit on Your Graves* hereafter) (1959). In *Native Son* (1951), the impoverished Bigger (Richard Wright, starring in the film adaptation of his own novel), the white Dalton family's newly appointed chauffer, smothers to death young white debutante Mary Dalton (Jean Wallace) after her blind mother enters the room while Mary is kissing him on her bed. Bigger, whose father was lynched, is sure of his own eventual lynching if he is discovered. So Bigger dismembers Mary and burns her in the furnace and, when the body is discovered, he hides out in an abandoned tenement. The specter of lynching haunts the text: the police and the courts, the benevolent and the malevolent, all become would-be lynchers, so Bigger pre-emptively kills to protect himself. Police raid his hideout and chase him across rooftops. It is only after shooting him with a fire hose that the police capture Bigger. A policeman proudly proclaims, "It's gonna be a hot time in the old town tonight!" and an angry mob at the jail chants for his lynching. On first review, New York, Ohio, Maryland, Pennsylvania, Kansas, and Virginia banned the film. This was the largest cluster of state-level rejections accompanying the release of any film dealing with Black-white American race relations of the decade. The film eventually passed muster in Pennsylvania, Virginia, New York, and Massachusetts but only with extensive eliminations. The eliminations reveal the racial politics of each board.[114] But a striking commonality among the deletions was the "legal lynching" of Bigger. New York censors removed the word lynching

FIGURE 18. Marsha (Ginger Rogers) is whipped in the face by Klan members. Frame captures from *Storm Warning* (1950).

from the dialogue, and evidence of police support for the lynch mob, as well as their brutality toward Bigger.[115] New York, Massachusetts, and Virginia removed a line that offers the film's stinging moral: "All my life I have heard of Black men being killed because of white girls." Virginia also removed a voiceover where Bigger introduces his father as a man whom "the white folks had lynched when I was a kid." Even these verbal descriptions of lynching, when crafted by a Black (communist) author, were racially subversive enough to prompt censorship.

The Respectful Prostitute, based on Jean-Paul Sartre's play about the Scottsboro incident, featured one of the most realistic racial lynching scenes of the era. When Lizzy (Barbara Laage), a white northern prostitute, is nearly raped, two Black men are her only witnesses, and her assailant kills one of them. Later the assailant is revealed to be a southern senator's son, and police and politicians collude in a cover-up designed to frame the surviving Black witness, Sidney (Walter Bryant), for murder and attempted rape. Lizzy initially refuses to go along with the story, but the love of the senator's son Fred (Ivan Desny) and the power of the senator seduce her. Once she has signed the affidavit, the spectacle of racist violence begins. Television cameras flood in. The town, whose racial animosity has been funneled solely into their use of the word nigger, turns a brutal hand against its Black residents. A lynch mob sweeps the streets. Sidney breaks into Lizzy's house through the window; she shelters him out of remorse and eventually decides to tell the truth. In the final scene, Lizzy and Sidney escape the mobs by running to National Guard troops brought in to restore order. As a military vehicle ushers them to safety, Lizzy smiles and takes Sidney's hand. The film, which began on racially contested, mobile terrain, ends similarly in the National Guardsmen's jeep, another "racialized vehicle," and this motif of movement reflects the film's implicit link of the vagabond nature of both the prostitute's existence and the existence of marginalized African American accused.

Not only did the film trouble the narrative of miscegenetic rape by suggesting it was a white politician's lie, but it also revealed its impact on Black men: Sidney, the innocent surveyor of white wrongs, is forced to flee the white mob, a fact stirringly rendered by a cinematography marking him as a subject of the shadows. The moments of stark realism come, however, when the lynch mob captures another man, mistaking him for Sidney, and drags him behind a truck (see figure 19). "That's not him!" Lizzie protests. But the mob pushes her away and proceeds to string him up in an abandoned lot. One man even says, "You're hysterical," and slaps her down into a pile of rubble.

The film confuses many aspects of American race relations and Black community life. The film's unusually cohesive and bitter Black community appears more colonial than American; Black people resist white racism by vanishing en masse from "their place" in service to whites, as opposed to Hollywood's more individualized comic resistance and backtalk as embodied by Hattie McDaniel's roles. (*The Respectful Prostitute*'s resistance is limited, however: the film's Black

protagonist, Sidney, is no militant and calls Lizzie "ma'am.") Nevertheless, there is spectatorial value in the film's alterity, as it linked transnational Black dissent to the African American case. Like *Senza Pietà*, the film's ending unites a Black man and white woman in ways taboo on American screens. Most importantly, its realistic scenarios of congressionally generated American racial violence far exceeded Black representability in Hollywood films, not only incorporating the graphic regimes of the early civil rights struggle but presenting a foreign refraction of the demented white southern racism Hollywood films repressed.

Accordingly, it was censored. The film's distributor, Times Film Corp., sought PCA approval but refused to change the content and title enough to please industry self-regulators.[116] Though both Kansas and Virginia banned the film, their reasoning differed. Kansas cited "immorality and prostitution," but Virginia said the film "would tend to incite to violence," a rationale suggesting opposition to the film's racial violence.[117] State documentation suggests that Virginia banned the film because of its racial content and, despite lengthy legal battles, the board never approved the film.[118]

I Spit on Your Graves, with its bold and intimate view of racial lynching, was similarly unable to overcome state banning. Jimmie (uncredited), a harmonica-playing Black teenager, works on the Memphis docks with his light-skinned older brother, Joe Grant (Christian Marquand). In the film's second scene, a white mob lynches Jimmie for his relationship with a white woman. Joe cuts Jimmie's corpse down from the tree, drives it home, lays it on the family tabletop, and sets it aflame, burning the entire ramshackle house with it (see figure 20). These scenes represent lynching with a difference. As Joe discovers the lynched body, we see it as well, giving us an intimacy with the dead that is absent in films such as *Intruder in the Dust* (1949) and *The Lawless* (1948), where the mob's target escapes with the help of a white liberal. Unlike these films, *I Spit on Your Graves* never attempts to account for the mob's logic or sadism—or to exploit its violence with action aesthetics. Rather, it treats a nexus more central to the Black experience of lynching: tragedy and disgust. What it delivers is a sense of abjection—of flesh turning cold, of standing in the wake of the dead, of handling dead bodies, being with the dead, of coping with the corporeal realities of death—giving viewers access to the attendant sense of loss and grotesquerie. In presenting the body of the lynched one, effaced in previous film dramas, this film removes the lynched one from the imaginary space of horror and places him in the cold reality of immobile Black flesh: of lifelessness. The inexplicable, destructive act of burning the body, one that Joe rather than the lynch mob enacts (and which is set to jazz music), catalyzes Joe's revenge and becomes a revolutionary sign of his agentic transformation of his brother's body into fodder for his own

FIGURE 19. *Facing page*: Brutal shots of racial violence divaricated from Hollywood's lynching iconography. Frame captures from *The Respectful Prostitute* (1952).

FIGURE 20. *Above and facing page*: Intimacy with the lynching body is followed by fire in *I Spit on Your Graves* (1959). Frame captures.

body's rage. Throughout the film, Joe will use his lightness (both his light skin and his consequently easy mobility) to lure white women into acts of miscegenation, becoming a "serial miscegenator" as revenge for his brother's killing (though in the film, unlike the book, Joe cannot go through with the rapes and killings and is only able to have consensual sex with white women).

The narrative that surrounds the lynching hopelessly muddles American geography and culture. It melds cacophonic Americana from differing moments, each preposterously transposed in translation. It treats Trenton, New Jersey, as a

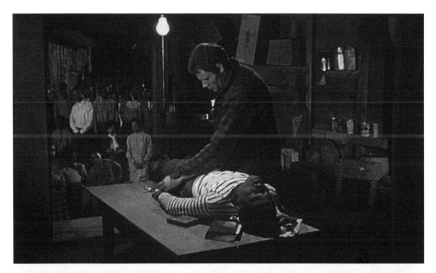

cultural destination—like Paris or New York—giving it southern-style plantation houses and horse stables; by contrast, Memphis is an industrial city. Characters' costumes hail from a range of eras: Joe dresses like James Dean while the
other Black residents wear tattered, turn-of-the-century garb; white Southerners
wear neck scarves and riding pants, imitation American jeans or cheap, flashy
gangster-style suits and neckties; and the African American "district" looks like
slave quarters, though Joe drives to them in a 1950s convertible. White supremacy and real relations of racial power are overwritten with a European fantasy

of American Black rebellion that collapses it into the transnational visual idiom of juvenile delinquency.[119] Such inconsistencies make the film unacceptable as a representation of an American "real." But the film's brazen surrealisms and the provocative questions these juxtapositions raise release us from American race relations' hardened visual regimes. When viewed in the context of Hollywood's rigid and often mystifying fantasies of race, this film's novel iconography provides an important break. Indeed, mixing emblems of the plantation chronotope with emergent Black power motifs has the startling but meaningful effect of morphing the racism of the past with the present resistance—allowing viewers and characters to confront history—and the historical tools of racism with present-day deconstructions.

The symbolic value of this iconographic shift is significant. By blending youth culture with miscegenation and lynching, the film epitomizes a sensational, exploitation-driven approach to social problems that states censored because it challenged sexual and racial mores and hierarchies of taste. Virginia banned the film in toto before the formal application even arrived at the office.[120] The distributor, Audubon Films, appealed the ban. While the files do not reveal whether Virginia accepted the film upon appeal, the film did eventually show, whether legally or not, at the Black-patronized Dixie Theater in March 1965. But this was three years after Audubon's initial application and five years after the film's making.

Through banning, eliminations, and delays, state censors greatly altered Black spectatorial possibilities in connection with foreign and independent films treating lynching. Yet we can suspiciously regard exploitation values in these films, where Black political resistance is often swept up in a blazing streak of affect and where, as Eileen Julien has noted of Josephine Baker's films, European filmmakers exploit American racism as a wedge against culpability for their own colonial oppressions.[121] Indeed, these filmmakers' lack of study of American conditions—their rendering of America as surrogate, extension, even colony—of European life, does, as James Baldwin has argued, limit greatly their ability to bring Black America realistically into relief.[122] Nevertheless, if I Spit on Your Graves, Native Son, and The Respectful Prostitute aided denial of colonial repression, they also operate as a cinema of guilt whose primary pleasure is seeing the American white man (or woman) writhe—a powerful proposition for Black spectators and one that foreshadowed the pleasures of Blaxploitation. Each film features the return of the some of the racial realities that Hollywood repressed, whether in the form of murdering Bigger Thomas, Sidney's shadowing presence that haunts Lizzie's residence, or Joe who fucks and nearly kills across the color line. Furthermore, European cinema's American noir offered Black spectators a far more direct and historically truthful representation of segregation and racist brutality. Crucially in each of these censorship cases, distributors, exhibitors, and civil rights leaders fought censorship of these dark films so that a broader set of images of race relations could be shown, though persevering state censors most often thwarted them.

State Censors and Race Riots

In the late 1950s, several of the films that most poignantly revealed Black anger and resentment at racial injustice centered on the motif of race riots. Race riots were crucially if indirectly related to civil rights. Historically, race riots were a response of disenfranchised Black people to centuries-long denials of civil rights. Further, the postwar decline in lynching and the rise in race riots indicated Black mass resistance to white mob rule. To many whites, however, riots were evidence of Black unfitness for equality. These films are vital to the narrative of racial censorship because they, more than even the lynching films, mirrored contemporary violence and depicted empowered Black militant resistance. Both *No Way Out* (1950) and *The Well* (1951) suffered heavy cuts despite PCA approval. But unlike the aforementioned European films, state boards worked with producers to reconstruct them so they fell in line with Hollywood's patterned racial repression. In *No Way Out*, a white mob plans violence against Black Dr. Brooks and the segregated northern city ghetto where he lives. But Lefty (Dots Johnson), a Black hospital employee, alerts and organizes Black men to launch a preemptive strike. Under PCA influence, the film focused on the preparation for the riot, cutting to brief, bloodless, medium-long shots once the fight began. This indirection was enough for New York, Kansas, and Massachusetts, which approved the film without eliminations. But in Maryland, Ohio, Virginia, and Pennsylvania, censors made major deletions, cutting all planning and preparation for the riots.[123] They removed the tangible signifiers that suggested violence, and thus left evidence of its suggestion only in the scenes' tension.

In Maryland, the board consulted with members of Baltimore's Black community and the Maryland Interracial Commission to view the film as censor's consultants. The group was nearly unanimous in its decision that the film should be shown as submitted. But the Maryland state censor ignored them and, as with *Betrayal*, let the state attorney general handle the film's censorship. He removed epithets, sexually suggestive dialogue, a hint of miscegenation, and, of course, racial violence, whether enacted by a mob or by an old white woman spitting on Dr. Brooks.

When Walter White vociferously protested the film's censorship, the chairman of Maryland's censorship board, Sydney Traub, responded that he, as a World War II veteran, also "deplore[d] racial prejudice and . . . am equally mindful of the danger that can flow from such hatred. But I cannot see how you can hope to eradicate the disease by depicting violence by mobs in utter defiance of law and order."[124] Traub's refusal to withhold censorship gained steam through an internal NAACP rift. As I describe in a later chapter, Carl Murphy, an NAACP board member (and editor of the *Baltimore Afro-American*), wanted to bar the word "nigger" from all American life and thus found the film highly censorable. But yet another NAACP perspective vied for prominence. For Baltimore NAACP activist Lillian Johnson, who also corresponded with Traub, the film's civil rights virtue was not its "lynch atmosphere" (praised by the national NAACP) but rather its replacement of Hollywood's tired lynching narrative with Black men finally defending themselves:

> Instead of the colored people being attacked, driven out of their homes and raped, the white hoodlums were annihilated almost to a man! Instead of the hospital wards being filled with the intended colored victims, they overflow with the white mobsters, as a result of the colored veterans organized defense of their homes, their women and children.... The NAACP feels ... that the deleted scenes should be restored so that the real impact of the picture will be maintained.[125]

Maryland delayed the release of *No Way Out* by three months (and even then only gave it a provisional seal with many eliminations) and never restored the scenes of organized Black resistance.

Another PCA-approved race riot film, *The Well*, was also widely censored. In *The Well*, a Black girl (Gwendolyn Laster) has fallen down a well, but suspicion in her disappearance falls on the white man (Harry Morgan) with whom she was last seen—a stranger who bought her flowers and appears to have kidnapped her. Moved by tension and misunderstanding, the girl's father (Ernest Anderson) approaches a relative of the suspected kidnapper, an encounter that ends in physical struggle. Crucially, an organized Black community rises up to find and defend the girl, first by reasoning with the town's leaders and later, after whites' violent attacks, with defensive violence. Finally a racially liberal sheriff restores order, discovers the girl, and unites the entire town in the effort to extract her from the well. In *The Well* white people are disproportionately the violent offenders. And the film credibly builds the atmosphere of riots—through sound and fast-paced editing—without showing it directly.

State censors removed violent scenes, carefully shot though they were. But they also cut Black townspeople questioning justice across the color line. In one scene, three laborers, two Black and one white, are moving boxes while they discuss the missing girl. The white mover says of the accused kidnapper, "Give him a break. Maybe he didn't do it." To which one of the Black men responds to his Black co-laborer: "Tell him what kind of a break we'd get if it were one of us." Later a Black student who sits at an integrated lunch counter boldly remarks in white earshot: "You can get away with murder—as long as you're the right color." Maryland removed all these lines, and all scenes where violence and epithets reached a fever pitch, despite protests of this censorship from Walter White and Judge Francis Rivers, a civil rights leader and the first Black member of the New York City Bar Association and City Court. Rivers opined that the film was honest and unique in its belief "that race-hate's dread power to divide a community into two warring mobs, white against colored, can be conquered by the cohesive power of universal aspiration."[126]

Not only did Maryland cut the film, it delayed its release by ten months. In the Cold War environment, *The Well*'s censorship transcended the local arena and moved to the international stage when the U.S. State Department blocked the film's premiere at the Berlin Film Festival.[127] With race riot films, censors cut not only interracial violence but also film elements they thought would stir Black militancy and upset the state's racial norms. As the case of Maryland's censorship of race riots reveals, state censors worried that showing any organized Black resistance or the logic behind Black self-defense would be a danger to "law enforcement." This parallels their broader censorship of racial violence in foreign and independent films, where, again, they worried about maintaining the racial status quo, as much as they worried about morality or violence.

CONCLUSION

The PCA guidelines showed filmmakers how to build deniable signifiers of touchy racial issues. But state censors consistently cut suggestion itself. This rendered already ambiguous racial scenes even more remote and elliptical. When it came to race in foreign, B, and independent films, both southern and nothern state censors cut tramontane views of miscegenation, racial strife, epithets, and racialized sexuality. They were concerned not only with disciplining images but also with disciplining looks, "views," spectatorship itself, by limiting the gaze's purview and its stirring effects. In doing so they greatly narrowed Hollywood's already limited interracial imaginary, as well as the unofficial racial lexicon offered by more marginal films. The question of why the PCA did not modify its policy to correspond with state censors' policies forces us to look back to the industry. Individual studios took calculated risks and pushed back against the restraints of state censors, a fact that sometimes put them in the position of advocating for a more thorough covering of the issues central to civil rights struggles. It is to an exploration of how one studio head measured these risks that I turn next.

3 · RACIAL TRAUMA, CIVIL RIGHTS, AND THE BRUTAL IMAGINATION OF DARRYL F. ZANUCK

We have explored the impact of industry and state censorship on cinematic images invoking key civil rights questions. Up to this point, producers such as Universal's Carl Laemmle—who tried to produced *Lulu Belle,* brought *Imitation of Life* to the screen, and brought *Stevedore* to Joseph Breen—have appeared relatively valiant in their attempts to address racial politics. But whether—and how—producers consistently pressed for representation of civil rights issues deserves greater scrutiny. What was the role of the individual Hollywood studios in representing and censoring civil rights issues? Although this story could be told in many ways, an important figure in any rendition would be Twentieth Century–Fox production head Darryl F. Zanuck. "I believe I can say without immodesty," said Zanuck, "that I have sought more than any other person in the industry to break new ground in touching on social and political causes."[1] And perhaps Zanuck wasn't completely wrong. Yet Twentieth Century–Fox's resumé on racial representations is rife with contradictions. Certain cinematic sequences mocked people of color, and even their suffering, while others presented their historical agony with great sympathy.[2] Not only did Zanuck happily sanction blackface but, in the 1930s, southern films replete with stereotypes became virtually a genre at the studio. *The Littlest Rebel* (1935), *In Old Kentucky* (1935), *Can This Be Dixie?* (1936), *Kentucky* (1938), and *Belle Starr* (1941), though not without subtle critique of the South, treated Black servitude as a natural and indispensable part of southern life for which the films were intensely nostalgic. Zanuck not only presented violence against Asians as comic in *The Bowery* (1933), *Son of the Gods* (1930), and *Old San Francisco* (1927), but his crowning insult came during the "war for democracy" when he okayed *Little Tokio, USA* (1942), a film that so celebrated the Japanese internment with an orgy of police violence against unabashedly caricatured yellowface "spies" that the Office of War Information called it an "invitation to witch hunt" and attempted to restrict its foreign distribution.[3] Nor did the war end his anti-Japanese racism. "Dig Ya Later," a song in Zanuck's postwar Carmen Miranda film *Dollface* (1945), gloated about bombing the Japanese: "It was mighty smoky over Tokyo . . . A friend of mine in a B29 dropped another load for luck as he flew away he was heard to say: 'Yuk-Yuk.'"

On the other hand, Zanuck consistently broached unresolved racial traumas and miscarriages of justice, using cinema to try to help resolve them by his own standards of justice.[4] Zanuck was fixated on and fascinated with repressive regimes—with the iconography of brutal, excessive discipline that seemed to haunt American systems and institutions. Many of his personal productions disclosed historical and contemporary racial upheavals, sometimes lingering with painful sentimentality on their human toll on people of color.[5] Under his leadership, Fox developed four postwar racial/ethnic problem films, outstripping its competitors.[6] And although Fox often backed down from its most revolutionary Black characters, Zanuck repeatedly attempted to depict militant, armed Black men with relative sympathy, as in *Crash Dive* (1943), *No Way Out* (1950), *Lydia Bailey* (1952), and *Island in the Sun* (1957).

Twentieth Century–Fox's board chairman, Wendell Willkie, a white, liberal politician and NAACP board member, may have been the mastermind behind Fox's liberalism. And Lamar Trotti, as a screenwriter for Fox, labored increasingly to balance the South's lost cause against the region's obvious abuses.[7] But Zanuck was the engineer behind the strange racial messages of the studio's films. As production files for *Slave Ship* (1937), *Crash Dive*, *Pinky*, *No Way Out*, and *Island in the Sun* show, Zanuck led studio decision making about how to depict racial traumas and Black empowerment in the films bearing his name. Further, his interest in Black politics and history strongly influenced Fox's house style of polysemic expressionism to distract from and embellish these sensitive issues.

Zanuck was not ignorant of injustice toward African Americans. He recognized at least the basic unfairness of slavery and understood the historical relationship between the Great Migration and white backlash. He sympathized with the plight of African Americans under segregation. But Zanuck's fascination with these "scenes of subjection" deserves to be connected to Saidiya Hartman's point about the "ease with which scenes of racial trauma are usually reiterated, the causalness with which they are circulated, and the consequences of this routine display of the slave's ravaged body."[8] Zanuck's films raise complex ethical questions about revealing Black suffering in mundane, normalizing, and even blithely entertaining ways.

Studio documents reveal that Zanuck's racial fantasies interfered with the effective showcasing of civil rights issues he was cognizant of and sympathetic about. He consistently restrained representations of racial wrongs out of personal judgment, his sense of the bottom line, and what American (white) movie

audiences could tolerate. Zanuck's use of gestures of interpersonal white tolerance, song and dance, Technicolor, and (indeed) blackface to redress racial
injustice shows his preference for symbolically figured interracial utopias rather
than more realist, narrative resolutions. Though Zanuck is not representative
of all studio heads, if even he—the studio head who fashioned himself as the
Hollywood vanguard of interracial representation—could so restrain the representation of civil rights, this gives a powerful indication of the studio system's
overall racial reticence.

However, despite their conflation of pain and entertainment, in their return
to historical traumatic events, Zanuck's films were, in Althusserian terms, symptomatic—and they drew the specter of racial suffering into the sphere of public
discourse (and commerce).[9] Though Zanuck's model for understanding American race relations was limited, these films, often with incongruity and sudden-
ness, invoked, pictured, and instantiated more about America's racial past than
they could adequately explain, leaving audiences to ponder important civil rights
questions the films patently effaced, and courting the revolutionary implications
Fox rendered in soft focus.

REMEMBERING SLAVERY AT FOX

Zanuck would produce several films that expanded the purview of the plantation
melodrama by revealing the brutality of slavery and disturbing the myth of the
happy darkie. The first of these, *Slave Ship*, was one of Hollywood's first consci-
entious treatments of the Middle Passage.[10]

Indeed, the film's title and images centralize the slave trade's injustice in ways
its narrative does not. Its source, the historical novel *The Last Slaver* by George S.
King, clearly presented slavery as a catastrophic wrong. It reworked the little-
known true story of *The Wanderer,* the last known illegal American slave ship
(one masquerading as a yacht), whose notorious exploits heightened the call for
civil war.[11] In the novel, white northern seaman James Kane joins the ship's crew
not knowing that he will be transporting slaves. When the crew mutinies on its
return voyage, the ship's cook Kalva, a former slave seeking to avenge his people's
suffering, kills the captain, after which he and Kane steer the ship back to Africa.
In a utopian ending, crew and cargo unite, initiating the fair trade of ivory with
African villagers. Though the story castigates the illegal slave traffic rather than
slavery as an institution, it evoked slaves' subjugation through historically accurate descriptions of the Middle Passage, speaking to a history of mass suffering.

The finished film omits both Kalva and the slave revolt, though the Middle
Passage sequences are lengthened and reveal slave suffering with veracity and
intimacy. But the slaver's captain, Jim Lovett (Warner Baxter), is the film's
hero—a man who comes to conscience about the wrong of slavery. He stops his
heartless mutinying crew after they have cast a long line of slaves chained to an

anchor overboard. Rather than restoring the enslaved people to their home and establishing trade with them as in the book, he releases them into the waters surrounding St. Helena Island. And, after proving himself a reformed slaver before the law, he settles with his southern bride (Elizabeth Allen) on a plantation in Jamaica in an ending that sidesteps the question of Black humanity raised in the Middle Passage scenes and visually restores the racial servitude and plantation chronotope. How did—how could—the studio adaptation process yield such revelation and repression? The answer exposes the mix of compulsion, compassion, sadism, and denial that guided Zanuck's treatment of race throughout his years at Fox.

The initial treatment was more racially daring, in many ways, than the book. Though it gave Captain Lovett a large, sympathetic role, it also revealed Black suffering, celebrated Black slave rebellion, and made Kalva a prominent character.[12] Nancy, the captain's fiancée and a belle of the plantation South, comes to conscience when forced on the slaver's journey. "Passing through the barracoon, Nancy for the first time sees the 'raw material' of American plantation slaves. It is an unhappy sight indeed, and she reacts to it." Enslaved people are "kept below . . . without a breath of fresh air"; "slaves who suffocated during the voyage are hoisted up and dumped overboard"; when brought on deck, "two slaves, manacled together, commit suicide by leaping into the water." The hold is so full that slaves can "only lie on their sides," and the women are brought up for illicit purposes.[13]

The first treatment also had prominent, empowered, and sympathetic Black characters. In place of the book's paternalistic relationship between the "faithful" Kalva and his "massa" Kane, the treatment showed a far more independent Black rebel.[14] Kane (who became Duncan, an undercover officer) rescues Kalva (renamed Sam and now lacking dialect present in the novel) when he falls overboard. As he does so, Duncan notices an "ugly scarred groove an inch deep . . . [on his] ankle. . . . Sam explains that this was caused by chains."[15] Sam is a protagonist in the treatment. He uses Congo drum rhythms to alert African cargo of the danger awaiting them. He instructs Duncan on how to send a message to shore in a bottle. Sam has almost superhuman strength—and he uses it to secure retribution against whites for enslavement. He strangles the first mate. He engineers the mutiny—breaking open the ship's gun locker, stealing ammunition, and holding Lovett at gunpoint so he will not throw the enslaved men overboard to "get rid of the evidence" of slavery. In a dramatic sequence, Sam kills the ship's captain with the help of "the voluptuous half-breed girl, Salamba."[16] "Shots are fired at the huge negro, and though some take effect . . . he goes on—a marlin-spike in his hand. . . . With a shriek Salamba dashes into the scene and pinions Lovett's arms just long enough for Sam to bring the spike down on Lovett's head, killing him."[17] Sam, however, never made it into the second draft of the treatment.

Zanuck was deeply invested in this difficult property, as he wrote over 100 pages worth of memos on the film before it was shot. Zanuck wanted the film to be an exciting, hardboiled adventure story. He saw slaving as a business not too different from bootlegging, one of his pet subjects during his tenure at Warner Bros. He attempted to lighten *Slave Ship* with comedy, making the film a vehicle for the youthful Mickey Rooney.[18] Through vignettes and details, Zanuck meticulously authored the backdrop and framing of the slave ship drama, creating a twisted, turbulent, darkly comic atmosphere.

Seeing the difficulty of maintaining audience sympathy with brutal slave handlers, Zanuck waffled about whether to show white brutality against slaves. At first he emphatically called for "technical research" so they could *"go into detail about the feeding and care of slaves in the hold."*[19] At times brutality was designed merely to increase the sense of "danger and suspense," however.[20] Zanuck's attitude toward slave suffering in this memo was incredibly cavalier. Soon after deciding to include such violence, Zanuck reversed himself, asking screenwriters to remove brutality altogether to avoid morally impugning the protagonists. In this draft, Zanuck removed "the slave stuff"; there should be *"no children on the slave ship,"* he instructed, and "eliminate all the business of the beating of the slaves and that sort of thing. Slave-running is simply a trade with them and we don't want to go out of our way to make them heavies."[21] It is evident that Zanuck sometimes saw slaving more as a masculine sport—a last frontier for the toughened white man—than as part of a brutal institution at odds with America's democratic promise of freedom.

But he was distracted—curious if not conscience-stricken—by slave suffering and wanted the captain to come to conscience. He finally decided that the film could be lighthearted *and* brutal—as long as its protagonists came out on the right side of the slavery question. He restored Middle Passage brutality scenes less than a month after eliminating them. With an unremitting aesthetic and social grimness consonant with *I Am a Fugitive from a Chain Gang* (1932) and *Two Seconds* (1932) (both films he supervised at Warner Bros.), he called for an opening sequence with "eight or ten angles showing the slaves being piled up in tiers . . . while they are showing them in we should hear the word 'blackbirds'—'come on, you blackbirds, get in there,'" one that made it into the finished film.[22] He plotted an opening title that dubbed slave running "the vilest, most despicable business of the time—an outrage on humanity," which also made it into the finished film. Zanuck himself wrote a sequence designed "to show how cheap life is," where a slave handler strikes an African attempting escape on the head and matter-of-factly throws him overboard, a scene that remained, with minor revisions, in the finished film.[23] He also added dialogue where Captain Lovett fondly reminisces on throwing slaves overboard to avoid capture.[24] He consistently added material suggesting forced interracial sex. In one draft, Nancy discovers that a bracelet Lovett gave her belonged to a slave girl.[25] He submitted scripts to the PCA in which Lovett's Portuguese slave-procurer has a "half-breed" mistress and a child so dark he is almost mistakenly enslaved, which Breen found unacceptable.[26] And the finished film he submitted to the PCA had African women "marching in line with their breasts exposed," all details that, while historically accurate, would have signaled to American audiences coercive interracial sex. Zanuck's brutal imagination produced a strange, jarring mix of historical veracity and light entertainment.

Zanuck never discussed racism in his memos. But the spectacle of half-nude Black bodies being beaten by white men insisted on a color-bound logic to enslavement. The idea of the revolt, too, is preserved when the enslaved people, hearing the mutiny above decks, struggle under their chains. Revealing medium shots of one Black male extra show him contemplating his fate and then tearing angrily at his chains in a manner that stirs and inspires the rest of the Black men and women. He stands in for Sam, providing a point of focalization for the anger, anguish, and defiance of the Black men (and women) below decks. Despite numerous, stern Production Code Administration warnings that censors would delete slave beatings, whippings, and killings, the finished film contained not one but three relatively accurate scenes showing the Middle Passage's vile density and brutal treatment, including one in which a line of chained enslaved men are thrown overboard so that the ship's captain will avoid being charged with illegal slave-running.[27]

The cruel severity of slave treatment is perhaps best articulated through an expressionistic tracking shot that unsparingly confronts audiences with a *mise-en-abyme* of Black bodies being whipped by punishing white slavers. The medium shots frankly revealing the faces of the enslaved bring a terrific realization of their frail humanity (see figure 21). The sound track is loud and the diegetic sound of the slave-handler's shrill commands and cracking whips competes with the score's staccato drumbeats and shrieking strings. Aesthetically, both sound and image indicate these to be the film's most epic scenes. But while the sequences are lengthy and compel sustained audience attention to relatively accurate below-deck conditions, they also perversely revel in the beauty of the mass suffering, the writhing bodies moving in wave-like, symphonic unison (see figure 22).

Zanuck had the realistic, brutal slave scenes he had originally sought. But whether they heightened the suspense of the white narrative above decks was doubtful. Censors and reviewers, Black and white, could focus on little other than these scenes, despite the film's tidy ending. Daughters of the American Revolution, perhaps complaining, said "cruelty and brutality to slaves . . . nullify one's interest in the romance of a Salem girl and the ship's captain."[28] For the *Omaha Bee*'s reviewer there was "something of a sensation in the scenes where [Wallace] Beery . . . orders the human cargo weighted down by the anchor and drowned to destroy the evidence."[29] Some accused Zanuck of sadism, a charge

FIGURE 21. These shots lend an indirect but palpable sense of slave rebellion to the finished version of *Slave Ship* (1937). Frame captures.

FIGURE 22. Even press photography proclaimed brutality toward slaves. Publicity still from *Slave Ship*.

his films would frequently face. Several states censored clubbing and flogging scenes as did censors in England, Australia, British Columbia, and Quebec.[30] The film's few Black critics mostly did not read these as pertaining to civil rights questions, although several had praised King's novel.[31] Sensing an insult in their perpetual screen bondage—and perhaps feeling the lightness with which slavery was incongruously, even uncritically, mixed with comedy and white romance— most did not even praise the film's Middle Passage sequence. Some, reading extra-textually, praised Fox for using a Black casting agent and employing 750 Depression-era Black actors for three days.[32] Black entertainment columnist and *Slave Ship* extra Harry Levette thought the violence misappropriated Black experience and applauded actor Warner Baxter's emotional protest during a particularly brutal scene.[33] But for at least one Black critic, the *Pittsburgh Courier's* Louis Lautier, *Slave Ship* helped viewers to publicly remember slavery, though he hungered to see the successful 1841 slave revolt aboard the *Creole* onscreen.[34] (see figure 23)

The script development process reveals that Zanuck understood that the Middle Passage's suffering was grave, unjust, and racialized. Although his decision to excise Kalva/Sam indicates a desire to downplay the centrality of Black rebellion, his notes reveal a competing desire—that of dramatizing incomprehensible, unending Black suffering, even if this violated white expectations about

FIGURE 23. Captain Lovett (Warner Baxter) prepares to force his Black cargo to jump ship in order to get rid of the evidence of his illegal slave trading. Publicity still from *Slave Ship*.

how Black people should function in entertainment. But his capitulation to the southern-style plantation at the film's closing indicates a submersion of the film's most racially provocative images and failure to address the broader question of white culpability that his narrative raised. His stunted, compulsive drive to reveal white brutality, one that was never completely compassionate toward his African American characters, was matched and ultimately overcome by his drive toward an aesthetically driven repression of racial injustice behind the veil of white romantic happiness.

CRASH DIVE, VISUAL EXPRESSIONISM, AND THE EMPOWERED BLACK SERVICEMAN

Slave Ship is an early example of a pattern: expressionism and incongruous comedy were frequently Zanuck's strategy for diffusing onscreen racial controversy. With racially integrated submarine combat film *Crash Dive* (1942), for the first time Zanuck would test these elements in color. Prompted by a government-sponsored OWI initiative to increase Black morale, Hollywood studios produced several combat films where multi-racial units worked together. Because the American armed services were not, in fact, integrated during World War II, these films could achieve this image of harmonious integration only by narrative device; in *Sahara* (1942), *Bataan* (1943), and *Crash Dive*, multi-racial war-torn regiments combine in the field out of necessity. Of all the integrated combat films of World War II, *Crash Dive* is the most perverse and incongruous—but it showcases the tensions and awkwardness of the makeshift combat integration that really took place in World War II's segregated military. It also makes clearest, perhaps unwittingly, the existing white racism in the military.

A love triangle dominates the main action. But original scripts prominently featured Anatole, a French Canadian cook, as comic relief. As a result of a conference with Zanuck, Anatole became a witty, yet human, Black mess man—Oliver Cromwell Jones (Ben Carter). When the submarine crew is short of men, Jones joins his white comrades in the film's climactic raid. His hardboiled, heroic bravery makes him the only one to stay with Lt. Ward Stuart (Tyrone Power) in the German stronghold, for which he receives a medal of valor.[35] The image of Jones with a machine gun links him to a real-life Black mess man, Dorie Miller, who ascended from below deck, manned his dead captain's machine gun, and brought down several of the Japanese planes attacking Pearl Harbor. Given the taboo of showing armed Black men onscreen, it is surprising that in Fox's film, Carter not only sports a machine gun but also, unlike *Bataan*'s Wesley Epps (Kenneth Spencer), is shown in shot-reverse-shot gunning down white enemies (see figure 24).

Oliver Jones differed from the other studios' Black soldiers in other ways. By contrast with Kenneth Spencer's imposing, physical brawn in MGM's *Bataan*, and Rex Ingram's dignified Sudanese Sergeant Major Tambul in *Sahara*, *Crash Dive*'s portly, long-haired Carter intimated that average Black men "in service" could easily become heroic servicemen. By showing Jones's transformation from cook to hero, the film took the risk of addressing stereotypes onscreen and revising them there. The result was a fascinatingly messy, risky depiction of integration, one that mixed blackface with historical fact and racial good will.

Jones was also integrated through the craft of Technicolor filmmaking. The film, the only one in this cycle of racially integrated war films shot in color, used color's visual textures to question the color line. Deep color tinting not only represents opposing sides in the conflict (the Americans in the submarine are cast in red, while the German territory is marked by blue light) but makes skin tone difficult to decipher. The film further complicates racial identities by having the white men slather black camouflage on their faces, an idea that Zanuck himself developed.[36] Jones, laughing at his white counterparts blacking up, proclaims, "I am the only *born* commando here." Rather than asserting Jones's other credentials for service, the joke makes his dark skin seem like his most relevant qualification. The moment is awkward, and blackness and blackface are still the subject of humor. But in a cinematic economy where black skin most often figured lack, this joke reversed these racial standards and allowed a Black man to engineer the racial joke. Technicolor could have easily been used to sharpen

FIGURE 24. Oliver Cromwell Jones (Ben Carter) chuckles that he is the only "born" commando among the lot. In the lower frame, Jones raises his machine gun in a rare image of Black onscreen militancy. Frame captures from *Crash Dive* (1943).

the visual color line. But instead the (Techni)color scheme in *Crash Dive's* final combat sequence combines tinting with blackface to reduce the visibility of race and racial distinction—a move that parallel's the narrative's assertion of Black equality. *Crash Dive's* visual logic extends the film's argument for social integration and equality.

As with *Slave Ship,* audiences did not know what to make of *Crash Dive.* The *New York Times'* Bosley Crowther was embarrassed by Fox's "clumsy and patronizing" decision to "drag" Carter—a "grinning jazzbo"—into the picture and read the film as a tongue-in-cheek racial slight.[37] But Walter White of the NAACP saw the film as evidence of Hollywood fulfilling its pledge to improve Black images on screen. Of Jones, White stated: "He's no cretinish, grinning, Uncle Tom. He is a sympathetic, courageous fighter who—in battle and out—stands on absolute par with other members of the crew."[38] In private correspondence he highlighted the film's potential as a tool to goad the army toward civil rights: "I can imagine a good many people seeing it and wondering why Negroes are not allowed to serve as sailors and officers in the Navy when a Negro mess man can act and be treated by his associates as is done in this picture."[39] In sum, Zanuck was clearly moved by the story of Dorie Miller. But rather than portraying Miller's story as a film of its own, Zanuck worked it into a semi-comic subplot. While the machine-gun-toting, militant Black everyman had historical veracity and boldness, the mixing of blackface humor with Technicolor aesthetics made for an uneven blend of minstrelsy with realism. Zanuck's Dorie Miller story is another example of his drive to create cutting edge interracial drama and his simultaneous desire to repress the image of Black equality beneath the weight of comic and color-bound signifiers.

ZANUCK'S RACE RELATIONS CLINIC: *PINKY* AND *NO WAY OUT* AND THE MEDICAL TURN

Between 1948 and 1950, Zanuck worked intensely on two racial problem films. While these films are typically treated separately, they are linked not only by their producer but by their shared address of civil rights questions through medical melodrama. The medical analogy proffered that America's race problem could be diagnosed and treated individually, personally, and with a clinical precision. But the gradual dilution of this metaphor over the course of these two scripts into weird science, sadism, and horror-noir represented the allusion's failures at racial containment.

Doctoring the Story of a Nurse: *Pinky,* Southern Discrimination, and Segregation

The story of how Fox, with *Pinky,* crafted highly differentiated spectatorial positions and managed largely to evade censorship even of its depiction of miscegenation reveals the increasing complexity of Zanuck's racial filmmaking of the postwar era, a time when strategic wartime racial liberalism waned, but questions about Black equality still loomed large. *Pinky*, like *Crash Dive*, focused on an exceptional Black individual. This reduced the scope of the narrative's moral implications for the nation.

Pinky was based on Cid Ricketts Sumner's 1945 novel *Quality*, which was serialized in *Ladies' Home Journal*. Sumner, a self-identified white Southerner, never advocated integration. But Zanuck employed liberal screenwriters Dudley Nichols and, later, Philip Dunne to adapt the novel, blending her gradualism with their liberalism. In *Quality* the protagonist (whose name is spelled Pinkey in the novel) passes for white while in the North training to be a nurse and falls in love with white doctor Chester Morris.[40] Nearly discovered, she flees to the southern home where Dicey, her washerwoman grandmother, raised her. Chester follows Pinkey to the ramshackle former slave quarters where she lives, but when she reveals that she's Black, he betrays his disgust and she sends him away. Pinkey stays in the shadow of the "Big House," a former plantation owned by Miss Em, a sickly old white woman who used to own Pinkey's family. Jake, an underemployed Black neighbor, introduces Pinkey to Arch Naughton, an inspiring Black newspaper reporter and political activist. When Miss Em takes ill, Pinkey cares for her at her grandmother's behest, eventually developing respect and affection for her. Miss Em dies and wills her estate to Pinkey, hoping she will use the money to build a hospital for the Black community. But Miss Wooley (Miss Em's cousin by marriage) contests the will, claiming that Pinkey drugged her ailing patient. Pinkey defends her right to the property in court and the judge ultimately awards her the land. Before she can actually do anything with the house, however, "white trash," as granny calls the arsonists, burn it to the ground.[41] The novel closes as Pinkey, standing in the embers, is consoled by a Black doctor she met in the North, Frank Canady, who has come to work with her on her hospital project and who harbors secret affection for her.

Although *Pinky* seemed to center on passing and miscegenation, Zanuck indicated his view that these were an indirect way to discuss discrimination and segregation. On the first pages of the notes from his first conference with Dudley Nichols, Zanuck states:

> I don't believe you could ever get me to read a book which was strictly about segregation of Negroes in America. . . . Seeing it in terms of the adventures of a girl [audiences] will accept it much more readily than if we tried to give it to them in terms of [the newsreel] March of Time. I am convinced that if we really want people to see the horrors of grinding poverty as suffered by these people, if we want the audience to see the results of lack of education and poor medical treatment, this is the way to do it.[42]

Accordingly, Zanuck told writers to interlace the passing narrative with sequences of discrimination from the book.[43] Zanuck wanted to suggest that discrimination, rather than her love for Morris, motivates Pinky's desire to return to her northern white life. He wanted to highlight her southern degradation by having Judge Walker offer Pinky—a "graduate nurse"—a cleaning job. He also wanted to highlight the problem of insufficient Black public health measures in the South through two Black youngsters who are suffering from diseases easily curable through vaccines (though these characters never made it into the finished picture). Where *Lost Boundaries,* the film about passing produced by Louis De Rochemont a year earlier, suggested that the stain of Black blood was horrific to the passing subject, *Pinky* began to posit that the horror was instead white racism.

The writers invented vignettes of southern racism, gesturing toward the systemic abuse that Zanuck and the writers openly invoked in the script draft. They spoke explicitly in memos of "white supremacy," "segregation," "North" and "South," "lynching," and the "horrors of grinding poverty"—concepts that they could never name in the finished film. Southern courts may appear fair because one awards Pinky her land. But in Pinky's encounters with the police, Zanuck's team made a choice to show southern-style civil rights abuses from a Black woman's perspective.

The team also added a scene where two white men attempt to rape Pinky. Zanuck wanted to dramatize southern terror more vividly through a lynching sequence in which a white lynch mob, unable to find its victim, seizes Pinky from her bed and nearly rapes her. But Philip Dunne developed the sequence that would appear in the finished film, one in which the specter of lynching is absent but Pinky is still sexually assaulted on the roadside.[44] It is in this sequence that we can most clearly see the expressionistic diffusion of the film's racial discourse, one Zanuck also used, as I have shown, in *Slave Ship* and *Crash Dive.* Throughout the film, light and shadow speak to racial and class divides: Dicey's home and front yard stand not only beneath an ensconcing weeping willow but are figuratively in the shadow of the "Big House." Thus the obscuring darkness, which visually fractures the figures onto which it falls, seems to speak to the real damage of slavery as casting a shadow from the past on the modern lives of impoverished southern Blacks. The language of light and shadow also poetically marks the dialogue. Jake states: "I got a feelin' that a fast letter like that is like a shadow moving forward. Things is comin' and they come treadin' on their shadows." The enduring visual darkness of the film's ending reminds us that there is never a conventionally happy conclusion for Pinky—the heavy cloud over her never fully lifts. But nowhere is the contrast between light and dark more clear than in the attempted rape scene. While walking in the woods to clear her mind, two white motorists offer Pinky, whom they assume is white, safe passage through the Black neighborhood. But when she tells them her race, they pursue her sadistically and relentlessly with a sexualized anger. Pinky's assailants shine a bright white spotlight on her from their car illuminating her body. The light transforms Pinky from a white-skinned woman into a black silhouette. Even after the men release her, they continue to haunt her as *light,* shining the spotlight after her as she disappears into the thick darkness of the woods.

By contrast with this subtle, expressionistic treatment of gendered racial oppression in this sequence, the film script's most direct address of civil rights came through Arch Naughton's dialogue. Arch, whom Sumner described as a "small yellow man," was to wear a black beret, already a signifier of militancy because of its use in the military attire of various nations.[45] Although Zanuck suggested cutting Frank Canady in his initial memo, Zanuck liked Arch. He called the sequences between Pinky and Arch (whom Nichols had made a stronger and more resolute character) "excellent."[46] Indeed, Zanuck's initial conference notes contain more than two full pages developing dialogue for Arch. Nichols gave Arch lines referencing civil rights decisions like the Dred Scott case and reminding audiences of the nation's constitutional promise to racial equality for Black people—a promise that many, after World War II, were willing to forget. Although Arch's rhetoric was a radical, prescient signifier of a Black revolution yet to come in 1948, it compelled even conservative Miss Em: "He's trapped in anger because Negroes get lighter but white folks never get darker," she observes, departing from the novel.[47] While in the book Jake is shiftless and ignorant and wants his rights but is afraid to fight for them, Arch's speeches catapulted the film into contemporary civil rights discourse:

ARCH: They say 'Go slow, go slow. Got to think about the white folks. Can't do that. White folks wouldn't stand for it.' (eyes burning). Where has all that got us in the last eighty years? Nowhere! We're going to take our stand now and fight it out. We've got all the principles of freedom and equality that we fought for in the last war back of us. We're bound to win!

PINKY: You really believe that?

ARCH: If I didn't I'd shoot myself. Oh, I'm not working alone—we've got organization now, big organization! We're going to get equality! . . . Aren't you the equal of anybody?[48]

Arch not only invokes the principles fought for in World War II as an argument for civil rights, but here and in other speeches, he argues for a militant approach and evinces his commitment to achieving change—even if it costs his life. More importantly, he confronts the audience with questions—like the final one in the above speech—directly challenging viewers to see Pinky's equality. Arch even bluntly tells Miss Em that segregation is "nothing more than an imposed system of degradation" and connects it to slavery.[49] When Miss Em says Blacks will be granted equality in due time, Arch rejoins, "*That,* Miss Em, is exactly what good people have been telling us since the days of Lincoln. The rights you talk about are guaranteed to everyone under the Constitution . . . Men have died before for this freedom and I would rather die than submit to this humiliation."[50]

Perhaps more contentious for producers than Arch's politics was his tender relationship with Pinky. It is clear that Pinky is romantically drawn to Arch's strength, activism, and intellect, that her destiny is entwined with the revolution of which he speaks. Arch deeply understands Pinky and predicts her moods, reasoning, and actions in an almost authorial way. Of Pinky's time up North, Arch plainly states: "You got scared of passing. . . . The man you're such a fool about is young, good-looking, just starting out in the world . . . and absolutely blind to the hell you are going through."[51] For much of the first screenplay and novel, the audience's rooting interest is in Pinky and Arch's union. Indeed, Zanuck himself plotted a scene in which Pinky promises Arch she will run away with him if the court does not award her the house.[52]

For all his virtues, however, the screenwriters' Arch was a flawed— "yellow"—character. He misuses publicity and delights in trouble and racial confrontations. For instance, he writes an article for the Black press denouncing the court's decision against Pinky before the judge has decided the case. When the white men in the gallery discover Arch's article, they begin to form a mob. Arch flees, leaving Pinky to face their wrath. This scene, one incongruous with Arch's earlier heroism, is the last one in which the character appears.

It was on September 20, 1948, four months into production, that Zanuck decided to eliminate Arch Naughton. This was less than a month after Walter White and other NAACP members had criticized the screenplay, roiling particularly at the negative turn in Arch's character.[53] White faulted the film's Black militancy particularly: "The story pictures every Negro who protests or otherwise attempts to correct injustice as being ether a charlatan or a crook or a fool."[54] Zanuck's angry response suggests that the studio head cut Arch partially to punish White for what he clearly saw as an overall lack of NAACP cooperation.[55] Zanuck was emphatic that the film must not be propaganda. And Arch was his way of condemning the emerging civil rights movement's propagandistic excesses.

It was Jane White, the NAACP leader's light-skinned actress daughter, who Zanuck thought captured the problem with Pinky best. "Pinky," she penned, "is a little disturbing. She has strength and forthrightness but not enough. . . . What is the motivation behind Pinky's lack of militance? Why is she so astonished at the idea of Negroes fighting for their civil rights? She is intelligent and aware and didn't she see Negroes living in comparative freedom in the North?"[56] Not only did Zanuck and Nichols conference with Jane further, but they developed the script along lines she prescribed. Pinky rather than Arch would "battle with Miss Em" and contend for militant action.[57]

Jake would also be "patterned after . . . Arch," said Zanuck, but he described Jake as pitiably unintelligent.[58] "He has read a good deal about the Negro problem but much of what he reads he either does not understand or he misinterprets. Nevertheless, he quotes from these books without having any real notion of what it is all about. They are just nice sounding words to him and he repeats them parrot-like."[59] This contrasts with earlier drafts where Jake's belief in the idea of freedom is the centering hallmark of his character. At their first meeting, Jake says to Pinky:

> I'll tell you what's coming to us. . . . We is going to get our share of jobs. We is going to get our share of relief when relief time come. We is going to get a new deal with po-lice and judges what we had a say in electing. We is going to ride the cars for free . . . free moving, Ms. Pinky! No more Jim Crowing. Nor in the movies. Nor in the schools. Nor in the eating places. Nor nowhere. No more bowing and scraping and going in the back door. No more being looked down on and set apart.[60]

Though laced with dialect, there is poetry in Jake's lines. But the Zanuck-led writing team chopped any mention of civil rights from this speech, opining that Jake "should not . . . elaborate on what the Negroes will get when they get their rights. He should quickly and shrewdly guess that the reason Pinky has returned home is because she got into an emotional jam with a white man up North."[61] Zanuck amended Jake's character, at least in part because Michael Abel, one of the script's readers and another producer at Fox, did not

> quite understand the delineation of Jake's character. Apparently he is supposed to be a shifty, dishonest, low-class Negro, a sort of agitator. Yet his aims are those of intelligent democratic liberalism; of social security and socialized medicine. . . . I recommend changing Jake's ideology to make him more of a rabble rouser, aiming at Negro control of the government, overthrow of existing authority and a life of indolence.[62]

Adhering to the stereotyped binary between the Black rank and file and intelligent "Negroes," Abel could not imagine that Jake could be downtrodden, revolutionary, and intelligent. His comments suggest Fox's hesitation in depicting a politically empowered working-class Black man. Although New Yorker Frederick O'Neal played Jake as a savvy trickster, he focuses on his own gain and his unflagging excitement for equality is lost. He steals Pinky and Dicey's money and even the mise-en-scène in his shack, lined with liquor bottles and cards, conspires against him.

Thus Zanuck, who wanted to show segregation and discrimination, erased the dialogue of the Black male militants who challenged it. And though Pinky did legitimately take on much of Arch's anger (but none of his hope in a civil rights movement), this anger is domesticated—reduced to a few arguments with Miss Em. Neither the image nor the rhetoric of a broader movement can be glimpsed in *Pinky* as it could in *Pinky*'s script. To his credit, Zanuck influenced the expression of Pinky's militance: "Pinky is an educated girl," he stated, "and with her new awareness of the plight of her people, she should have arguments which are just as forceful and logical as are Miss Em's."[63] When her grandmother asks her why she is so "set" against Miss Em, she states: "Look at her house. Slave built, slave run, and run down ever since," alluding to the history of slavery as a structuring reality of her relationship to Miss Em. But by making the film's Black political mouthpiece a light-skinned woman, Zanuck also made resistance sexy. Not only did several memos emphasize Pinky's sex appeal, but her humiliation—as she is frisked by police and nearly raped in the forest—is tinged with an erotic dimension in the film that was absent in the novel. Zanuck was clear that Pinky could not end up with either a white or Black man. But through Pinky's political sassiness, he could eroticize her—and Black politics—in a way he could not with either Arch or Jake. And because of this change, the film condemns interracial lechery and white snobbery with greater effectiveness than it condemns systematic segregation. Although white actress Jeanne Crain plays Pinky as more frustrated, fussy, cold, stern, priggish, snobbish, unhappy, and bitter than defiant, demanding, angry, and righteous, the script team had developed some powerfully charged moments.

Zanuck's decision to cast Crain as Pinky may have been the most damaging act of racial self-censorship in the film's production: first, in doing so, he avoided casting Dorothy Dandridge whom, according to Elia Kazan's biographer Richard Schickel, he had also considered for the part.[64] Second, the casting of a white woman who, as Kazan noted, "didn't have any fire," severely limited the film's (and Pinky's) potential to communicate Black militancy. As Kazan would put it, "The only good thing about her face was that it went so far in the direction of no temperament that you felt Pinky was floating through her experience without reacting to them, which is what 'passing' is."[65]

The script also limited Pinky's centrality and moral high ground by subordinating her to Miss Em's old southern wisdom. Perhaps the best example of this comes when Granny states that "she has lived in this world . . . long enough to know that if there is something white folks don't want for you to have—want for theyself, might as well forget all about it." In response, Pinky argues not that Granny's words are flawed by an Uncle Tom logic but rather that Miss Em wanted her to have the property. Thus civil rights questions are entangled with the wishes of a white southern plantation owner; Pinky's struggle for the house has become a battle to honor Miss Em's legacy rather than for her own civil rights. The subsuming of Pinky's power and voice into the sea of white southern "tolerance" is nowhere better demonstrated than in the finished film's trial scenes. Unlike the early drafts of the script, Pinky has no voice in the trial—she never testifies. It is the white judge, who like Miss Em is a valued part of the white southern community, who speaks for her. Pinky gains the house (white hoodlums don't burn it down as in the novel) and her medical mission replaces her romantic engagement. What has been lost, however, is her voice—and the film loses its polyphonic authenticity.

The limits to Pinky's power were not the only casualty of Zanuck's desire for mainstream box office success. Zanuck moderated potentially censorable racial problems by suggesting a "personal," "individual" approach rather than an institutional critique. Indeed, it was his concern about the problem taking over the picture that led to his replacing Nichols with Dunne as the screenwriter. Rather than centralizing Black poverty, inadequate healthcare, and white racism as structural limitations, *Pinky* focused on the drama of Pinky's choice to live as Black in spite of discrimination. While at one level this decision spoke to her emerging racial pride, at another Pinky's vision is motivated by the wishes of a woman who once enslaved Blacks.

In sum, Zanuck's desire to be at the forefront of progressive racial representation led him to take heed of African American women in the scriptwriting process and yielded Hollywood's most central and militant Black female heroine to date. But *Pinky* also demonstrates the limits of studio civil rights. The prominence of tolerant white characters as heroes, and the impossibility of Arch Naughton as a militant and Pinky's romantic interest on the screen, overcame the film's structural critique of southern racism and the impulses its liberal screenwriters displayed. In compressing these elements, the film presented a circumscribed and limited conception of the emergent movement and suggested that America's civil rights problem could be solved with white tolerance rather than radical redistributions of power.

No Way Out: Of Integrated Hospitals, Race Riots, and Organized Rage

Walter White blasted *Pinky* in the Black press, though he praised almost every other postwar racial problem film. Even Zanuck's own contract employees complained that *Pinky* had pulled punches. In response, Zanuck funneled much attention into another racial prestige project—before *Pinky* had even reached the screen. At the outset of this project, Zanuck resolved to be safe but to boldly delve into America's mid-century racial troubles, including racism and riots.

Between the making of *Pinky* in 1948 and the making of *No Way Out,* the racial politics of the nation shifted. Civil rights had gone from being a regional to a national issue. In mid-1948 it divided the Democratic National Convention, but by 1949, not only had President Truman issued executive orders 9980 and 9981, integrating the Armed Forces and creating a permanent Fair Employment Practices Commission, but his victory the previous November seemed to suggest national support for these efforts. The voice of the Supreme Court in *Shelley v. Kraemer,* a decision barring restrictive covenants, further moved national discussions on race relations toward an increasing federal consensus on the illegality of segregation in the workplace or the neighborhood.

Rather than celebrating integration, Zanuck chose the 1943 riots as the referent for his drama. These riots had exposed racism in the midst of a war for democracy. To invoke these riots in the wake of the Second World War was an act of pessimism which pointed out the war's unfulfilled promises. Indeed, this was the grimmest of Zanuck's films on race relations—with the least narrative closure, ideological coherence, or clear message.

Unlike *Pinky, No Way Out* villainized white racists and showed sympathetic *and* politically empowered Black men, building, through characters and mise-en-scène, a space for even politically militant Black spectators. Zanuck referred to *Pinky* as "tea" and *No Way Out* as "dinner."[66] Where *Pinky* had depicted racism as a southern problem internally and interpersonally solvable through domestic discussion, *No Way Out* expressionistically rendered racial violence and argued for what Zanuck would call "professional equality" for Black doctors in the North. According to screenwriter Lesser Samuels, his screenplay depicted the "corrosive effect of hatred, especially as it pertains to the bitter, unreasoning animosity of the ignorant white man for his Black brother living in a world that has been made impossible for him."[67] As a sign of his boldness, Zanuck assigned Joseph Mankiewicz to direct the film shortly after he criticized Zanuck for pulling punches by having a white woman play Pinky.[68] As with *Pinky,* however, *No Way Out* would skirt the line on full-fledged racial equality, even as it reveled in racial controversy and championed conditional racial integration.

I have discussed *No Way Out*'s censorship in earlier chapters, but here I cover the film's repressed conception in greater depth. In *No Way Out,* Luther Brooks (Sidney Poitier), the first Black doctor at an all-white county hospital in a northern urban center, gets an unlucky first assignment: the graveyard shift in the prison ward. His first patients are brothers Ray (Richard Widmark) and Johnny Biddle (Dick Paxton), two racist white men wounded while holding up a gas station. Ray taunts Dr. Brooks with the word "nigger" as he treats his brother. When Johnny dies during a spinal tap, Ray vows revenge. Brooks, a new doctor, fears he made a mistake, but his mentor, Dr. Wharton (Steven McNally), cannot get a nervous hospital director to assent to an autopsy without family consent. Ray is determined to see Brooks dead. Though in police custody, he uses his lover (who is also his brother's ex-wife, Edie Johnson [Linda Darnell]) to gather white neighbors and friends to "go over to Niggertown" to kill Brooks and any other "Black boys" they meet along the way. But Black hospital elevator operator Lefty Jones (Dots Johnson) coordinates a preemptive strike against the white men while they are preparing for the fight in a junkyard. Brooks, unlike his brother (Ossie Davis) who joins the fight, makes frantic calls to avert the showdown and, later, compassionately nurses white victims until a grieving white mother spits in his face and he walks off the job, stunned. In concert with his wife, Cora (Mildred Joanne Smith), Brooks turns himself in for Johnny's murder to force an autopsy, one that ultimately proves his innocence—that is, to everyone except Ray. Under threat of violence, Ray forces Edie (who is repentant) to set up a meeting with Brooks. Ray ambushes and shoots him. Brooks's bullet wound is not fatal, but Ray, still ailing and in need of a doctor, has torn something in his leg. In the final frames of the film, Brooks slowly spins a tourniquet, cutting off circulation to Ray's bleeding leg, saying through clenched teeth: "Don't cry, white boy. You're gonna live." The film's sadism and nihilism would challenge the racial problem film's conventional conciliatory ending, as epitomized in films like *Home of the Brave* (1949) and even Zanuck's own *Pinky* and *Gentleman's Agreement* (1947).

Zanuck's early story conferences set the drama's tone and scope. He worked with three writers. Lesser Samuels, from whom he bought the property, would work only on the first draft. Philip Yordan, known for writing *Anna Lucasta*, was brought in presumably to strengthen the Black dialogue. And Joseph Mankiewicz came in as scriptwriter at draft six. Across the screenplay's seven drafts, it underwent drastic revisions of its focus, characterization, and ending.

Zanuck altered the script in several racially progressive ways, tinkering with strategies of racial focalization. Samuels's version focused on Brooks's white supervisor Dan Wharton and his romance with a nurse. It is Wharton who introduces us to segregation and angrily laments its effects. He invokes Black accomplishments to remind a flagging Brooks that he can be a doctor in a "white world."[69] But Zanuck argued that Wharton, "the Abraham Lincoln of our story," was too heroic and too central.[70] He wanted to focus on Luther Brooks, a position that was likely informed by the NAACP's letters lambasting *Pinky*, which, given Zanuck's defensive ten-page response, had clearly touched a nerve.[71] Accordingly, Zanuck's "first criticism" was "of the character Luther Brooks, our leading role. I have the impression that Luther is a weakling. I am disturbed about his being a doctor. I resent his bowing and scraping."[72] Throughout the scriptwriting process, Zanuck set parameters for Brooks's character development. Zanuck contextualized Brooks by showing his family: "I would like to see us go into Luther's home. I would like to see how real Negroes in a metropolitan city live. I would like to see them as human beings. Perhaps Luther has a mother and a father; he is part of a family."[73] Zanuck's desire for Black familial realism correlates to the positive image of Black Americans that Walter White called for. And, indeed, in the finished film Luther and his wife, Cora (a character Zanuck changed drastically from a showgirl to a housewife), are the most stable and most loving couple. He also suggested presenting a hospital setting in which integration was normalized: "Possibly," he wrote, "we should introduce Luther in a regular staff meeting . . . and play the scene as though Luther were just another white doctor. At this point there is no awareness or condescension on the part of others."[74] This more direct integrationism is crystallized in scenes where Brooks angrily refuses to work in a lucrative segregated clinic with pompous Dr. Clark (Frederick O'Neal, who played Jake in *Pinky*). These scenes attempted to revise *Pinky*'s timidity along NAACP lines. But Dr. Clark ended up on the cutting room floor, perhaps because producers saw the film's disdain for this middle-class figure as potentially offensive to the NAACP.

Zanuck also finally brought a politically empowered Black working man from script to screen. Lefty, the leader of the Black resistance, is a softer, more complicated figure than Samuels's original story suggested. Samuels's Lefty responds violently to Ray Biddle's racism: " 'Some day mebbe I gets to tangle with that no-good man. They don't call no ambulance, just the meat wagon,' he said savagely."[75] Zanuck revised Lefty's line to remove the heavy dialect.[76] In the finished film, although his menacing language and scarred face intimidate, Lefty explains his anger with a story: when Luther was still in school, a white mob from Beaver Canal left his sister in a wheelchair and him with the scar on his face. When Brooks claims that preemptive attacks make Blacks "no better than" whites, Lefty powerfully responds, "Ain't that asking a lot for us to be better than them when we get killed just trying to prove we're as good?" Luther can offer no reply. The finished film's Lefty also seems more sympathetic. He's a World War II veteran, as we learn from the "navy flare gun" he uses to signal the attack. This connection to World War II is strengthened by the casting of Dots Johnson, who starred as a Black soldier in *Paisan* (1945).

Zanuck rendered the Black rebellion sensitively by showing Brooks's own brother, John (Ossie Davis), a student and future postal worker, as one of its members. When he tells his wife (Ruby Dee) he's going "for a walk," she sees through his lie and begs him to stay. But his mother, without looking up from her knitting, says, "Go ahead, John, take your walk," thus, in veiled language, justifying his participation in the rebellion. These scenes make obvious that it is not just Black gangs but Black families that have a stake in this fight, a fight that amounts (as many riots did) to a resistance against white lynching. Zanuck retained sequences of Black college students leaving class to fight in the Black uprising—which suggested a much broader base of Black discontentment and also that the "riot" was more like a movement—until draft six.

But despite Zanuck's interventions, Lefty was still a morally contradictory character. At first, he seems a parallel in Black to Ray Biddle, evincing Brooks's claim that "there are Negroes who are pathological white-haters." Lefty's followers, whom Brooks describes as a preexisting "gang," are linked to noir's criminal underclass through their costumes—fedoras, wife-beaters, and gold chains—and their pool hall hangout. Lefty's cruelty shows through in his rallying cry on the night of the attack when he tells Black fighters to "shut up" and calls one of them "boy." Rather than invoking pride or retaliation—or defense of Black homes—Lefty seems to delight in violence. Depicting the "gangster" as both sympathetic and cruel was not new to Zanuck but a throwback to his work on films such as *The Public Enemy* (1931) at Warner Bros. Thus, by writerly design, Lefty was a character with contradictions that Zanuck made appear righteous in his anti-white sentiments at some moments and savage at others. Similarly, Black reasons for participating in the resistance—and thus the civil rights implications of Black self-defense—were deniable and never clearly stated. These reasons became even less clear as Zanuck cut scenes emphasizing Black student and veteran participation.

While Zanuck began with a zeal for cutting-edge Black representation, the arc of script development shows his increasing, neurotic, racial constraint. Early drafts explained the institutional sources of white working-class race hatred rather than rendering racism as sensational, symbolic, violent action.[77] In one draft Black residents move into Ray Biddle's neighborhood, Beaver Canal, "coming up from the South by the carload," a clear link to the Great Migration. "Pretty soon," the script has one white man remark, "it won't be safe for a white woman to walk the street."[78] Another early draft had a Beaver Canal vigilante named Whitey incredulously report: "The Supreme Court just decided that a Negro can move right next door and you can't do a thing."[79] Other Beaver Canal residents feel African Americans are getting an education "ahead" of them. "They're grabbin' up the earth, they ain't satisfied shinin' shoes and diggin' ditches—they're goin' to college and becomin' lawyers and doctors—they're openin' banks, runnin' for Congress—pretty soon we'll have a nigger President."[80] But Zanuck himself cut much of this dialogue late in production. While the lines he cut are not entirely convincing, the issues borrowed directly from contemporary headlines and school integration cases. Zanuck's choice to entirely omit them— rather than improve them—left a vacuum and further personalized Ray Biddle's racism.[81] Most disturbingly, these script drafts intimate that Zanuck understood the everyday logic of white working class racism but shied away from directly representing it. Zanuck's modifications and censorship of *No Way Out* display white liberalism's calculated moderation. He upheld the mantle of unrepresentability of the institutional sources of white racism and focused instead on the spectacular melodrama of Black/white racial conflict.

And even racism's spectacular elements had to be tamed. Zanuck stated early that, to serve the bottom line, the film could neither center on a "problem" nor show "social equality" between the races: "I visualize an exciting, violent story dealing with a very profound American problem. However never at any time do I want the problem to become bigger than the story."[82] Accordingly, Zanuck instructed the script team to minimize social equality and the riot because while he was resigned to losing "about 3000 accounts in the South . . . it would be a terrible thing [to] give the so-called white cities a chance to turn us down. . . . It is fine to be courageous but . . . not too courageous with other people's money. . . .

This story argues for professional fairness and equality. It opposes prejudice and intolerance. It does not seek, nor should it, for total social equality."[83]

As a result, a series of visual and verbal substitutions supplanted the film's realist potential. Although the film's slim PCA file suggests limited self-regulatory input on the script's riot scenes, Zanuck and the production team strategically muted *No Way Out*'s style of articulation to fit a racialized version of the PCA's "principle of deniability."[84] Verbally, the grating, offensive sound of the word "nigger" becomes the means for revealing civil rights abuses but without verisimilitude that might produce audience action. Rather than calling Black people "nigger," whites talk about "niggers" in the abstract, thus lessening its edge, making censorship less likely, and relieving Brooks of the burden of responding. As the word ceases to be used for social exchange, it can become more fully ensconced in and removed to the white racist imagination and psychosis.

What is striking is how little *No Way Out*'s dialogue actually says—and how much is left to the audience to figure out. For example, Lefty dramatically but vaguely addresses Luther about why he "hates whites":

LEFTY: I'm not ridin' no elevator tonight. Trouble's coming over from Beaver Canal and I'm gonna get me some. Jonah heard them talking . . . about you and what they are going to do to niggertown tonight because you killed Johnny Biddle.
LUTHER: We've got to stop them!
LEFTY: Stop who? Beaver Canal?
LUTHER: It won't help! It only makes things worse.
LEFTY: Not for us it won't. Not tonight! We're going to be ready tonight.
LUTHER: You're talking like a crazy man!
LEFTY: Yea, sometimes I do get a little crazy when these things happen. Like six years ago when Beaver Canal came over. You were still in school. My kid sister's *still* in a wheelchair. I got this [pointing to his scar] from a broken bottle.

With some difficulty we can discern that Lefty is describing a pattern of white racial violence. But he never explicitly mentions riots, racism, or even white or Black people, opting instead for myriad ambiguous signifiers. Although the film boldly touted the word "nigger" (and that thirty-two times), if the studio wanted to avoid alienating the white mainstream audiences it had charmed just a few years earlier with Bill Robinson's tap dances, it had to temper *No Way Out*'s discussion of northern segregation, race riots, white racism, or justifiable Black reasons for rebellion. More detailed realism in these sequences might have prompted real audience engagement with the question of how and why riots occurred and their relationship to civil rights abuses that typically preceded them.

Visually, the studio's combination of repression and representation is best evinced in its handling of the Black rebellion sequence. In Samuels's story the riot smoldered on the film's margins: we hear of it only from the relative safety of the hospital. Zanuck increased the stakes of his "exciting" and "thrilling" riot by involving sympathetic characters, but he advocated several minor acts of violence rather than one big clash to diffuse censorable violence. "I worry about the race riot, no matter how small we keep it." Writing and development of the story, he suggested, would be crucial so as to "avoid any pitfalls that might wreck us from the standpoint of police or political censorship."[85] To avoid censorship, the violent activity and the name-calling come *before* the riot (during the preparation scenes). The riot remains, as Zanuck wanted it, on the scale "of a street fight."[86] The junkyard setting obviated concerns about the destruction of property. No visible evidence of injury, attack, or death appears, except when white people arrive at the hospital in the scene after the riot. Instead, long shots of men with raised sticks crosscut with invading Black bodies maintained the kinesthetic energy without showing actual violence. Violence is also rendered sonically— as noise. As the white sadistic mob breaks bottles and cracks whips, Edie reacts strongly to this cacophony, as if imagining the rehearsed violence. Expressionistic music accompanies the image of men mounting a tall pile of metal to find weapons, making this nighttime scene feel like a dystopian, postindustrial bonfire. Rather than depicting physical blows that might communicate real enmity, the film engages in an expressionistic, surreal tableau vivant that allows us to study the scene—a technique best exemplified right before the fighting begins, when the flare gun goes off. For several seconds both Black and white men stand still, both poised to fight but mesmerized by the glow of the flare, which lights their faces. The film makes a clear link between what it projects as an apocalyptic—no way out—racial situation and the nuclear age in the eerie light of the flare gun that silently simulates the Cold War's ultimate form of annihilation—an atomic bomb. Thus, despite mounting disavowals of racial violence in the text, the text amplifies the danger of race riots only by way of expressionistic allusion.

Zanuck had helped develop these techniques to diffuse violence in the pre-Code era. In films like *The Public Enemy*, the effects of violence took the form of resonant echoes—shadows, silhouette, and percussive gunshots set against the sounds of a rainstorm—that were projected in the surrounding environment, rather than visible blood and guts.[87] This elaborated and creatively extended moments of violence. But in *No Way Out*, so great was the social threat of race riot violence that Zanuck and his team opted to displace it almost entirely into the environment. In a social problem film it was rare for such large-scale violence to be so indirectly represented, the reasons for enmity so unclear, or the film's message so vague. With *No Way Out*, Zanuck, who had ruthlessly engineered a moral in *The Grapes of Wrath* (1940) and *The Ox-Bow Incident*, let the latent nihilism that had saturated *Pinky*'s unsatisfying ending fully bloom into a largely messageless, bloody conclusion.

The studio made more cuts after state censors previewed the film.[88] Despite this preemptive action, Virginia, Ohio, and Maryland made plot-altering cuts to the final release print, some deleting the riot entirely. Through many memos on minor plot elements, Zanuck, with his writers, had made *No Way Out* into a web of ambiguous signifiers that could be read in remarkably opposing ways by audiences with vastly different ideas about Black rights and equality. Though *No Way Out* showed sympathy for its Black doctor, Zanuck waffled about the film's message on integration and how big to make the riots—both ideologically and physically. Ultimately he opted to condemn rabid white racism and show Black militancy, but the idea of mass movement implicit in Black self-defense scenes remained veiled and repressed.

ISLAND CIVIL RIGHTS DURING THE MASS MOVEMENT

Pinky and *No Way Out* had announced America's racial problem to a mainstream Hollywood audience, suggesting in the first instance interpersonal tolerance as the solution and in the second, with noir's signature despair, that perhaps there was no way out of racial turmoil. As the U.S. mass movement for civil rights began, however, Hollywood studios became notoriously and increasingly bashful about directly presenting these struggles onscreen. Not only had the "problem" cycle ended, but the civil rights narrative could no longer be compartmentalized as an individual story. And, as the U.S. State Department's desire to stifle *Blackboard Jungle* (1955) on the international festival circuit indicates, both state and Cold War national forces were invested in repressing interracial screen violence.[89] The beginning of the civil rights movement engendered a shift in representational politics that is more worthy of discussion. Although several important court and legislative governmental reforms had come almost a decade earlier, in 1955 two major events would signal the mass movement's commencement: the lynching of Emmett Till followed by the perfunctory trial of his murderers, and the Montgomery bus boycott (from December 1955 to December 1956). The camera lens would be vital to the social meaning of both these events. Internationally circulated images of masses of Black people coming to see Emmett Till's mangled body in the open casket in Chicago would remind the world that white America had a greater tolerance for lynching than for Black people. And unbussed Black Montgomery residents, moving en masse to and from work and school, would unsettle American TV screens, and white American televisual spectatorship, as Sasha Torres and Mary Dudziac have suggested.[90]

Fox films *Carmen Jones* (1954), *The King and I* (1956), *Island in the Sun* (1957), and *South Pacific* (1958) made aesthetically bound, indirect commentary on racial difference and civil rights, sublimating political "problems" under the apparently carefree logic of the musical or the dramatic veil of melodrama.[91] Although most of these films are set away from U.S. shores, in *South Pacific* and *Island in the Sun* the use of African American actors to play those suffering from U.S.-style race discrimination encoded civil rights in the guise of island escapism, repurposing the island genre—long a site for displacing interracial desires—to reveal colonial relationships at home and abroad.[92] Of these films, the most important to American civil rights is *Island in the* Sun, which deals with several issues relevant to civil rights: miscegenation, white violence, and both organized Black resistance and Black riot violence. Its creative team adopted a number of strategies to distract both censors and racist whites from its connection to pressing American news items concerning civil rights, while maintaining its edge in controversy. Specifically, it dampened the physical intensity of interracial engagement by literally stopping the movement by means of melodramatic tableaux. It invoked the visual image of mass movement but never in a threatening way, always combining masses with arguably apolitical music. While television showed carefully circumscribed documentary images of the movement in programs like Edward R. Murrow's "Clinton and the Law" (1957) and Charles Guggenheim's *A City Decides* (1957), *Island* used Cinemascope and Technicolor to aggrandize the proportions of the masses. It invoked the visual aesthetic of Black mass movement, but in ways that rearranged this narrative, divorcing civil rights struggles from the contexts in which Americans were used to seeing them on their television screens.

Zanuck indicated his eagerness to film *Island* by purchasing the rights before author Alec Waugh even finished writing the novel. It was also his first independent production off the studio lot. Careful adaptation was crucial to maintaining balance among politically, racially, and regionally differentiated spectators. The book takes place in Santa Marta, a fictional Caribbean island on the verge of colonial uprising. Feeling Black pressure, the island's governor introduces a new constitution obliterating income and literacy requirements and enfranchising Black residents. Maxwell, the protagonist, is a frustrated planter's son who is brutal toward plantation workers and resents the eclipse of colonial authority. He thinks Blacks are savage and unable to handle self-rule. Maxwell's sister Jocelyn contrasts with her brother physically (she is blonde and pale where Maxwell is dark) and, to some extent, ideologically. She is a member of a clique of planters' daughters calling themselves "the inseparables," who struggle with their racist parents. Not only is one of the inseparables (Doris) clearly part Black (although no one discusses it), but Mavis, who is from one of the island's oldest planter families, falls in love with Black cricket star and assistant district attorney Grainger Morris, an "exceptional" Black man thoroughly invested in the welfare of his people. Midway through the novel, Maxwell and Jocelyn make a potentially life-changing discovery—that their father is part Black—a fact that threatens Jocelyn's plans to marry the son of Santa Marta's governor, Euan. Attempting to capitalize on his newfound blackness, Maxwell unsuccessfully runs for office courting the Black votes by falsely claiming affinity with the island's workers. When Hilary Carson, an ex-naval officer whom he suspects of an affair with his wife, refers to Maxwell as having a "touch of the tarbrush," Maxwell brutally strangles him and makes the crime look like a burglary. Maxwell's political rival is David Boyeur, a rowdy, color-conscious, and arrogant mulatto leader who ruthlessly controls the island's "savage" Black populace. Boyeur is going steady with Margot Seaton, a beautiful Black shopgirl who will eventually marry the governor's white aide de camp, Denis Archer. Out of pride and after being ignored by the colony's planter-dominated governing body, Boyeur engineers a strike of all the island's Blacks for wage increases. During the strike, Maxwell, in a fit of Dostoyevskian despair, kills himself by goading the protesting Black workers to attack him. The governor prosecutes Boyeur for inciting the mob that killed Maxwell, but Grainger successfully argues that Maxwell was responsible for his own death. To restore order, the governor calls in a heavily armed British barge to stop the violence and threaten the strikers back to work, despite the legal dubiousness of this action. Meanwhile, Jocelyn discovers that she is the product of her mother's indiscretion with a fully white man and thereupon decides to marry the governor's son. Grainger, however, decides for chaste dedication to his people rather than marrying Mavis.

The book was a swan song of colonial culture focalized through racist whites. As with *Pinky*, Zanuck took a racially conservative but popular book and gave it to white, left-wing writers hoping for balance.[93] In this case, Zanuck chose a particularly progressive group. Alfred Hayes, a British leftist associated with Italian neorealism, adapted the screenplay (with assistance from Nunnally Johnson), while Zanuck also consulted with blacklisted screenwriters Irvin Shaw and Robert Rossen, the latter of whom he selected to direct.[94] From the vantage point of leftist race politics, the book offered both promise and challenges. It hinged on Santa Marta's new constitution, which granted voting rights to Blacks. It dramatized a strike of the island's Black workers for fair wages and an end to segregation. And its climax was a physical confrontation between Blacks and whites ending in violence. All these occurrences resonated with the concurrent American struggle for civil rights. But Waugh's novel also depicted the island's Black residents as ignorant and savage and its Black leaders as criminally greedy and inept. Its omniscient narrator had described West Indians as "superstitious."[95] The novel insinuated that Maxwell's blackness was to blame for his uneven temperament. These were characterizations Zanuck did not want to emulate. Zanuck's script team downplayed the intergenerational struggle against colonial racism—and in fact would downplay colonial racism altogether, representing it as a far more benign force. The governor's racist statements and action against strikers would be omitted. And certain characters—Doris and Grainger, most importantly—would be cut.

Casting, which Zanuck engineered, did much to link the narrative to civil rights questions. Harry Belafonte, a visible part of the American civil rights movement, added intertextual layers to Boyeur. In May 1957, only a month before *Island in the Sun* was released, Belafonte would perform before 30,000 people at a prayer vigil led by Martin Luther King Jr. at the Lincoln Memorial to commemorate the third anniversary of *Brown v. Board of Education*.[96] Casting also heightened the suggestion of miscegenation—linking the onscreen characters involved in interracial affairs with their offscreen loves (Belafonte and Dandridge, most prominently).

Screenwriter Hayes initially suggested restricting the focus to the white Fleury family. "To me," he wrote, "the underlying theme of the book [is] the burden of colonial guilt, the burden of sin or secret which oppresses the oppressor."[97] But in Zanuck's eyes, the book did more than dramatize white guilt. Black revolt and transgressive interracial love—these were the elements of greatest interest to Zanuck. Hayes had removed some Black characters, but Zanuck wanted to preserve the epic feel by maintaining a brimming ensemble. "I think we have lost the size and scope. We tell a nice love story . . . but that's all it is, just a nice love story."[98] Zanuck explicitly asked that future script drafts include more racial conflict and be more about a "problem."

> Throughout the years I have learned in making pictures like . . . PINKIE [*sic*], and GENTLEMAN'S AGREEMENT, that it is foolish to get into a . . . controversial story and then try to white-wash it. . . . In Island in the Sun, we would be foolish to go into a black-versus-white story and then avoid the situations which are controversial. There is utterly nothing controversial in this script.[99]

Zanuck clearly saw the film not as a "South Seas" or even "colonial" genre picture but specifically in terms of "black-versus-white":

> I always had the feeling, from the book, that in this story the people were sitting on a keg of dynamite due to the explosive nature of the Black-and-white situation in this spot. I thought we would tell our personal stories in the foreground, while in the background would be this seething mass of Black people straining against the domination of these few whites.[100]

Though he wanted more racial conflict, having learned from *No Way Out*, he did not want face-to-face interracial violence. The "riotous" mob that kills Maxwell and the colonial reprisals tested the limits of censorship. In the book, Maxwell incites the mob by invoking the voice of the colonial oppressor. Calling newly enfranchised Blacks "slaves," Maxwell says they should be whipped into order.

> You are idle, stupid, ignorant. You'll work only when the whip's cracked behind you. You can't think for yourselves, you follow your master: the man with the loudest voice. . . . The white people flatter you . . . they tell you that you're as good as they are. They give you a vote, they give you self-government, they finance your projects. I know how wrong they are.[101]

While the suicide-by-mob had exploitation value, Zanuck cut it—and all violent racial conflict between the colonial oppressor and the Black masses.[102] While excising the riot (which presented Africa's descendants as angry animals under the dominating control of a ruthless, power-hungry, half-breed leader) improved the film's depiction of Black people, the wholesale elimination of the strike—like the removal of Arch Naughton from *Pinky*—allowed the studio to avoid taking a stance on the book's clearest reference to contemporary civil rights struggles.

In place of the strike and riot, Zanuck opted for a series of restrained conflicts. And even in these, Zanuck was cautious. Hayes wanted to have Boyeur punch Maxwell during a political debate in the square.[103] Though here, as elsewhere, Hayes muted violence through tableaux, Zanuck's next memo stated unequivocally: "You cannot have a Negro hitting a white man as you do on page 104. . . . It has got to be staged so that the police jump in between and pull them apart—or Boyeur controls himself and pulls back."[104] Zanuck preferred conflict to remain repressed—if only barely. Zanuck sketched out a scene—one retained in the finished film—where Maxwell, angry with his wife, recklessly drives his sports car into a Black crowd, nearly hitting a Black cyclist.[105] What had been merely a disconnected group of passersby quickly congeals into a concerned Black mass. This seemingly insignificant moment reveals in small brushstrokes white colonial privilege and indifference, the narrow contingencies that barely restrain everyday interracial conflict, and the dynamics and potential of Black response. He also wanted the film to end with the white authority figures giving a summation of the problem and its solutions. The conclusion should be, he stated, "Keep it orderly and keep it civilized. As long as the changes are in an orderly, civilized manner without violence then we have nothing to worry about."[106]

To Zanuck's credit, he seems to have surrounded himself with talent likely to steer him away from the kinds of equivocation on Black civil rights that marred *Pinky* and left *No Way Out* only vaguely militant. He had indicated early that Hayes should emphasize the "problem" more clearly.[107] He then sought out Irvin Shaw to help him define that problem in leftist—or leftish—terms. Zanuck directly invoked Shaw in memos to Hayes, suggesting "more violence, . . . emotional eruptions" that would reveal the "basic racial problem."[108] Shaw, Zanuck told Hayes, suggested a scene at Governor's House where "the calm, placid atmosphere is shattered by the arrival of a native band led by a couple of men carrying banners. They are, of course, uninvited guests and they are led by a half-cast [sic] agitator."[109] Instead, the writers converted Boyeur's demonstration into disdain: he comes late to the governor's party with Margot as his unannounced companion, and then pointedly brings up the issue of equal rights in conversation—a less obvious disruption but a politicized break with white colonial ceremony nonetheless.

Rossen's visual effects also manifest civil rights in extra-narrative ways. Although the film, sans riot and strike, depicts no mass movement, Rossen and

FIGURE 25. As Black bodies countermand public space, Carnival communicates the uncontainability of Black masses and provides a space for the staging of indirect, deniable challenges to the colonial order. Frame capture from *Island in the Sun* (1957).

Zanuck made this movement palpable in epic Cinemascope crowd sequences, where music and dance replace politics and diffuse the threat of Black bodies moving en masse. Heightening realism, Zanuck assented to film these sequences in Grenada, which was under intense anticolonial pressure in the mid-1950s and which, like Santa Marta, had shifted from British to French rule.

The film's lengthy Carnival scenes demonstrate this indirect, "apolitical" revelation of the power of Black masses. Black people of varying hues occupy the street with incredible vertical and horizontal volume, reversing its typical direction, use, and order (see figure 25). As Bakhtin has suggested, the carnival presents a particularly powerful opportunity for reversal of the social order.[110] In *Island in the Sun*, we learn that Carnival hosts not only figurative countermanding of colonial property and order (as Black bodies laboring in dance and song rather than field work), but that it becomes a place where "grudges are settled." Black folks typically disempowered by colonial relations mask themselves and perform vengeance upon specific whites who have harmed them. This completes the portrait of Carnival as an anticolonial space, a space for resonant, if transient, reversal of fortunes and justice for Black people, one that stands in for the movement politics the film effaces.

Musicalized masses also replace political ones in Boyer and Maxwell's townsquare confrontation. Here steel drums, rather than Black verbiage or violence, interrupt and drown out Maxwell's speech and introduce Black mass discontent. The melodic shouts and percussive music of Black people lead Fleury to double over fetally in agony and to clasp his hands full-force against his ears.[111] The town square and carnival's Black masses consciously play on concurrent press photography of the civil rights movement—particularly of the Montgomery bus boycott, which lent iconic status to large masses of African Americans arrayed around King but also brought the concept of mass mobilization (as well as its effectiveness) to the forefront of national consciousness.

Although he had removed the strike and violence, Zanuck not only instructed Hayes to build up individual Black characters but took to the project himself.[112] Zanuck was particularly interested in Boyeur. In the book, Boyeur had been a power-hungry man who wanted to be white and was willing to sell his people out for his own prestige. But Zanuck and Hayes wanted to change this:

> The point has to be made that Boyeur, despite the role he plays in the story, is not a heavy: it would be unfortunate if the story should emerge with a West Indian as the drama's villain. It must be clearly shown, as the Governor indicates, that Boyeur is dangerous 'only if he is handled tactlessly'; if, in short, he is snubbed or ignored or slighted as Maxwell so obviously does slight him. . . . Boyeur is young, brash, a labor leader, ambitious, vain but immensely proud too; and at thirty, he has succeeded in organizing the first important organized labor movement in the islands. It is a question of racial pride; it is a question of Boyeur's expressing the rising self-consciousness of the West Indian; he has to be written with tact.[113]

Zanuck initially agreed. Boyeur, Zanuck stated, would "take on some of the characteristics of Grainger Morris," the book's sympathetic mulatto attorney.[114] This hybrid character combined civic-minded idealism with anticolonial insurgency, implicitly courting audience sympathy for anticolonial resistance. Zanuck clearly stated: "Boyeur can be just as tough as he is in the script, but we will see, also, that he is a dedicated man; the welfare, present and future of the colored people of Santa Marta, are his main interest in life."[115] Strangely, however, in mid-stage drafts, Zanuck openly called writers to emphasize Boyeur's arrogance and self-promotion—to have him claim "the name of David Boyeur will be known wherever there is injustice or inequality," combining civil rights activism with selfishness, as in the book—and as Arch had in *Pinky*.[116] Notes in the margins of these memos (probably from Hayes to whom the memos were sent) and Hayes's slow compliance with suggested changes may indicate his disagreement with Zanuck about his changes to Boyeur.

The development of David Boyeur was influenced by happenings outside the studio walls. The MPAA was so anxious about *Island*'s presentation of Black folks that it submitted the script to the African American attorney and Special Assistant on Negro Affairs during World War II, Truman Gibson. Gibson, who read both the book and the script, lamented the excision of Grainger, the more relatable character. In a letter that circulated from the MPAA New York offices to the PCA and to Fox, he stated in reference to an early script draft that "the development of Boyeur as a cynical exploiter of his people diverts attention from some of the reasons why people in that area are now actively and rapidly pushing towards dominion status; and also why the Caribbean World has so radically changed in the last few years."[117] But even this did not immediately prod Zanuck to change Boyeur's character.

It wasn't until Rossen began working on the script in September (the film would be shot in December) that Boyeur's character attained the humanity he has on screen. In a joint memo Rossen and Zanuck changed the ending where Mavis's assessment of Boyeur as a fraud stands unchallenged, allowing Boyeur to defend himself. "She does not," they amended, "question his deep convictions," although she questions his motives.[118] They also converted Boyeur's introduction at the governor's party from a showcase for his arrogance to a platform for his call for equality, further developing this scene along the lines Shaw suggested. Most importantly, they changed the confrontation between Maxwell and Boyeur on the waterfront. Rather than Boyeur hitting, chiding, or threatening Maxwell, Zanuck and Rossen decided he would be utterly civil and fair:

> It is Boyeur who stops the mockery of Maxwell and . . . who insists that Maxwell be given a chance to state his position and Maxwell does, rather well. . . . However, he cannot stand up against the inner truth of Boyeur's argument which is primarily the fact that Maxwell cannot gain victory because he has now discovered himself to be part negro but must gain on the basis of being an equal. The issue of color should not be involved. It's now man against man. One man in tune with the people he addresses, the other allied to them merely by accident of birth and color but not by living, breathing experience.[119]

After Rossen commenced involvement, the script also bore veiled references to integration. Even the conservative Maxwell tells Black Santa Martans that the two worlds, white and Black, cannot exist "cut off from each other by suspicion and fear," thus suggesting the need for some sort of integration.[120]

Although Rossen, a victim of the Blacklist, could no longer make films directly advocating left-wing views, after he became involved in *Island* the plot became conspicuously more about class than it was about color alone, illuminating a broader definition of island civil rights and guardedly highlighting the connections between the American civil rights movement and the international workers' struggle. New scenes were added where Boyeur recounts how as a child he, like most native islanders, had "no money . . . no opportunity to become anything and nobody paying any attention. That's why I began organizing."[121] Scenes between Mavis and Boyeur no longer took place primarily on an old plantation where discussion of a slave revolt foregrounds color politics, but rather as Boyeur shows Mavis (and audiences) the island's impoverished communities—in a market on a bus showing natives who "seem to be carrying all their belongings with them," and, crucially, on the coasts with the fishermen.[122] In Boyeur's confrontation with Maxwell, he asks whether Fleury thinks "the only issue here is color." Raising the question of class, Boyeur boldly suggests that the issue is who is the owner and who the slave rather than who is Black and who is white.[123]

Not long after Walter White's death in 1955, with the help of Hayes, Shaw, Gibson, and Rossen, Zanuck finally oversaw the creation of a Black revolutionary of which White would have been proud. Boyeur has the stature of Henry Carter in *The Ox-Bow Incident*, Tom Joad in *The Grapes of Wrath*, and Lincoln in *Young Mr. Lincoln*—all men whose integrity, civic duty, and social responsibility led them to stand, perilously, for justice, even when it was unpopular. Like Arch Naughton of *Pinky*, Lefty of *No Way Out*, and Kalva/Sam of *Slave Ship*, Boyeur went through transformations in the scriptwriting process that drastically shifted the size of and potential sympathy for his role, evincing the trouble Zanuck's production team was still having with an empowered Black male hero. But in the case of *Island in the Sun*, the movement was consistently in the direction of making the Black revolutionary character more important and more sympathetic, a marked contrast to the script development toward marginality, ignorance, and unsympathetic rage as in earlier films. And in *Island* no white man was responsible for solving the race problem. No white men would save David Boyeur, except, of course, Zanuck and Rossen themselves.

But Boyeur's political potency and iconic centrality came with a price: his love life had to be frustrated. As in the book, Boyeur, in Zanuck's words, would "give up the white girl he could have had, in order to devote himself entirely to the welfare of his people."[124] Sexual self-sacrifice modeled on that in *Pinky* was Zanuck's solution to the dangers posed by so significant and political a Black character.[125] However, Zanuck did allow Boyeur's rejection of Mavis to be tinged with revolutionary fire. He is rejecting her, he tells her, because she has "never experienced ignorance or prejudice." He could never marry a white woman because of the "inevitable . . . day [that] she would forget herself and call me 'nigger.' "[126] It is the threat of racism—not noble sacrifice to white custom or noble self-castration—that ultimately prompts their separation.

Although the Production Code no longer banned miscegenation, the depiction of interracial love in *Island*'s script was an even bigger problem than violence or revolution. In *Pinky*, when the title character kissed her white lover, white audiences could be reassured by the racial identities of the actors that the interracial kiss was only a narrative illusion. However, in *Island*, Dandridge's Margot would marry her white lover and Belafonte's Boyeur would respond to overt sexual overtures from a white woman. For Zanuck, adding this narrative intensity seemed to require scaling back the physical intensity. Although the script called for an interracial kiss, Zanuck's second memo stated: "I think we are in trouble censorshipwise [*sic*] with the kissing."[127] Instead, he opined, Margot and Archer should "continue to dance on and on and we can end on the dancing."[128] Thus Zanuck let carefully choreographed intimacy and music dissipate and play out smoldering interracial tensions. Even with the kissing out, Zanuck's fear—particularly about pairing a Black man with a white woman—seemed to mount as production got closer. "We should keep the feeling of romance or sex out of [Boyeur and Mavis's] relationship. Their story should be different than the other three love stories. We will naturally have a feeling of sex in it in spite of whatever we do. But we need to get a sort of intellectual approach and underneath this approach we feel there is always an element of sex."[129] But even as he saw this element as a potential censorship problem, he returned to it almost obsessively. He continued to draw and redraw scenes between Mavis and Boyeur that would build their connection, if on nonsexual grounds.

Black actors publicly denounced Zanuck's restrictions on interracial romance. Dandridge told *Jet* that "John [Justin, who played Archer] and I had to fight to say the word 'love.' At first his line was 'You know how we feel,' as though it could have been pain that we felt." When the pair protested, Rossen did not make the decision himself but cabled Zanuck, who okayed changing the line to "You know I'm in love with you, don't you?"—a line that preserved the doubt that would cement, for Zanuck, his signature deniability.[130] Joan Fontaine told reporters that she had to convince Zanuck to let her drink from the same coconut as Belafonte. Belafonte concurred, stating that although the picture courageously dealt with colonialism and portrayed the Black man as the "winner" in an explosive political contest, "the romantic impact . . . is only strongly implied and the conclusions are left to the viewer's imagination."[131] Elsewhere he opined: "The tacit romance between Joan Fontaine and myself winds up with nothing. . . . The audience may get the feeling we're drawn to one another because at one point I even touch her elbow."[132]

Despite the fact that the film takes place on a fictional island, one that never becomes an integrated society (all interracial couples leave the island for England), Zanuck wanted to further limit the implications of the film's message about interracial marriage and integration. He proposed to do this through the film's final conversation, one held between the island's governor and chief of police. The conclusion Zanuck wanted audiences to draw, he stated in these memos, was that "what is good for Margot and Archer," the interracial couple with the happiest ending, "isn't necessarily right for any other two people here on the island . . . [and] is not necessarily good for Mavis and Boyeur."[133]

But as he minimized direct representations of interracial love, he permitted—even authored—subtle, deniable polysemic signifiers of it. For example, although Boyeur and Mavis never kiss, the camera lingers on a two-shot of the couple locking eyes as they share a drink from a coconut shell (see figure 26). The length of the sequence and its clear pregnant pauses are what gesture toward the omitted action, another example of the film's tableaux effect. Margot Seaton and Denis Archer's love is similarly signaled by a substitutionary embrace in Archer's closed quarters as they are dancing (figure 26). On the cusp of a kiss, they pause in a frozen tableau that stands in for the kiss that Zanuck would not

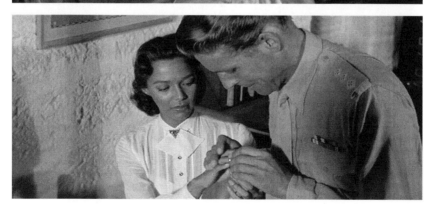

FIGURE 26. Mavis (Joan Fontaine) and Boyeur (Harry Belafonte) share a coconut shell; Margot (Dorothy Dandridge) and Archer (John Justin) exchange an ecstatic embrace. Both scenes were designed to avoid the need for kissing. Though we never see Archer and Margot marry, the bottom frame gives us an image of their exchanging rings that stands in for the unfilmable interracial wedding. Frame captures from *Island in the Sun*.

allow.[134] Likewise, although we never see the marriage between Margot and Archer, he publicly places a ring on her finger in the governor's office (figure 26).

Studio documents reveal that Twentieth Century–Fox president Spyros Skouras was an early advocate of restricting *Island*'s miscegenation. Though Skouras wanted "courage," confidentially he told Zanuck not to "have Negro actors making love to white actors."[135] When the studio's northern and border states sales departments expressed concern, Skouras asked Zanuck to alter two scenes and omit the "provoking" line "people are white and black" from advertisements.[136] Specifically, Skouras asked Zanuck to "delete cheek to cheek dance between Margot and [the Governor's] Aide and if you have additional footage for finish where Boyeur rejects Mavis to show her reprimanding more strongly, as you did in *Pinky,*" it would help them avoid a "ban."[137] The American civil rights movement figured prominently in sales discussions. Alex Harrison projected that the film would lose nearly one million dollars because it reminded Southerners of the "school integration controversy."[138] The film was banned in Atlanta and confiscated by the sheriff at a drive-in opening outside the city limits. The governor threatened a state censorship bill if the film showed.[139]

Despite the threat of losses, Zanuck defended the film, arguing the narrative integrity of both scenes on the chopping block.[140] Most strongly, he argued that the company should ignore this "audible but fanatic minority" that threatened to make Twentieth Century–Fox "a victim of prejudice" and that the same Southerners who threatened protest would be the first to purchase tickets. When Fox executive Murray Silverstone argued that whites come off badly in the picture because of "murder, illegitimacy, [and] pregnancy" while the colored people come off "spotless" and that the "marriage of colored girl 'with' white man . . . and rejection [of] white girl by negro may result . . . [in] implications [of the] inferiority of the white race," Zanuck would argue that "there is absolutely no way the ending can be altered without mutilating [the] climax."[141] He used his signature deniability against his own company by telling Silverstone that Boyeur leaves Mavis because of his career, not because of her race.[142] He would also deny the relationship between his film and the American movement for civil rights.[143]

> Spyros showed me your letter concerning governor of Georgia and his request to Harry Balance. . . . You must energetically fight such un-American censorship as our film is produced with dignity and taste and we do not advocate anything. There are no obvious interracial love scenes and no overemphasis on sex. We deal with British West Indian problems and conflicts which have nothing in common with southern racial issues. . . . We are not dealing with Harlem or Tennessee and the West Indians are mixed blood which has developed for generations. . . . I can possibly understand but never condone the attack on 'Edge of the City' but I repeat our film does not have any relation with these current American problems.[144]

But with his marked inability to distinguish racial from racist representation, Zanuck compared *Island's* box office potential to *The Birth of a Nation*, which "was banned in eleven states and ended up grossing 50 million dollars."[145] Skouras withdrew his objections and let the picture stand without changes. But his financial worries, based on the American civil rights situation, clearly influenced Zanuck. Though the MPAA no longer prohibited miscegenation, studio bottom line made it enduringly anathema.[146]

Throughout the film, controversial racial material melted into aesthetics and affect. The conversation about slavery, revolt, and contemporary Black labor between Boyeur and Mavis dissipates into song. In place of riot and rebellion, we are given Carnival and political mass meetings, in which subversive forces are encased in steel drums and revolutionary potential is masked in play, spectacle, and "the glittering robes of entertainment."[147] But inasmuch as the signs of censorship are everywhere in the text, the film highlights its own racial repression. The obviously muted energy and emphatic passivity of the text—its consistent resort to melodramatic tableaux and dramatic blocking—herald loudly the threat of censorship and the air of repression that marked the American family melodrama of the 1950s. These signs seem to hold a Sirkian metatextual drama all their own, one designed to taunt and draw audience attention to the censor's limits. Thus, although the film, like *No Way Out*, constrains racial violence and, like *Pinky*, masks miscegenation—limiting these themes to the industrially defined visual and aural tropes of the melodrama—its depiction of a Black revolutionary character and the self-evidence of its restraint represent an evolution of the studio's subtle methods of racial representation. In the film's manifest insufficiencies, the deliberately random vain whims of its inconsequential white protagonists, and its self-loathing, the text seems to admit that rendering the colonial narrative through white characters is inadequate and reductive. With the rise of the mass movement, Fox relocated the representation of civil rights to a narrative landscape outside the United States. Black masses were pictured, sometimes even in situations adjacent to politics, but representations of political violence and miscegenation were still muted by Zanuck's own productive censorship.

CONCLUSION

As the case of producer-auteur Darryl Zanuck demonstrates, the studio could both generate and repress civil rights images. With one hand, Zanuck pushed for greater revelation. With the other, he neutralized controversial images, neatly packaging them to avoid upsetting racial norms and PCA and state censorship. Zanuck created and honed a complex set of strategies for depicting controversial racial issues in ways that could be read differently by civil rights activists and by racially reactionary whites. Although *Pinky* was a box office success—even in the South—the polyphonic and uncompromising *No Way Out* became for the studio an unprofitable limit text, whose excesses, though they appear tame by modern standards, would guide future treatment in films such as *Island in the Sun*. As the civil rights movement intensified and as Zanuck-helmed films broached bolder and more contemporary racial themes, his approach became more restrained and his messages about racial trauma and civil rights less resolute. Although courting controversial political issues in early script drafts, Zanuck ultimately buried many of these themes—or burdened them with elaborate, deniable signification in later drafts. And while the studio continued to depict "true stories" of racial unrest and trauma, it focalized these narratives through white folks or interracial ensemble casts. Zanuck and his writers also had trouble depicting politically empowered Black men, although their work shows an evolution in this area, culminating in *Island in the Sun*. Nevertheless, Zanuck's films engaged with controversial racial themes, and, as the civil rights movement progressed, he depicted unafraid Black men fighting back against white oppression. He aestheticized Black resistance, making it an indelible part of the text's fabric, though often not its main narrative. In doing so, he made these representations a part of the mainstream cinema, if at tremendous cost to their incisive edge.

4 · SHADOWBOXING

Black Interpretive Activism
in the Classical Hollywood Era

Black activists looking to the screen for some meaningful representation of their experiences in a segregated America faced a wall of repression. As I have shown, not only did the PCA censor civil rights issues, but studios and state censors also repressed the interracial imagination. Even the "liberal" films of Darryl F. Zanuck muted Black struggle and avoided crisply and clearly addressing the civil rights issues at stake. But Black audiences did not accept the limits Hollywood imposed on the screen figuration of lynching, miscegenation, and integration. As Anna Everett, Jacqueline Stewart, Manthia Diawara, and others have shown, Black audiences instead actively interpreted Hollywood films, seeking signs of truth and illumination among the shrouded symbols of Black civil rights abuses. Especially important in this interpretive work were the efforts of Black activists.[1]

The question of how and when Black people took political action about film's civil rights questions provides an important corollary to the creative (and repressive) processes I have discussed in earlier chapters. With consistency and diligence, Black activists turned classical era cinema's faltering representations of issues like lynching, racial violence, and segregation into fodder for public argument. Unlike many other arenas of struggle (Jim Crow buses, voting restrictions, and housing discrimination), where racism's wrongs were achingly clear and where activists could use legal means to secure their rights, the cinema's meanings were far more nebulous. Film required *interpretation* to become the basis for activism. Though activists differed in their film readings and course of action, the internal debates and the moments of congealing sentiment effectively recast the screen's civil rights narrative. Through what I call "interpretive activism," African American activists used public discourse—pickets, resolutions, commendations—to foreground pressing civil rights issues that Hollywood left in the shadows. The NAACP placed itself at the center of Hollywood–African

American relations. But Black voices from within and outside the organization competed with that of NAACP executive secretary Walter White.

For activists, the issues that consistently reemerged as grounds for mobilization were somewhat different from those for Hollywood and its censors. Lynching and integration were battlegrounds for both censors and activists. But for activists the fight against Black primitivism and the plantation chronotope— and the use of epithets—were part of an African American bill of image rights that emerged during the period. Notably, miscegenation is absent from this list. Interracial romance was an issue so taboo that it became difficult for many activists to publicly advocate.

The Birth of a Nation has a seminal—near legendary—place in the history of Black film activism and sparked the largest, most coordinated Black protest that relied upon film interpretation, one the budding NAACP skillfully conjoined with its anti-lynching struggle.[2] However, its centrality has obscured smaller-scale but nonetheless crucial activism, which consistently and gradually defined the relationship between the screen and rights. For the purposes of this chapter, I define "activism" as the call for or engagement in public action to end racial bias. I do not address either activism that did not have an interpretive element or interpretation that did not amount to large-scale discursive formations or action because these are beyond the scope of this chapter. However, I do address activists' numerous techniques—pickets, demonstrations, boycotts, and discursive, "soft activism" (press releases, letter writing campaigns, and public "resolutions").[3] Often news items in the Black press were not merely reporting on the protest, they *were* the protest. That is, Black newspapers constructed a discursive weapon—an image of dissent and disillusionment meant not only to galvanize readers but to warn Hollywood. Beyond protest, activists strategically embraced films they adjudged useful to their cause, like *Fury* (1936), *The Ox-Bow Incident* (1943), *The Burning Cross* (1947), and *No Way Out* (1950).

The Black press was a major venue for interpretive activism. Black journalists, whose newspapers were the primary venue for African American dissent and civil rights coverage, knew their medium's value for highlighting the battles for racial equality that were essential to their papers' missions. They used print media to augment the cinema, sharpening and pinning down film's meaning so that it could become the basis for activism. While this activism routinely failed to significantly alter industry policy, it often wrought small changes and may have succeeded in reorienting readers to films' meaning to Black freedom struggles.[4] This history reveals the polysemic social meaning of films and their role in the activist-honed iconography of the emergent civil rights movement.

SOUNDING BACK: NASCENT BLACK ACTIVISM, 1929–1934

Few African American protests during the early sound era were based on film content. Perhaps because not many films matched *Birth*'s virulent racism, for the remainder of the silent era evidence of NAACP film protest seems almost nonexistent.[5] Indeed, the NAACP often focused on legitimate theater rather than film, and although NAACP investigation of complaints against specific films began in the 1930s, it was limited to a few films.[6] The earliest picket lines of the sound era demanded equal employment and integration of movie venues rather than egalitarian film content. Sometimes, however, content seeped into these struggles. For example, in 1929, *Hallelujah!*'s music director Eva Jessye wrote a scathing, serialized exposé of the racial politics of the film's production in the Black press. She condemned MGM for its treatment of the Black cast, a slight that she said was registered in the original script's use of the word "nigger."[7] Beginning in the 1920s, Black projectionists and other movie house workers also fought for employment and equal wages at northern movie houses—striking, negotiating, and picketing (amid violent confrontations with police)—in New York, St. Louis, Philadelphia, Baltimore, and Chicago.[8] Their "Don't dream where you can't work" campaigns reclaimed Hollywood's performative space for a more worthy drama—that of civil rights demands. But though they recognized Hollywood's racism in employment, these protests were not based on film interpretation.

Between 1930 and 1935, the Black press records several protests of screen use of the plainest possible insult: the word "nigger." Black resentment so peaked with Paul Robeson's thirty-three utterances of the term in *The Emperor Jones* (1933) that theater owner Abe Lichtman petitioned United Artists for an epithet-free print.[9] In 1934, African Americans threw bricks at the screen in five cities during showings of *Carolina,* in which "nigger" was repeatedly uttered.[10] As a clear sign of derision poised among far more nebulous white-authored gestures, narratives, and images during the early sound era, the word became a complex metonym for Hollywood inequality. However, existing records suggest that activists did not explicitly address epithets as a civil rights issue, discussing it instead in terms of "insult" and "offense."

During this period of critical nascency, the Black press was nevertheless developing an analytical standard to evaluate screen presentation of civil rights issues—and its impact on viewers. For instance, Black press reviewers recognized *I Am a Fugitive from a Chain Gang* (1931) as exposing civil rights abuses practiced disproportionately against African Americans in the penal system. African American journalists recommended the film as "of real interest to our group" because "a large percentage of the men who work on these Georgia chain gangs are Negroes."[11] Not only did the *Chicago Defender* serialize Warner Bros.'

narrative on its pages, but several news stories recontextualized the film in terms of the "real experience" of Black chain gang victims.[12] Harry Levette, bit actor and Hollywood columnist for the Associated Negro Press, boldly revealed to readers that he had appeared in a lynching scene in *Hell's Highway,* one that, after PCA disapproval, ended up on the cutting room floor. His behind-the-scenes account, which refers to the film by its working title, *Liberty Road,* also revealed that a Black man had acted as assistant technical director for the camp scenes. It read:

> If you have never seen a manhunt following a bloody prison break, if you have never seen men shot down like dogs, treed by bloodhounds or chased into throttling quicksands, then when *Liberty Road* . . . is released, it will give you a portrayal of the real thing. But it will also give you a glimpse into the awful life of the southern prison camp lightened only by the chanted labor songs of the Negro convicts who as a rule are in the majority. . . . Your movie gossiper gets chased up a tree by bloodhounds. . . . Then we are captured by the posse which is nothing more than a mob and all hang on the spot to the limb of a big live oak. That's a little too realistic too and an unconscious hush would fall over the whole tense company at each rehearsal of the terrible scene. It is doubtful if the censors leave it in but if they do with those bodies shown dangling in the air, it may react as a terrible indictment of the lynching evil, as the Negro convicts are shown as unarmed and the least murderous of the desperate convicts. . . . Harry Smith, the famous middle-weight boxer . . . has a bit in the picture that shows him running blindly against a bank and shot down by a dozen rifles, falling covered with blood.[13]

Despite censorship, viewers could still see "the bloodhounds treeing us," said Levette. But perhaps because the censorship eviscerated the racial angle and most visible signs of lynching, no major civil rights organ used *Fugitive* or *Hell's Highway* to further the movement. Black press critics recognized the "social equality" in *Baby Face* (1933) and *Massacre* (1934) as well. One unnamed reviewer exclaimed that Lily and Chico are "inseparable all through the astounding picture. . . . Though Theresa . . . acts and dresses as a maid, she still acts and is treated as a companion of Barbara."[14] In *Massacre,* an unnamed reviewer noted that not only was Muse a "pal and confidant" to Barthelmess, but the film, in portraying "many injustices practiced upon the American Indian by the government agents," presented "a fine tie-up between the American Indian and the American Negro fighting for justice."[15] Reviewers also strained to find references to the Scottsboro Boys in films like *Wild Boys of the Road* (1933), where a white girl is raped on a train car—but by a white engineer.[16] However, these were interpretations only, limited to one or two critics and without direct links to activism.

One of the earliest indications of a move toward combining film interpretation with overt action was the response to *Imitation of Life* (1934). Black critics more widely debated the film's intended stance on civil rights. Some said it suggested, through melodrama, the pain of segregation. According to Black press critic Fay Jackson, "Fredi Washington utters a cry 'I want the same things other people enjoy,' that found an echo in the hearts of 12 million Negroes throughout the United States [a cry that had been smoldering] probably . . . since their so-called emancipation. . . . Washington expresses the desire for freedom and equal justice."[17] Even the Black leftist paper the *Negro Liberator* called *Imitation of Life* "without a doubt Hollywood's best picture of Negroes and Negro life," praising its "flashes of genuine understanding and sympathy for the Negro characters in the story."[18]

But Hollywood's best was still "just an imitation," said the *Negro Liberator*. "Subtly woven into the picture is the old, old theme of the loyalty of the Negro," and the film's conclusion reinforced the color line by sending Peola to a segregated school in the South.[19] For other Black press reviewers, Delilah, the Black cook who gives away her fortune—and control of her life—to the white woman whose house she tends, was so illogical that she became "propaganda" against Black people attaining their full rights.[20] The appearance of the word "nigger" in the original script, an element that the *Afro-American* discussed, seemed further evidence of racist intent.[21]

Despite reviewers' dissatisfaction in this era, I could find evidence of only one African American who took action against a film on the grounds of its position on civil rights questions. It was artist/activist Shirley Graham, who would later become the wife of W.E.B. Du Bois. She was, in 1934, a college student working at a laundry to support her two children and her education.[22] Graham not only disliked the film—and said so in print—but strove to keep it out of theaters. "Where in all the world will you find a black mother so stupid, so blind to the welfare of her child that she will thus utterly throw away her future and her happiness?" she asked of Delilah in an open letter to the manager of the Apollo Theater in Oberlin, Ohio. "We're proud of our mothers. We see them, stretching back of us, a long line of deep bosomed, proud, black women who have given of the last ounce of their strength and being that we might come into the full share of manhood and womanhood." Responding to the film's symbolic blocking, which situated Delilah and Peola in the basement, Graham insisted that Black mothers "never taught us to accept a 'basement' standard." Graham, who complained of being "forced into an apologetic explanation of the psychology" of *Emperor Jones* to her fellow students, found a similar psychological enigma in *Imitation of Life:* Graham reviled the idea of trying "to explain [to white collegiates why Peola] a colored girl in the City of New York . . . and who, we are led to believe, is well supplied with funds, [is] spending her evenings hanging around a basement staircase trying to catch a glimpse of the 'white folks' party. Imagine such a thing in New York!"

Based on more than mere offense, Graham's anti–*Imitation of Life* campaign was designed to protect the image of Black women struggling for their rights and who were actually autonomous participants in New York's cultural and political scene. "Peola throws a contemptuous veil across the young women who are today striving towards and demanding the best in life. We don't want *Imitation of Life* in Oberlin. We are working too hard to obtain the real thing."[23] Graham's impassioned protest stands against the grain of most other Black critiques of the film in its militancy. Speaking for a cadre of modern Black mothers, she told Hollywood that even the modish *Imitation of Life* left much to be desired in terms of cultural realism. Graham's criticism, as opposed to *The Birth of a Nation* protests earlier, was personal as well as political. It focused not on obvious racial insults but instead combined careful interpretation of mise-en-scène, reference to the film's effect on race relations, and a corrective view of Hollywood's Black women. In doing so, Graham's missive simultaneously discovered, described, and protested insults to Black womanhood grievous enough for her to call for the film's banning. Though apparently acting alone, Graham's protest was a flinty foreshadowing of the militancy to come.

FILM ACTIVISM AND THE POPULAR FRONT, 1935–1939

As I have suggested, during the 1930s the PCA and SRC generally ignored Walter White and the NAACP. Though this was clearly due to the industry's racism, it was also because the NAACP had not developed a solid film campaign in the early 1930s. While White wrote Will Hays protesting the sound version of *The Birth of a Nation,* he did not write to the industry regularly.[24] In the mid- to late 1930s, both the NAACP and Black leftists began to put to use film's potential for decrying injustice on the cultural front. A major issue during this era was lynching, which activists took up, as I describe below, in relation to *The Barbary Coast* (1935), *The Frisco Kid* (1935), *Fury* (1936), *They Won't Forget* (1937), and *Black Legion* (1937). *Gone with the Wind* (1939) raised various other civil rights issues for Black activists, who linked its depiction of slavery to the conditions of enslavement suffered by African Americans during the Great Depression. It is significant that Black journalists and activists used these films to stage increasingly complex public interrogations of the civil rights issues they engaged.

This discourse on the racial politics of the lynching film did not come out of thin air. Between 1931 and 1934, the communist newspaper the *Black Liberator* had pioneered a nuanced, interpretive critique of Hollywood-style screen lynching. The *Liberator* opined that downplaying Black suffering for international audiences was "good business for Wall Street," so Hollywood lynchings were inaccurate, absurdly motivated to enhance a love narrative, or worse, warned

Black spectators against resisting white southern justice.[25] Between 1933 and 1934, the paper called on Black workers to protest two films displaying Hollywood's lynch logic. One was Pathé's newsreel of the lynching of Claude Neal (1934), which not only glorified lynching but proved the filmmakers' inhumane participation in Neal's murder.[26] The reel was "so complete" that it could only have resulted from Pathé's extensive foreknowledge and complicity. The *Liberator*'s other call to action targeted *The Bowery* (1933), where, in a sequence played for comedy, three Chinese people burn to death as rival volunteer fire companies tussle over the right to use the hydrant. "While the ridiculous battle rages, the Chinese are calmly allowed to burn."[27] The *Liberator*'s calls apparently failed to result in pickets. But the Black left press's wave of inciting film interpretation (on lynching, Scottsboro, and Black representation more generally) challenged readers to make decisions and broadened Black attention beyond obvious insults like epithets to the ideology undergirding Hollywood's brutal disregard for suffering from racism and poverty.[28]

The NAACP's mid-1930s anti-lynching film activism began with the branches rather than the national office. In 1935, the Jersey City branch in conjunction with white communist Sylvan Pollack launched a nationally syndicated, bold publicity protest against two Hollywood films that "glorified lynching": *Barbary Coast* (1935) and *Frisco Kid* (1935).[29] Ironically, these seemingly pro-lynching films were the result of PCA self-regulation at work. In 1935, after moral reformers furiously attacked the industry for films sympathetic to gangsters, Breen and Hays sought a moratorium on gangster films.[30] Judging by their PCA files, Breen was so anxious on this front that he allowed gangster characters to be lynched onscreen in *Barbary Coast* and *Frisco Kid*, both set in turn-of-the-century San Francisco. The death-by lynching was one of several techniques filmmakers used to keep audiences from identifying with the gangster. But not only did the films show lynching, they seemed to justify it. In *Barbary Coast*, Breen took care to remove Black prostitutes from the film and warned filmmakers that censors might cut shots of the rope and silhouettes of the lynched men.[31] But he did not ask that they remove the lynching scenes nor did he mandate that the "Vigilantes" be punished according to Hollywood's standard compensating moral values. Similarly, in *Frisco Kid*, an erudite Vigilante leader claims "law has become a farce." Lynching is necessary "because it is better to have vigilance" than "anarchy," a line he utters only moments before his mob drags two men at gunpoint from prison and hangs them to the cheers of thousands. (They later shoot and trample another under their feet; see figure 27.) While Breen curbed gangster violence, he raised no questions about the vigilantes who lynched.[32]

The lynching scenes are graphic and facilitate identification with retributive violence. In *Barbary Coast*, this is displayed when, as the hitman Knuckles (Brian Donlevy) asks for a trial and for justice, the tightening noose interrupts his pleas

as it snuffs out his life. In *The Frisco Kid,* lengthy sequences reveal the victims as they are noosed and pushed out the window. The camera only cuts away after their fall from the ledge is sure. As the lynchers quietly leave the scene, a body swings with an ominous slowness in the back corner of the expressionistically shadowed frame. Notably, the mobs are far larger than in later films such as *Fury* (1936) and *They Won't Forget* (1937), and their orderly, mechanized energy resembles "town lynchings," which citizens attended in their Sunday best, unmoved while witnessing en masse the victim's frenzied struggle. Of course lynching's racial element is missing in both films; reputable white gentlemen in top hats lynch less reputable white gentlemen.

But African Americans invested in civil rights connected these lynchings to the much more common practice of white-on-Black lynching. A consistent and thoughtful critic of lynching in film was New York journalist Roi Ottley, whose creative treatise on civil rights, *New World A'Comin,* would be adapted into one of the most important civil rights radio shows of the 1940s.[33] Ottley left Harlem's Alhambra Theater "nauseous . . . because I heard my brothers loudly and vociferously applauding lynching." To Ottley, the film actually made "an *effort* to encourage and justify lynching when the law machinery breaks down" by having an orderly, self-righteous public lynch "evil" men. Ottley reminded entertainment column readers of the twenty lynchings in 1935. "Negroes . . . should be the first to resist and protest against this type of picture. We are the first to feel its adverse effects. Mob rule is never right . . . even when it is palmed off under such romantic labels as the 'Liberty League,' 'Vigilantes,' [and] 'Ku Klux Klan.'"[34] Despite the absence of Black characters in the film, Ottley connected the romantic, self-righteous *Frisco Kid* lynch mob to the anti-Black KKK. *Frisco Kid* and *Barbary Coast*—and local protests against them—complicate our notion that Hollywood's lynching films of this period were decisively anti-lynching, revealing the underbelly of this cycle. The Jersey City NAACP (and Ottley) brought public attention to the political implications of Hollywood's (conditional) support for lynching upon Black civil rights.

Ignoring local activists' critical view, the national NAACP and the *Daily Worker* publicly supported Hollywood's 1936–1937 prestige anti-lynching cycle. *Fury* arrived in Washington while Walter White was petitioning for the passage of one of the "thirty-odd" anti-lynching bills. Calling *Fury* "the most effective picture dealing with lynching yet," Walter White stopped just short of bringing the film to the halls of Congress; he scrambled to coordinate a screening for Eleanor Roosevelt and those congressmen important to the passage of the Costigan-Wagner anti-lynching bill before Congress adjourned because *Fury* was "just the stimulation to see that something is done."[35]

FIGURE 27. *Facing page:* Direct, even celebratory images of lynching were a problem for Black critics with *The Frisco Kid* (1935). Frame captures from *The Frisco Kid.*

Black journalist-activists crafted nuanced public interpretations of *Fury* that directly explained its relevance to Black civil rights.[36] These reviews are fascinating not only for their value to the public debate on lynching but because of how adeptly reviewers read the political and ideological significance of textual details. African American *Daily Worker* editor Benjamin J. Davis, who was a longstanding critic of capitalist Hollywood, praised the film but, unlike White, acknowledged Hollywood's contradictions in presenting lynching. He said *Fury* demonstrated that "anti-lynching sentiment now has a box office value for Hollywood" and was capable of making "new friends in the nation-wide movement against lynching."[37] While *Fury's* lynching was "engendered by the tongues of gossipy women" rather than the "background of race superiority poison, lynch terror and rape-frame ups against the Negro people," Davis noted that spectators were forced to recall "the horrible lynchings of more than 5,000 Negroes in this country since the Civil War" and to feel "the strong urge to do something about it." To Davis, *Fury's* mob implicated "the political and economic structure of the capitalist system": the Chamber of Commerce organized the lynch mob, which "received [protection] from the Governor down to the sheriff and his deputies."[38] Though they read *Fury* differently, White and Davis used the event of *Fury's* release to amplify existing public discussion of racial lynching and to augment social movement against it.

Similarly, Black journalists pushed for public recognition of *Black Legion's* connection to anti-lynching legislation, though the film erased the Legion's racism. In his column, Charles Isaac Bowen, a syndicated entertainment critic, reprinted for readers all of the judge's speech at the film's conclusion, claiming that "radio and moving pictures are playing an important part in molding public sentiment against lynching and secret terrorist organizations." Bowen admitted that *Black Legion's* closing speech might be "propaganda . . . but," he stated, "it makes you feel like a real American."[39]

In 1937, the national NAACP continued its use of film as a cultural component of the anti-lynching campaign by recommending Warner Bros.' *They Won't Forget* (1937) to its branches.[40] The NAACP's Youth Council even threw a picket line around the Times Square premiere supporting the film and linking it to lynching legislation.[41] Black press reviewers saw the film as yet another Mervyn LeRoy indictment of southern justice in the tradition of *I Am a Fugitive from a Chain Gang* (1932); some even claimed it featured "scenes and dialogue suggesting the Scottsboro case," a contemporaneous real-world drama Hollywood treated only indirectly.[42] Most Black press reviews focused on Tump Redwine (Clinton Rosemond), the Black man who only "barely escape[d] the necktie," and whose "moans," future Black filmmaker St. Claire Bourne claimed, contained a "resonant realism which is hard to dispel from the mind even after the picture is ended."[43]

Though Roi Ottley proclaimed that erasing lynching's interracial angle would earn the issue greater national support, several other Black critics tempered their praise because of the studio's questionable focus on a *white* lynching victim.[44] "You'll read what excellent propaganda against lynching it is," said Frances Ball of the *New York Amsterdam News,*

> but to my mind . . . the marked inference that a Negro janitor was really guilty of the crime for which an innocent white man was unlawfully lynched defeats the whole anti-lynching purpose. The truth of the matter . . . is . . . that the Negro is the worst victim of mob violence . . . and in too many instances the scapegoat for his white brother's crime. Turning the situation around only makes it seem as if they skip some Negroes who should be given a rope necktie.[45]

Baltimore Afro-American columnist Lillian Johnson pointed even more clearly to the film's racial repressions. Cleverly playing on the film's title, she mused, "I wonder if even the motion picture company wouldn't have forgotten to make the film if it had been the janitor who was lynched."[46]

Segregation was another issue Black activists took on in the late 1930s. In 1938, Black Greensboro students boycotted exhibitors that censored racial equality from films, in a protest that dynamically connected the politics of the segregated theatrical space with the ideological effects of the images screened there. When, at Independent Theater Owners Association meetings, exhibitors from five states (Mississippi, Arkansas, Tennessee, North Carolina, and South Carolina) announced their intention to ban images of "Negroes in scenes with white people on an equal social basis," and specified films like *One Mile From Heaven* (1937), *Artists and Models* (1937), *Vogues of 1938* (1937), and *Second Honeymoon* (1937), thousands of Greensboro citizens, led by the Black women students of Bennett College, enacted a month's long counter-movement to retain social equality.[47]

By the end of the 1930s, so many activists were engaged with the film question that even those protesting the same film often disagreed on what civil rights issues were at stake, as *Gone with the Wind* (1939) suggests. Despite David O. Selznick's subtle self-censorship, the racism of Margaret Mitchell's novel prompted preemptive Black protest before cameras rolled.[48] Through directly rhetorical confrontations such as resolutions and open letters, organizational activists struggled to name the film's danger and alert scriptwriters to its potential impact on Black citizenship.[49]

Upon the film's release, the most militant reviewers said it incited civil rights regressions. St. Claire Bourne heard one youthful Atlanta spectator tell his Black caregiver, "You'd be a slave too if it wasn't for the Yankees and my daddy wouldn't have to pay you," an ominous sign.[50] *New Amsterdam News's* Dan Burley called the film "pus" still "oozing" from the nation's civil war wounds: "The Negro . . . is still a chattel slave in the eyes of his former master." It was more than dangerous nostalgia; it explained the southern worldview that "kept Angelo Herndon on the chain gang" and "why the State of Alabama persists in holding in shackles the remnants of the nine Scottsboro Boys."[51] *GWTW* was not about the past but pressingly pertinent to contemporary denials of Black civil rights.

Walter White quietly exchanged letters with Selznick about *GWTW*, beginning in 1937 and spanning several years. But his minor role in the controversy indicates not only the nascence of NAACP counter-film activism, but also White's misgivings about complaint. Selznick was warm toward the national NAACP's representatives.[52] And White, as would become his practice, opted to "discuss" rather than protest, avoiding public criticism (White's second-in-command Roy Wilkins even wrote a sympathetic review in the *New York Amsterdam News*).[53]

But after its release, Selznick's polysemic film seemed akin to *The Birth of a Nation* to White. White warned both Selznick and the MPPDA that the revival of the Klan, *The Birth of a Nation,* and Confederate sentiment all seemed to be "by-products" of *GWTW's* popularity.[54] "Who knows how far this will grow?" White asked Selznick, or "what will be the repercussions upon the minorities in the United States and upon democratic government for us all?"[55] White's "protest" was articulate but came in the form of questions rather than demands—and even this came only after the film's release and through back channels.

Leftist labor organizations highlighted a different set of civil rights issues than White, lambasting the film's "bourbon ideology" and elision of slave suffering.[56] To Benjamin Davis, the film was culpable not for the resurgence of the Klan but rather for "moral justification" of Black slavery—and denial of Black people's "demands for full and complete democratic rights" during a Depression where "approximately half of the Negro population . . . is without work [or] relief of any kind." Such an obvious ideological maneuver deserved public disavowal.[57] The difference between White's reading and those of the left indicate the disparate historiographies of the civil rights struggle that these organizations held.

Differences in tactics also divided civil rights movie activists and bespoke differing views of what a freedom movement should look like. Black left activists opposed *GWTW* in the press and via "live" protests because they saw the film as a weapon against their own progressive movement.[58] Pickets were a crucial part of their arsenal because they saw the space in front of the theater—where the "palace" met the street—as a place of counter-discourse. In the case of *GWTW*, pickets, largely orchestrated by the National Negro Congress (NNC), met the film in four cities (see figure 28) and used a leftist lexicon to dramatically demonstrate that there was something wrong, something going on—and to demand that bystanders pay attention to the issues they addressed and take a stand for or against them. The NNC, through local councils, engineered hundreds of

FIGURE 28. Pickets and protestors interrupt easy spectatorship of *Gone with the Wind* (1939). Courtesy of the *Baltimore Afro-American* and the *Chicago Defender*.

interracial (though mostly white) pickets in Chicago and Brooklyn with placards boldly claiming that "*Gone with the Wind* incites race hatred," "*Gone with the Wind* is a blow to American democracy," "You'd be sweet, too—under a whip!" and "Negroes were never docile slaves."[59] These protests not only deterred patrons and confronted spectators with chattel slavery's brutality but they were public agitation: the physical presence of protesters around the movie house disrupted the easy flow of commercial entertainment and converted sites of pleasure into theaters of struggle.[60]

Black leftists abroad, more coordinated than the NAACP, followed suit. In London, C.L.R. James and George Padmore's International African Bureau and the League of Coloured People called for a boycott and asked that the Home

Secretary ban *GWTW* because, in Padmore's words, it showed African Americans as "lazy, stupid . . . and willing to remain in slavery, just the same way as some Britishers today defend the system of imperialism by alleging that Africans and Indians are not interested in their national independence."[61] For Padmore, *GWTW* could be linked to an international labor struggle—and the struggle of colonial people's throughout the world. Though White was a member of the NNC, he kept a firm distance from this and other leftist film campaigns, which broadened the implications of civil rights iconography to include issues like labor and colonialism.

In sum, in the Popular Front era, activists linked film to Black politics in ways that relied upon incisive cultural semiotics and film interpretation. No longer did activists point only to obvious racism and racial insults. Increasingly, activist responses—to the lynching film cycle and *Gone with the Wind*—built on the nuances of film content and its ideological effects on American racial politics. It was clear to activists that the cinema's lynching, its Black chattel, and its segregation had to be dealt with through decisive, premeditated activism. But widely differing views about Hollywood's relative racial malice and how to confront screen racism hampered a single concerted effort in the tradition of *The Birth of a Nation*.

THE RISE OF NAACP FILM ACTIVISM

Walter White and the War to End the Civil War

As the film industry grew and solidified, the national NAACP intensified its Hollywood campaign and became the civil rights group most influential and consistent in critiquing the cinema. However, during this era, NAACP branches and other groups and individuals seeking to expand the NAACP's purview and tactics challenged Walter White but were rebuffed in White's alliance-averse campaign of Hollywood diplomacy.

In the 1940s, the NAACP began to track Hollywood's treatment of Black people, although never comprehensively. OWI's push for the image of racial equality emboldened the NAACP, as did the pledge to improve Black representations White received when he and Wendell Willkie visited the studio heads in 1942.[62] Thus the national NAACP condemned more films in the war years than in the entire preceding decade.

The Supreme Court's decision in *Thornhill v. Alabama* (1940) had firmed up the right to picket. But though White would allude to this right, he would rarely exercise it.[63] As civil rights historians Martha Biondi and Beth Thompkin Bates suggest, the NAACP established a concessions-based program in the 1940s, one Bates argues led the organization to ask for—rather than demand—equality.[64] White was a businessman. He believed in civil discourse more than civil disobedience, and that through "friendly, frank facing of the facts," he could move Hollywood executives.[65] His mode was educational, and he sought to build upon Hollywood executives' liberal instincts. Because film was a creative field, White believed that too much protest was tantamount to censorship, which he generally opposed. His approach was to protest only when public relations failed and avoid pickets and boycotts in favor of open letters that brought NAACP concerns into the public sphere of community dialogue. In the process he managed to become the single most consistently influential civil rights activist with regard to classical Hollywood cinema. But Hollywood studios also used White. Studios banked on the hope that White would vent his disappointment through conversations with public relations agents instead of protests and that he would consider the long war for influence more valuable than the battle over any individual film.

Three central cinematic concerns dominated White's wartime agenda: the depiction of the Civil War era, civil rights abuses, and integration. The Civil War was White's greatest point of emphasis. So great was White's sense that Blacks' fate during World War II was tied up with the cinematic presentation of the Civil War that he was more concerned about films depicting white public figures who influenced the slavery debate—John Brown, Andrew Johnson, Thaddeus Stevens—than he was about Black representation. In 1941, he wrote to the "gentlemen" at Warner Bros. to "most vigorously condemn" *Santa Fe Trail's* (1948) "distortion of the facts," not in its characterization of Black slaves but rather of John Brown as an abusive father and crazed warmonger, condemnable in part for his irrational commitment to Black people. "We were shocked because Warner Brothers has shown an enlightened point of view on so many social issues. . . . Your picturization of those who were willing to destroy the union in order to perpetuate slavery as admirable characters cannot but do infinite harm."[66] White carefully walked the line between "trusted friend" and "protestor."

White criticized the same elision of the South's Civil War era racism with *Tennessee Johnson* (1942). As Koppes and Black note, White's involvement with the film began when OWI's Lowell Mellett asked him to read the script.[67] White's letter read like a history lesson: the film heroized Senator Andrew Johnson (Van Heflin), a Southerner who opposed Black emancipation and suffrage and created "the black codes" that effactually kept Black folks enslaved after the Civil War, while it condemned Thaddeus Stevens (Lionel Barrymore), the northern senator who fought hardest for Black franchise. How could such anti-Black sectionalism be squared with the democratic war effort OWI existed to support?[68]

Claiming that the *Daily Worker* was behind Black dissent, MGM told Mellett that the film would not affect Black morale because average African Americans knew too little about history to care.[69] Yet under OWI pressure, MGM reshot many sequences. Even in the finished film, however, Johnson, who claims that he and other "mudsills" are denied equality, seems the hero of the underdog and champion of voting rights. By contrast, Thaddeus Stevens thrives on Black subjugation, employing the film's only Black characters as his servants. When accused of having no sympathy for Blacks, Johnson counters that Stevens is "making slaves of the whites." "Here at the desk where Lincoln freed the slaves, I will free their former masters," he proclaims to surging musical accompaniment.

White tried to convince MGM that even the modified version was a danger to Black morale. He flew in Judge William Hastie (who would resign his position as civilian aide to Secretary of War Henry Stimson in protest against military segregation) to see the film in New York when changes were still possible before the national release. To Hastie, MGM's revisions left unchanged the impression it was right to "welcome [slave owners] back into the Union without any guarantee of change of heart. . . . A not too far-fetched analogy . . . would be for the United Nations to win the war and then welcome Hitler and Nazi Germany back into the society of nations, turning over to them the disposition of the lives and fortunes of Jews and other minorities."[70] Though MGM ostensibly removed the race question, Hastie linked the film's southern appeasement to contemporary civil rights: "The viciousness of the Bilbos, Connallys, and Rankins in 1942 is a heritage which all of us have to combat today because of the mistakes . . . made immediately after the Civil War."[71]

Though the NAACP and NNC reviled *Tennessee Johnson,* again their strategy and rhetoric contrasted. The NNC immediately publicized their dissent. In a mass petition signed by Black actor Canada Lee and Black musicians Teddy Wilson, Dean Dixon, and Hazel Scott, the NNC demanded that the OWI ban the film:

> Johnson once wrote: 'The Negroes have shown less capacity for government than any other race of people. No independent government of any form has been successful in their hands. On the contrary, wherever they have been left to their own devices they have shown a constant tendency to relapse into barbarism.' We are not going to stop Hitler with films like this to help him.[72]

By linking poll taxers of the past with those of the present and suggesting that the film "serves . . . the theory of white supremacy," the NNC made public and plain both the film's implicit denigration of Black people and its vaunting of white privilege.[73] In the wake of *Gone with the Wind* and in the early part of the war, White (and more vocal civil rights groups) fought primarily not against stereotypes, but against those films whose position on slavery worked against full African American citizenship.

Another issue that bothered White was the absence of civil rights abuses in Hollywood narratives. Before World War II, White called for direct screening of civil rights abuses very infrequently. During the war, however, White was firmer in his insistence that these abuses be aired. For example, White wanted *They Call Him Cooperation,* a short film about African American insurance company owner William Spaulding, to include a graphic beating: "On a very hot summer day, Mr. Spaulding went into a store in a building which he owns in Durham. He sought to buy a bottle of Coca Cola to quench his thirst. The young white Southern clerk beat Mr. Spaulding so unmercifully for daring to drink his Coca Cola in a 'white' store that he required hospital treatment." White pushed for engagement with brutal American racism, although he argued along lines that would appeal to Hollywood executives, suggesting that the episode showed Spaulding's "fortitude."[74] Southern civil rights issues again reached the screen in *In This Our Life* (1942). White told Warner Bros. that the scene where Parry Clay laments a Black man's chances in the southern legal system was "the outstanding example to date of honest [film] treatment of Negroes."[75] When censored prints showed in Harlem, White fought for restoration of expunged scenes. He also championed *The Ox-Bow Incident* (1943) as an anti-lynching film, one in which one of the victims—a Mexican often referred to by his race—is a person of color. A Black preacher, Sparks (Leigh Whipper), also delivers a conscience-searing speech about Black lynching. White further controlled the film's reception by confronting negative reviewers.[76]

But White did not get much traction on this front. As chapter 1 suggests, even the liberal OWI generally counseled studios against depicting interracial conflict during World War II. So White turned to commending Hollywood's interracial teamwork in films like *Bataan* (1942), *Sahara* (1943), and *Crash Dive* (1943) and pressed filmmakers to depict the reality of everyday, homefront integration in films like *Stage Door Canteen* (1943). For instance, White repeatedly insisted that producer Sol Lesser show racial intermixing in *Stage Door Canteen* despite recent race riots.[77] By missive, White commended the writer and director Preston Sturges for his "dignified and decent" integrated church sequence in *Sullivan's Travels* (1942), calling it "one of the most moving sequences I have seen in a motion picture for a long time."[78] The sequence is integrated in various senses; not only does a predominantly white chain gang respectfully and reverently enter the all-Black church (removing their hats as they enter), but the congregation receives the group with the spiritual "Let My People Go," thus likening the condition of chain gang laborers to both biblical and African American slavery. We also see that the chain gang is in fact integrated. Even more powerful are the crosscut images of Black parishioners and white prisoners laughing at the Mickey Mouse cartoon that is being screened in the church, which furthers the feeling of integrated cinematic space. The pastor emphasizes the equality of the congregation, stating, "We're all equal in the sight of God"—a statement that could refer as well to the racial differences between the gathered men as to the fact that the group contains both free and imprisoned men. As White's responses to films featuring integration and showing civil rights abuses evinces, he increasingly called on Hollywood to do its part in representing the ideal and reality of African American wartime civil rights.

Wartime NAACP Criticism Beyond Walter White

Though White's criteria became more civil rights–focused during the war, his centrality to the national NAACP's film activities actually receded, especially when he went abroad as a foreign correspondent. In White's absence, Roy Wilkins and several women at the organization developed a critique of Hollywood—and a campaign of action that was more militant than White's. Even when White was on the scene—and despite his dominance in public relations—he could not singlehandedly keep up with the films featuring African Americans. Accordingly, as he did with potential civil rights violations, White sent staff to investigate and report on pictures about which NAACP members, film reviewers, or concerned citizen complained, or which had content relevant to the race. The NAACP's roughly two-page review memos began with a film summary followed by an argument about the film's racial politics, using evidence, sometimes quite nuanced, from the film itself. When the NAACP did not share the perspective of the complainants, they instructed them to correspond directly with the theater manager or the studio.

Though most of the architects of the NAACP's film campaigns were women, they strategically mobilized the concept of "Black morale" to combat negative screen images of Black men. For example, it was national staffer Charlotte Crump who initiated the national's protest of *Tarzan's New York Adventure* (1942), flooding MGM's New York office with angry calls. It was not just that the Tarzan films seemed more racist in a wartime context, but that the franchise's imputation of Black savagery extended, with intended comedy, to African Americans in modern-day New York City. This smacked of recidivism, or worse: backlash. As letters of complaint and a review in *PM* reported, an African American janitor (Mantan Moreland) had a "long telephone conversation with an ape," an insult to Black humanity, masculinity, and modernity.[79] Crump called the scene "ridiculous . . . and . . . degrading to Negroes." Even more offensive, she claimed, was a scene where Tarzan, visiting the big city, identified an African American porter as being from the "Tambeezi . . . tribe. They put clothes on him, too." Beyond racial offense, MGM's escapism and lack of civic conscience bothered Crump. She concluded that "MGM is wasting a lot of time and money producing these [Tarzan] pictures at a time when the motion picture industry could be devoting its efforts more valuably and practically to portraying . . . the deep human drama inherent in any one of a thousand incidents growing out of the war," including those of the "colored allies of the United Nations . . . entirely neglected by the motion pictures."[80] Crump herself orchestrated the "telephone protest" and, as a publicity worker, also probably sent out the press release that was picked up by the Associated Negro Press distributed to Black readers nationwide.

The most important NAACP staffer with regard to film was Julia Elizabeth

Baxter, whose nuanced film readings set standards for the organization's official policy (see figure 29).[81] During her twenty-five years with the NAACP, Baxter became the head of the Information and Research division, which was responsible for numerous tasks vital to the organization's functioning, including monitoring statistics on housing and educational discrimination, lynching, and police brutality; keeping track of goals and achievements; feeding information to the legal and press divisions; and also, crucially, recommending organizational strategy.[82] Although Baxter played a crucial supporting role in the organization, she has been little discussed in historical accounts of the NAACP.[83] Baxter's memos, more than any other single source of information on film, set the organization into protest mode: the national NAACP launched official public complaints based on her reports on *Scrub Me Mama with a Boogie Beat* (1941), *Coal Black and the Sebben Dwarfs* (1943), *Duel in the Sun* (1946), and *Feelin' Alright* (1949).

During World War II, Baxter fought against disgraceful caricatures of Black soldiers, but also of Black women. She recommended a full-scale publicity campaign against *Coal Black and the Sebben Dwarfs,* Warner Bros.' racist animated short from 1943. In it, a mulatta chargirl named "So White" works for "Coal Black," a "wicked sepian queen of amazing physical proportions, exaggerated orange lips, [and] billowing bust." When Prince Chawrmin falls in love with So White, the queen hires Black mobsters to kill her, but the sexually available chargirl overcomes the mobsters with kisses. After the queen puts her into a deep

FIGURE 29. Julia Baxter, head of the NAACP Research Division. Courtesy of the *Baltimore Afro-American.*

sleep with a poisoned apple, a kiss from a dwarf soldier awakens her—and produces American flags at the end of her pigtails. Baxter lambasted the use of the Black woman's body as a site of grotesquerie and conquest. Obviously the story's Black dwarf soldiers were, as Baxter put it, "disgraceful"—a random, morale-bruising addition that derailed the Grimm Brothers' tale. But Baxter went further: the film's racist presentation was, in a sense, an irony worse than segregation itself. "The segregation and indignities to which colored soldiers are subjected is in itself damaging to national unity. That they should also be held up for derision by theatergoing audiences is inexcusable. Ironically enough, the American flag floats over the camp in which these boys are quartered."[84] She called for the film's complete withdrawal. But the official NAACP press release, which quoted Baxter's memo, omitted mention of the offense against Black women, perhaps because Baxter (or White) recognized that the outrage would more quickly follow a perceived strike against the Black soldier.

While White focused on civil rights historiography, Baxter engaged in a much more careful and elaborate analysis of dialogue, narratives, and visual evidence. Baxter's readings swiftly chopped Hollywood's fantasies down to size, cutting away the fluff to reveal their ideological work. For example, Baxter succinctly called MGM's *Music for Millions* (1944) "a mediocre film of uneven quality which capitalizes upon the theme of war to achieve a cheap, melodramatic sentimentalism."[85] Baxter appraised both characterization and the film's overall quality and tone. The movie's two "negligible" and "regrettable" Black characters were a porter played by Willie Best with his "customary eye-rolling, Stepin Fetchit act," and Jessie (Lillian Yarbo), a Black maid. Baxter focused on Jessie: "Insidious anti-Negro propaganda is spread throughout the film, focusing upon the Negro Jessie. A finer dramatic effect would have been achieved had Jessie never put in an appearance, but remained an invisible servant. . . . Her brief but surly entrance upon the scene fixes in the minds of the audience . . . the personification of questionable attributes ascribed to the negro domestic."[86] Baxter critiqued not the fact that African Americans were menials in the film, as White and Wilkins typically did, but *how* the maid was played and how this characterization would be interpreted in a wartime context. Although Jessie only appears once, and very briefly, the white women protagonists accuse her of sleeping all the time rather than working and even speak of kicking her in the pants. In light of Black wartime activism, the mock militancy and laziness of the Black maid seemed particularly egregious. "A far greater step toward . . . cementing race relations might have been . . . achieved had M-G-M distributed a few Negro soldiers or sailors in service camp audiences before whom the stars of the picture supposedly performed."[87] Also in her wartime portfolio was Baxter's review of Lester Cole's left-leaning *None Shall Escape* (1944), a film imagining postwar Nazi punishment at war crime tribunals. She resisted overpraising even this "democratic" film, noting in it the troubling studio tendency to tell even stories about racial persecution through "benevolent" white surrogates. The film admirably showed Jewish persecution, and its racially mixed tribunal (which included a silent Black member) showed that "all races are . . . affected by the war, and all will participate in the judging of its perpetrators." But "like the Negro in so many of our current movies . . . the Jews' story is not told by a Jew . . . but by . . . the benevolent . . . white majority." With her signature close attention to editing and mise-en-scène, Baxter suggested that "the flash back technique could have been utilized" to give Jewish subjectivity greater centrality.[88] Baxter thus went beyond critiquing anti-Black insults to shed light on Hollywood's ideologically bound omissions of the subjectivities of various marginalized peoples.

After the war, Baxter's review of *Duel in the Sun* took to task White's "close, personal friend" David O. Selznick.[89] *Duel in the Sun* is best known for challenging Christian morality, for which it received a "Condemned" rating from the Legion of Decency. Baxter, however, insisted that the film adopts a traditional racial morality, reinforcing the axiom that dark women are passionate and sexually immoral. Keenly observant of the intricacies of diction, dialect, and dress, Baxter felt that Vashti (Butterfly McQueen) served "primarily to bring humor to an unconvincing, heavy film," though she acknowledged that the role, albeit marginal, was "neither overwritten nor overplayed. While Miss McQueen is bandanna'd throughout . . . her costumes are quiet, there is no ogling, eyerolling or . . . hamming." But within its narrative context, even McQueen's unexaggerated character made the argument that "Negroes are stupid unreliable, delightfully naïve. They do not make the best servants but can be readily tolerated." Together Vashti, "half-breed" Pearl Chavez (Jennifer Jones), and her full-blood Indian mother (Tilly Losch) suggested that

> 1) Miscegenation is never successful. Indian women are immoral and make unfaithful wives who degrade the honorable names bestowed on them through marriage to white men. 2) Half breeds cannot constrain their violent elemental passions. In constant conflict because of the diversity of background which is theirs, they remain, essentially, children of the earth.[90]

Although *Duel in the Sun* bore no obvious insult to African Americans, in Baxter's reading the film's formation of Black and Indian women's "innate" qualities made a silent argument that the film's cinematic pleasures were based on the idea of racial inferiority. Unlike White, who was supremely concerned with developing relationships with Hollywood executives, Baxter closely read Hollywood films and edged the organization toward protest on the basis of the films' subtle ideological ramifications.

Prompted by Baxter, the national NAACP protested *Duel in the Sun* through an open letter to Selznick. Using Baxter's lexicon, Wilkins told him that the film contained stereotypes of "half-breeds" and of Black servitude. The board of directors decided against a "comprehensive, widely-publicized attack." But because of the "frequently expressed desire and intention to improve the portrayals of Negroes in [Selznick's] films," Wilkins felt obliged to share the organization's "disappointment over the old stereotype presented by the character Vashti and . . . the vicious underlying theme," a message that he also sent out via press release to many Black newspapers.[91]

Wilkins's willingness to offend White's Hollywood friends in the case of *Duel* was not exceptional. His tenure as acting secretary while White was abroad produced direct-action film activism on a level White would not have countenanced. In two months, Wilkins called for three film investigations (*None Shall Escape, Lifeboat, Sahara*), initiated two film protests against the studios (of *Lifeboat* and newsreels omitting Black soldiers), and issued a commendation for Columbia's depiction of a Sudanese soldier in *Sahara* (1944). Wilkins's most important campaign protested Hollywood's segregated newsreels, a protest that, as mentioned earlier, alarmed the MPPDA. All-American, a film company distributing to Black theaters, produced newsreels of Franklin D. Roosevelt at the Tehran Conference commending Black and white troops, but mainstream Hollywood newsreels enacted a kind of segregation by editing, going so far as cutting out the best shots of Roosevelt in order to avoid showing *any* Black troops. The NAACP branch of Petersburg, Virginia, the *Pittsburgh Courier,* and several Interracial Councils joined the national NAACP in protesting this form of screen segregation. The magnitude of protests so frightened studios that they asked the MPPDA to help manage it.[92] During the same period, Wilkins also openly stated that he did not think that White's Hollywood campaign was working. Since White's Hollywood visit, Wilkins argued that, "while some slight improvement has been noted here and there, and while two all-colored feature pictures have been issued, the results thus far have been disappointing."[93]

For Wilkins, the "keenest . . . disappointment" among Hollywood's postpledge offerings was *Lifeboat* (1944), a film he argued enacted a kind of segregation.[94] Though the Black and left press had high hopes for *Lifeboat,* since it starred dignified leftist actor Canada Lee, in the finished film Lee's character Joe Spencer is generally more ghettoized than the captured Nazi POW (William Yetter Jr.).[95] Giving Fox no time to explain itself, Wilkins issued a press release critiquing the film on the same day he sent William Goetz his protest. The OWI also worried about *Lifeboat* but focused on its seeming justification of mob violence and its Black stereotypes. But Wilkins focused on Joe Spencer, who could have been "easily . . . extended into real significance" but instead was segregated to his own corner of the raft, was called "Charcoal," only spoke when spoken to, and behaved "in the manner of a steerage passenger rather than an equally beset participant in the grim struggle for survival."[96] The length of Wilkins's brash letter, its lack of praise, and its simultaneity with the press release mark a sharp departure from White's low-pressure tactics and indicate the militancy that might have taken shape if Wilkins had been in control. Through the course of the war years, with the combined efforts of a more direct Walter White and the openly critical Baxter and Wilkins, the national NAACP strengthened its critical voice in regards to the cinema and began to combine praise with strategically measured grit and militancy.

PUSHING BACK FROM HOLLYWOOD'S LUNCHEON TABLE: WARTIME PROTEST OUTSIDE THE NAACP

Black impatience with continued denials of equality in media representation was palpable outside the NAACP. When asked in a 1943 *Pittsburgh Courier* poll "Should Negroes boycott motion pictures which portray them as inferiors?" a startlingly high number of respondents—82.7 percent—said yes, implicitly challenging Walter White's polite strategies. Among northern respondents the number advocating protest was even higher—92 percent.[97]

During the war years, Black film activism increased outside the NAACP as well. But the national NAACP largely ignored these struggles, despite invitations to join them. Outside the organization, Black journalists, whose critiques became increasingly sophisticated, were essential to this growing screen militancy. One fascinating wartime protester was Almena Davis-Lomax, editor of the Black *Los Angeles Tribune.* She and Leon Washington of the *Los Angeles Sentinel* set pickets on *Tales of Manhattan* (1942), a film without direct racial insults, but which, despite its urbane title, depicted African Americans as ignorant sharecroppers rather than modern citizens. Their protest raised the bar for Hollywood's treatment of the race, making "Hollywood's apparently endless number of Negro caricatures" picket-worthy.[98]

Tales of Manhattan followed a tailcoat on its surprising migration from owner to owner. The film was produced by Boris Morros (who was later revealed to be a Soviet double agent) and had progressive undertones.[99] In the film's final episode, the tailcoat—with $43,000 in the pocket—falls from a plane into a remote, all-Black, sharecropping community. Esther (Ethel Waters) chastises her husband, Luke (Paul Robeson), who wants to use the money himself, and she insists that he give it to Reverend Lazarus (Eddie "Rochester" Anderson), who decides the money should be equally shared by all community residents. In the final sequence, Luke heralds the day when "there will be no more rich and no more poor," signaling the sequence's leftist message. But the episode demonstrated that even left-leaning white producers could engage in stereotypes. As *PM* noted, why did the all-Black sequence in a film called *Tales of Manhattan* have to be set in a space of timeless backwardness, rural primitivism, and fantasy? Harlem was a structuring absence. Not only was the sequence and its community segregated, but all of the Black characters speak in heavy dialect, and, seemingly ignorant of modern technology, they assume that the money has come from "hebben" rather than an airplane. Robeson, a friend of Morros, reportedly failed to persuade him to conclude with images of the community after it had benefitted from the money.[100]

Rather than writing resolutions, Almena Davis-Lomax showed up in person to protest. She lacked the bonhomie with Hollywood moguls that White had. But she knew how to get to them. Not only did she send copies of her published film review to the actors, director, and producers, but she organized pickets at the film's first showing in Los Angeles, where the producers lived and would presumably be forced to watch her counter-spectacle unfold. Her picketers' signs read, "Hollywood, take your feet off the Negroes' neck," and, more apocalyptically, "*Tales of Manhattan* is the bitter end!" She also organized protesters under the banner of the "March on Washington Movement–West Coast Branch," linking the struggle against screen caricatures explicitly to A. Philip Randolph's threatened militant civil rights March on Washington.[101] Her protests, unlike White's, made Black militancy quite literally visible to studio officials at the Los Angeles premieres.

Davis-Lomax's correspondence with White evinces her careful study of Hollywood films and their depiction of Black folks—one honed by her consistent film reviews for her paper and attendance of L.A. preview screenings. She sent White a long list of "Anti-Negro films" worthy of pickets—*Gone with the Wind* with its "happy, carefree, well-cared-for" slaves; *Harlem's Black Magic,* where newsreel company March of Time "hired Negro actors to make stupid grimaces and then used pictures in short about 'voodoo' in Harlem"; "Jungle Films," in which Blacks were "shown as timid" and "afraid of whites"; and *The Little Colonel* (1935), where "Hattie McDaniel is made to say she didn't want to be free," just as Louise Beavers had in *Rainbow on the River* (1936).[102] A running theme for Davis-Lomax was the critique of Black timidity. Black slaves in Hollywood films were "anxious to be servants only" while white confederates were valiant fighters for a "noble cause." When Davis-Lomax approached White for help with her protests (and with countering Black entertainment columnists who "traitorously" supported Hollywood), White rebuffed her, perhaps because of his budding relationship with Fox (which made *Tales of Manhattan*) and to avoid attacking films that stood somewhere between open racial disparagement and "improvement."[103] Davis-Lomax claimed her direct-action campaign was effective. She told White that several Black actors reported that MGM's decision to remove crap-shooting from *Cabin in the Sky* was a direct result of her work.[104] Throughout her career Davis-Lomax drew the hardest line of any Black activist in terms of film depictions of the race. She was the most consistent picketer of Hollywood films of any Black activists of the Hollywood era. In her careful, sustained interpretation of Hollywood's Black backwardness as itself a kind of racism, she discovered insult among deliberately polysemic representations.

Where Davis-Lomax attempted to enlist White's support, Leon Washington,

Davis's collaborator in the *Tales of Manhattan* fight, challenged White's Hollywood politeness. "With all due respect to Mr. White and his method of attack
via the luncheon table," Washington felt a more grassroots campaign was in
order. "Hollywood is the most vicious race-baiting, jim-crow, propaganda dis-
seminating agency in America. . . . Hollywood could contribute much to Negro
morale and to the progress of the win the war campaign by sabotaging its Uncle
Tom, Aunt Dinah, buck dancing, and crap shooting scenes."[105] Washington
and Davis also campaigned for equal hiring in Hollywood—especially of Black
skilled workers, writers, and creative talent. Though most Hollywood Black
actors resented Davis and Washington, Paul Robeson joined their protest and
called the film "ridiculous, fantastic, and a slur upon the race." Feeling duped, he
agreed to join pickets if they formed in New York.[106] *Tales of Manhattan's* protests evince a growing sentiment among Black journalists that cinematic representation was worthy of more vigorous and sustained activism than the NAACP
would countenance.

STEREOTYPES AND CIVIL RIGHTS: LATE WAR
AND POSTWAR BLACK FILM PROTEST

By the end of World War II, Black activists and reviewers were increasingly pushing for a major break with Hollywood's racist past. Over the course of 1944, 1945,
and 1946 some of the most effective protests of narrative films of the classical
era emerged. Black activism caused the shelving of two films, both prospec-
tive Lena Horne vehicles at MGM—*Uncle Tom's Cabin* in 1944 and *St. Louis
Woman* in 1945—and altered production plans of a third—*Song of the South.* The
national NAACP, though, steered clear of central involvement in the public out-
cry over these films and privately supported *Uncle Tom's Cabin.* In each of these
cases, activists engaged in careful interpretation of films to relate them to pressing civil rights issues. But the national NAACP had an increasingly offscreen
role in these protests, as new upstart organizations became the public voice of
Black dissent.[107]

The primary issue for activists in each of the era's major film protests was the
nostalgia for Black docility, backwardness, and primitivism—that hazy, grease-
lensed historiography that wrote out Black militancy and left Black folks still in
image-bound enslavement. Cinema's exploitation of the Black primitive—and
refusal to acknowledge Black modern existence—had caused several protests in
the 1930s. Pseudo-documentary films like *L'Afrique Vous Parle* (1931), where filmmakers reputedly fed an African native to lions, and *Ingagi* (1930), which suggested
that "African women have had children whose fathers were gorillas," brought
protests from civil rights activists such as Ida B. Wells.[108] Black primitivism even
became the basis for the NAACP's first wide-scale publicity protest, leveled
against March of Time's "documentary" short *Harlem's Black Magic,* a newsreel

claiming that one-third of Harlem residents were addicted to voodoo (over images of exaggerated hand-waving, occult voodoo charms, and Black bodies writhing in spiritual ecstasy) that the NAACP wanted withdrawn and replaced with real Harlem news.[109] The wartime all-Black features were supposed to stoke Black morale, but even white mainstream critics Archer Winsten and Manny Farber lambasted the Jim Crow backwardness of Cabin in the Sky (1943).[110] And Black composer William Grant Still resigned in protest from his role writing the score for Stormy Weather (1943) because of racially demeaning demands that he make his music less "refined."[111] Delta Sigma Theta Sorority joined Still's Stormy Weather protest, asking Irving Mills to abate his insistence on crass movement and music in a film supposedly focused on Black accomplishments.[112]

Such negative publicity had often succeeded in putting the studios on the defensive after a film's release. But in the postwar era, even before their release, films featuring chronotopes of Black premodernity seemed a direct impediment to Black attainment of full citizenship, one so important that it often replaced concern about screen depictions of major civil rights issues as the centerpoint of activists' agendas.

In September 1945, many Black and labor organizations condemned the theatrical restaging and proposed cinematic remake of Uncle Tom's Cabin, with Lena Horne and Paul Robeson slated to star. In the postwar era, it became to Black critics yet another reassertion of the entrapping plantation chronotope. The Los Angeles Tribune and Los Angeles mayor Fletcher Bowron's Committee on Homefront Unity recommended that Will Hays ban the film on the ground that it would cause "racial tension." Leon Hardwick's Interracial/International Film and Radio Guild (IFRG), one of the many anti-racist film groups formed at the war's end, directly confronted the film's slated producer Arthur Hornblow in an interview: "We tire of seeing ourselves depicted constantly as bootblacks, porters, maids and now—of all things—slaves."[113] When Hardwick warned of "international repercussions"—that "Negroes, labor unions and liberal whites all over the country would arise" to fight filming of Uncle Tom's Cabin—Hornblow, genuinely surprised at this Black resistance, retorted "Uncle Tom's Cabin is an American Classic." MGM's production, he averred, would be no burlesque but rather "entirely serious." "Our sympathetic treatment . . . will smoke out all the Simon Legrees of today." Hornblow claimed he was a "liberal," personally acquainted with "several colored leaders for some time," and that the Black "home life, . . . joy . . . and sorrows on the plantation" would be shown as "no different from those of any other peoples."[114]

This did not placate the Black press. For many the problem was the screen "revival and re-portrayal" of slavery itself. Any film showing "America's dark days" of slavery on screen, E. B. Rea of the Baltimore Afro-American stated, would be strongly resisted.[115] Capitalizing on the rhetoric of "morale" and the motif of Black wartime militancy, Rea made a claim that was perhaps a veiled threat of

Black violence against the film—that *Uncle Tom's* "March of Slaves" would be "propaganda as inflaming" for Black Americans as the Bataan "March of Death" campaign was for all Americans.[116] Other critics directly linked *Uncle Tom's* production to the repeal of wartime civil rights promises and the resurgence of American racial conditions dangerously similar to Black slavery. "Too close and too apparent are the everyday efforts of the 'white supremacy' advocates to restore a new slavery. If MGM wants a couple of first-class race riots stemming from moving picture theaters, it could provoke them quickly," said one unidentified journalist.[117] Another explained that in its day, "*Uncle Tom's Cabin* pointed out the brutality that the slave masters wreaked upon pitiful helpless victims" but it enshrined "Uncle Tom . . . the mealy mouthed Negro who was afraid to lift his voice in protest even after protest became possible. . . . Now is not the time to release this classic in a film medium. We are in effect still fighting the Civil War and all it represents. . . . Southern Congressmen are locked in battle with liberals because . . . the Federal government [is, in the eyes of the South,] giving too much equality to Negroes."[118]

By contrast with the Black press, the national NAACP (deriving its opinion from Julia Baxter's review of the play) argued for *Uncle Tom's Cabin*. The organization emphasized Stowe's importance to abolition and that protestors were taking the term "Uncle Tom," which had acquired new meanings since the book's writing, out of original context. "Uncle Tom," White wrote to Reverend John Haynes Holmes, "was a revolutionary."[119] Following local NAACP branch protests, White circulated a memo discouraging local branches from protesting the play.[120] Ultimately, under public pressure from vice presidential candidate Henry Wallace, the Black press, and Lena Horne (who refused the offered role "in protest"), MGM shelved the film.[121]

Black journalists spearheaded yet another protest in 1945 against a proposed MGM project—*St. Louis Woman,* a play that Countee Cullen and Arna Bontemps were adapting from Bontemps's 1931 novel *God Sends Sunday.* This play also failed the developing standard of respectable, dialect-free Black urbanity. For Leon Hardwick of the IFRG, the list of objectionable elements—which included the racetrack setting, the "Dis and Dat" dialect, all the "killing, vice, trash, and passion"—was topped by the intention to cast Horne as the "loose" Della. The film threatened Horne's respectable position as "an idol to her people, a symbol of the highest type of Negro womanhood."[122] Actress Fredi Washington, who publicly opposed the film in her *People's Voice* column, took a position less grounded in the middle-class politics of respectability: the problem was not that Horne would play a fallen woman but the character's lack of genuine humanity.[123] Nevertheless, the *St. Louis Woman* protest, perhaps more than any other of the period, instantiates the move away from concern about concrete civil rights issues and a venture into the realm of intuited intangibles linked to the primitive.

The national NAACP believed the film was not enough like the white social problem films Walter White championed. White worked to avert the production, likewise building up an argument on the grounds of "decency" and stereotype rather than civil rights proper. According to White, the work figured Negroes as "pimps and prostitutes with no redeeming characteristics."[124] In a draft of a letter from White to producer Arthur Freed, the leader explained in social scientific language that stereotypes were "a stimulant in racial friction through . . . breeding of contempt" and were "an obstacle to the attainment by the Negro of his rightful place as a first class American citizen."[125] Privately to Countee Cullen, White spoke in franker terms of "this critical juncture of the Negro's history as the war ends. . . . What an irony it is that white people should do a play" like " 'Deep are the Roots' . . . one of the hardest hitting and most uncompromising plays on the Negro . . . while two colored authors should do one which portrays every cliché and every hoary myth about the Negro which our enemies have attempted to perpetuate."[126] White also desired to protect Lena Horne, for whom he had a fatherly affection. Though Horne had almost been a femme fatale in *Cabin in the Sky* and in her first radio appearance on the program *Suspense,* White and Hardwick wanted to keep her from menial or sordid roles.[127] Responding to this pressure, Horne publicly turned down *St. Louis Woman,* a protest that likely imperiled her status at MGM but which certainly helped seal the film's fate.[128]

Song of the South was the third in Hollywood's cycle showcasing the Black primitive to draw protest in a two-year period. Though Disney sought deniability by making it unclear whether *Song of the South* was set before or after the Civil War and by prominently featuring Academy Award winner Hattie McDaniel, many Black onlookers read the film as a veiled attack on civil rights, as Matthew Bernstein suggests.[129] Though *Song of the South* protests have been discussed before, the local activism that was the mainstay of this struggle has remained underexamined. Protests greeted the film's announcement from the American Council on Race Relations (ACRR), the National Negro Publishers Association (NNPA), the American Jewish Council (AJC), and the IFRG, among others. In September 1944, the National Negro Publishers Association (NNPA), headed by *Sentinel* editor Leon Washington, challenged the film's dialect and "these antebellum roles."[130] The Black press also reported that two Black actors (Clarence Muse and Tiny Bradshaw) quit in protest against the film's racism, evincing the important and continuing significance of the movie set as itself a racial battleground in the screen struggle for equality.[131] As with *Cabin in the Sky,* even mainstream sources like the *New York Times* saw the film's racism.[132]

The national NAACP's role in opposing *Song of the South* was minor, as Matthew Bernstein and Thomas Cripps argue, employing a campaign of personal letters.[133] In fact, White's public statement on the film, one issued before he had seen it, audaciously praised its technical elements while condemning its depiction of the master-slave relationship.[134] After *Parents Magazine* gave the film a medal, White stepped up his opposition, protesting the award in a press release. But even then his wording suggests that he was ambivalent. White said the film "glorifies racial stereotypes and virtually justifies slavery by picturing it as an idyllic system," suggesting that such "half-truths" were the underlying cause behind "racial friction."[135]

Upon the film's release, some NAACP locals with a more radical, leftist bent again challenged White's reticence, picketing for the film's ban. For example, when the manager of the Warner Bros. Theater in San Pedro, California, told the local NAACP branch to admit that *Song of the South* pictured a "beautiful period in our lives . . . and in yours," they defied this interpretation by amassing thirty NAACP, National Maritime Union, and Council for Civil Unity picketers to corral the theater, claiming that "the only 'Song of the South'" was a dirge for all the Blacks "lynched since VJ day."[136]

The National Negro Congress was even more active than it had been with *Gone with the Wind,* using *Song of the South* as a tool to unmask "white supremacy" through performative dissent in the streets. The NNC held picket lines in both Brooklyn and Times Square and also at the Pantages RKO Hillstreet Theater in Los Angeles.[137] Drawing on the entertainment politics of New York's Café Society, in this protest and others the NNC asked film actors to "star" at protest rallies. The "soft politics" of stars' participation turned protest into a kind of performance. Using Brechtian techniques to link popular culture and activism, they helped convince spectators that actors were not studio property and could publicly stand apart from racist spectacles. *Bataan* star Kenneth Spencer, the NNC Theater division spokesman, led a group of picketers at the film's Times Square exhibition and called on New York City to refuse a permit to the film and others "entrenching the evils of Bilboism in this country."[138] "The NNC understands *The Outlaw* was banned due to your efforts on the basis of its immorality. We call on you to stop the showing of *The Song of the South, Abie's Irish Rose,* and any other pictures which unfavorably stereotypes any nationality or race of people," read one press release.[139] Stars not only employed political oratory but made the viability of integration visible, audible, and, by their energy, palpable. Nineteen picketers, Black and white, marched with signs stating, "We fought for Uncle Sam not Uncle Tom" and "The 'Song of the South' is slightly off-key because Disney says it's wrong to be free." The protests engaged in elaborate counterspectacle, topped by burning "Jim Crow" in effigy.[140] Police arrested protestors in New York for disorderly conduct.[141]

In Los Angeles, the Mayor's Committee for Civic Unity, which had stood against *Uncle Tom's Cabin,* sent a letter of protest to Disney.[142] The American Youth for Democracy of Ohio, under the leadership of local activist Sylvia Hashmall, fought for the film to be withdrawn in Cleveland.[143] For Hashmall, screening "Negroes as bandanna-headed, illiterate, ignorant people" served to prove that they "rate nothing better than second-class citizenship because of their inherent inferiority."[144] Several locals of the American Federation of Teachers also raised their voices in protest. Paul Cook of the Local 27 in Washington, D.C., reviled the use of supposed Negro dialect for the cartoon animals and claimed that Disney had missed a valuable opportunity: "Although Negroes could have been portrayed as artisans and business people . . . the picture offers . . . the Negro . . . whose only thought is to help solve the problems of white people."[145] The ethos behind *Song of the South*'s Black and labor protest was summed up by a *Chicago Defender* critic who suggested Remus's relationship to white adults showed him to be an "ineffectual Uncle Tom. . . . As long as Hollywood refuses to portray modern Negroes truthfully, flights into the servile past, no matter how sincere, will always be resented."[146] As *St. Louis Woman, Uncle Tom's Cabin*, and *Song of the South* suggest, Black and left-wing organizations connected Hollywood's postwar nostalgic throwbacks to Black abject primitivism directly to the retrenchment against Black civil rights—casting each film as a fantastic extension of the logic of segregation.

Activism demanding screen civil rights and an end to Black backwardness also emerged in unexpected places. An interracial group of ninety inmates at Connecticut's Danbury Prison, which had recently won a battle against "Jim Crow seating" in the auditorium, wrote the warden protesting *Col. Effingham's Raid* (1946), a B-film produced by Lamar Trotti featuring both a white man (Charles Coburn) who fights to preserve a Confederate monument and an easily frightened Black servant (Nicodemus Stewart). The inmates claimed that films "showing Negroes as naturally inferior people fit only to be servants and lackeys of the white 'master race'" were incommensurate with rehabilitation.[147] But whether protesters targeted A- or B-films in the postwar era, the focus had shifted from using film activism to publicize civil rights abuses to calling for repression of films that denied equal Black citizenship by dwelling on the segregated or plantation past.

Although most civil rights activists critiqued the return to the plantation, one postwar plantation film seemed on the edge of showing the grit and rebellion that was a constant undercurrent in the lives of actual enslaved people. The film was *The Foxes of Harrow*, based on a novel by Black author Frank Yerby. Yerby's novel had been epic—spanning from before the Civil War to the end of Radical Reconstruction. It had also been focalized equally through Black and white characters, and even these white leads were markedly off-white: Stephen (played by Rex Harrison) was Irish and Odalie (Maureen O'Hara) was Creole. The Black characters included not only a mulatta woman who comes to be Stephen's mistress but also a Black child, Lil' Inch, whose mother, sensing his greatness, tries to save him from a life of slavery by throwing him into the Mississippi River. She fails but drowns herself in the process. L'il Inch grows up to become a government leader during Radical Reconstruction. Twentieth Century–Fox, with pressure from the Hays Office, removed miscegenation from *Foxes* and any inkling of rape (both miscegenetic and within the Black and white races). Zanuck also all but cut the entire Reconstruction period, one that had caused much trouble with earlier films such as *Tennessee Johnson*. But standing firm is the scene of La Belle Sauvage (Suzette Harbin) proclaiming her son a "warrior for him people" and fighting off her master's insistence to take the child from her. Her desperation to kill her child rather than see him enslaved flies in the face of the film's portrayal of Stephen as a benevolent, sympathetic slave master and raises the question of slavery's unseen abuses, one of which, this bedroom scene strongly suggests, is rape. However, even this more revelatory narrative failed to impress many Black press critics familiar with the novel on which it was based. Alvin Moses of the *Philadelphia Tribune* reviled how cavalierly Hollywood could "meat chop a great plot."[148] Bob Queen of the *Afro-American* claimed that even the "camouflaged" mulatto lacked warmth with Stephen and made it impossible to rewardingly pretend she was mixed.[149] Black press columnist Harry Kegan called the destruction of Yerby's book "complete and tragic!" Yerby's book, he noted, was the only one since *Uncle Tom's Cabin* to condemn "the entire social system of the antibellum [*sic*] South." In the finished film, the only "flash of Yerby was the instant at which the slave girl kills herself rather than see her son grow up a slave."[150] Lillian Scott, one of the most important film critics of late 1940s civil rights images, reviled particularly a scene where the slaves refuse to cut the cane until their white mistress, "like a true lady of the old South, whipped them out of hiding. They cut that cane. Yes, suh."[151] The critics of *Harrow* felt bitterly the changes to the script and critiqued even this atypically rebellious plantation melodrama for its ultimate insistence on Black servility.

POSTWAR SOCIAL PROBLEM FILMS

By the late war years, many local leaders and even national NAACP staffers believed White's Hollywood diplomacy had failed and wanted the branches to initiate a mass movement.[152] Public relations man Neil Scott counseled White: "We feel that entirely too much energy has been devoted to the individual motion picture companies rather than to the theatre owners and exhibitors whom the individual motion picture companies depend upon to sell their product."[153] In a long memo, Scott outlined a coordinated branch campaign to convince exhibitors to keep scenes with Black performers in films—and encouraged the NAACP to publicize any racial omissions in the Black press. Even Wilkins publicly departed from White, touting the merits of a boycott strategy. In 1946, Wilkins wrote:

> While we have made mighty protests and have used persuasion and other kinds of arguments with Hollywood, we have not had any real power to change the situation. Real power would be the boycott to force the picture makers and exhibitors

either to make better use of Negroes or suffer the loss of profit. . . . Under the new federal court ruling abolishing block booking, . . . if [an exhibitor's] patrons are 50 per cent Negro and he knows they will boycott films showing their race in a bad light, he will refuse to buy those films.[154]

But White believed he was finally making headway. Between 1945 and 1949, he asked numerous Hollywood producers if he could read scripts on liberal/democratic themes.[155] The year 1949 represented the pinnacle of Walter White's influence among Hollywood studio executives. As the studios sought to do social problem films on race, they not only featured African Americans in major roles, but also began to deal with American civil rights violations. At the studio's request, Walter White reviewed scripts for *Intruder in the Dust* (1949) and *Pinky* while Jane White, his daughter, reviewed the script for *No Way Out.* This active vetting by the NAACP made White, temporarily and unofficially, into the Black film czar he had sought to be in 1946 when he tried to create a Negro Bureau in Hollywood.[156] Finally, White had the opportunity not only to shape the discourse on civil rights–centric films but to shape the films themselves.

But while White highly praised many studio films broaching civil rights issues, he failed to publicly support a burgeoning independent film movement that more forcefully addressed these themes. For example, in 1947, White praised *Gentleman's Agreement,* arguably the first studio postwar ethnic problem film, but disregarded the first film to show Black people as lynching victims, *The Burning Cross.* Although NAACP representatives attended a preview screening—and the film broached Black voting rights—the national NAACP did not lend publicity support to the film, opining that although the treatment of civil rights issues was "alright," the film was of low technical quality.[157] By contrast, several NAACP branches saw the civil rights mettle of B- and independent films like *The Burning Cross, Strange Victory,* and *Storm Warning* and used them to publicize their voting drives and anti-Klan activism.[158]

What is more, NAACP records on *Pinky* showcase the fragility of White's concessions-based protest strategy and the limits of studios' civil rights tolerance. Darryl Zanuck sent White the script in July 1948 and White distributed it to staff and others whom he trusted, including white *Ladies' Home Journal* columnist Poppy Cannon, Jane White, and Roy Wilkins. These consultants agreed that the film subtly advocated segregation and attacked Black civil rights advancement. Pinky's "childish" need to seek advice from her "mammy" and Miss Em, an unreconstructed plantation segregationist, seemed illogical and an implicit southern concession. Granny, hoping to reciprocate the care the white woman once gave her, compels Pinky to volunteer to nurse sick Miss Em. In this, Wilkins saw a philosophy that, while "Granny undoubtedly believes" it, "is a part of slavery days and should not be projected into a film for exhibition in 1948–9. When the slavery era really becomes history, and when we have ceased fighting the Civil War all over again in our search for interracial peace and justice, producers and writers can project the slavery philosophy in its proper perspective."[159] Although White's cover letter was polite, the NAACP's overall mockery rankled Zanuck. He marveled at Wilkins's statement that "although Granny undoubtedly believes" her philosophy, it should not be in the film, a position he thought made Wilkins into a kind of censor. Citing his own bravery on social issues, in *Gentleman's Agreement* he admitted he had to balance "enthusiasm with . . . responsibilities to the stockholders, to the public and to the truth as I see it." The best a Hollywood liberal like Zanuck could do was "make the white majority experience emotionally the injustice and daily hurts suffered by colored people."[160] Zanuck's response revealed Hollywood's glass ceiling for Black representation and the end of Fox's cordial relationship with the NAACP, one ironically, but not coincidentally, timed with the tapering of war and postwar liberalism. Though the NAACP failed to radicalize Zanuck's liberalism, their efforts clearly inspired Zanuck and announced with a bitter cynicism the postwar militant position of the organization.

NO WAY OUT, CENSORSHIP, AND THE N-WORD

As I have suggested in chapter 3, though Zanuck was angered by NAACP members' unveiled criticism, their reaction to *Pinky* influenced him. Their critique gradually took effect and contributed to his creating a stronger, more viable treatment of race in *No Way Out*. White recognized in *No Way Out* the candid treatment of race hatred that the organization had long promoted. Accordingly, the national NAACP's response to the film was immediate and ecstatic. White positively reviewed it in the Black press; he told branches that it was "one of the most forthright films ever made . . . against race prejudice," and he hosted a luncheon honoring Twentieth Century–Fox.[161] White even claimed that "nationwide concern about human rights is in part due to the new type of pictures Hollywood is making about the Negro" and that *No Way Out* was helping to "close the gap between protestation and practice of democracy."[162] When Pennsylvania, Boston, and Chicago threatened to ban the film as "hate-arousing," White staunchly—and with much effort—defended it, calling branches to resist its censorship.[163] White used the film to call attention to civil rights struggles in the North, claiming that Chicago (which had seen more "bombings and mob attacks on Negro homes" than Birmingham) was full of "bigots like Ray Biddle" and needed "to see the picture" as public education against racial violence.[164]

It was at this moment that the NAACP began to protest not representation but censorship. As I have suggested, the protest of what was missing or absent from Hollywood—of repression itself—was not new.[165] In the postwar era, as White realized the difficulty and dangers of direct creative criticism, he steered the NAACP toward a method at which they could be more effective—the legal struggle against racist film censorship. When, as I have discussed, in 1947, MPAA president Eric Johnston filed suit against the Memphis censor's banning of Hal Roach's *Curley,* he opened up a new era in the fight against racial censorship. Thereafter, NAACP lawyers used the legal strategies developed in housing discrimination and voting rights cases to fight censorship of racial tolerance films, even in cases where the NAACP did not like the film. For example, Walter White offered to file an *amicus curiae* brief against *Pinky*'s Texas censorship (a case that would reach the Supreme Court) because "if so mild a picture . . . can be banned, all of the work that [Eric Johnston], Wendell Willkie, and I have put into the fight for more decent roles for Negroes . . . may go down the drain."[166] White and the NAACP's legal team also attempted to legally reverse southern snipping of scenes with Cab Calloway and Lena Horne and films like *The Burning Cross* (1947), *Lost Boundaries* (1948), *No Way Out* (1950), *Native Son* (1950), and *The Well* (1951).[167] Increasingly influential in these censorship struggles was Thurgood Marshall. Marshall asked the ACLU to amplify its anti-censorship efforts for the African American case: "Censorship as such is bad. But censorship of race is one of the worst evils that can be imagined in the field of censorship."[168] This was part and parcel of the NAACP's new legal strategy for correcting movies' racial wrongs.[169]

The NAACP's pro–*No Way Out* protests, made only thirty-five years after the struggle against *The Birth of a Nation,* epitomized the national NAACP's changing approach to film: both *No Way Out* and *Birth of a Nation* depicted racial violence—and white racism. But in the case of *No Way Out,* the national NAACP so believed in the film that it would counter its own branches to fight *against* the film's censorship, a mighty shift in perspective on Hollywood's good will. The pro–*No Way Out* stance of the NAACP was such a departure from earlier approaches—and in some locales went so strongly against the better judgment of local branch officers—that White sent a form letter to each of the organization's branches at Twentieth Century–Fox's behest, asking them not to aid in the film's ban.[170]

However, White's defense of a film containing thirty-odd epithets ("nigger," "black boy," and "coon" among them) put him in conflict with branches that unconditionally opposed these words as an affront to civil rights. The film created an interpretive crisis over the civil rights questions it raised—and over the right of the (white) movies to speak epithets, supposedly in the name of African American rights. Carl Murphy, leader of the Maryland NAACP chapter, publisher of the *Baltimore Afro-American* newspaper, and member of the NAACP board of directors, directly asked Maryland censors to remove all epithets in *No Way Out,* regardless of inflection, direction, or the film's overall message. For Murphy, epithets were the most important postwar issue in terms of racial representation and equality.

As a newspaper editor, Murphy knew well that casual use of epithets in national media was shockingly common, even during and after the war for democracy. For example, in January 1946, an Army Radio station announcer had supposedly slipped on live radio and used the word "nigger" to describe Cab Calloway, a term that Black soldiers protested.[171] Black publishers like Murphy had effected some change in the casual use of the term during the war. In Warner Bros.' *The Adventures of Mark Twain* (1944), Twain (Fredric March) called Black folks "darkies," and joked during a speech that he "had an old colored woman who fell in the fire and burned," whose tombstone read "well done good and faithful servant." This prompted uninhibited laughter from his onscreen audience. In response, the *Pittsburgh Courier's* Pacific Coast offices wrote to all the major studios requesting them to ban the use of the term "darky" from films. Though the brutal joke seemed the bigger offense, the use of epithets was a clear and manageable issue for the *Courier* and one with a history.[172] As a result of the *Courier's* protest, executives at RKO, Twentieth Century–Fox, and Universal pledged to avoid the use of offensive words.[173]

In the case of *No Way Out*, Murphy directly conflicted with White. It was true that the national NAACP had occasionally stood against the use of racial epithets. White had even warned MGM boss Dore Schary that Black folks would be offended by the word "nigger" in *Intruder in the Dust*.[174] And though the national NAACP generally opposed censorship, there were exceptions: they supported the ban on rescreenings of *The Birth of a Nation*. But films that both uttered epithets and condemned racism often won White's approval, as his defense of the "logical" use of "nigger" in *Emperor Jones* (1933) suggests.[175] White backed down. Although he continued to fight a ban on *No Way Out*, he carefully acquiesced to the branches, asking Fox's Ed Harrison to delete "epithets . . . from future showings if this is technically possible and artistically feasible."[176]

This would be one of the last film controversies of White's career — an ironically muted and exasperating conclusion. But in it, White also refused to force his branches into line for the sake of the studios. The contrast between Murphy and White on *No Way Out* highlights the different ways this polysemic film could be interpreted by advocates of civil rights who represented the same organization, each pursing different aspects of the battle for equality in different locales.

Outside the NAACP, Black critics noted *No Way Out's* boldness but doubted whether it was good for integration or the movement. Lillian Scott noted that Poitier's Brooks was "not quite as professional or mature" in his bearing as "the young interns, white or colored, one sees in hospitals. . . . It is, of course, a great relief to see Hollywood portraying Negroes as highly intelligent, trained people for a change but why do these superior qualities always come packaged in an overly receptive, humorless individual. . . . Is there no such thing as an intelligent phlegmatic individual?"[177] Although *No Way Out* was recognized as a departure, in its revised form it had not gone far enough for many African Americans.

The Black responses at the preview screening held at Baltimore's Regent Theatre reflected disappointment that censors had clipped the film's most powerful scenes: "Let it show," said Mrs. Hilda Purvey, "that the colored race is finally
fighting back."[178]

Some NAACP activism continued into the early 1950s. After Universal invited them to a preview screening, Walter White, Ralph Bunche, and Alain
Locke lauded the metaphor of blindness in *Bright Victory* (1951), the story of
blind veterans, one white, one Black, who clash and then become friends. Fully
embracing the film's metaphor, for Locke, the film was as much about the "social
conquest over the blindness of race prejudice" as about the war veteran's physical blindness. For Walter White, similarly, the film celebrated "those who cannot
or will not see color as a barrier to human decency." However, the film would be
one of the last the NAACP would seek to link to the civil rights struggle.

Outside of the NAACP, Black journalists carefully distilled the hidden civil
rights angles in a number of important films. Though, as I stated earlier, civil
rights–minded film activists rarely celebrated miscegenation, *Ebony* plastered
images of interracial romance throughout its pages in its review of *Pool of London, The President's Lady,* Minoru Shibuya's *Yassamossa* (1953), the Italian *Senza
Pietà,* and *Anna's Sin* (1952). With *Pool of London, Ebony* suggested this film's
value for civil rights: "There are no passionate clinches, no bodily contact but
even the restrained love story of Johnny and Pat will be irritating to white Americans because of its profound implications."[179] For some, it was easier to discuss
the touchy subject of miscegenation when the plot involved Native American–
white romance. *Broken Arrow,* which Twentieth Century–Fox marketed to Black
audiences, prompted discussion on how important the love narrative was to full-
fledged equality. One reviewer said the film's love story was "one of the strongest
indictments of racial misunderstanding," highlighting the conflicts between the
"bronzed first Americans and whites," a comment that highlights the similarity
in skin color between Native and Black Americans.[180] *Baltimore Afro-American*
reviewer Lillian Scott took pleasure in the "poetic" wedding ceremony where the
blood of the two mix and they become one.[181]

One of the largest discursive formations of the Black press in the postwar era's
civil rights–oriented film offerings surrounded criticism of *The Jackie Robinson
Story.* Because southern exhibitors refused to book a film with so frank an integrationist stance, W. J. Heinman of United Artists proposed that the national
NAACP join with UA in "putting together a . . . road show operation" using a
"large truck . . . a generator, portable machines, both 16 mm and 35mm, portable screen and a loud speaker system for . . . ballyhoo" and setting up exhibition "deals with halls, churches, etc." with the NAACP to provide the truck and
equipment and get 50 percent of the profit. The NAACP declined.[182] But the
film became the focus of civil rights activism. The Bluefield, Virginia, chapter
of the NAACP announced urgently that African Americans should boycott a

segregated showing of the film, using the film's progressive racial politics against the segregationist exhibitors showing it. But the local radio station refused to air the NAACP's boycott announcements on racial grounds—prompting the NAACP to seek Federal Communications Commission intervention. The FCC invested the complaint but it is unclear from the NAACP files what action, if any, the commission took.

A groundswell of discursive support greeted this independent, low-budget film. Among the most artful of the reviewers was Marion Jackson, who called the film "a candid close-up of an American—of color and hope—who through his physical prowess and genuine skills liberates baseball from the ghetto."[183] For Eustace Gay of the *Philadelphia Tribune* it was crucial that the film emerged in the midst of Jackie's moment of glory and the unfolding controversy about integration. Unlike so many other problem films, *The Jackie Robinson Story* did not "end in frustration . . . disappointment, discouragement, and a sense of futility."[184] Similarly, William Gunn called the film a " 'must-see' for Roy Harney and other Pirate officials who . . . stubbornly refuse to accept the credo that baseball is an American pastime . . . and should be played by ANYONE who . . . can make the grade."[185] For several reviewers the incidents of segregation and degradation were the most important in the film: Alvin White of the Associated Negro Press wrote of the film's brutally "honest portrayal of democracy," such as it was, in the United States, "especially that portion which showed the mighty Mack Robinson, elder brother of [Jackie], himself an Olympic hero and college graduate reduced to the status of a street cleaner!"[186] For Swig Garlington, progressive entertainment columnist for the *New Amsterdam News,* while the film was laudable, it seemed ultimately opposed to the militant struggle for Black civil rights:

> Too much emphasis is placed on the "don't fight back" attitude which Jackie sells. How is the Negro ever going to get any place without fighting—mostly fighting back? There are only a few Jackie Robinsons among our group who can gain by "not fighting back." This philosophy is likely to be misinterpreted. . . . A white man—especially southern whites and prejudiced Yankees, who think the Negro has a place in which to stay—may use Jackie as the ideal example to follow, and probably tell Negroes seeking improvements and their rights: "don't fight back," be a nice fellow like Jackie and everything will be O.K.

Though Swig praised the film as showing "how Democracy can work," he also said the film would be successful partly because it contained nothing "which could possibly offend even an anti-negro white."[187]

Black press critics denied the boundary lines between cultural and textual politics, claiming, in the vein of the Cultural Front, a continuity between racial politics onscreen and in "real life," and seeking to underscore the value of fighting back to the emerging civil rights agenda.

NAACP FILM TACTICS IN THE WILKINS ERA

In 1955, NAACP youth council member Camille Carter wrote to find out if the national NAACP had protested *Untamed* (1955), a film she claimed "glorifies the white settlement of South Africa [following] an Indian-Cowboy theme with the Zulus in the Indian role." The moment where Richard Egan proclaims his desire to run the Zulus "off the face of the earth!" seemed plainly racist. "I *want help*. Personally I favor a council picket line. Advise me on the best way to express my indignation."[188] The reply was negative. By 1955, the national NAACP had stopped assessing films for their ideology or propaganda value, nor did they generally protest them.[189] Neither the Black press nor the national NAACP would engage with film in the same manner as they had during the war and immediate postwar years.

White died in 1955, leaving Wilkins to finish the organization's film work. Wilkins's strategy varied widely from White's, as did his understandings of the place of film in the civil rights agenda. The rise of the L.A. branch's Hollywood activism in 1957 and of television as a potentially more dangerous staging ground for stereotypes that undermined civil rights claims contributed to Wilkins's replacement of wartime assertiveness with strategic neutrality.[190]

Wilkins made several significant changes to the NAACP's film policy when he took over for Walter White in 1955. First, at a meeting of the MPAA, he issued a general statement on the NAACP's film policy, a move that White was reluctant to make. In doing so, he fixed and solidified the organization's position on film: that the organization was not a censor and that it did not oppose the depiction of "comics, maids, [or] menials" wholesale. What the NAACP did oppose were Hollywood limitations on Black actors and the depiction of Black life, and the "stereotyped . . . eye-rolling, shuffling, grinning and obsequiousness . . . that perpetuates the images of the Negro as a buffoon whose claims to equality need not be taken seriously."[191] Wilkins reminded the MPAA that since 1942, when White and Wilkie made their first visit, Black people had migrated from the South in large numbers, becoming union members and white-collar workers. Public schools had been desegregated. But this changing Black reality was largely absent from film. If the movie industry had been doing its job in portraying Black people, Wilkins argued, international scandals like Little Rock would have carried less weight. Wilkins also confronted producers with the "changes in the Negro himself. He is more alert, more aware of himself and of the place of his nation in the world. . . . He has seen India and Indonesia gain independence." In closing, Wilkins promised continued "scrutiny and criticism." The NAACP would not "seek to dictate to the industry but will attempt to see that sixteen million Americans struggling to attain their rightful place in the light of the nation and the world are not handicapped by misrepresentation in a medium which speaks powerfully to people everywhere." But it wouldn't be the national NAACP that would do the scrutinizing.

Wilkins's second major change was that he allowed for increased branch control over the organization's film policy, even if this control was still concentrated in a single branch, the Los Angeles/Hollywood branch. Again, Wilkins did what White wouldn't, placing the actors and Hollywood at the center of black film criticism. Third, he generally refused to give official statements on emerging films. For example, in 1958, when Almena Davis spearheaded a protest of the backward-looking film adaptation of *Porgy and Bess* (1959), *Hollywood Close-up* asked the NAACP about whether they would protest the film. John Morsell (assistant executive director under Wilkins) indicated the organization's inability to comment:

> The Association has taken no official stand on the proposed 'Porgy and Bess' film, and it is unlikely that it will do so. Our principle reason should be apparent, namely that we have no wish to set ourselves up as censors. . . . If motion pictures or plays or other cultural productions are demonstrably malicious or harmful, we would have reasons to make such facts known. Our devotion to the principle of freedom of expression is such, however that we would prefer to exercise this kind of judgment in narrow rather than broad limits.[192]

The NAACP's own anti-censorship campaigns had trickled down into a more consistently civil libertarian film policy. Though NAACP members and youth leaders conveyed concerns about several films, including *Cinerama Holiday* (1955) and *The Snows of Kilimanjaro* (1953), under Wilkins's leadership these concerned citizens were told to handle the protests themselves locally.[193] Although Wilkins and staff attended the screenings of *Gone Are the Days* (1963) as well as *Anna Lucasta* (1958) and the organization still vigorously opposed showings of *The Birth of a Nation*, it is clear from Wilkins's correspondence and, perhaps more dramatically, his silence, that in his eyes the national NAACP had little place in film affairs.[194] The national NAACP praised isolated films, like George Stevens's *Giant* (1956) and *The Roots/Raices* (a 1954 Mexican documentary film), the latter of which it recommended to its branches.[195] Wilkins even sent Morsell to evaluate *Voice of the Hurricane* as late as 1964.[196] But the cultivation of a cinematic voice and a cinematic hermeneutic was no longer a part of the organization's function, as the organization no longer stood at the epicenter of film criticism and reception for the Black community. As the mass movement for civil rights became a center-stage issue, the NAACP no longer focused on film in its civil rights program.

CONCLUSION

In 1959, twenty-five years after Shirley Graham's protests of Stahl's 1934 *Imitation of Life,* Almena Davis-Lomax organized pickets and a boycott of Douglas Sirk's remake. "Imitation of Life . . . is a libel on the Negro race," she said. "It libels our children and the Negro mother [and] should be banned in the interest of national unity, harmony, peace, decency and inter-racial respect. The *Tribune* is refusing all advertising of it and will picket it in the Los Angeles area and call upon the N.A.A.C.P. to condemn, oppose and picket it, too." Davis picketed the film with her children and her protest was carried in the *Hollywood Reporter*.[197] Likewise, disappointed with the NAACP Hollywood branch's negotiations efforts, Black actor (and former IFRG leader) Caleb Peterson formed the Hollywood Race Relations Bureau (HRRB) and led pickets of theaters, studio gates, and the 1962 Oscars ceremony, claiming that African Americans were still segregated both from Hollywood jobs and onscreen.[198] Later that year, the HRRB joined with CORE to picket Darryl Zanuck's World War II picture *The Longest Day*, which failed to show even one of the thousands of Black soldiers who fought on D-Day.[199] Davis's and Peterson's persevering protests suggest the continued, organizationally unaligned struggle against the Hollywood screen, one that countered the NAACP's slow and steady, non-aggressive approach.

From 1930 to 1960, African American activists fought Hollywood—and sometimes each other—to meaningfully relate Hollywood films to Black claims for equality and civil rights. Many voices other than Walter White contributed to the battle to link films to African American struggle. While this story has generally been told in terms of the NAACP, a broader portrait that extends beyond the organization gives a richer view of Black screen activism and how Hollywood's limited iconography became grist for activists fighting for civil rights. Walter White generally attempted to privately convince producers to improve Black images; NAACP staff members, many of them women, more closely monitored the ideology and politics of Hollywood images and favored mass strategies and open protest; local and leftist activists engaged in elaborate counter-spectacle that turned the theater into a venue for discursive engagement about civil rights; and journalists often developed complex, sophisticated, and well-informed critiques of the American screen's repressed civil rights images. While Black activists could not control Hollywood's production of Black images, they could influence films' reception—and sometimes local censorship. With varying levels of success, activists wielded this control as an ideological wedge against various kinds of image-bound inequality, often through careful and poignant readings of a film's social value and historical weight.

CONCLUSION

My focus in these chapters has been on the policies and textual patterns that restrained the cinematic envisioning of issues pertinent to Black civil rights. In the years before the full-fledged mass movement for civil rights, there was significant struggle over not only how to define this agenda but also how to represent it. Various institutions, ranging from the Hollywood studios to the Black press, were engaged in negotiating these representations and in marshaling their meanings. The cinema became an important site of inscription for both filmmakers and Black activists, who often differed in their understanding and interpretations of the signifiers these films projected.

Extremely influential was the MPPDA, the most centralized force of repression governing the American screen—and it had an "industry policy" against strong interracial images, whether of lynching, racial prejudice, miscegenation, or integration. The PCA modulated its policies in reaction to criticism and to changing national—and industrial—imperatives about race, especially in the postwar era. Though the PCA did eventually soften its repression of miscegenation, mob violence, and integration, it only did so when the impact of such representations on developing civil rights struggles was less powerful because they were already being addressed in a federal narrative of civil rights, one dramatically revealed in the nation's courts.

State censors, with an instrumentalist fear of Black sexuality and, to a lesser extent, of racial violence, cut images that might trouble the racial status quo more harshly than the PCA, excising miscegenation from films without Black people and "shadows" or verbal mentions of lynching. States cut even the suggestion of themes or action they thought inciting, obviating Hollywood's indirect representation. The PCA did not always adapt its policy to state censors' standards and routinely suffered state-level cuts. State censors were most effective, however, in repressing foreign, independent, and race cinemas, which represented Black desire and Black abuse more directly.

Hollywood studios had to contend with the PCA and the state censors in treating racial controversy. But the case of Darryl Zanuck shows that the producer and the studios were also a force of repression. He converted real-world examples of civil rights violations into a visual regime governed by fantasy and the imperative of fiscally responsible entertainment. We can see this clearly because as the PCA weakened, Zanuck and Twentieth Century–Fox president Spyros Skouras embarked on a campaign of auto-censorship designed to protect the studio from costly controversy. Zanuck's desire to reveal racial injustice was not based on selfless personal convictions but often on a desire to exploit controversy and excitement surrounding racial mixing as well as the idea of change and movement.

The representations of America's civil rights violations that made it through the vetting system were marred by a remoteness that strains the imagination. Certain important concepts never made it through. The substitutes that stand in their place may be evocative—and may even have an added spectatorial value in their openness to interpretation. But what is lost is the straightforward simplicity of direct treatment that unburdened white cinematic representations were afforded. Most obviously, the figuration of civil rights in oblique ways left the politics of such images unclear. Black characters were often confined to the role of witness rather than actors or victims; they could be psychic but not physical victims of violence. By avoiding Black victimization and aggression, the industry largely sidestepped admitting the scope and depth of American racism and the history of Black resistance. The absence of explicit links to race moved lynching images into a vague discourse on democracy rather than one specifically tied to racism. The loss of racial specificity in lynching images—as well as those of interracial romance and segregation—had profound effects on the possibility of cinema striking public conscience and consciousness in racially specific terms.

However, oblique signifiers persistently remained: the noose, the implicit link between the Black man and the gallows; the angry white rural mob; the tanned, liminal body of the South Seas island maiden; Black servants talking back; film titles like *Slave Ship;* the mother-love of the Black mammy for her white charge; the mention of race in oratorical condemnation of mob violence; or, perhaps most importantly, a vague sense of racial "trouble" with no definite links to race. State censors cut some of these, making the representation of civil rights issues even harder to grasp. These signifiers were deniable—but they were also nebulous, nascent, half-developed, and often strange, troubling the narratives in which they appeared. They permitted only limited views and vantage points on the issues they addressed, distancing them from the heat of contemporary racial discourse and debate. In holding together an incongruous series of substitutive icons for real-world violence and passions, films of the classical era often yielded representations that were weirder than fantasy, though often sutured seamlessly with Hollywood's signature continuity style. Yet as I have labored to show, many of these films gave off an air (or, as Breen might put it, "a flavor") of the very relations they repressed. Built into the reversed narratives and substitutive iconographies that compressed civil rights issues was often a furious and forceful resonance, a palpable sense of something real to which they refer but that never makes a screen appearance (and indeed, as Stanley Cavell notes, that the screen itself hides). Black activists raised the issue of whether these oblique signifiers were enough, attempting both to speak what was absent and to use the half-revealed images to strike a blow for freedom. Their "interpretive activism" powerfully marshaled these signs to the purposes and needs of the movement.

CIVIL RIGHTS AND REPRESSION
AFTER THE CLASSICAL ERA

In the mid-1950s and 1960s, civil rights images exceeded their fetters and sprawled across television screens, piercing the American conscience as the events of the mass movement took shape. In the 1960s, though film censorship declined, the studios, fearing financial losses, maintained the mantle of civil rights repression. We can see this because the films of the civil rights era—films like *Guess Who's Coming to Dinner* (1967) and *In the Heat of the Night* (1967)—bear out the pattern of repression evident already in the films of the 1950s like *Island in the Sun*. Yet at the same time, an alternative to this staid approach was emerging, one evident already in Douglas Sirk's *Imitation of Life* and, later, in Samuel Fuller's *Shock Corridor* (1963). Borne in *Imitation of Life's* excessive images and dialogue was a pastiche of melodrama that evinced a fatigue not only with that genre but also with the oversimplifications of preceding racial problem films. Fuller, who trained in the studio system under Darryl Zanuck, demonstrates well the trajectory of racial repression in the years immediately following the decline of censorship. *Shock Corridor*, set in a mental institution, is framed around a narrative of reform and (medical) treatment, as with earlier racial problem films. But it mocks and exceeds the existing racial formula in the Black patient's automatic memories of the KKK South. Both these films reveal the insufficiency of the social problem formula and the high seriousness of the racial problem discourse. In these films, repression left another legacy: shock. The taboo had made an imprint against which filmmakers—Black and white—would be doomed to consistently react.

The classical era's system of vetting has left a powerful and enduring legacy in the present. A cinema without walls (and without the industrial apparatus of classical Hollywood) has altered fundamentally the constraints.[1] Actors and directors are purportedly free agents without the dominating pressure of studio heads such as Zanuck. However, the mechanisms of repression have been surprisingly perseverant. The continuation of minstrelsy and dominance of a relatively narrow formula governing narratives of Black life in most Hollywood films demonstrates the failing creativity of this neoliberal style of directorial freedom. While the studio system may be a thing of the past, creative decisions still often rest with a powerful few, whether they are embodied in the casting director, the

Hollywood agent, or the producer. However, New Hollywood's free-agent system has, in limited ways, expanded the possibility of representing civil rights issues, even if Black representation largely exists in a structured marginal space. The rise of independent cinema, which was an indirect effect of the fall of the Hollywood studio system, has become a venue for Black filmmakers. Not only have Black independent filmmakers and documentarians been able to work with independent distributors in ways that sidestep the Hollywood's vetting and formulae, but African American stars such as Danny Glover have used the relative ease of shifting from actor to producer to push the envelope on questions of justice. The cost, however, has been a lack of financing and smaller audiences. In a world of narrowcast media, designed just for you, we choose our own messages. Indeed, some of the 1970s' and 1980s' most revolutionary Black filmmakers (like Charles Burnett and Julie Dash), when confronted with meager financing, turned to making television movies for the Disney and Hallmark channels between feature film projects.

RIGHTS YOU CAN BUY: CINEMA CIVIL RIGHTS IN THE ERA OF NEOLIBERALISM AND THE ONE PERCENT

In the last decade, we have seen signs and symbols of Black equality that Walter White and Martin Luther King's generation only dreamed of, chief among them the election of Barack Obama. The decade has also given rise to an intense neoliberalism, however, that has led to the defunding of an already crippled government safety net. Thus symbolic victories seem unrelated to any broader plan of aid to African Americans. We are in a moment when the words "civil rights" evoke immediate images of the past, symbols of hope and promise, but when an ultra neoliberalist state has transformed discourses of rights into the lexicon of the marketplace. As one of my students put it, "In America we don't have freedom; instead we have rights and liberties"; rights are "property" for which people and now corporations can barter and negotiate. In many ways the analogy of "rights" that so helped the African American cause in the 1940s through the 1960s has limited our view of what (Black) American freedom can be. At the same time, we enter a moment where the specific racial histories (that once mattered to legislating equality) are silenced in the sweep of neo-color blindness. We can witness this in the legal undoing of affirmative action as a kind of "special right" for minorities, the Supreme Court's self-imposed blindness to the history of southern discrimination in its attack on the Voting Rights Act, and in the nation's unabated silence on the question of reparations. The adoption of the term "civil rights" and its iconography by various other groups has represented a hopeful widening, but at its worst it has also represented a dilution of the concept, a reduction to analogy that is blind to the current needs of African Americans, rather than as grounds for coalition building. In many quarters of public discourse, dominance of the civil rights analogy has supplanted and replaced real discussion of contemporary Black civil rights.

How do we account for the status of Black civil rights representability in an era that enshrines the images of King and Obama through medals, memorials, and photographs, but which fails to grant equal justice to Trayvon Martin, Amadou Diallo, Ramarley Graham, or Shaaliver Douse? In many senses visual memorialization has itself become an obstacle to realizing the continued need for racial justice and equality—and to denaturalizing and uncovering the tortured, entangled thread of contemporary racism in our cultural imagination.[2] As Thomas Holt and Michael Katz have brilliantly argued, increasing socioeconomic polarities within a once insular Black community have facilitated American cultural blindness about continued racism. Indeed, the very visibility of Black celebrity in the twenty-first century has made it possible for those seeking to deny racism's continued existence to point to the contemporary Duboisian talented tenth, and to ignore the masses of Black people whose inequality is increasingly invisible and unfelt.[3] Contemporary civil rights issues (e.g., global inequality, mass incarceration, the widening income gap, and the deep persistence of institutional racism in a purportedly postracial era) have remained largely marginal in both media and public discourse.

PACKAGING CIVIL RIGHTS

So where do we look? In this era concerned with neatly tying up racial narratives with the false moniker "postracial," abuses of civil rights still appear indirectly on the screen. In the 1990s, Paul Gilroy smartly recognized that a yearning for civil rights that had become inappropriate in the Black public sphere could be found in the wildly sexualized lyrics of R. Kelly and Snoop Doggy Dogg.[4] As Roopali Mukherjee has discussed, mainstream cinema of the 1990s gave rise to cinematic modes seeking to package, get over, and dismiss civil rights. One such vehicle was the civil rights nostalgia film, which helped to ensure that civil rights discourse would remain frozen in memoriam, enshrined with a warm sepia gloss that allowed audiences to celebrate how far we have come.[5] Even still, sometimes visual evidence manifests the repressed issues beneath the narrative surface. I would argue that Spike Lee's *Malcolm X* (1999), for example, challenged this representational strategy. The film's close brings the narrative up to the contemporary moment, examining in a montage the legacy of Malcolm X as a living addendum to history. In its brevity and its reliance on the catchphrase "I am Malcolm X," this sequence could be considered a commercialization of his memory. But it could also be read as breaching the neatness of the historical past, a signifier of the unresolved past's tendency to erupt into the present—a sign of civil rights history's stubborn, radical uncontainability. Lee, with his signature Brechtian incongruity and confrontational aesthetic, forces viewers to consider

Malcolm X's legacy as puncturing the veil of pastness and coming boldly into the present. Many more recent Black-themed films overtly representing civil rights abuses of the past fall into a pattern similar to that which Mukherjee recognizes in the 1990s. *Django Unchained* (2012), *The Butler* (2013), and *Twelve Years a Slave* (2013) break with tradition in some ways by acknowledging a "long civil rights movement" that existed before the 1950s. But have they made visible the links between the harsh racism of the past and the oppressions of the present? Or have they, instead, reveled in the stylized fantasy on the one hand and self-celebratory distancing in the other? And to what extent do their narratives praising great men obscure the mass power that is the root and marvel of any mass movement?

Dominant Hollywood cinema still yields striking, though subtle, manifestations that gesture elliptically toward the movement's incompleteness. The sound of Candie's dogs tearing a slave apart in *Django Unchained,* the ghastly white of the post-Katrina medical relief center that both pronounces and accelerates Wink's death in *Beasts of the Southern Wild* (2012), the death-defying persistence of Black reporter Luisa Ray (Halle Berry) in *Cloud Atlas* (2012) against not only corporate nuclear energy but the atomization that alienates her cross-racial, human connection with others—these circuitous signifiers reveal everyday, greed-wrought injustices of the past, present, and future and sometimes imagine the possibilities of coalition building as an alternative to oppression.

12 Years a Slave demonstrates well the splintered ideological trajectory of the civil rights films of 2012–13. On one hand, the film, which relates the discrete narrative of a northern free man kidnapped and sold into slavery, literally renders slavery as a memory. Also, the total freedom of Solomon Northrup (Chiwetel Ejiofor) in the North that the film sets as its initial narrative premise is a myth, one that fails to complicate America's racial landscape by showing northern racism.[6] Northrup, also, is no revolutionary. In slavery, Northrup, unlike most other slaves of the era, does not make strong "fictive kinship" networks. Nor does the film champion rebellion of the soft or violent kind, as the demise of Robert (Michael K. Williams) and the living death of Eliza (Adepero Oduye) aver. Despite his tortures, Northrup perseveres in believing in white men's honor, and it is this faith that is ultimately rewarded when the enshrined white liberals, a Canadian Quaker named Bass (Brad Pitt) and Northrup's Saratoga neighbor, Parker (Rob Steinberg), come to save him. It would seem, then, that the spectator can not only put racism in the past but can identify herself with clear moral heroes as they castigate the film's twisted villains and sympathize with its Black victims cum heroes. But this would be too hasty a judgment. Though the narrative scenarios of *12 Years* are as didactic as those in *Roots* (1978), British director Steve McQueen uses the frame itself to capture nuances, psychological complexity, and contradictions of slavery. The film's visual juxtapositions and sonic overtness often cast the narrative against itself, revealing its staged construction and introducing a subtext that holds greater depth. For example, in one scene a racist, unskilled white field hand (Paul Dano) tries to hang the competent, defiant Northrup. But the overseer, who knows Northrup's value as property, interrupts him. Rather than cutting Northrup from the hangman's noose, however, the overseer lets him hang with the tips of his toes barely touching the ground, barely sparing him a choking death. The camera gives us several deep-space shots of Northrup half-hanging in the foreground as slaves ignore this visual symbol of white supremacy: slave children play in the background, the sun wanes, and the slaves go about their routines. In this sequence, McQueen poses the violent vignettes of slavery in a tableau of living death that resonates with the work of African American silhouette artist Kara Walker. Slavery is visible not as past alone but as a haunting hanging. Northrup exists in a corporeal torture measured in the careful tip-toe dance and studied partial breaths that thinly separate him from death and that cause his body to drift about aimlessly in a space of mortal urgency somewhere outside of time. The very motionlessness of the camera in several of the shots allows viewers to study and dissect Northrup's physical and social lot, caught between death and life but always noosed. Through these subtleties, the film resists the easy closure of its narrative. It is the failure of easy closure—the dredging up of the repressed living message of these films for today's oppression—that advances the complexity of civil rights representability.

The Night Catches Us (2010) represents a far better active civil rights memorial, one that more crisply disrupts a neatly packaged movement nostalgia by showing its links to contemporary struggle. Director Tanya Hamilton articulates the transition from Black power to the 1980s' imploding urban rage in a way that indicts the failure of American responsiveness to Black crisis and the racism of American "law and order." Not only does Hamilton keep returning us to Philadelphia cops' everyday civil rights violations that make it impossible for Black women and men to live outside the shadow of criminalization, but her visuals reveal the role of poverty in undermining Black civil rights struggles (see figure 30). Among the film's final images are those of the police executing the twisted, utterly sympathetic cop killer, Jimmy Dixon (Amari Cheatom), a Black man who could have been a revolutionary. His alleyway killing, hidden from street- and camera-view, evokes for me the alleyway behind 6221 Osage Avenue, where, as Jason Osder's documentary Let the Fire Burn (2013) indicates, police likely fired shots at MOVE members trying to escape the burning house. In Osder's film, the undisclosed, unsurveillable alleyway is treated with what Osder calls a "Rashomon effect," as viewers decide whether shots were fired at those leaving the flaming inferno. In Hamilton's film, however, the condemnation of police action is much squarer. The police force surrounds a beret-wearing, crouching Dixon as he recedes into the roots and rubble of his makeshift hideout. We cut to the image of the police lights seen through firefly-dimpled high grass. The shots are fired amid the same ominous stillness of the Twelve Years a Slave image—the

FIGURE 30. Jimmy (Amari Cheatom) shoots into the rubble, figuratively confronting the forces of poverty that leave him with no way out. Frame capture from *The Night Catches Us* (2010).

persistent dead calm that haunts ever-expected Black state-sponsored murder. The film forms a lament that is more indicting than nostalgic—a warning about political dreams deferred and the very legal noose that defers them.

Perhaps the most important civil rights issue of the twenty-first century, the penal system's colonization of Black lives, remains marginal to Hollywood cinema. In an era where *Law & Order* is one of the most watched American television shows, films, too, have taken on a "law and order" ethos that has largely defined Black criminalization as the fault of disobedient Black men rather than the civil rights movement's unanswered cry for equality. Bold moments of civil rights pedagogy, like Furious Styles' "gentrification" speech in *Boyz N the Hood* (1991) or John Sayles's roaming camera in *City of Hope* (1991), which reveals how politicians' decisions affect life on the street, offer brief glimpses of the real structural sources of Black inequality. But, more often, systematic critique remains mired in a web of intangible, deniable images. Too often it is white men, like Jean Valjean (Hugh Jackman) in *Les Misérables* (2013) or Jake Hoyt (Ethan Hawke) in *Training Day* (2001), who become the "white slaves" with whom Americans are called to identify in their plight within the criminal justice system.

In the contemporary era, while Hollywood still sidelines Black screenwriters and directors and keeps historical and contemporary civil rights issues locked in limited narrative formulae, African American independent cinema has effectively begun to circumvent Hollywood's reticence in ways recognized by the independent filmmaking establishment. For example, *Fruitvale Station* (2013) and *Middle of Nowhere* (2012), both honored by top prizes at Sundance, rise above the repression-reaction dynamic to clearly represent the racial and gendered dynamics of mass incarceration. Though contemporary Hollywood films like *The Hurricane* (1999) have given similar glimpses, rarely does the massiveness of this problem ever make a screen appearance, even in the most realistic and poignant of independent film renderings.

Fruitvale Station, and perhaps this Black independent film activity more generally, offers hope for a more revelatory way of addressing even controversial contemporary civil rights issues about which there is no national consensus. The film is a circular narrative based on the true story of the last day of a young Black man, Oscar Grant (Michael B. Jordan), murdered by the transit police in Oakland. The film both follows and departs from earlier racial problem films I discuss in this book. Like *No Way Out* and *Pinky,* it is a timely narrative, one that seeks to make sense of recent issues and to reflect on contemporary race relations. The film also shares these earlier films' embrace of melodrama—the emotion and suspense of "just in the nick of time" and "too late" structures our identification with Grant.[7] However, the film breaks from the containment strategies of its forebears. Its introductory images replicating the actual cell phone video of the murder are mirrored in the film's continual use of handheld camera shots. This ultra-realist photography penetratingly communicates the authentic, not only because it imitates the unsteadiness of actual vision, but, in the case of the cell phone video, because it links the film to Grant's actual story. This phone video also turns surveillance away from the Black body and onto law enforcement officials who are typically the surveyors, showing the usefulness of such guerilla film technology for counteracting cultural dominance based on the visible.

In several flashbacks to Oscar's time in prison, we finally receive on the screen a poetically nuanced perspective on Black incarceration, one that admits the violence of prison and of the life that sends Black men there, but also the vulnerability and need of these men. The film's final sequences break with traditional narrative filmmaking and bring us documentary images of a memorial protest staged in memory of Oscar Grant. The implication of this ending, as in *Malcolm X,* is the need for movement—the need for action. This ending contrasts with the social problem formula of the classical Hollywood era that sought to avert activism and avoid a movement. The value in films like *Fruitvale Station* lies not so much in that that they pioneer new techniques but in that they use the cinema to invoke contemporary civil rights issues in a direct way, a way that attempts to redress the complexities of the history of cinematic repression I have outlined in this book. *Fruitvale Station's* triumph is that it manages to do this about an issue that, like so many addressed in this book, is, in its moment, still nascent and undefined in the American conscience and consciousness. *Fruitvale Station* announces that cinema still has an important role to play in dramatizing and affectively reinforcing contemporary civil rights struggles. And in light of the weight of the denial and reversal of civil rights gains in the contemporary era, such an activist cinematic stance is even more necessary.

NOTES

INTRODUCTION

1. Donald Bogle, *Toms, Coons, Mammies, Mulattoes, and Bucks: An Interpretive History of Black Film* (New York: Continuum, 2004).

2. See, for example, Pearl Bowser and Louise Spence, *Writing Himself into History: Oscar Micheaux, His Films and His Audiences* (New Brunswick, NJ: Rutgers University Press, 2001).

3. Walter White, letter to William Goetz, December 4, 1942, Papers of the NAACP, Library of Congress (NAACP LOC hereafter).

4. Ed Guerrero, *Framing Blackness: The African American Image in Film* (Philadelphia: Temple University Press, 1993); Thomas Cripps, "The Absent Presence in American Civil War Films," *Historical Journal of Film, Radio and Television* 14:4 (1994), 367.

5. Jane Gaines, *Fire and Desire: Mixed-Race Movies in the Silent Era* (Chicago: University of

Chicago Press, 2001); J. Ronald Green, *With a Crooked Stick: The Films of Oscar Micheaux* (Bloomington: Indiana University Press, 2004).

6. While many race filmmakers, including Oscar Micheaux, Spencer Williams, and Powell Lindsay, revealed civil rights abuses in their films, the absence of white people and the focus on internal class divisions within Black communities in many cases made their direct engagement with civil rights and interracial struggle infrequent.

7. Michel Foucault, *The History of Sexuality*, Vol. 1 (New York: Vintage, 1990), 15–19.

8. Christian Metz, "Censorship: Barrier or Deviation?" in *The Imaginary Signifier* (Bloomington: Indiana University Press, 1977), 253–265.

9. Patricia White, *Uninvited: Classical Hollywood Cinema and Lesbian Representability* (Bloomington: Indiana University Press, 1999), 16. Using methodological tools honed and gleaned by African American media scholars such as Pearl Bowser and Louise Spence, Manthia Diawara, Jacqueline Stewart, and Robin Means Coleman, as well as tools utilized by scholars of censorship, we can encounter the mechanisms of the forces of racist repression in the cinema with greater precision. See Bowser and Spence, *Writing*; Manthia Diawara, "Black Spectatorship: the Problem of Identification and Resistance," *Screen* 29:4 (1988), 66–79; Jacqueline Najuma Stewart, *Migrating to the Movies* (Berkeley: University of California Press, 2005); and Robin Means Coleman, *African American Viewers and the Black Situation Comedy: Situating Racial Humor* (New York: Taylor & Francis, 1998). For an important grounding in the methods of examining censorship, see Matthew Bernstein, *Controlling Hollywood: Censorship and Regulation in the Studio Era* (New Brunswick, NJ: Rutgers University Press, 1999).

10. Even early government censorship of the movies, dating back to 1908, regulated screen representation of race. See Lee Grieveson, *Policing the Cinema* (Berkeley: University of California Press, 2004). Indeed, as historian Nell Painter points out, it is only by a forceful forgetting that we can deny the racial meanings of concerns about "white slavery," which, as Shelley Stamp and others have shown, was a structuring issue in early film regulation. See Nell Irvin Painter, *The History of White People* (New York: W. W. Norton, 2010), 34–59; Charlene Regester, "Black Films, White Censors," in *Movie Censorship and American Culture*, ed. Francis Couvares (Washington, DC: Smithsonian Press, 1996), 159–186; J. Douglas Smith, "Patrolling the Borders of Race: Motion Picture Censorship and Jim Crow in Virginia, 1922–1932," *Historical Journal of Radio, Film and Television* 21:3 (August 2001), 273. Further, it was racial control and only secondarily sexuality and violence that motivated the most significant and large-scale act of early censorship: the federal restriction on the movement of the Jack Johnson films. My examination of the *Legislative Journal* for the Commonwealth of Pennsylvania suggests that these fight films were the original censorship concern in the state. See "An Act to Prevent the Exhibition of Moving Pictures or Motion Pictures or Other Pictures of Prize Fights, Prize Fighting, Boxing Matches, Pugilistic Contests or Any Indecent or Immoral Pictures within the Commonwealth of Pennsylvania," *Pennsylvania Legislative Journal of the House*, January 24, 1911, 104. This act did not pass, but later a modified version did pass, creating the Pennsylvania Board of Motion Picture Censorship. This was the first state-level legislation regarding motion picture censorship in the country. For more on race in the fight film, see Dan Streible's work in *Fight Pictures: A History of Boxing and Early Cinema* (Berkeley: University of California Press, 2008).

11. Important scholarship by Anna Everett has explored how Black press critics used a competing medium to explore, explain, and counteract Hollywood's oft-demeaning images. Anna Everett, *Returning the Gaze: A Genealogy of Black Film Criticism, 1909–1949* (Durham, NC: Duke University Press, 2000). But Everett's groundbreaking contribution leaves room for exploration of explicitly political and directly confrontational screen engagement. Thomas

Cripps provides an encyclopedic exploration of Black representation of the World War II and postwar era but has left room for nuanced work on the meanings of specific films and protests. Thomas Cripps, *Making Movies Black: The Hollywood Message Movie from World War II to the Civil Rights Era* (Oxford: Oxford University Press, 1993). Historians interested in the national NAACP's film campaigns have begun to explain the importance of film to the organization's overall policies. But rarely do they engage with the films themselves, with the local branches or with the complex politics of interpretation these activists forged. See Lauren Sklaroff, *Black Culture and the New Deal* (Chapel Hill: University of North Carolina Press, 2009); Jenny Woodley, "In Harlem and Hollywood: The NAACP's Cultural Campaigns, 1910–1950," in *Long Is the Way and Hard: One Hundred Years of the NAACP*, ed. Kervern Verney and Lee Sartain (Fayetteville: University of Arkansas Press, 2009), 15–28; Steven Tuck, "'You can sing and punch . . . but you can't be a soldier or a man': African American Struggles for a New Place in Popular Culture," in *Fog of War: The Second World War and the Civil Rights Movement*, ed. Kevin Kruse and Stephen Tuck. (Oxford: Oxford University Press, 2012), 103–125; Justin T. Lorts, "Hollywood, the NAACP and the Cultural Politics of the Early Civil Rights Movement," in *Freedom Rights: New Perspectives on the Civil Rights Movement*, ed. Danielle L. McGuire and John Dittmer (Lexington: University Press of Kentucky, 2011), 39–70. On the tensions between the national NAACP and the branches, see Verney and Sartain, *Long Is the Way*, and Barbara Ransby, *Ella Baker and the Black Radical Tradition* (Chapel Hill: University of North Carolina Press, 2003).

12. Martha Biondi, *To Stand and Fight: The Struggle for Civil Rights in Postwar New York City* (Cambridge, MA: Harvard University Press, 2006), 16.

13. Jessie P. Guzman and W. Hardin Hughes, "Lynching—Crime," in *The Negro Yearbook: A Review of Events Affecting Negro Life, 1941–1946* (Atlanta: Foote and Davies Press, 1947), 306–308.

14. Jolie A. Sheffer, *The Romance of Race: Incest, Miscegenation, and Multiculturalism in the United States, 1880–1930* (New Brunswick, NJ: Rutgers University Press, 2012), 15–19.

15. Jacquelyn Dowd Hall, "The Long Civil Rights Movement and the Political Uses of the Past," *Journal of American History* 91:4 (March 2005), 1233–1263.

16. Harvard Sitkoff, *A New Deal for Blacks: The Emergence of Civil Rights as a National Issue: The Depression Era* (New York: Oxford University Press, 1978), 34–36.

17. Robin Kelley, *Hammer and Hoe: Alabama Communists during the Great Depression* (Chapel Hill: University of North Carolina Press, 1992), 156–157.

18. Michael Denning, *The Cultural Front: The Laboring of American Culture in the Twentieth Century* (New York: Verso Books, 1998), xvi.

19. Cornelius Bynum, *A. Philip Randolph and the Struggle for Civil Rights* (Urbana: University of Illinois Press, 2010), 174.

20. For more on the northern dimensions of the civil rights movement, see Thomas Sugrue, *The Origins of Urban Crisis: Race and Inequality in Postwar Detroit* (Princeton, NJ: Princeton University Press, 1996); Matthew Countryman, *Up South: Civil Rights and Black Power in Philadelphia* (Philadelphia: University of Pennsylvania Press, 2007).

21. Beth Tompkin Bates, *Pullman Porters and the Rise of Protest Politics in Black America, 1925–1945* (Chapel Hill: University of North Carolina Press, 2010).

22. Guzman and Hughes, *The Negro Yearbook*, 307.

23. Patricia Sullivan, *Days of Hope* (Chapel Hill: University of North Carolina Press, 1996), 134. She cites Henry Louis Gates, *Colored People: A Memoir* (New York: Vintage, 1994), 84–85.

24. Guzman and Hughes, *The Negro Yearbook*, 309.

25. Dorothy Beeler, "Race Riot in Columbia, Tennessee, February 25–27, 1946," *Tennessee Historical Quarterly* 39:1 (Spring 1980), 49–61.

26. John Nickle, "Disabling African American Men: Liberalism and Race Message Films," *Cinema Journal* 44:1 (Fall 2004), 25–48.

27. Mary Dudziak, *Cold War, Civil Rights: Race and the Image of American Democracy* (Princeton, NJ: Princeton University Press, 1995).

28. Martha Biondi, "The Struggle for Black Equality in New York City, 1945–1955," Ph.D. diss., Columbia University, 1997.

1. REGULATING RACE, STRUCTURING ABSENCE

1. Some prefer the term "self-regulation" to "censorship" because industry regulation was less harsh and could be negotiated, unlike most state and municipal censorship, as I show. But I frequently use the term censorship here because the MPPDA, though more prone to negotiation, did require cuts and changes as a condition of approval.

2. In 1939, the Code was amended to include a clause "taking cognizance" of the fact that racial epithets, including "nigger," were offensive to audiences. MPAA General Correspondence File (GCF, hereafter), Reel 6, Academy of Motion Picture Arts and Sciences (AMPAS, hereafter).

3. Ruth Vasey, "Beyond Sex and Violence: Industry Policy and the Regulation of Hollywood Movies, 1922–1939," *Quarterly Review of Film and Video* 15:4 (1995), 65–85.

4. Vasey and Jacobs point out the ways in which audiences both perceived censorship and read controversial material back into the text. Vasey, "Beyond Sex," 102–129, and *The World According to Hollywood* (Madison: University of Wisconsin Press, 1997); Lea Jacobs, *The Wages of Sin: Censorship and the Fallen Woman Film, 1928–1942* (Berkeley: University of California, 1995). Also see Stanley Cavell, *Pursuits of Happiness: The Hollywood Comedy of Remarriage* (Cambridge, MA: Harvard University Press, 1981), 83. Cavell put it this way, referring to the makeshift screen Ellie and Peter erect between them for privacy's sake in *It Happened One Night* (1934): "If the screen works like a kind of censoring, elaborating the effect of what it covers, how will you censor *that?*"

5. Thomas Doherty argues that "pre-Code Hollywood was more casual about the enforcement of Jim Crow codes of segregation and hierarchy than Hollywood under the Code." *Pre-Code Hollywood: Sex, Immorality, and Insurrection in American Cinema, 1930–1934* (New York: Columbia University Press, 1999), 276. Playwright Lynn Nottage suggests this as well: "If that Code hadn't set in ... the whole trajectory of Hollywood would have been different, and some would argue that race in America would be different because the representations of people of color and particularly of women would have been much more expansive" (see Manohla Dargis, "Theresa Harris, a Black Actress who Left an Impression" *New York Times,* April 21, 2011).

6. MPPDA internal memos reveal that in 1930 the matter that generated "the greatest number of protests" from the public was not screen sex or violence, but a proposed remake of *The Birth of a Nation* (1915) with sound. Lamar Trotti, memo to Will Hays, March 30, 1931, GCF, Reel 1 (reel numbers denoted by R1, R2, and so on, hereafter).

7. *The Last Mile* was never able to receive approval from the SRC or, upon rerelease, the PCA because it encouraged audiences to side with criminals. *Last Mile,* PCA file, AMPAS, Margaret Herrick Library, Beverly Hills, CA. (All SRC and PCA files in this book were viewed at AMPAS. Hereafter they are denoted by their name only. I refer to all files, whether they emanated from the SRC or PCA, as "PCA files" [and denote them PCAF] because AMPAS has used this general term to designate all self-regulation files in this collection.)

8. Though Trotti averred opposition to the Klan, he warned Hays that if the MPPDA opposed *The Mating Call* (1924), a film that argued that "there is a time and place" for Klan "lawlessness

. . . there'd be a big increase in the sale of nightshirts to guard against this 'Catholic-Jew con-trolled industry.' " "We can't probably afford to alienate a large group of citizens who thrives on attacks." Lamar Trotti, memorandum to Will Hays, MPAA GCF R4, August 28, 1928. On Trotti, see Matthew Bernstein, "A 'Professional Southerner' in the Hollywood Studio System: Lamar Trotti at Work, 1925–1952," in *American Cinema and the Southern Racial Imaginary*, ed. Deborah Barker and Kathryn McKee (Athens: University of Georgia Press, 2011), 122–150. Bernstein highlights the strange liberal/southern conservative dichotomy in Trotti but, since I focus on his role as conservative censor, I emphasize this side.

9. In *I Am a Fugitive from a Chain Gang*, a chalkboard at the prison reveals the prisoner count—thirty-three whites and sixty-nine Negroes.

10. Jason Joy to David O. Selznick, June 8, 1932, *Hell's Highway* PCAF.

11. Ibid. Joy to Selznick, May 31, 1932; B. B. Kahane to Ned Dipnet, August 19, 1932, RKO Production Files, UCLA Special Collections.

12. Joy to Hays March 25, 1932, *Laughter in Hell*, PCA file (*LIH* PCAF hereafter).

13. Ibid.

14. Lamar Trotti, "Memorandum Re: Laughter in Hell," March 31, 1932, *LIH* PCAF.

15. Joy to Carl Laemmle, August 23, 1932, *LIH* PCAF.

16. Joy to Laemmle August 30, 1932, *LIH* PCAF.

17. Ibid.

18. Laemmle to Joy, September 13, 1932, *LIH* PCAF.

19. Censors reports, *LIH* PCAF.

20. Ibid.

21. Ibid.

22. I. Auster, Memorandum for Mr. Breen, re: Miscegenation, March 13, 1934. The memo contains a direct quote from Hays. Emphasis added. Hays made this comment in reaction to *The Love Mart*, whose SRC file has not survived. The PCA file on *Imitation of Life* (1934), how-ever, shows that the International Federation of Catholic Alumnae would not recommend *The Love Mart* because it depicted interracial love.

23. No SRC file exists on *Golden Dawn*, but according to the MPAA GCF [R1], the film was "produced on the Coast . . . without any contact with Colonel Joy whatever" (Carl E. Mil-liken to Will Hays, interoffice memo, August 1, 1930). It is interesting to note that the MPP-DA's qualms with *Golden Dawn* were dancing girls and the words "damned" and "wop"—not miscegenation. The film was not a success and appears not to have been rereleased during Breen's tenure. The song instructed white colonialists to woo African maids by asking for "Koochie koo" and if she answers "yes," then ask "her if she'd care to share your jungle bunga-low with you."

24. Susan Courtney suggests that the South Seas was an alternative site for projecting misce-genetic desires. Susan Courtney, *Hollywood Fantasies of Miscegenation: Spectacular Narratives of Gender and Race* (Princeton, NJ: Princeton University Press, 2004), 134.

25. On the casting, see "Motion Pictures Drama," *California Eagle*, October 18, 1929, 10.

26. R. E. Plummer review for SRC, September 14, 1931, *Five Star Final* PCAF.

27. Joy to David O. Selznick, April 4, 1932, *Is My Face Red?*, PCAF.

28. On Mandelstamm, see Vasey, *World*, 82.

29. Joy also worried about *Morocco's* racial violence and, out of deference to the French colo-nial authority (and perhaps also to avoid the specter of a Black uprising), asked Paramount to cut scenes showing Sam ("Tom Brown" in the finished film), a Legionnaire, killing two or three Moors. Jason Joy to B. P. Schulberg, April 15, 1930, *Morocco* PCAF.

30. "Bevy of Girls in New Play," *Pittsburgh Courier*, June 20, 1931, 5

31. Col. Joy's Resume, February 22, 1929, *Hallelujah* PCAF.

32. On *Lulu Belle*, see James Wilson, *Bulldaggers, Pansies, and Chocolate Babies: Performance, Race, and the Harlem Renaissance* (Ann Arbor: University of Michigan Press, 2010).

33. Gaylyn Studlar, *This Mad Masquerade: Stardom and Masculinity in the Jazz Age* (New York: Columbia University Press, 1996), 8.

34. Ibid., 220.

35. H. M. Warner to Will Hays, August 12, 1932, *Lulu Belle* PCAF.

36. Robert Cochrane wanted her to be French (Hays to Robert Cochrane, November 1, 1930). Lou Edelman wanted her to be "part-Creole-part-French-Canadian," according to Breen (memo for the files re: *Lulu Belle*, Warner Bros., April 5, 1940). Irving Thalberg wrote to Hays that "the story would be changed from negro to white people, which would greatly add to the difficulties of recognition to the public," but he did not mention whether this "white" Lulu Belle would be American (Thalberg to Hays, August 4, 1932), *Lulu Belle* PCAF.

37. I. Auster to Breen, March 13, 1934, *Lulu Belle* PCAF.

38. Richard Maltby, " 'To Prevent That Prevalent Type of Book': Censorship and Adaptation in Hollywood, 1924–1934," *American Quarterly* 44:4 (December 1992), 554–583.

39. Though Joy worried much about offending foreign nations, he was not concerned about protests from Black civil rights leaders. He and his successor, James Wingate, did call producers to omit "nigger" from some film scripts. But this policy was extremely inconsistent. For example, there is no evidence that the SRC wanted the word "nigger" removed from *The Emperor Jones*, in which characters—Black and white—use it over twenty times.

40. Lamar Trotti to Jason Joy, October 19, 1928, *Hallelujah* PCAF.

41. Trotti to Carl Milliken, August 13, 1930, MPAA GCF, R1.

42. For instance, during the scriptwriting for *The Big House* (1930), citing "sales resistance," Joy asked for the removal of a southern accent from one character to avoid offending the South. Jason Joy to George Kann, February 17, 1930, *Big House* PCAF. With *Blonde Venus* (1932), Trotti and Joy expressed concern about the "Hot Voodoo" number in which Marlene Dietrich "is shown singing in a negro café operated by negroes," a "questionable" element for "Southern states where such equality is frowned upon." Resume: Lamar Trotti, May 16, 1932, *Blonde Venus* PCAF.

43. Gene Markey and Katheryn Scola, *Baby Face* story outlines, November 21, 1932, 3, and November 9, 1932, 1, Folder 2769, Warner Bros. Archive, University of Southern California, Los Angeles (WBA hereafter).

44. Script outline of November 9, 1932. Script outline of November 21, 1932, 24, Folder 2769, WBA.

45. This is one of many pre-Code films in which Black people "sing sex." In *Hell's Highway* (1932), unnamed Black convicts sing "Frankie and Johnny" to tell the story of a love affair turned fatal. In *Cabin in the Cotton* (1932), after a kissing scene fades to Black, Madge (Bette Davis) sings "Willie the Weeper" in butchered Black dialect and with the accompaniment of a Black jazz band.

46. James Wingate to Darryl F. Zanuck, January 3, 1933, *Baby Face* PCAF.

47. *Belle of the Nineties* PCAF.

48. Joseph Breen to Harry Zehner, October 17, 1935, *Show Boat* PCAF. "Aunt Jemima" was the stage name for Italian American actress Tess Gardella, who played Queenie in the 1927 Broadway production of *Show Boat.*

49. Susan Courtney has done an important analysis of the ambiguity present in the miscegenation narrative from *Imitation of Life*, shedding light on how the PCA's response to the film evidence "Hollywood's ongoing cinematic participation in shaping cultural conceptions of the very meaning and location of racial identity, particularly as it is conceived of as a visible category." Susan Courtney, "Picturizing Race: Hollywood's Censorship of Miscegenation and Production of Racial Visibility through *Imitation of Life*," *Genders* (27) 1998, unpaginated. In private correspondence with Will Hays, Breen would admit that the film violated the miscegenation clause only "in spirit"; March 22, 1934, *Imitation of Life* PCAF (*Imitation* PCAF hereafter).

50. Breen to Harry Zehner, March 9, 1934. This was a supposition that Wingate, who stated that miscegenation was "not the main theme of the story," did not share. Wingate to Hays, June 26, 1934, *Imitation* PCAF.

51. Breen consistently referred to Peola as the product of miscegenation, whereas Wingate called Peola "a light skinned colored girl." Wingate to Hays, June 26, 1934, *Imitation* PCAF.

52. Quote from Breen in letter from Hays to Robert Cochrane, May 18, 1934, *Imitation* PCAF.

53. Breen mentions passing as the reason for the film industry's difficulties in four separate correspondences. Breen to Zehner, March 9, 1934; Breen to Hays, March 22, 1934; Breen to Hays, April 2, 1934; Breen to Hays, June 7, 1934, *Imitation* PCAF.

54. J. B. Lewis, memo to Breen, March 10, 1934, *Imitation* PCAF.

55. Ibid.

56. Breen to Will Hays, March 22, 1934; Breen to Maurice McKenzie, March 26, 1934; Alice Field, memo to Breen on *Imitation of Life*, undated, *Imitation* PCAF.

57. Maurice McKenzie to Breen, April 3, 1934, *Imitation* PCAF.

58. Will Hays to Robert Cochrane, May 18, 1934. As production on *Imitation of Life* continued, Breen would describe its central problem as "the negro question" or "an inflammable racial question," one that the film left dangerously unresolved. Breen to Zehner, July 20, 1934. Breen to Hays, August 3, 1934, *Imitation* PCAF.

59. J. B. Lewis to Breen, March 10, 1934, *Imitation* PCAF.

60. Harry Levette, "Hollywood Respects Star's Word on What Is Offensive," *Chicago Defender*, September 12, 1942, 20. It is important to note, however, that Levette credits Louise Beavers's complaints to the producers about the word "nigger" with the change in the scene.

61. J. B. Lewis to Breen, March 10, 1934, *Imitation* PCAF.

62. Though Harry Zehner, Universal's assistant general manager, had removed the lynching scene from the script sent to the PCA, in a letter to Joseph Breen he confessed that he planned to shoot it anyway. Zehner to Breen, July 17, 1934, *Imitation* PCAF.

63. Breen, memo to Hays, *Imitation* PCAF.

64. The New York office told Breen that the word "nigger" was unacceptable, "even though it is put in the mouth of a colored person and refers to one of her own race." McKenzie to Breen, April 4, 1934, *Imitation* PCAF.

65. For more on costuming in the fallen woman film, see Jacobs, *The Wages of Sin*, 68–85.

66. Zehner to Carl Laemmle, January 12, 1935, *Imitation* PCAF.

67. For a fuller account of this struggle, see Robert Zangrando, *The NAACP Crusade against Lynching: 1909–1950* (Philadelphia: Temple University Press, 1980), 139–153, and Harvard Sitkoff, *A New Deal for Blacks: The Emergence of Civil Rights as a National Issue* (New York: Oxford University Press, 1978), 282–294.

68. Harry Levette, "Hollywood Working on Anti-Lynch films," *Pittsburgh Courier*, January 23, 1937, 12.

69. Breen to Joy, October 21, 1935. *The Prisoner of Shark Island* PCAF.

70. Matthew Bernstein, *Screening a Lynching: The Leo Frank Case in Film and Television* (Athens: University of Georgia Press, 2009), 78. Bernstein explains how Breen coerced executives to change direct evidence of railroading in early script drafts of *They Won't Forget* (1937) to far more ambiguous signifiers (80–82). Breen required wholesale rewriting on *They Won't Forget* to eliminate its "stark perversion of justice" and the mob's lack of punishment. In reviewing

Fury, Breen called on MGM to take care that "there be no travesty of justice or the courts and that the forces of law and order are not treated unfairly" and insisted that a corrupt senator be changed to a political boss to decrease the condemnation of government officials. Breen to L. B. Mayer, August 26, 1935, *Fury* PCAF. With *Outcast*, Breen insisted that "the sheriff should not be made to appear to condone the illegal act of the mob, who seek to lynch Dr. Phil. This is important." Breen to Emanuel Cohen, November 2, 1936, *Outcast* PCAF.

71. In censoring *They Won't Forget*, Maryland's state board had called for elimination of a "police officer giving negro the first degree" (a Freudian slip?). *They Won't Forget* PCAF. The PCA required that the racist methods of a district attorney in *Knock on Any Door* (1949), a film adapted from a novel by Black author Willard Motley, be changed in order for the film to attain a seal (Joseph Breen to Robert Lord, June 29, 1948, *Knock on Any Door* PCAF). Similarly, though script drafts for *The Ring* (1952), a boxing film condemning anti-Latino prejudice, had shown police racism, Breen opined, "We feel it would not be good to infer that the police discriminate against these boys because of their nationality," a change screenwriters made. Breen to Franklin King, November 19, 1951, *The Ring* PCAF.

72. He suggested changing the term "lynch" to "kill" or "punish" or "burn." Breen suggested changing "you string him up" to "you fix him" and later "let Hattie have it." He also asked that the lines "neck-tie party" and "They tell me you never forget how the body of a man looks swinging from a tree" be changed. Breen to Emanuel Cohen, November 2, 1936, *Outcast* PCAF.

73. Though Breen complained of "too much realism" and asked for the excision of shots of children playing at the lynching, mentions of dynamite, and "any . . . suggestion that Joe is actually immersed in flames," Breen's significant creative input enabled the representation of lynching. For example, he suggested that certain problematic sequences be shot in long shot to reduce detail. He even permitted scenes of Joe's "frantic face behind the flames" in certain sequences. Breen to Louis B. Mayer, January 27, 1936, *Fury* PCAF.

74. Lang admitted that a lynching film "should have a white woman raped by a colored man and . . . still prove that lynching is wrong. . . . But I . . . saw the possibility of saying something against lynching—even if it was not as it should be done. I had various scenes with Negroes in them. One . . . had Sylvia Sidney looking out a window; she sees a colored girl hanging laundry . . . and singing a song 'When all the darkies are free.' This scene was cut out [as] 'not necessary'" (though it appears in contemporary prints). When the D.A. rails against lynching in the courtroom, Lang's version cut to Black Southerners listening to the speech on a car radio, with an old man "nodding to himself," also cut, Lang said. Peter Bogdanovich, *Fritz Lang in America* (London: Studio Vista, 1967), 32–34.

75. Bernstein, *Screening a Lynching*, 99.

76. *Stevedore* opinion cited in "Commenting upon document entitled 'Code, Extra-Code and Industry Regulation in Motion Pictures,'" June 22, 1938, MPAA GCF AMPAS, R5.

77. Breen to Hays, June 30, 1936, *Stevedore* PCAF. According to scholar Sarah Buchanan, Freulich later collaborated with Paul Robeson and his wife to make the film in London, and had concrete plans to make the film in April 1937. But the project floundered and was eventually impeded by the approach of war in Europe. Sarah A. Buchanan, "The Photography of Roman Freulich from Poland to Hollywood," *History of Photography* 35:4 (2011), 416–438.

78. "Commenting upon . . . 'Code,'" GCF.

79. Lawrence Reddick, "Educational Programs for the Improvement of Race Relations: Motion Pictures, Radio, the Press, and Libraries," *Journal of Negro Education* 13:3 (Summer 1944), 367–389.

80. Breen to L. B. Mayer, November 29, 1938, *The Adventures of Huckleberry Finn* PCAF.

81. Breen, to J. L. Warner, June 18, 1936, *Black Legion* PCAF. The Warner Bros. script collec-

tion indicates that early drafts of the treatment explicitly showed the Klan's terrorism against Blacks, Catholics, and Jews. Klan members particularly objected to a Black (housekeeper), Jew, and Catholic living in a house together as "disgusting and dangerous." They were meant to plainly say, "Down with the Catholics, Jews, niggers, and communists. America for Americans." WBA, *Black Legion* Production File, B1, F1739.

82. I. Auster Memorandum, June 19, 1936, *Black Legion* PCAF.

83. Rex Hale and Leon d'Usseau, "The Avenging Angels" synopsis, undated, *Nation Aflame* PCAF.

84. Ibid.

85. Breen to Maurice Conn, June 5, 1936, *Nation Aflame* PCAF.

86. Breen to Conn, June 29, 1936, *Nation Aflame* PCAF.

87. Breen to Victor Halperin, November 17, 1936, *Nation Aflame* PCAF.

88. Marie Presstman to James Wingate, November 13, 1936, *Legion of Terror* PCAF.

89. Breen to Harry Cohn, February 28, 1934, *Black Moon* PCAF.

90. Mrs. Alonzo Richardson, "The Censor Has His Say," *Variety*, November 18, 1932, 10.

91. Raye got her start in vaudeville and worked on Al Jolson's radio show. Her first musical appearance on screen was in the Bing Crosby vehicle *Rhythm on the Range* (1936). Raye appeared in a sequence similar to *Artists'* in *The Big Broadcast* (1938), again singing about Harlem and in similar garb but without blackface.

92. Michael Rogin *Blackface, White Noise: Jewish Immigrants in the Hollywood Melting Pot* (Berkeley: University of California Press, 1996), 45–70. Just because the sequence stoked southern ire does not mean that it was pleasurable or empowering to Black spectators. It burlesques—rather than humanizes—Harlem, making it a musical fantasyland filled with hep cats who slavishly succumb to rhythm.

93. E. V. Richards Jr., to Ben Piazza, Louis B. Mayer, Y. F. Freeman, Sidney R. Kent, Cecil B. DeMille, and Will Hays, September 3, 1937, *Artists and Models* PCAF.

94. Frantz was "displeased with the intermixture of negroes and white persons." Posing himself as a southern statesman rather than a fringe racist, Frantz called himself a friend of "negroes" provided "of course . . . they . . . stay in their place and do not try any social equality plans." Frantz's asserted the southern policy on racial visibility, one he desired to see extend to film: "Our newspaper . . . will not publish negroes as Mr. and Mrs. nor will it publish negroes' pictures, but unfailingly it publishes worthwhile things they do." Claiming friends in the local film industry who shared his views, Frantz warned the MPPDA of potential southern backlash. Dolph Frantz to Adolph Zukor, August 25, 1937, *Imitation of Life* PCAF.

95. Richardson's perspective is revealing about the logic of southern racism but particularly illuminates that one of the problems the South had with social equality in films was that it implicitly imperiled white women. Richardson wrote to Breen on August 31, 1937. In a column in *Film Daily*, she expounded: "The Harlem cabaret scene . . . would lose the value of the picture to a Southern audience. The South knows, understands, and helps the Negro as no other section can, but half-naked Negro women dancers do not appeal." "The Censor Has His Say," *Film Daily*, November 18, 1932, 10.

96. Joseph Breen, interoffice memo to Maurice McKenzie, *Imitation of Life* PCAF.

97. Joseph Breen to John Hammell, October 16, 1937, *Big Broadcast of 1938* PCAF.

98. Cripps, *Making Movies*, 10.

99. L. H. to Breen, February 8, 1938, *Big Broadcast of 1938* PCAF. Breen to J. R. McDonough, September 14, 1938, *Story of Vernon and Irene Castle* PCAF.

100. Breen to J. R. McDonough, July 2, 1935; Breen to McDonough, September 3, 1938; *Mad Miss Manton* PCAF.

101. The PCA "urgently" recommended that "Kit's line addressed to the Negro, Rex, 'C'mon,

Rex—Keep me company' be changed as possibly offensive to Southern audiences." Production Code Administration to William Gordon, October 7, 1941, *Syncopation* PCAF.

102. "Eight Film Plays Are Named Best of Three Months by Will H. Hays National Previewing Committees," *Washington Post*, September 10, 1937, 12.

103. Flora's widowed status, of which we are reminded, makes possible that her deceased husband was as light-skinned as she—and thus that Sunny is indeed Black and her child.

104. On the suspense narrative and race, see Linda Williams, *Playing the Race Card: Melodramas of Black and White from Uncle Tom to O. J. Simpson* (Princeton, NJ: Princeton University Press, 2001).

105. Charles Wolfe, "Vitaphone Shorts and *The Jazz Singer*," *Wide Angle* 12:3 (July 1990), 58–78. Wolfe describes a similar moment in *The Jazz Singer* where "looks lock . . . characters into an imaginary field of relations were Oedipal and assimilationist tensions have dissolved, but the narrative itself seems suspended." The final sequence in *One Mile From Heaven,* as in *The Jazz Singer,* "occurs outside of causal logic, outside of (all but cyclical) time" (74).

106. Although a Mississippian, Harmon, who lived in New York, operating a two-man PCA branch for foreign and East Coast productions (Doherty, *Breen*, 145), was more racially liberal than Trotti. At Breen's request, he drafted PCA guidelines on "what should not be approved in motion pictures dealing with whites and negroes." Harmon developed twelve principles, suggesting, in the main, avoidance of sequences of interracial enmity, inferences of racial superiority, the sectional aspects of interracial problems, inflammatory names or epithets ("Boy," "nigger," "blackamoor," etc.), and stereotypes; crimes of violence should not be linked to the offender's racial heritage; and the Code's clause stating "the history, institutions, prominent people, and citizenry of foreign nations should be represented fairly in pictures" should be extended to American racial groups. His last recommendation referred directly to the recent southern exhibitors' protest, which he recognized reflected "existing prejudices of many Southern theater-goers." But Harmon believed it was "proper for white people and negroes to appear together in the same scenes in motion pictures," and that the film "industry must seek to formulate principles for its guidance in interracial relations on a national rather than a sectional basis" (Francis Harmon, "Memorandum: Suggesting Guiding Principles in Connection with Motion Pictures Dealing with Negroes and Whites," November 5, 1937, MPAA GCF, R4). Harmon admitted that his policy varied from "prevailing sentiment" in the South, but argued that it captured the perspective of "thoughtful leaders both black and white, with whom I have been working for nearly twenty years in the realm of interracial relationships" (Francis Harmon to Breen, November 5, 1937, MPAA GCF, R4). Harmon's track record evinces his difference from Trotti. In direct contradiction of Trotti, he advocated PCA condemnation of *The Birth of a Nation* and helped Breen decide against approving a cartoon parody of *Green Pastures*, which mocked Harlem's Heaven as "Pair-o-Dice." Harmon argued the film's religious offense to the Code, seeking to end the PCA's double standard on Black religious representation that began with *Hallelujah!* (MPAA GCF R4). He approved, apparently without cuts, *Song of Freedom* (1938), a British film featuring Paul Robeson, in which a white woman comes on to him and the two get drunk together (Harmon signed the PCA seal on April 20, 1938; *Song of Freedom* PCAF). Harmon wanted the PCA to stand against antisemitism in *Oliver Twist* (1948); when it came to miscegenation, he argued to end the ban on *Shanghai Gesture* and later told Darryl F. Zanuck on how to use *Pinky* to confront the South about its history of white rape of Black women (Harmon to Zanuck, March 18, 1949, *Pinky* PCAF).

107. Breen, Memo, undated, *Spirit of Youth* PCAF. Dan Streible, "A History of the Boxing Film, 1894–1915: Social Control and Social Reform in the Progressive Era," *Film History* 3:3 (1989), 235–259. Indeed, the governmental ban on interstate commerce involving boxing films

was not lifted until 1940 ("Government Removes Ban on Fight Pictures," *Chicago Defender*, July 13, 1940, 2).

108. Breen consulted not a white representative but Paul Williams, an African American architect considered a "friend of Mr. Hays" and a "Dr. Hudson," who appears, from the meager evidence we have, to also have been African American. According to Breen's report to Hays, both men assured him that the film would leave "little to be feared . . . from the standpoint of the better elements among the negroes in this country." They found the film "so thoroughly unobjectionable on the usual grounds" that they thought "it would help their people much, if this story, glorifying a negro athlete could be distributed wide-spread." Joseph Breen, Memo for the files, December 3, 1937, *Spirit of Youth* PCAF.

109. Breen thought Southerners were "not likely to be disposed to look with favor on this kind of picture, and we respectfully suggest that you proceed with the greatest caution in your attempts to distribute it." Breen to Shanberg, December 7, 1937, *Spirit of Youth* PCAF.

110. Ibid.

111. Breen to Lewis Milestone, February 14, 1938, *Of Mice and Men* PCAF.

112. See Clayton Koppes and Gregory Black, "What to Show the World: The Office of War Information and Hollywood, 1942–1945," *Journal of American History* 64:1 (June 1977), 87–105, and "Blacks, Loyalty, and Motion Picture Propaganda in World War II," *Journal of American History* 73:2 (September 1986), 383–406.

113. Koppes and Black, "What to Show," 103, indicate that even Paramount discussed its stories with OWI "in general terms." And my research indicates that Paramount did submit some scripts.

114. Ibid., 88. See also Jessica Wagner, "An Unpleasant Wartime Function: Race, Film Censorship, and the Office of War Information, 1942–1945" (master's thesis, University of Maryland, 2007).

115. For example, in reaction to *The American Story*, the OWI reviewer noted, "From the overseas standpoint, the presentation of members of the United Nations is inadequate and misleading and could be resented aboard." Feature review, "The American Story," July 22, 1943, National Archives (NA hereafter). Though the United Nations was not formed until 1945, Roosevelt had coined the term in 1942 to describe the twenty-six nations allied in the fight against the Axis.

116. Feature review, *Charlie Chan in the Secret Service.* July 29, 1943, NA. Bernais asked the studio "to modify this exuberance to some extent"; William S. Cunningham to Phil Krane, August 30, 1943, NA.

117. In response to the unproduced script *The Land of the Free*, OWI reviewers Roth and Ruthven complained that reducing "Nazi espionage" to "ordinary gangsterism" obscured "the real menace and character of the enemy." Feature review, *Land of the Free*, May 20, 1943, AMPAS. Regarding *God Is My Co-Pilot* (1944), they wrote, "Perhaps with a few revisions or deletion . . . it would be possible to indicate the nature of the Allied coalition which is fighting a common enemy, international fascism, rather than certain groups fighting a 'personal' or 'natural' enemy, Japan." Feature review, *God Is My Co-Pilot*, March 9, 1944. Two references to "the yellow rats" and "their 'buck teeth' " supplanted racial characteristics with ideology as the basis for war. Feature review, *Little Tokio USA*, July 9, 1942, NA.

118. Peculiarly employing epithets themselves while chastising the producers, the OWI reviewers suggested Ollie "should hate the Japs not just because they are Japs but because they represent the doctrine of militarism—the age-old idea that people cannot co-inhabit the earth unless a few men dominate all others through physical force." Feature review, *Joe Navy*, April 22, 1943, AMPAS. Indeed, OWI preferred a diplomatic politesse in its films about America "because the overseas audiences are particularly sensitive to any implication of an

American attitude of superiority." "Perhaps," they suggested, "the line which refers to our army as 'the finest in the world' (p. 5) could be changed to 'one of the finest in the world.'" Feature review, *Christmas Holiday*, September 26, 1943, AMPAS.

119. Koppes and Black, "Blacks, Loyalty," 386.

120. A notable and important exception to this policy was Eddie "Rochester" Anderson, Jack Benny's sidekick, whom the OWI gradually recognized "has been pretty well established in this country simply as a member of a comedy act rather than as a Negro servant of a white employer." Feature review, *The Meanest Man in the World*, March 31, 1943, NA.

121. Feature review, *All Out for Rhythm* (aka *Sing a Jingle*), May 3, 1943, NA.

122. Feature review, *Cabin in the Sky*, January 19, 1943, NA.

123. The part was important to OWI not only because it showed "the heroic role of dark-skinned soldiers in this war" but also "by implication, the American negro." Feature review, *Somewhere in the Sahara*, February 1, 1943, NA.

124. Ibid.

125. Feature review, *Somewhere in the Sahara*, July 8, 1943, NA.

126. This MGM script was eventually scrapped in large measure due to the Maritime Commission's unwillingness to cooperate on a film dealing with "the race problem."

127. Feature review, *Liberty Ship*, September 14, 1942, NA.

128. Feature review, *Stormy Weather*, January 11, 1943, NA. OWI rankled at the term "zoot suits" in *Girl in the Case* (feature review, January 15, 1944) because it was "internationally associated with an American minority problem, could these references be eliminated?" It also strongly opposed "Pachucos," a short film by Karl Kamb on Mexican Americans that the Coordinator for Inter-American affairs asked MGM to produce. Both Mexican American lawlessness and "their persecution complex" bothered OWI, as well as "Carmen Esperanza, who cannot get a job as a teacher because she is Mexican," aspects that, OWI opined, gave "no recognition to the great progress that has been made in breaking down barriers against Mexicans in war work." The film's "Anglo Saxon Americans" (a policemen and "petty politician who brings pressure against the Mexican boys") were misrepresented, OWI stated, as "unjust and intolerant" while "the thousands of Americans seeking justice and equal rights for minorities are ignored." They called the film's line "The Negro . . . has been a part of the American population ever since the Revolution and hasn't made a home for himself yet," a "misrepresentation of the Negro who has been making great strides toward achieving equality." Feature review, *Pachuchos*, August 5, 1943. Ulrich Bell, the director of the Bureau of Motion Pictures' Overseas Branch, felt the OWI's continued stand against the picture "will probably mean that MGM will not make it" (Ulrich Bell to Robert Riskin, August 27, 1943, NA). For more on regulating Latinos in wartime Hollywood, see Catherine Benamou, "Dual-Engined Diplomacy: Walt Disney, Orson Welles, and Pan-American Film Policy during World War II," in ¡Américas Unidas! Nelson A. Rockefeller's *Office of Inter-American Affairs* (*1940–46*), ed. Gisela Cramer and Ursula Prutsch (Frankfurt: Iberoamericana-Vervuert, 2012), 107–141.

129. They were concerned that when Joe is called on to vote on what to do with the Nazi, "he is surprised and prefers not to participate. This presentation of a Negro unwillingly follows Nazi propaganda lines which attempt to divide the United Nations by strengthening racial barriers." Feature review, *Lifeboat*, July 31, 1943; October 8, 1943, NA.

130. I cite the AFI catalog entry because the film's NA OWI file is now lost. Warners did some censoring of their own. It cut a line where William tells Craig that he will only hire him if he gets rid of certain Black clients, arguing that his properties, which Craig wants to condemn, are "plenty good enough for Negroes" (Draft of November 3, 1941, 61). Also, Stanley, saying of Parry and Black people, "I know them. They'll do anything to save their own skins!" (blue pages dated December 1, 1941, in draft of November 3, 1941), was marked for cutting and is absent in the film. In this draft, when Stanley tells Parry to "say that you took the car," he retorts, in part, that "lies won't help me," indicating that this white woman is lying. This was slated for cutting (blue pages dated November 10, 1941, in draft of November 3, 1941). Also, Stanley's mother Lavinia says, "But he's a negro and they're used to that sort of thing. It [jail time] won't make so much of a difference to him" (blue pages in draft December 8, 1941, in draft of November 3, 1941). Indeed, in each case awkward cuts aver that Warners' cuts were applied not to the script but to the celluloid print itself. Atlanta censored the film because of the line "Colored boys don't have a chance anyhow," and the jail scene where it is "the word of a white woman against that of a negro boy" (Mrs. Alonzo Richardson to Breen, June 6, 1942, *In This Our Life* PCAF). Warners cut these sequences in prints destined for various places, including Harlem and Brooklyn (though not in downtown New York City), "to obviate any disturbances since . . . there were several riots between white and Negro troops—in the East as well as the South—plus some lynchings in Dixie. Warner Bros. figured it was better to risk censure than to aggravate the then hair-trigger tempers." Brooklyn Black spectators protested until the scenes were restored. "Win Victory over Warner Movie," *New York Amsterdam News*, August 29, 1942, 11; Walter White to Joseph Hazen, July 10, 1942, Papers of the NAACP.

131. Many PCA files contained "Daily Progress reports" that commented on the war angle and other OWI concerns.

132. Blacks appeared in 124 of 406 pictures produced during this span. "Studies of Negro Performers Appearing in Feature Pictures Approved by the Production Code Administration of the Motion Picture Association," MPAA GCF, R9.

133. "Negro Performers," undated, MPAA GCF, R9.

134. Change 11 showed too much of Horne's chest. Breen to Joy, February 18, 1943, *Stormy Weather* PCAF. Certificate of Approval, January 25, 1944, for *Rhapsody in Blue* states, "This certificate is issued with the understanding that the present scenes of the pianist in the Paris café have been changed to get away from the objectionable breast shots."

135. Between January and September of 1944, the Illinois Interracial Commission, the *Pittsburgh Courier*, the Petersburg, Virginia, NAACP, and the national NAACP, all under separate cover, wrote letters, some signed by their considerable constituencies, protesting the excision of Black troops from newsreel footage. The problem so overwhelmed Paramount, the company responsible for releasing the censored newsreels, that they turned to Hays for public relations help. Claude Lee of Paramount would write to Hays that he planned to handle the problem by stating that "the newsreel cannot concern itself with a 'cause.' . . . No one has a 'right' to newsreel coverage." Claude F. Lee to Will Hays, undated memo. Hays, according to Lee, stated that "the stand should be firmly taken that we cannot yield to anyone or any cause our prerogatives of editorial discretion." Claude Lee, memo to Russell Holmon, March 17, 1944, GCF R9.

136. Joel Fluellen, who played in *The Respectful Prostitute* on stage and in *The Burning Cross* (1947) on screen, also appeared as a near lynching victim in the western *The Moonlighter* (1953). Rex Ingram appeared as a rebellious near lynching victim in *Stevedore, Huck Finn*, and later *Moon Rise* (1948). Leigh Whipper condemned white racism in *The Ox-Bow Incident, Of Mice and Men*, and, on the stage, in *Stevedore*.

137. See "Moonrise: Rex Ingram's Role Called 'Best Ever Written,' " *Ebony*, July 1, 1948.

138. Breen to William Gordon, October 15, 1942, *I Walked with a Zombie* PCAF.

139. Breen to Trem Carr, January 17, 1945, *The Scarlet Clue* PCAF.

140. Breen, Memorandum for the Files Re: China Sky (RKO) November 9, 1943.

141. Ibid.

142. Breen, Memorandum for the Files: Re: China Sky (RKO), November 10, 1943.

143. For more on Breen's leave of absence, see Thomas Doherty, *Hollywood's Censor* (New York: Columbia University Press, 2009), 132–147.

144. Breen to Paramount, December 26, 1940, *Flame of New Orleans* PCAF.

145. Alternate titles include *Ouanga, Drums of the Jungle, Drums in the Night,* and *Crimes of Voodoo*. The film, however, was reviewed by the British Board of Film Censors and did show in Britain in 1935. Steve Chibnall, *Quota Quickies: The Birth of the British B-Film* (London: BFI Press, 2007), 110 and 148.

146. Later she says to Eve, "A passive, white-blooded thing like you make Adam happy? Adam needs a woman of fire like me." Although Clelie's dark arts make her a "bad" woman, in the horror/exploitation lexicon this only makes her more fascinating.

147. Hazel Plate, memo for the files, August 21, 1941, *The Love Wanga* PCAF.

148. See Approval sheet dated September 10, 1941, for the scenes required cut.

149. Ibid.

150. Breen urged "the advisability of omitting any negresses" from the dance hall and requiring, in a fight scene, that an unspecified "woman will not be shown clinging to a negro's leg, but to a white man's." Breen to Albert Lewin, January 30, 1942, *Moon in Sixpence* PCAF. Responding to the script for *Shanghai Gesture*, Breen required omission of the line "Shore look like a tasty little dish of chop suey" as "offensive, inasmuch as it is spoken by a negro." Breen also damped down the white/Asian desire in these films, removing lines such as "Just as some white men pant for yellow women, so Chinamen pant for English girls" (Breen to Arnold Pressburger, April 25, 1941, *Shanghai Gesture* PCAF).

151. The play on which the film was based had called Tondeleyo a "negress" and as a result ended up on the industry's forbidden list. The British version, released in the United States in 1930, had caused controversy and been banned in the United States and elsewhere. Breen said the film was unacceptable because "for nine reels the whole flavor of the picture will be one of miscegenation and inasmuch as this is such a very questionable subject, we feel that the present treatment would not prove acceptable. . . . We would like to venture the suggestion that, in order to make this story acceptable from the standpoint of the production code, as well as unobjectionable to audiences generally, it will be necessary to remove any flavor whatever of miscegenation, and to establish from the very beginning that Tondeleyo has no negro blood in her at all." Breen to Mayer, October 15, 1941, *White Cargo* PCAF. On November 12, 1941, Breen would "strongly urge that there be no actual discussion of the alleged Negro blood in Tondeleyo. This we believe could be handled largely by inference, up to the point where you clear the matter up and indicate that she is white." According to AFI, the Catholic Legion of Decency still put the film in its "C" (condemned) category.

152. Breen to Disney, August 1, 1944, *Song of the South* PCAF.

153. Breen to Disney, July 31, 1944, *Song of the South* PCAF.

154. Ibid.

155. On *Song of the South*, see Karl F. Cohen, *Forbidden Animation: Censored Cartoons and Blacklisted Animators in America* (Jefferson, NC: McFarland, 1997), 49–71.

156. Emphasis added. "Passed June 15, 1945," MPAA GCF R10.

157. George Houser to Eric Johnston, October 22, 1945, MPAA GCF R10.

158. Francis Harmon, memo to Eric Johnston, November 2, 1945, MPAA GCF R10.

159. Eric Johnston to George Houser, November 2, 1945, MPAA GCF R10.

160. Memphis censor Lloyd T. Binford rejected the picture because "the South does not permit Negros in white schools nor recognize social equality between the races." "Movie Moguls Sue to End Ban of Movie with Interracial Cast," *Daily World*, September 27, 1947.

161. See Cindy Patton, "White Racism/Black Signs: Censorship and Images of Race Relations," *Journal of Communication* 45:2 (Spring 1995), 65.

162. Peter Roffman and Jim Purdy, *The Hollywood Social Problem Film: Madness, Despair, and Politics from the Depression to the Fifties* (Bloomington: Indiana University Press, 1981), 305.

163. Fox submitted story synopses for the source material, a magazine story called *Quality*, to the PCA on February 25, 1948. Geoffrey Shurlock and Stephen Jackson reviewed these in February and flagged *Quality* as possibly offending "industry policy." They set it aside for Johnston, who did not consider the issue of pressing importance and, as of the end of March, had still not given his official opinion on it, due to his mother's illness. S.S.J., "Memo for the files," March 31, 1949, *Pinky* PCAF.

164. Leonard Leff and Jerold Simmons, *Dame in the Kimono* (Lexington: University Press of Kentucky, 2001), 169.

165. Steven S. Jackson, "Memo: Re: Pinky" March 31, 1948, *Pinky* PCAF.

166. In this case, W. L. Gelling, operator of the Paramount Theater in Marshall, Texas, showed *Pinky* according to the distribution arrangements of eastern Texas theaters, but in defiance of the town's censor board, which had been created to stop the film. See *Gelling v. State*, 247 S.W. 2d 95 (1952) and *Gelling v. Texas*, 343 U.S. 960 (1952).

167. Ibid.

168. This suggests that perhaps before the MPAA changed the miscegenation clause of the Code in 1954, the PCA had unofficially shifted its definitions. Joseph Breen to Jason Joy, February 28, 1949, *Pinky* PCAF.

169. Jason Joy to Joseph Breen, March 2, 1949, *Pinky* PCAF.

170. Ibid.

171. Francis Harmon, "Some comments and suggestions re *Pinky*," March 18, 1949, *Pinky* PCAF.

172. Darryl Zanuck to Francis Harmon (cc: Joe Breen), March 30, 1949, *Pinky* PCAF.

173. Breen removed a sequence from an initial script of *Baby Doll* (1956) of a "Negro girl offering herself to Vaccaro for sex purposes" but did not invoke the miscegenation clause and rather complained of its "illicit sex" angle. Breen to J. L. Warner, August 1, 1952, *Baby Doll* PCAF. In *Lydia Bailey* (1952), a film about the Haitian revolution, Breen acknowledged, without critique, the presence of mulatto women but forbade the presentation of "these mulatto women in any way as prostitutes" or the insinuation of "loose sex between the white" crewmen and "the black women on the island." Breen to Jason Joy, November 2, 1948, *Lydia Bailey* PCAF.

174. Breen to Ed R. Svigala, May 14, 1951, *Angelo* PCAF.

175. Breen to Joy, June 24, 1952. Breen repeated this warning to Joy in a letter of September 5, 1952, *The President's Lady* PCAF. *Ebony* called this "the first time that Hollywood has ever openly represented a Negro female and white male as lovers." "The President's Lady," *Ebony*, February 1953, 72.

176. Breen to George M. Thorton, July 25, 1950, *Pool of London* PCAF.

177. Ibid.

178. Though Breen was uncritical of the film's ineffective and corrupt law enforcement officials, he dampened the racial dynamics of the story, eliminating ungrammatical English and "subservience" from the film's Black characters and eliminating references to Klan members as "white." Breen also recommended the elimination of the words "nigger" and "shine" from the script, and removed the film's linkage of the KKK to patriotism and anticommunism. Breen asked for the removal or muting of the KKK's brutal lashing of Charlie with a whip until he is unconscious. In the lynching scene Breen indicated that shots of the Klan leaders striking "the old Negro grandfather in the face should be carefully photographed . . . and the blow should not be too brutal." Breen to Walter Colmes, May 12, 1947, *The Burning Cross* PCAF.

179. Breen similarly made no attempt to dampen the near lynching in John Ford's *The Sun Shines Bright* (1952) where, despite the horror of the scene's depiction of the mob's fury (and the mob's clear racism), the town's white moral leader is able to dissuade the mob. However, he did attempt to dampen the "abject fear" of a Black boy's prayer during a lynching scene in *The Moonlighter* (1950), indicating his continued sensitivity to the issue.

180. While hiding in a barn, Paul inadvertently frightens a young white girl who hits her head on a pole, an incident the papers drum up as an attempted rape. Breen sought to minimize the insinuation of interracial rape by removing the line ". . . and I looked at his hands and thought of them touching lovely little Mildred Jenson and it made my blood run cold." Breen to Luigi Luraschi, October 17, 1949, *The Lawless* PCAF.

181. Ibid.

182. For more on Code regulation in the Shurlock era, see Jerold Simmons, "The Production Code under New Management: Geoffrey Shurlock, *The Bad Seed*, and *Tea and Sympathy*," *Journal of Popular Film and Television* 22:1 (Spring 19940), 2. And Kevin Sandler, *The Naked Truth: Why Hollywood Doesn't Make X-Rated Movies* (New Brunswick, NJ: Rutgers University Press, 2007).

183. Garth Jowett, *Film: The Democratic Art* (Boston: Focal Press, 1976), 420. Jowett cites John Sergent, "Self-Regulation: The Motion Picture Production Code, 1930–1961" (Ph.D. diss., University of Michigan, 1963), 222–223.

184. Susan Courtney suggests that there may have been a racial undertone to restrictions on *Band of Angel's* adultery, since Shurlock cites the fact that the pair are "master and slave" in his objection to their adulterous relationship. Courtney, *Hollywood Fantasies*, 125.

185. Shurlock to Harry Cohn, February 13, 1954, *Reprisal* PCAF.

186. Shurlock to Harry Cohn, May 13, 1955, *Island in the Sun* PCAF.

187. Hazel Garland of the *Pittsburgh Courier* read the film not only in terms of its extratexual commentary on interracial romance (according to *Confidential*, white actress Meg Myles met lover Sammy Davis Jr. on the film's set), but also the civil rights struggles implied on screen: "You'll see [James Edwards's] facial muscles twitching as he watches a brutal mob beating a helpless customer . . . unable to stand it. . . . [He] enters the fray. Because of his act, his little girl is brutally murdered in one of the most shocking scenes in the movie. If you think the Emmett Till case was a real shocker, see 'The Phenix City Story.'" Hazel Garland, "Things to Talk About: Don't Miss 'The Phenix City Story' . . . A Must!" *Pittsburgh Courier*, October 8, 1955, 12.

188. EGD, Memo for the Files, November 5, 1954, *Phenix City* PCAF.

189. Shurlock's letter complained of "the repeated and offensive use of the word 'nigger,'" which he felt should be used "a couple of times for characterization" but in accordance with the revised Code should be "avoided as highly offensive to the negro race." Geoffrey Shurlock to Roger Corman, July 3, 1961, *Intruder* PCAF.

190. Ibid.

191. Shurlock, undated memo for the files.

2. STATE CENSORSHIP AND THE COLOR LINE

1. Lea Jacobs, *The Wages of Sin* (Berkeley: University of California Press, 1990), 31.

2. It is worth noting that the PCA did not keep such careful tabs on the actions of local municipal censors.

3. Edna J. Carroll, letter to James M. Jerauld, editor of *Box Office*, March 27, 1953, PA State Archives, Harrisburg, PA (PSA hereafter).

4. Although past their prime in the 1940s, race films were still crucial articulations of Black life and were submitted regularly for censorship, evincing their continued distribution.

5. State censor boards operated under the supervision of various parts of the state bureaucracy, ranging from the attorney general's office to the governor's office to the board of education. Massachusetts's statute did not bar exhibition of all films on Sunday (commonly known as "blue laws") but required proper morals for Sunday films. Louisiana, Florida, and Connecticut had censorship laws but not active censorship boards. According to Neville Hunnings, *Film Censors and the Law* (London: Unwin Press, 1967), 187–189, the statute that created the Connecticut board was repealed in 1927 and replaced with an entertainment tax law; the Florida law stipulated that only those films approved by the National Board of Review could be shown in the state (189); and the Louisiana law (191–192) was never enforced. For more on these laws see Richard Randall, *Censorship of the Movies* (Madison: University of Wisconsin Press, 1968).

6. Nevertheless, it is important to note the limitations of existing material: complete records of excision and rejection in Virginia and Maryland are available only from 1945 to 1960, though I was able to find deletions to some specific films before 1945.

7. The PCA monitored Pennsylvania's and Massachusetts's eliminations, however.

8. Catherine Mackinnon uses this term. Cited in Valerie Smith, *Not Just Race, Not Just Gender* (New York: Routledge, 1998), 7.

9. Two fascinating examples are *The Liar* (1918), where white Franklin (Edward F. Rosemond), after being jilted by white Sybil (Virginia Pearson), tampers with her birth certificate to make it seem as if she is the daughter of a Black laborer (Albert Roccardi). She perseveres with plans to marry a white man. The board removed both her nightmares of bearing a Black baby with her fiancé and dialogue where Franklin condemns Sibyl, whom he calls Black, for her planned marriage (*The Liar* review card, August 20, 1918). Similarly, the Kansas Board of Review (KBR hereafter) removed the idea of miscegenetic illegitimacy from *Who's Your Father* (1918), a Tom Mix western short featuring Madame Sultewan as the Black mother, from which the board eliminated all "action indicating Negro suspects white man as father to his baby" (*Who's Your Father* review card, July 18, 1918, Kansas Historical Society, Center for Historical Research). A nearly complete index of film eliminations and rejections is also available through the KHS website (http://www.kshs.org/p/board-of-review-movie-index/13820).

10. For instance, Virginia's state censors banned the Hollywood short *Cracked Wedding Bells* (1923), a comedy that, like Edison's *What Happened in the Tunnel* (1903), played on the idea of white men's "accidental" miscegenation. According to the Virginia censor's description, a white reporter covering a Black wedding dons blackface. When the groom is killed the bride chooses the blacked-up white man to take his place. The ceremony never occurs, though, because the wedding party disperses to catch a wagon full of chickens. Though Virginia censors acknowledged that this comedy was premised on unbridgeable Black inferiority, they still feared its miscegenation. "There is a statute making the marriages of whites and blacks a felony," the board wrote in its rejection letter. "To ridicule any law is to lessen its effectiveness if not indirectly to bring it into disrepute." "Reasons for the Rejection of Cracked Wedding Bells," October 5, 1923, VA General Correspondence and Controversial Films file (GCCFF hereafter), Box 53, Folder 90. The Virginia board also rejected *The Love Mart* (1927), in which a white "lady," falsely taken for an octoroon, is sold as chattel, because of "offense" to whites and "irritation" to Blacks. "In a state where the best feeling prevails between the two races, it is always unwise to present . . . any entertainment which emphasizes race prejudice or suggests injustice to the colored race." Rejection of First National Film Entitled 'The Love Mart,'" Evan Chesterman, February 11, 1928. GCCFF.

11. New York Motion Picture Division (NYMPD hereafter) Elimination Bulletin (EB hereafter), *I've Got Your Number*, January 24, 1934.

12. Ohio Division of Film Censorship (ODFC hereafter) EB, March 15, 1940.

13. Censorship report, *Shanghai Gesture* PCAF.

14. ODFC EB, November 14, 1942.

15. State boards sporadically cut dark men's desire for white women—when it was considered too shocking or mentally torturous or involved white slavery. For example, KBR cut a slave-market scene from the silent serial *Bride 13* (1920), in which Black cabaret performer Florence Mills, rumored to have loved men across the color line, may have appeared as bride 9 (other brides were white). Cut scenes entailed "struggle . . . between brides and blacks," a "black [man] looking appraisingly at girl's figure," and "black boys looking lustfully at bride 12 and attempting to embrace her" (Review card, *Bride 13 #15*, May 13, 1921).

16. *Within Our Gates* (1919), Ohio Certificate of Censorship: Rejected—No. 856—April 7, 1920; Jane Gaines, *Fire and Desire: Mixed-Race Movies in the Silent Era* (Chicago: University of Chicago Press, 2001), 179.

17. EB, August 26, 1929.

18. Darlene Clark Hine, "Rape and the Inner Lives of Black Women in the Middle West," *Signs* 14:4 (Summer 1989), 912–920; Valerie Smith, *Not Just Race, Not Just Gender: Black Feminist Readings* (New York: Routledge, 1998), 9. As Smith points out, Black women's rape is largely invisible in America's cultural imaginary.

19. James Wingate, Memorandum, April 12, 1934, *Laughing Boy* PCAF.

20. Wingate described the film's problems to Hays by saying: "In addition to the element of prostitution, the story implies an attack on the general treatment of the Indians by the whites." *I've Got Your Number* PCAF; James Wingate to Will Hays, November 25, 1933.

21. EB, *Laughing Boy*, April 4, 1934, NYMPD Records.

22. Actor's credits are not available. All eliminated the italicized portion of the following speech: "She took a brooch. They kept laying it around in her way. It was that Sam Awkright. *He wanted her to*—Oh Peter, it's too terrible." See PCA file for *Birthright* for censors reports. New York was explicit that race, not coerced sex, prompted the cut, stating parenthetically in its elimination order: "Sam Awkright is a white man."

23. *Pinky* PCAF.

24. From the beginning, media were centrally linked to the dramatic "last stand" Interposition struggle: journalist James Kilpatrick of the *Richmond News Leader* was influential not only in the propagation but in the authoring of the Interposition strategy. Robert A. Pratt, *The Color of Their Skin: Education and Race in Richmond, VA 1954–1989* (Charlottesville: University of Virginia Press, 1992), 5. And James Ely, *The Crisis of Conservative Virginia: The Byrd Organization and the Politics of Massive Resistance* (Knoxville: University of Tennessee Press, 1976).

25. On the *Miracle* decision, see Garth Jowett, "A Significant Medium for the Communication of Ideas: The *Miracle* Decision and the Decline of Motion Picture Censorship, 1952–1968," in *Movie Censorship and American Culture*, ed. Francis Couvares (Washington, DC: Smithsonian Institution Press, 1996), 258–276.

26. One citizen exclaimed that the allowance of any film where "Sidney Poitier . . . slap[s] a white woman across the room in a tantrum of rage" showed its lack of cooperation "with Senator Byrd's most commendable plan of Massive Resistance to integration." The letter's author also included counter-propaganda—a pamphlet including photographs from the popular press decrying the national spread of integration. Bruce Dunstan, letter to Lollie C. Whitehead, September 3, 1957, Virginia Division of Motion Picture Censorship Records, Library of Virginia, State Record Center, Richmond (VDMPCR hereafter).

27. Although the main mulatto character, Amantha, is played by a white woman, *Band of Angels* was one of the first films to feature an African American woman (Carol Drake as Michele) in the part of a white man's mulatto mistress.

28. Elimination Record, *Band of Angels*, August 5, 1957, VDMPCR.

29. The very idea behind this "Integration Movie" made it a rallying point for segregationist backlash. Mrs. Fred Laidy, letter to Lollie C. Whitehead, July 15, 1957, VDMPCR. Citing imagined scenes where Harry Belafonte kisses his white co-star, one writer suggested that the board "put the ban" on *Island in the Sun* and "let our law department deal with the films in the same manner it is dealing with the rest of" the anti-integration struggle. Randolph McPherson, letter to the Board of Censors, August 15, 1957, VDMPCR.

30. J. Lindsay Almond, letter to Mrs. Amos R. Sweet, July 22, 1957, VDMPCR.

31. NYMPD EB, *Youth of Russia*, September 27, 1934.

32. ODFC Rejection. April 14, 1934.

33. ODFC EB, November 17, 1939.

34. Ohio Rejected Films List, Undated, Series 1448—Rejected films, 1919–1954, Certificate of rejection, November 2, 1938.

35. The lack of eliminations from *The Vicious Years* (1950), about a white Italian war orphan, seems to suggest that race, not illegitimacy, was the issue. See board minutes, December 12, 1951 (*Angelo*) and March 28, 1951 (*The Vicious Years*). Maryland State Board of Motion Picture Censors Records (MSBMPCR hereafter).

36. See board minutes, March 7, 1951, MSBMPCR.

37. Virginia censors trimmed a scene from *Razzia sur la Chnouf* where Lea, a hysterical, drug-addled white woman, dances in a tight embrace with a shirtless Black man and then allows a crowd of drugged Black natives to engulf her on the dance floor of a Black night club (VDMPC Elimination Records [ER hereafter], Series 10, Box 48, Folder 8, July 1, 1958). The board also cut a sequence of a jungle-attired blonde nymphette dancing in the presence of adoring African natives from *The Nature Girl and the Slaver* (1957). VDMPC ER, Series 10, Box 48, Folder 9, May 6, 1960.

38. As late as 1964, the state even cut remote verbal mention of miscegenation from *Black Like Me* (VDMPC ER, Series 10, Box 48, Folder 10, September 9, 1964) in lines such as "Did you ever get a white woman? I hear they're nuts about colored fellows over in Australia" and "There's plenty of white women round here would like a good buck nigger." VDMPC also cut two consensual interracial love scenes from the French art house/exploitation film *My Baby Is Black*, totaling over 130 feet of film (GCCFF ER, March 2, 1965). Shirley Clarke's *The Cool World* was also trimmed.

39. Indication of the censorship of *Pool of London* (distributed by Universal) is given in United Artists' memo from Bernard Kamber to W. J. Heineman et al., February 11, 1952, in "Re: Ohio censorship of *The Well*."

40. The board also excised expressions of racism prescribing that "where Owner [*sic*] of 'Dive' [bar] throws Johnny, the negro boy out . . . eliminate remark by him—'They're all the same.'" Censors' Slip, *Pool of London*, October 15, 1951, ODFC Series 1596, Ohio Historical Society Archives, Columbus (ODFCF hereafter).

41. On October 9, the KBR sent a telegram to the ODFC to see whether they had taken action on the film, which suggests that the OFDC had reviewed it. But there is no record of their decision. KBR, telegram to ODFC, February 12, 1952, ODFCF.

42. Kitzmiller, a Detroit GI turned actor, would become the first African American—and first Black man—to win an actor's prize at the Cannes Film Festival. "Without Pity," *Variety*, December 14, 1949.

43. According to *Variety*, the film "was banned in American and British occupation zones in Germany. Much of the story makes the American Military Police its villain." Ibid.

44. *Variety* stated: "*Without Pity* is about miscegenation. . . . Perhaps this subject can be

handled for the screen in good taste but this pic does not get by. Pic has too many sordid twists and over-reaches its sexy scenes to make for general theater consumption." Ibid.

45. "Questionnaire-Censorship" respondent Fred Slayer, November 2, 1950. Controversial Film File (CFF) on *Without Pity*, ODFCF.

46. "In re: Chicago board decision, E. J. Stutz to Susan [*sic*] Warfield," October 7, 1950. "In re: communist showing, Stutz to Susan [*sic*] Warfield," October 23, 1950, ODFCF. Stutz invited members of the local Community Relations board, the municipal court of Cleveland, and the American Council on Human Relations. One respondent, John H. Sears, said, "If we have grown up, I don't see any harm in showing this film. We talk democracy but act something else." See CFF *Without Pity*, ODFCF.

47. E. J. Stutz to Susannah Warfield, January 10, 1951, CFF *Without Pity*, ODFCF.

48. NYMPD EB, April 9, 1951, and December 26, 1950.

49. NYMPD EB, May 17, 1934.

50. *Vogues of 1938* PCA file. Censor's Report, September 8, 1937.

51. NYMPD EB, April 9, 1951.

52. NYMPD EB, October 31, 1934; May 16, 1947; April 21, 1952; March 8, 1948.

53. For more on Micheaux's censorship, see J. Ronald Green, *With a Crooked Stick: The Films of Oscar Micheaux* (Bloomington: Indiana University Press, 2004); Charlene Regester, "Black Films, White Censors: Oscar Micheaux Confronts Censorship in New York, Virginia and Chicago," in Couvares, *Movie Censorship and American Culture*, 159–186; Patrick McGilligan, *Oscar Micheaux: The Great and Only* (New York: Harper and Row, 2007); Pearl Bowser and Louise Spence, *Writing Himself into History: Oscar Micheaux, His Silent Films and His Audiences* (New Brunswick, NJ: Rutgers University Press, 2000).

54. *Daughter of the Congo* is no longer extant, but AFI describes it as a complex transnational narrative of a mulatto girl captured first by an African tribe and then by Arab slave traders and rescued by a Black Amero-Liberian U.S. cavalryman.

55. EB *Harlem after Midnight*, April 24, 1934, NYMPD.

56. Ohio required major deletions from every reel and removed most of the discussion of drug use and selling women into prostitution. ODFC Bulletin, September 8, 1934.

57. Board minutes, July 1 and 2, 1948, MSBMPCR. The cuts focused on passing rather than miscegenation, excising the verbal recounting of a light-skinned African American man in the military passing for white who commits suicide when his secret is discovered. See board minutes, August 8, 1948, MSBMPCR.

58. Though Ohio was the only board consistently cutting violence from race films, several boards severely censored or banned *Gang War* (1939) and *Bargain with Bullets* (1937), which sensitively portrayed the Black gangster. Maryland ultimately approved the former film, but it eliminated even the threat of violence, a standard discordant with the board's treatment of gangsterism in Hollywood films.

59. See board minutes, January 2, 1948, MSBMPCR.

60. Board minutes, August 29, 1947, MSBMPCR.

61. Jacqueline Stewart, "The Films of Spencer Williams," 4th Annual Barnard College Mellon Mays Distinguished Lecture, December 5, 2013.

62. The board's records do not give a full list of deletions, but its partial list indicates that they wanted to remove sexuality in dance and dialogue. EB, October 1941.

63. Board minutes, January 14, 1947, MSBMPCR.

64. Board minutes, November 7, 1947, MSBMPCR.

65. Robin Kelley, *Race Rebels* (New York: Simon and Schuster, 1996), 169–170. Kelley and Eric Lott note that several jazz musicians of the era (some of whom were featured in Black films) echoed this idea that bebop, jazz, and Black sound more generally gave place for an overflow of repressed Black working class political expression not possible in the policed image. Eric Lott, *Love and Theft: Blackface Minstrelsy and the American Working Class* (New York: Oxford University Press, 1993).

66. Paul Gilroy, "After the Love Is Gone: Bio-Politics and Etho-Poetics in the Black Public Sphere," in *The Black Public Sphere: A Public Culture Book*, ed. Black Public Sphere Collective (Chicago: University of Chicago Press, 1995), 58.

67. Stewart, "Films of Spencer Williams."

68. On municipal censorship of racial equality, see Whitney Strub, "Black and White and Banned All Over: Race, Censorship, and Obscenity in Post-War Memphis," *Journal of Social History* 40:3 (Spring 2007), 685; Margaret T. McGehee, "Disturbing the Peace: *Lost Boundaries, Pinky,* and Censorship in Atlanta, Georgia, 1949–1952," *Cinema Journal* 46:1 (Fall 2006), 23–51; and Matthew Bernstein, "A Tale of Three Cities: The Banning of *Scarlet Street*," in *Controlling Hollywood: Censorship and Regulation in the Studio Era*, ed. Matthew Bernstein (New Brunswick, NJ: Rutgers University Press, 1999), 157–185.

69. In the 1920s, the KBR removed an intertitle critical of train-car Jim Crow from Micheaux's *The Virgin of the Seminole* (1923) (KBR Review card, May 5, 1923). Earlier, Virginia banned Micheaux's *Son of Satan* (1924) in part for showing "an intermingling of the races that would prove offensive to Southern ideas" in a scene with a "'fashionable' dance where a white orchestra furnishes music for blacks" (Reason for Rejection, *Son of Satan*, July 22, 1924, VDMPC GCCFF; Box 55, folder 4).

70. "Any case where Negroes would try to associate with the Whites in Virginia would incite to crime." Director to Micheaux Picture Company, April 21, 1932, VDMPC files, GCCFF Box 56, folder 5.

71. Magnum, *Legal Status of the Negro*, 57; Murray, *State's Laws*, 480. Murray lists the year of adoption for public school segregation as 1928 and public place segregation as 1926. Indeed, in 1930, a few years before the film's debut, Virginia passed its first classification legislation naming those with any African heritage "Negro." Thus it may be that in the moment of segregation's retrenchment, an aristocratic, self-possessed Black woman deciding her own racial destiny was more transgressive than miscegenation.

72. ODFC records, Ohio State Archives, Rejected films, Series 1518. *Harlem Sketches* (16 mm), submitted by Garrison Film Distribution Inc., New York City. Maker Vanguard Prods, Reels-1, Rejected August 26, 1935, Cert. 283.

73. "Show Movies of Riots in New York to Prove Who Was at Fault," *Chicago Defender*, April 20, 1935, 1. Russell Campbell and William Alexander suggest that the film was a Film and Photo League property in *Cinema Strikes Back*, 49. "Film and Photo League Filmography," compiled by Russell Campbell and William Alexander, *Jump Cut*, no. 14 (1977), 33.

74. Rejected film list ODFC. Film rejected January 15, 1937. The board also eliminated lines condemning capitalism from *Wings of Victory* (1941) and *The Living Orphan* (1937). EB, January 19, 1940, and January 1942. *New Masses* calls *A Greater Promise* a tribute to the "development of theater of the national minorities in the U.S.S.R." "Sights and Sounds," *New Masses*, October 20, 1936, 27.

75. These included *Fighter against Fascism* (1933), a documentary on the life of imprisoned German communist Ernst Thaelmann, *The Youth of Maxim* (1934), a narrative film in which the protagonist battles with and outsmarts police in support of the Bolshevik revolution, and *Spain in Flames* (1937), a pro-loyalist documentary that the board thought would "stir up the feelings among Germans and Italians in this country" (ODFC Rejected Film List).

76. Although the pretext is American race relations, the film's obsessive return to Hitler makes it more evocatively read as a Jewish filmmaker's ruminations on the impossibility of being in the wake of the Holocaust. The race problem becomes an insufficient shorthand for

a much bigger problem of consciousness. Nevertheless, the film's commentary on the "American Negro" provided stirring facts and figures arranged in a kind of poetic soliloquy: "Of 2000 archivists in the U.S. less than 100 are Negro. We keep the yellow star hidden in quotas for Negros and Jews.... 50,000 railroad conductors [and] not even fifty are Negro. But there is a reservoir for cheap labor, Negros provide very well. A people of fourteen million still waiting. Still knocking at the door. Still looking at the opportunity section. A strange victory. Nigger. Kike. Wop." *Strange Victory* is housed at MoMA's film archive.

77. PSBC *Strange Victory*, License Application, June 30, 1949.

78. The board removed "all close views of native girls with bare breasts (exploiting them)" from *An Adventure in Paradise* (1944) (NYMPD EB, October 6, 1944), and it excised "all views of exploitation of dancer's body as camera moves from her feet upward," citing indecency from *L'Amour Che Canta* (NYMPD EB, March 25, 1937).

79. Race was specifically mentioned in these brutality-based excisions. From *King Kong* (1933), New York eliminated not only "all views of monster holding girl as he tears clothing from her body" but also "all views of monster with natives in his mouth as he tears them apart" (*King Kong* EB, February 21, 1933). In *Shadows of the Orient* (1935) (EB, September 22, 1937), the board required the distributor to "eliminate man pulling lever and view of Chinese [slaves] falling from plane." These changes suggest that the prohibition on brutality had (perhaps unintentionally) the effect of reversing the doom of characters of color. Such brutality certainly reduced already strained identification with these characters, robbing them of dignity even in death and contributing to the sense of narrative expendability that surrounded them.

80. The KBR eliminated a number of scenes showing armed Black men, or Black men fighting with white men. From *Quicksand* (1923) the board cut a "negro shooting white man" (Review card, April 19, 1923); from *Fire Patrol* (1924) a "Negro choking [a white] man" (Review card, November 5, 1924). The board also cut several films that dared to show Black men in struggles with white women. From *Why Pay Rent* (1923), the board removed "all scenes of colored man and white woman engaging in fight," as it had removed such scenes from *Bride 13* (Review card, September 22, 1923). Because many of these films are now lost, the board's objections are difficult to pinpoint. But the amassed evidence of these numerous deletions where race was specifically mentioned—often the only deletions made to the films in question—suggests that race was at issue.

81. KBR Review card, August 25, 1933.

82. VDMPC License Application, October 8, 1935, GCCFF, Box 54, Folder 7.

83. Evan R. Chesterman, July 22, 1924, Reason for Rejection, "Son of Satan," GCCFF, Box 55, Folder 4.

84. This anti-revolt censorship, designed patently to protect those in power, was true across genre, and can be seen in the board's censorship of films ranging from Hollywood prison films (*Heroes for Sale* [1933], *Mayor of Hell* [1933], *I Am a Fugitive from a Chain Gang* [1932], and *Strong Arm* [1930]) to Soviet or socialist dramas (Isaak Babel's *Jimmie Higgins* [1928] and *The Weavers* [aka *Die Weber*, 1929]) to documentaries examining foreign politics (*Kash-Poosh* [1930]). EBs, June 6, 1933 (*Heroes for Sale*), May 29, 1933 (*Mayor of Hell*), October 31, 1932 (*I Am a Fugitive*), January 31, 1933 (*Jimmie Higgins*), and March 22, 1930 (*Khas-Poosh*). *Strong Arm* was rejected, April 25, 1930, as was *The Weavers*, March 27, 1929.

85. NYMPD EB, January 30, 1931.

86. NYMPD EB, September 17, 1936.

87. In the 1930s and 1940s, the board regularly removed the word lynching and any verbal incitement to or justification of the practice—even when such lines were uttered by condemnable characters and in films without explicit reference to race.

88. ODFC EB, June 4, 1936.

89. ODFC EB, May 8, 1943.

90. Many of the years between 1930 and 1940 saw double-digit numbers of Black lynchings. But between 1940 and 1951, the highest number of lynchings in any one year had decreased to six. The number of prevented lynchings, however, skyrocketed, indicating not that violent racism had subsided but that people were fighting back. In 1947, for example, there was only one lynching, but the number of prevented lynchings was thirty-one. In 1949, when there were three lynchings, the total prevented lynchings were eighteen in number. Jesse Park Guzman, ed., *The Negro Yearbook: A Review of Events Affecting Negro Life* (New York: H. M. Wise and Company, 1952), 278.

91. *Burning Cross* cutting continuity, Library of Congress Motion Picture Reading Room, Washington, DC.

92. The film explicitly mentions white supremacy as one of the Klan's goals. Ibid., 31. The Klan also asks Johnny if he is "white and a gentile"; ibid., 30.

93. Ohio feared particularly "boy gang leaders" moved by the film's "very forceful suggestion" to a "destructive adventure against helpless minorities in the region." Memorandum concerning Reactions to the *Burning Cross*, undated, 2, ODFCF.

94. Clyde Hissong, "Memorandum Concerning Reactions to *The Burning Cross*," November 24, 1947, ODFCF.

95. Undated board minutes, VDMPCR.

96. "Un-American 'Solon Hissed in Woodpile' Slur," *Los Angeles Sentinel*, November 13, 1947, 2.

97. In permitting the film, the board could have broken with "official acts of silence" that allowed misinformation "to become deep-rooted" in many Virginians' thinking. "Because of the wide-spread propaganda to which the public has been subjected for more than a score of years . . . in support of the Ku Klux Klan, especially through the showing of *The Birth of a Nation*, the NAACP feels that *The Burning Cross* should be shown." Walter Tinsley to Beverly Bradshaw, October 3, 1947, GCCFF, Box 33, Folder 45.

98. Walter White to Madison Jones, October 3, 1947, Papers of the NAACP, Library of Congress, Washington, DC (NAACP LOC hereafter).

99. "Film Which Attacks Ku Klux Klan Is Boldest Since 'Birth of Nation,'" *Cleveland Call and Post*, June 14, 1947, 10B. "Virginia Bans Showing of Film Blasting Ku Klux Klan," *New Journal and Guide*, September 27, 1947, A18. Not only was the film's producer left-leaning but the film's Black star, Joel Fluellen, became, in November 1947, the vice president of the Los Angeles chapter of the National Negro Congress. "NNC to Meet," *Los Angeles Sentinel*, November 20, 1947, 11.

100. "Boldest Since 'Birth . . . ,'" 10B. The *Afro*, which polled the preview audience, reported that one Black man claimed he felt like "'kicking' a player in the scene showing how the hooded Kluxers invade the homes of their prey." Another said of Grandpa's kneeling prayer as the KKK torches his house: "He's praying like a fool when he should be shooting." "Anti-Klan film Okayed with Reservations for Virginia," *Afro-American*, November 11, 1947. The *Richmond Times-Dispatch* reported that only two of the preview audience argued for deletions and two for complete banning: a representative of the YMCA termed the film "as bad as the Ku Klux Klan" and a former dean of Westhampton College called it "very unpleasant" and found "no point in showing it." Those suggesting deletions wanted connections between the Klan's rise and the Civil War excised. "Klan Film May Be Shown, Court Rules," *Richmond Times Dispatch*, November 21, 1947, section 2, page 1.

101. Elimination Record, November 17, 1947, VDMPCR. Racial deletions were required only in the North: the Chicago board of censors required elimination of seven scenes of brutality,

including the order to "eliminate shooting of Negro (Charlie West) by Klan leader. He may be seen on floor afterward." Detroit also initially followed neighboring Ohio in banning the film, although whether they maintained the ban is not clear.

102. "Kow-Towing Leaders Flayed by Speaker NAACP Official Tells Norfolk Group 'We Want Freedom Now,'" *New Journal and Guide*, April 10, 1948, 5.

103. "Tuck Assailed by Norfolk NAACP for Opposition to Civil Rights" *New Journal and Guide*, March 13, 1948, 10.

104. The film also received a Unity Award from the Interracial Film and Radio Guild. Herman Hill, "Interracial Unity Awards Presented in L.A.," *Pittsburgh Courier*, March 6, 1948, 15.

105. New York, Massachusetts, and Kansas approved it without eliminations, suggesting a divide between state censors about whether lynching was safe screen fare.

106. Thomas Cripps, "The Absent Presence in American Civil War Films," *Historical Journal of Film, Radio, and Television* 14:4 (1994), 367–376.

107. Breen wrote to Warner Bros., "Page 103: Again we must urge you to exercise extreme care to avoid unacceptable brutality in this scene where Hank is shown brutalizing his wife. We think it inadvisable to have him actually punch her; he should merely shove and push her and generally rough her up" (Breen to Warner Bros., February 6, 1950). From the PCA file, it appears that Adams's lynching was originally supposed to be much more brutal. Breen wrote, "The scene of the mob beating Adams must be handled with extreme care, to avoid unacceptable brutality." Breen to Warner Bros., November 8, 1949, *Storm Warning* PCAF.

108. Susannah Warfield, letter to A. S. Howson, August 22, 1950, ODFCF.

109. Warfield to Hugh Flick, September 1, 1950, ODFCF.

110. Warfield to Albert Howson, January 4, 1951, ODFCF.

111. Warfield to Howson, December 29, 1950, ODFCF. "Where Hank returns to his home and stands looking through glass in door, eliminate scenes of Marsha, not completely clothed, as she is being viewed by Hank, off scene." And the dialogue "Hank: 'A guy oughter [*sic*] be friendly with his wife's sister.' And 'Aw, you wouldn't mind that. You know, they say that what one sister goes for, the other goes for too'" (*Storm Warning* Censors' Slip, date received December 14, 1950, returned January 6, 1951), ODFCF. The following sadistic lines during the rape attempt were removed earlier: "Hank: What Lucy doesn't know won't hurt her. . . . A girl like you's been around, you know what it's all about. Marsha: You're hurting me. Hank: Some women like to be hurt (gasping continues behind following speech)."

112. *Storm Warning* PCAF, Censor's Report: December 27, 1950.

113. Courtney, *Hollywood Fantasies of Miscegenation*, 202.

114. Ohio banned *Native Son* because it "contributes to racial misunderstanding . . . [is] against public interest . . . and presents racial frictions when all groups should be united against everything subversive." *Native Son's* distributor, Classic Films, represented in court by Ephraim London, the same attorney who had months before successfully argued the *Miracle* case, fought its Ohio rejection (with the help of the NAACP's Thurgood Marshall) all the way to the U.S. Supreme Court. With two leftist, "subversive" films at the center of the case (the censorship of Joseph Losey's *M* [1950] was also at issue), London faced different challenges from what the religious censorship of *The Miracle* involved ("Ohio Ban on Film Upheld by Court," *Los Angeles Times*, October 16, 1952, 23). Although Ohio's Supreme Court supported the censors, the U.S. Supreme Court ultimately reversed the Ohio court's decision in *Superior Films, Inc. v. Department of Education of Ohio*, 346 U.S. 587 (1954). Virginia removed the word "nigger" and miscegenetic dialogue (as in "Bigger picked up a rich white chick," and Bessie's line, "I almost dropped dead when I saw him sitting there holding hands with a white girl") (VDMPC ER, July 11, 1952). Pennsylvania removed the words "white" and "nigger" when they were used as epithets and any inference that Mary was sexually loose (as in the line "Whose bed did they find her in?"). VDMPC ER, August 21, 1951. Massachusetts removed the scene of Bigger and Mary holding hands in the restaurant and several utterances of the word "nigger" (*Native Son* PCAF, Censor Report October 19, 1951).

115. *Native Son* PCAF, Censor Report, October 19, 1951.

116. *Respectful Prostitute* PCAF.

117. VDMPC ER, August 4, 1958. Newspapers also suggest this reason for deletion. The *Richmond News Leader*, for example, reported that "the censorship board's action was not because the film was sexually provocative but rather because of its dealing with the race problem in the South" (*Richmond News Leader*, February 25, 1961). In Maryland, although the board minutes reflect that the board required eliminations to the film (and did not ban it) in mid-1956, the board stopped recording eliminations in the minutes, except in special cases.

118. Kenneth C. Patty, Assistant Attorney General, letter to Mrs. Russell F. Wagers, February 5, 1959. Mrs. Russell F. Wagers, letter to Mr. Felix J. Bilgrey, February 6, 1959. Office memo, June 22, 1960, *Respectful Prostitute* Case file. Hugh Robertson, "Movie Ban Upheld by Judge Hening," *Richmond News Leader*, February 25, 1961, VDMPCR, GCCFF. "Film Case Appeal Will Be Dropped," *Richmond Times Dispatch*, July 22, 1961.

119. The film shows a subversive kind of miscegenation—surreptitious, guileful, indiscreet miscegenation showcasing the supraracial power of the Black passing subject in the act of masquerade—rather than the typical tragic entrapment, discovery, and relegation to social smallness we see in films like *Imitation of Life, Lost Boundaries*, and *Pinky*. The film had a distinctly rebellious flare, depicting Joe's domination of the raw, sadistic, immoral "white" "youth culture," of Trenton's beatnik gangs.

120. The reels had arrived before the application. Margaret Gregory, letter to S. Davis, November 27, 1962, VDMPCR, GCCFF files, Box 54; Folder 21.

121. Eileen Julien, "Now You See it, Now You Don't: Josephine Baker's Films of the 1930s and the Problem of Color," in *Black Europe and the African Diaspora*, ed. Darlene Clark Hine, Tricia Danielle Keaton, and Stephen Small (Urbana: University of Illinois Press, 2009), 48–62.

122. Baldwin states that *I Spit on Your Graves* contains only a "European dream of American . . . fully of envy, guilt, condescension and terror." Dreams like these were "now coming back to Europe, perhaps to drive Europe mad" but certainly "to render Europe obsolete." James Baldwin, *The Devil Finds Work* (New York: Random House, 2000), 45.

123. Ohio removed even discussion of racial violence and crudely cut a 153-foot block of footage, including all preparation for the riot and the riot itself (Censors' slip, September 18, 1950, ODFCF). Virginia eliminated all the riot preparation scenes, rendering the Black victory over the racist white mob a mere suggestion. Elimination order, August 24, 1950, VDMPC Records, GCCFF. Pennsylvania significantly dampened the riot scenes, removing all planning and preparation for the fight and "all views of Negroes moving in for riot," though it allowed two shots of Black men synchronizing their watches to coordinate the attack and two shots of fighting.

124. Sydney Traub to Walter White, October 30, 1950, NAACP LOC.

125. Edna B. Kerin conversation, dictated by phone to Ed Harrison, August 22, 1950, NAACP LOC.

126. Francis Rivers, letter to Clarence Green, enclosed in letter to Governor Theodore McKeldin, November 14, 1951, Governor's Papers, Maryland State Archives.

127. Jack Raymondbonn, "Berlin Sets Scene for Second Film Festival," *New York Times*, June 1, 1952, X3.

3. RACIAL TRAUMA, CIVIL RIGHTS, AND THE
BRUTAL IMAGINATION OF DARRYL F. ZANUCK

1. Zanuck to Walter White, September 21, 1948, Papers of the NAACP, Library of Congress (NAACP LOC hereafter).

2. For more on the complex ideology of Zanuck's films, see Russell Campbell, "The Ideology of the Social Consciousness Movie: Three Films of Darryl F. Zanuck," *Quarterly Review of Film Studies* 3:1 (1975), 49–71.

3. Clayton Koppes and Gregory Black, "What to Show the World: The Office of War Information and Hollywood, 1942–1945," *Journal of American History* 64:1 (June 1977), 87–105. Koppes and Black even suggest this film prompted OWI to situate an office in Hollywood.

4. This is noted by George Custen, *Twentieth Century's Fox: Darryl F. Zanuck and the Culture of Hollywood* (New York: Basic Books, 1998), 299. It may be that Zanuck's gentile status meant he could pursue such plots without fear of being considered too ethnic and not white enough.

5. These racial conflicts included the bombing of Hiroshima and Nagasaki and the Japanese internment (*Daisy Kenyon* [1947], *Japanese War Bride* [1952]), the Mexican Revolution (*Viva Zapata!* [1952]), the Holocaust (*The Diary of Anne Frank* [1957]), the genocidal "removal" of Native Americans from their land (*Ramona* [1936]), lynching (*The Ox-Bow Incident* [1943] and *Young Mr. Lincoln* [1939]), the race riots of 1943 (*No Way Out* [1950]), Margaret Garner's 1856 infanticide to save her children from slavery (*The Foxes of Harrow* [1947]), the Haitian revolution (*Lydia Bailey* [1952]), white rape of Black women (*Pinky* [1949]), the Middle Passage (*Slave Ship* [1936]), and Black anticolonial struggles (*Island in the Sun* [1957]).

6. *Gentleman's Agreement* (1947), *Pinky*, *Broken Arrow* (1950), and *No Way Out* certainly fit this description. But others (*The Foxes of Harrow* and *The President's Lady* [1952]) might also be considered.

7. Symptoms of southern racial violence (especially lynching) recurred in Trotti's scripts like *Young Mr. Lincoln* and *The Ox-Bow Incident*. Trotti even adapted two screenplays about genocide (*Ramona* and *Slave Ship* [1937]). But the stereotypical *Judge Priest*, *Can This Be Dixie?*, *Kentucky*, and *Belle Starr* (1941) championed the South's lost cause.

8. Saidiya Hartman, *Scenes of Subjection: Terror, Slavery, and Self-Making in Nineteenth-Century America* (New York: Oxford University Press, 1997), 3.

9. For discussion of symptomatic readings, see Louis Althusser's *Reading Capital* (London: Verso, 1998), 35.

10. Paramount's *Souls at Sea* (1937), based on the real story of the ship *William Brown*, was another treatment of the Middle Passage, but despite two graphic below-decks sequences, it focuses more on the abolitionists' suffering than on that of slaves.

11. After May 15, 1820, though owning slaves was still legal, transporting slaves to U.S. shores was punishable by death.

12. Sam Hellman and Gladys Lehman wrote the first draft. Later, Lamar Trotti, Nunnally Johnson, and William Faulkner contributed.

13. Hellman and Lehman, "The Last Slaver: Treatment outline," March 14, 1936. In the second treatment of April 21, 1936, Nancy is more racist: "Slavery is a filthy business. To her [Nancy], it is like living with niggers" (27). Doheny Library, Twentieth Century–Fox Collection, University of Southern California, Los Angeles. (Unless otherwise noted, all production files, including conferences, notes, treatments, and script drafts mentioned in this chapter come from this source.)

14. Dr. George S. King, *The Last Slaver* (New York: G. P. Putnam's Sons, 1933), 47.

15. Hellman and Lehman, Draft, March 14, 1936.

16. Ibid.

17. Ibid.

18. Zanuck developed a storyline where a crew member on the slaver reads *Uncle Tom's Cabin* because he thinks it is about a cabin boy (Conference, August 10, 1936, 20); in another draft, Nancy's governess sleeps through the mutiny and wakes up confused at the end of the film (Treatment of March 14, 1936); in yet another Zanuck suggested, "We can get a comedy point from Thompson [as] he remembers one time they were shipwrecked at so-and-so—had nothing to live on but human flesh . . . —and Jim wouldn't touch a mouthful!" (Conference, December 9, 1936, 11). In this effort, the writing team developed "Swifty," to be played by Mickey Rooney—a "spunky" stowaway cabin boy aching to prove himself among the rough crew. They initially toyed with having sixteen-year-old Swifty "adopt" a Black slave about his age. "We hope to get a running gag out of Swifty and the colored kid—Swifty's effort to teach him English, American ideas." Rough Revision of October 16, 1936, 2; Conference, November 16, 1936, 2–3.

19. Conference, August 10, 1936, 19, 5.

20. Conference, November 16, 1936, 11: "Maybe [Lovett] has to shoot or knock out a couple of them [the slaves] so that we get the feeling of danger and suspense."

21. Ibid., 1.

22. Conference, December 7, 1936, 1.

23. Ibid, 2.

24. Thompson says of a man captured for slaving, "Why didn't they take an anchor and throw them overboard like we did that time in the Azore? When they came aboard the ship, there was nothing." Conference, December 7, 1936.

25. Conference, August 10, 1936, 14.

26. Breen to Joy, December 5, 1936. Breen complained in successive letters about the brutality the slaves suffer in the film. Breen to Zanuck, December 5, 1936, and May 11, 1937, *Slave Ship* PCAF. The letter of May 11, 1937, also condemns breast exposures.

27. Zanuck wanted exposé-style images and openly flouted the PCA's suggestions to get it. Even at the PCA's second screening of the film, Zanuck still had not omitted the heartless killing of the sick slave that the PCA wanted excised or shots of the slave women's exposed breasts. The PCA was perhaps more troubled by the "physical contact" between the ship's captain and the "half-breed" slave, which Breen dubbed "very offensive" and insisted "should be dropped entirely." He also had a problem with Danelo, "a Portuguese white man" (played by Joseph Schildkraut in the finished film), having a Black son, which, he said, "is a definite violation of the Code on the grounds of miscegenation." Breen to Zanuck, December 5, 1936, *Slave Ship* PCAF.

28. AMPAS Clipping file, *Slave Ship*.

29. *Omaha Bee*, July 24, 1937, *Slave Ship* scrapbook, USC Doheny Library.

30. See censorship records for Ohio, Maryland, Virginia, and New York, *Slave Ship* PCA file.

31. HLM, "About Books," *New York Amsterdam News*, November 15, 1933, 6. Miss Victoria Hopkins lambasted the film before its release, saying, "Our foreparents would turn over in their graves if they know some of the roles played by actors of our group." "SLAVE SHIP," *New Journal and Guide*, April 17, 1937, 8.

32. Harry Levette, "750 Colored Actors Used in 'Slave Ship' Cinema," *Atlanta Daily World*, March 22, 1937, 2.

33. Because "the scene capitalized too much on the helplessness of the black man under great odds," Baxter opined, "they won't like it on Central Avenue or in any community of colored fans." Harry Levette, "Warner Baxter Checks Use of Scene from Film That Might Hurt Negro Race," *Atlanta Daily World*, March 6, 1937, 5.

34. Louis Lautier, "Lautier Gives Hollywood an Idea for a Great American Super Movie," *Pittsburgh Courier*, October 22, 1938, 6.

35. "Conference with Mr. Zanuck on Rev. Temporary Script dated July 6, 1942," July 13, 1942, 3.

36. Conference, July 14, 1942. Zanuck also developed new lines for the cook and decided that his outstanding bravery would earn him a medal at the finish.

37. Bosley Crowther, "Cleaving the Color Line," *New York Times*, June 6, 1943, X3.

38. Walter White, "People and Places," *Chicago Defender*, May 8, 1943, 15.

39. Walter White to Wendell Willkie, April 17, 1943, NAACP LOC.

40. Morris becomes Thomas Adams in the film.

41. Cid Ricketts Sumner, *Quality* (Indianapolis: Bobbs-Mill Publishing, 1946), 282.

42. Conference, May 26, 1948, 2.

43. The initial memo states that "Mr. Zanuck would like to put into the script the sequence from the book where Pinky goes into the dry goods store to buy something and is rebuffed because she is a Negro." Ibid., 12.

44. Conference, November 30, 1948.

45. Sumner, *Quality*, 110.

46. Conference, May 26, 1948, 12.

47. Script draft of May 25, 1948, 146

48. Script draft of June 24, 1948, 63.

49. Ibid., 105–106.

50. Ibid, 121–122.

51. Ibid., 64.

52. "Conference with Mr. Zanuck (on screenplay of 5/25/48)," 14.

53. Jane White to Darryl F. Zanuck dated "1948" (enclosed in Walter White's letter to Zanuck of September 5, 1948, NAACP LOC). Jessie Parkhurst Guzman, ed., *Negro Yearbook: A Review of Events Affecting Negro Life, 1941–1946* (Tuskegee, Ala.: Department of Records and Research, Tuskegee Institute, 1947), 238. Zanuck had a long if sometimes strained relationship of his own with the NAACP—the era's largest and most vocal civil rights organization. In July 1942, Zanuck hosted a luncheon to support an NAACP-led campaign for improved Black representations. Zanuck sent letters to dozens of Hollywood producers, compelling them to join him in creating "real life . . . normal . . . and integral" for African American characters onscreen (Darryl F. Zanuck to E. J. Mannix, July 21, 1942, NAACP LOC). In the same year, Zanuck further solidified his relationship with Walter White, sending him the script for *They Call Him Cooperation*, a short film script based on a *Saturday Evening Post* article about the first Black insurance company owner, Charles C. Spaulding (Walter White to Jason Joy, July 28, 1943, NAACP LOC). All told, Zanuck submitted four scripts-in-progress to the NAACP—a surprisingly high number. Those scripts were *Pinky, No Way Out, They Call Him Cooperation,* and *Carmen Jones* (1954).

54. Walter White to Darryl Zanuck, September 5, 1948. NAACP LOC.

55. Zanuck, letter to White, September 21, 1948. NAACP LOC.

56. Jane White, "Opinion on confidential untitled script of DFZ," 1948, NAACP LOC. Although she opined that "since the character of Arch has been deleted, I feel a definite need for a dark-skinned Southern Negro character of manifest the forthright militance that Arch possessed," Zanuck was more swayed by her ideas about Pinky. He also consulted her on *No Way Out.* Jane White, "Recapitulation of Major Points Made Jan. 26, 1949 to Mr. Zanuck," January 28, 1949, 1.

57. Zanuck to White, September 21, 1948, 8–9. To this end, Zanuck suggested that the story be perceptually focalized through the Black female character—and scripted a scene in which

Pinky drafts a letter to her former lover, one of the first sequences in film history where an African American woman's internal monologue usurps the voiceover and therein takes power over cinematic perception.

58. "Conference on Phillip Dunne's Notes of November 30, 1948," November 30, 1948.

59. "Conference on First Draft Continuity," September 20, 1948.

60. First draft screenplay, May 25, 1948, 48.

61. "Conference on Phillip Dunne's notes of 11/30/48," November 30, 1948.

62. Michael Abel to Darryl Zanuck, Memo, October 15, 1948, 4.

63. "Pinky: Conference with Mr. Zanuck on first draft of continuity of 7/7/49," 2. At this point he even suggested that Pinky call out white racism in court: "I hoped for some equality of justice. I know now that you have two sets of laws—one for the white and one for the Blacks. The question here is not whether Miss Em was sane. . . . The only issue here is that I am colored and I shouldn't get the house which Miss Em left me." None of this ended up in the finished film.

64. Richard Schickel, *Elia Kazan: A Biography* (New York: HarperCollins, 2006), 205.

65. Ibid.

66. Kenneth Geist, *The Life and Films of Joseph L. Mankiewicz* (New York: Scribner, 1978), 153.

67. Lesser Samuels, "No Place for Anger," *New York Times*, July 30, 1950, X5.

68. "All About Joe," Joseph Mankiewicz, interview with Peter Stone, 1989, in *Joseph Mankiewicz Interviews*, ed. Brian Duath (Jackson: University of Mississippi Press, 2008), 171. Mankiewicz claims that he brought Zanuck Lesser Samuels's story after having "a big fight" with him about depicting Blacks using minstrel techniques. "Goddammit, this is the last time I want to see a white girl play a black girl!" Mankiewicz recalls having said.

69. "What about Carver? And Paul Williams? Marian Anderson? And Dr. Brunche [*sic*]? What if they all said that [they don't belong]? No, that's not the answer, Luther. . . . The Ray Biddles of this world . . . don't belong." Dr. Wharton was to provide the vehicle for the film's nihilistic, borderline apocalyptic racial philosophy: "It's not only my hate and [Ray's]. Multiply it by . . . millions all over the world . . . ready to shout hurray for our side. . . . We've gone from chariots to jet propulsion—from smoke signals to television—and from savagery back to savagery. Never has it taken time so long to stand still. . . . Ellen: If only we'd stop making progress and start getting civilized, what a wonderful world this could be." "No Way Out" original script (property 2024), draft 1 (undated), 111–112. In the finished film, it would be Luther who invoked Dr. Carver in a discussion with his wife, Cora.

70. Memo, Zanuck to Lesser Samuels, February 1, 1949, 4.

71. Zanuck to White, September 21, 1949, NAACP LOC.

72. Zanuck to Samuels, February 1, 1949, 1.

73. Ibid., 4.

74. Zanuck to Samuels, February 1, 1949, 3.

75. "No Way Out" original script (property 2024), draft 1 (undated), 12.

76. "No Way Out Conference on screenplay of June 16, 1949, with Messrs. Zanuck, Mankeiwicz-MM," June 20, 1949.

77. Zanuck even brought in Malcolm Ross of the Fair Employment Practices Commission to consult on the film, a fact that was widely touted in the Black press. "Photo Standalone 18," *Chicago Defender*, August 26, 1950, 21.

78. *No Way Out* Screenplay (property 2420), draft 8, draft continuity, July 6, 1949, 1949, 57.

79. April 19, 1949, draft, 57. Whitey is referring to *Shelley v. Kraemer*, in which the Supreme Court decided by a 6–0 vote that restrictive covenants were illegal. 334 U.S. 1 (1948).

80. April 19, 1949 draft, 57.

81. The NAACP established its legal defense fund in 1940. *Sweatt v. Painter*, 339 U.S. 629

(1950) (which began in 1946), *Sipuel v. Board of Regents of Oklahoma*, 332 U.S. 631 (1948), and *McLaurin v. Oklahoma State Regents*, 339 U.S. 637 (1950) were all school segregation cases that reached the Supreme Court and that challenged the administration of "equal" educational provisions in their separate but equal schooling system.

82. Zanuck to Samuels, February 1, 1949.

83. Ibid. He would explain the limits of this social equality further in defining Luther's character: "Luther does not want to crash the white man's world. He does not seek admittance to the white man's society. All he asks for is civility, not condescension, in the work he has chosen. He can handle himself. He is a damned good doctor. He has an inner dignity of his own."

84. Ruth Vasey, *The World according to Hollywood* (Madison: University of Wisconsin Press, 1997). Lea Jacobs, *The Wages of Sin* (Berkeley: University of California Press, 1997).

85. Zanuck to Samuels, February 1, 1949.

86. Zanuck to Lesser, February 1, 1949.

87. Stephen Prince, *Classical Film Violence: Designing and Regulating Brutality in Hollywood* (New Brunswick, NJ: Rutgers University Press, 2003), 139–205.

88. The preview version more squarely treated segregation *as a problem*. When Dr. Wharton invites Dr. Brooks to breakfast, the latter responds: "Where would you take me?" It was also clearer in the pre-release version that rioters were veterans, which forged a stronger link to 1943 race riots and the failures of wartime ideology. "A one-armed white vet" tries "to stop his father from joining the race rioters." When the father calls the son a "nigger lover," the vet responds by saying: "As my father [and] as an American . . . I think you stink." "No Way Out," *Ebony*, March 1950, 33.

89. The *New York Times* reported that Clare Booth Luce, the U.S. ambassador to Italy, refused to attend the Venice Film Festival if *Blackboard Jungle* was to be shown. Her actions prompted the withdrawal of the film. "Mrs. Luce Upheld on Film Festival," *New York Times*, September 4, 1955, 44.

90. See Sasha Torres, *Black and White, and in Color: Television and Black Civil Rights* (Princeton, NJ: Princeton University Press, 2003), and Mary Dudziac, *Cold War Civil Rights: Race and the Image of American Democracy* (Princeton, NJ: Princeton University Press, 2002).

91. Jeff Smith argues that the sound track of *Carmen Jones*, which dubs white singers for Black characters, is a site for a "peculiar kind of integration" ("Black Faces, White Voices: The Politics of Dubbing in *Carmen Jones*," *Velvet Light Trap* 51 [Spring 2003], 29–42). *The King and I* also spoke to questions of racial difference. Multiple musical numbers build into a sung treatise on white liberal interpersonal racial politics, suggesting no need for fear of the other ("Whistle a Happy Tune") and the acceptability of "Getting to Know" someone different.

92. Strengthening this claim is the fact that Dorothy Dandridge was also offered the role as Tiptum in *The King and I* but turned it down. "Dorothy Dandridge to be 'Slave' in New Movie," *Jet Magazine*, June 2, 1955, 61. *South Pacific* maintained the play's link between its lead character's racism to her upbringing in Little Rock, Arkansas, even though the film script was being revised while the Little Rock school integration crisis was taking place.

93. *Island* was a conservative best seller that had been serialized, like *Pinky*, in *Ladies' Home Journal* in September 1955. There is no evidence that Zanuck consulted African Americans in *Island*'s development.

94. Hayes's first screenplay was *Paisa*. Irvin Shaw's novel *The Young Lions* was developed for the screen concurrently with *Island in the Sun* and would be released in 1958.

95. Alec Waugh, *Island in the Sun* (New York: Farrar, Strauss and Cudahy, 1955), 13.

96. Belafonte was far from an opportunist in his civil rights pursuits—in 1950, he picketed the hearings that indicted W.E.B. Du Bois as a Russian spy. For more on Belafonte's relationship with King, see Taylor Branch, *Parting the Waters: America in the King Years, 1954–1963* (New

York: Touchstone, 1988), 185, 209, 218. Zanuck had already decided on much of the film's casting by his second memo (November 1955) and thus drew the characters with the actors in mind. Under "tentative casting list," he stated that Boyeur would be "a double for Harry Belafonte." Next to Margot Seaton, he wrote: "She could only be played by Dorothy Dandridge" (Memo of November 29, 1955, 8).

97. Alfred Hayes, Proposed treatment for *Island in the Sun*, undated.

98. Conference, October 25, 1955.

99. At the end of the script, he had scrawled: "What do we solve or even propose—just a story—we must try to *prove* something—why deal with a ticklish issue unless you make *a* point? WE have whitewashed *all.*" Script draft of October 17, 1955.

100. Conference, October 25, 1955.

101. Waugh, *Island,* 398.

102. The decision to eliminate the suicide-by-mob was most likely due to the PCA's objections, as I detail in chapter 1.

103. Maxwell's taunt that Boyeur has lost his Black mistress, Margot, to a white man produces an "inarticulate snarl from Boyeur: his fist lashes out. Maxwell is knocked down. An ugly threatening movement from the crowd. On the veranda, Sylvia screams. A police whistle blows. Whittingham [chief of police] comes quickly down into the square. A beat. The tableaux holds—at the edge of violence . . . Then Boyeur suddenly laughs" [ellipsis original to source text], November 11, 1955 screenplay draft, 104.

104. Accordingly, rather than having Boyeur say, as he had in the book, "All right, boys, let him have it," thus inciting the crowd to kill Maxwell, Hayes has Boyeur state, "All right, boys. The fun's over. Let's go home" (ibid.). In the final film he would state only, "All right, friends. The meeting's over." These subtle changes in language shifted the mass gathering from a mob to an orderly, if tense, political meeting.

105. Conference, June 14, 1956, 10–11.

106. Zanuck to Alfred Hayes, November 29, 1955, 1–2.

107. Notes by Darryl F. Zanuck, April 5, 1956.

108. Ibid.

109. Ibid.

110. Bakhtin holds that "Carnival" develops relationships along the lines of carnivalistic misalliances—"All things that once were self-enclosed, disunified, distanced from one another . . . are drawn into carnivalistic contracts and combinations." These changes have the effect of challenging traditional hierarchies of social relationship to create a space-time governed by an alternative set of hierarchies. It is worth considering how many of Zanuck's films, particularly the musicals, engage with the carnivalesque, but certainly *Island in the Sun* highlights the political potential for undoing power that comes along with the cultural rituals involved in carnival, thus suggesting the power of cultural politics. Mikhail Bakhtin, *Problems of Dostoevsky's Poetics* (Manchester: Manchester University Press, 1984), 122–125.

111. Although the Black people are in part obscured by their massification, the camera stops short of entirely eliding their individuality. With a neorealist flare, it grabs hold of individuals' faces, movements, and even voices, revealing the personality, life, and diversity among enmassed individuals.

112. In his first memo alone, he plotted interaction between the interracial couples and the feuding Boyeur and Maxwell in four distinct parts of the script.

113. Alfred Hayes, Proposed treatment for *Island in the Sun*, undated.

114. Conference, October 25, 1955.

115. Ibid.

116. "Notes, by Darryl F. Zanuck" of April 6, 1956, 4–5.

117. Truman Gibson, letter to Col. Frank McCarthy, July 19, 1956, *Island* PCA file.

118. "Notes dictated in Paris by Rossen and Zanuck," August 11, 1956.

119. Ibid.

120. Script draft of October 5, 1956, 137.

121. Script draft of September 10, 1956, 28.

122. Ibid., 62–65.

123. Final Draft, October 5, 1956, 137.

124. Conference, October 25, 1955, 5.

125. Casting further undermined the plausibility of Boyeur's romance: the book's Mavis was a sexually attractive girl in her early twenties, but in the film she is played by a forty-year-old Joan Fontaine as a virtual old maid.

126. Final Draft, October 5, 1956, 149.

127. Zanuck, memo to Alfred Hayes, November 29, 1955, 4.

128. Ibid.

129. Zanuck memo of April 5, 1956, 3.

130. Dandridge says that she and Justin proposed creating two versions of the film—one for the American audience with no kissing and another for the more initiated European audience for whom these sequences strained credibility. "Dorothy Dandridge to Be 'Slave' in New Movie," *Jet Magazine*, June 2, 1955, 56–58.

131. Ibid. Reportedly, the studio also required Belafonte to refrain from mentioning interracial romance—or Joan Fontaine—in any press materials during the filming of *Island in the Sun*.

132. "Belafonte Says Studio Requested His Silence on Interracial Role," *Daily Defender*, June 10, 1957, 18.

133. Zanuck, memo to Alfred Hayes, November 29, 1955, 2.

134. In an interview with *The Worker*, Joan Fontaine stated that this was the result of actor interventions on the set: "At least I have made them agree that Harry and I can drink out of the same coconut together in a scene. But they insist on no kissing and that we give one another up at the end of the picture. We have tried fighting but it's like fighting with marshmallows." *The Worker*, February 3, 1957.

135. Spyros Skouras, wire to Zanuck, April 24, 1957, Stanford University Special Collections. Spyros Skouras papers (SSP hereafter).

136. Skouras to Buddy Adler, April 24, 1957, SSP. Skouras to Zanuck, May 25, 1957, SSP. Skouras would ultimately push for a trailer in which Zanuck appeared to introduce the film, personifying the noble white liberal the film lacked. Skouras to Zanuck, May 15, 1957, SSP. Harrison to Zanuck, June 3, 1957, SSP.

137. Skouras to Zanuck, June 1, 1957, and June 3, 1957, SSP. After screening the film for nineteen girls at the home office, two considered the ending "revolting," though seventeen found no objection. With the ending, Skouras said his suggestion was not an "elimination here but an addition, provided you already have it, to reprimand Belafonte for ruthlessness in pursuing his personal ambitions," as Zanuck had originally planned before Rossen came on board. Skouras to Zanuck, June 3, 1957, SSP.

138. Harrison wrote: "Ever since the picture was first released, we have had nothing but trouble in trying to book the picture in various areas in the South due to the intense feeling of the Southern people in view of the school integration controversy. This has been the most serious controversy in the South since the Civil War and feelings have been running very high and with a bitterness usually unknown in America." Harrison to Skouras, August 27, 1958, SSP.

139. Harrison to Skouras, August 19, 1957, SSP.

140. To convince Skouras, Zanuck used a four-fronted defense of the film, highlighting the story's proven appeal in *Ladies' Home Journal,* the PCA approval of the finished film, an absence of additional shots to change the final sequence, and Belafonte's contract, which designated "certain story points which cannot be altered or eliminated." Zanuck to Skouras, June 2, 1957, SSP.

141. Murray Silverstone to Zanuck, June 1, 1957; Zanuck to Murray Silverstone, June 2, 1957, SSP.

142. Zanuck to Murray Silverstone, June 2, 1957.

143. Ibid., SSP.

144. Zanuck, wire to Alex Harrison, March 18, 1957, SSP. Harry Balance was the southern division sales manager for Twentieth Century–Fox.

145. Zanuck to Murray Silverstone, July 2, 1957, SSP.

146. Zanuck to Skouras, February 16, 1957, SSP.

147. Zanuck admonished, "We must begin to deal realistically in film with the causes of wars and panics, with social upheavals and depression, with starvation and want and injustice and barbarism under whatever guise. That is why I call upon *writers* to lead the way—if they have something worthwhile to say, let them dress it in the glittering robes of entertainment and they will find a *ready market.* No producer who is worthy of the name will reject entertainment and without entertainment no propaganda film is worth a dime." Darryl Zanuck, *Saturday Review,* October 30, 1943, 12.

4. SHADOWBOXING

1. Anna Everett, *Returning the Gaze: A Genealogy of Black Film Criticism, 1909–1949* (Durham, NC: Duke University Press, 2000); Manthia Diawara, "Black Spectatorship: The Problem of Identification and Resistance," *Screen* 29:4 (1988), 66–79; Jacqueline Najuma Stewart, *Migrating to the Movies* (Berkeley: University of California Press, 2005).

2. See Thomas R. Cripps, "The Reaction of the Negro to the Motion Picture, *Birth of a Nation,"* in *Focus on "The Birth of a Nation,"* ed. Fred Silva (Englewood Cliffs, NJ: Prentice Hall, 1971), 111–124.

3. For the purposes of this chapter, film reviews are not activism, unless the reviewer explicitly calls readers to action.

4. This chapter is informed by emerging work on the modern politics of Black performance of race and self-hood, and it seeks to find traces of these performances in protest. Pickets, even resolutions and open letters, were as much performances counterposed against Hollywood, designed to bring out the gravitas and self-hood missing from the texts they critiqued. Stephanie Batiste, *Darkening Mirrors: Imperial Representation in Depression Era African American Performance* (Durham, NC: Duke University Press, 2011); Daphne Brooks, *Bodies in Dissent: Spectacular Performances of Race and Freedom, 1850–1910* (Durham, NC: Duke University Press, 2011); Jayna Brown, *Babylon Girls: Black Women Performers and the Shaping of the Modern* (Durham, NC: Duke University Press, 2008).

5. See Thomas Cripps, *Slow Fade to Black: The Negro in American Film, 1900–1942* (New York: Oxford University Press, 1977), still one of the most authoritative sources on NAACP film activities.

6. The first was the proposed sound version of *The Birth of a Nation* in 1930. Several years later, Roy Wilkins protested to Universal that a Harlem model was booed in *Beauty on Broadway* (1933). Roy Wilkins to Walter Winchell, August 9, 1933, Papers of the NAACP, Library of Congress, Washington, DC (NAACP LOC, hereafter).

7. Eva Jessye, "Movie News: The Truth about 'Hallelujah,'" *Afro-American,* July 19, 1930, A9;

Eva Jessye, "The Actors in 'Hallelujah' Didn't Get Enormous Salaries: 'Inside' Story on Filming," *Afro-American*, July 5, 1930, 8.

8. The operators were often backed only by local, sometimes Black-run, organizations like New York's Citizen's Civic Affairs Committee, the Motion Picture Projectionists Association, and Harlem Labor Union, and Chicago's Negro Labor Relations League, with only occasional help from major labor organizations like the AFL and CIO. "Motion Picture Men Protest," *Afro-American*, December 21, 1923, 11; "Movie Salary 3-Year Fight Close to End," *Philadelphia Tribune*, September 20, 1934, 1; J. Smith, "I.L.D Joins with Projectionists in Labor Dispute," *Afro-American*, December 7, 1935, 13; J. Smith, "Movie Operators Claim Victory at End of 4-Week Strike: Boost in Wage Scale Agreed Upon," *Afro-American*, December 14, 1935, 13; "Picket Theaters Where Moving Picture Operators Are Denied Jobs: Number of Operators in Chicago," *Pittsburgh Courier*, November 28, 1936, 21; "Art Theatre Employs Colored Ushers," *New York Amsterdam News*, August 14, 1937, 12; "Boycott Movie; Barred Race Operators: St. Louisans Carry on with Jobs Campaign Theatre Enters," *Chicago Defender*, April 22, 1939, 6; "Loew's Changes Policy, Colored Workers Hired," *Cleveland Call and Post*, August 31, 1939, 12; "Union Renews Job Campaign," *New York Amsterdam News*, October 21, 1939, 7.

9. "Delete Offensive Terms from 'Emperor Jones' Film," *New Journal and Guide*, October 7, 1933, 1.

10. Pro–Marcus Garvey spectators also threw bricks at the screen during a showing of Bud Pollard's *The Black King* (1932), a film burlesquing the leader. "Sans the Footlight or Even the Stage with the Drops," *Chicago Defender*, July 30, 1932, 5.

11. "'I Am a Fugitive' at the Roosevelt," *Pittsburgh Courier*, December 17, 1932, A7.

12. "I Fled the Chain Gang," *Afro-American*, April 15, 1939, 5; "A Georgia Convict Camp," *Afro-American*, January 27, 1934, 17.

13. Harry Levette, "GOSSIP of the MOVIE LOTS," *Atlanta Daily World*, July 21, 1932, 3A.

14. "Theresa Harris Baby Face of Films Scoring," July 29, 1933, *Afro-American*, 11. Harry Levette insisted that Theresa Harris was a "pioneer portrayer of the serious young girl types for colored actresses in major features" and that she "set a new style of colored girls in pictures—that of the sweet type." Harry Levette, "Thru Hollywood with Harry Levette: Off to Hollywood," *Chicago Defender*, October 30, 1937, 18; Harry Levette, "Coast Codgings: What, No More Scandal?" *Chicago Defender*, June 1, 1935, 7.

15. "Muse Stars in Film with Barthelmess," *Pittsburgh Courier*, December 2, 1933, A6.

16. Ralph Matthews, "What Were the Ten Best Films of 1933?: Many Movie Critics in Disagreement," *Afro-American*, January 6, 1934, 19.

17. Fay M. Jackson, "Fredi Washington Strikes New Note in Hollywood Film," *Pittsburgh Courier*, December 15, 1934, A8.

18. Camera Eye, "Screenings," *Negro Liberator*, December 22, 1934.

19. Ibid.

20. Rev. Horace White of Ohio, who read the book and saw the movie, decided to critique the film from the pulpit of his African American church. *Chicago Defender* included the text of his critique, which also followed along social justice lines, claiming that "Peola was unrealistic, a myth. There are no such Negroes who would give up wealth and respect simply to be a white cashier," and that, in the film's warped logic, Delilah "is subservient because she wants to be and not because of the white man. Such psychology shows that the Negro is unfit for proving his right to American citizenship." "Minister Raps Imitation of Life as Subtle Propaganda," *Chicago Defender*, January 26, 1935. A similar sentiment appeared in the Philadelphia Black newspaper the *Christian Recorder*: "The docility of Aunt Delilah cannot be found today. . . . It is not something which is to be held up to the modern generation of Negroes struggling for their place in American life." "Imitation of Life," *Christian Recorder*, March 28, 1935.

21. On epithets, see Louis Lautier, "Louise Beavers Wouldn't Use Epithet in 'Imitation of Life,'" *Afro-American,* March 2, 1935, 9. When the studio claimed the word was used between Black people, Beavers smartly insisted that the film's use made it "a fighting word" because it was not Blacks but "others" that were responsible for its use. The word "Black" was used in place of "nigger" in the finished film. Lautier reports that the NAACP wrote to the studio protesting the term but there is no evidence of this in studio or NAACP files.

22. Gerald Horne, *Race Woman: The Lives of Shirley Graham DuBois* (New York: New York University Press, 2000), 64–70.

23. Graham's open letter appeared as a news item in the *New York Age* and the *Baltimore Afro-American.* "Basement Standard of 'Imitation of Life' Riles Oberlin Students," *Afro-American,* March 9, 1935, 16; "Oberlin Students Turn Thumbs Down on *Imitation of Life,*" *New York Age,* March 9, 1935.

24. Walter White to Will Hays, August 12, 1930, MPAA GCF, Reel 1.

25. Camera Eye, "Screenings," *Negro Liberator,* December 23, 1933; Camera Eye, "Screenings," *Negro Liberator,* February 3, 1933. In 1934, the *Liberator* called *Laughter in Hell*'s lynching of Black chain gang prisoners "a warning to the Negroes of the South that this is exactly what may happen" if they "refuse to submit to the will of the southern ruling class." Camera Eye, "Screenings," February 10, 1934; "The Negro in the Movie," *Negro Liberator,* October 21, 1933.

26. Camera Eye, "Screenings," *Negro Liberator,* December 1, 1934.

27. On *The Bowery,* see David Platt, "Movie Snapshots," *Negro Liberator,* December 2, 1933.

28. In addition, the National Negro Congress, an umbrella organization with a branch-national structure similar to that of the NAACP, became more active during these years, protesting not only theater segregation, but also the revival of *The Birth of a Nation,* which they felt could be an obstacle to the passage of anti-lynching legislation. The NNC not only picketed *The Birth of a Nation,* but also ridiculed the film, suggesting that audiences found it dated and laughable. "Revival of 1915 Film Protested: Silent Movie Draws Hilarity Instead of Serious Reception," *New York Amsterdam News,* March 5, 1938, 17. For more on the National Negro Congress, see Erik Gellman, *Death Blow to Jim Crow: The National Negro Congress and the Rise of Militant Civil Rights* (Chapel Hill: University of North Carolina Press, 2012).

29. The *Chicago Defender* and the *Los Angeles Sentinel* covered the campaign in their national editions. "Hollywood Working on Anti-Lynch Films," *Pittsburgh Courier,* January 23, 1937, 12; "Ban Asked on Three Movies by N.A.A.C.P.," *Los Angeles Sentinel,* March 26, 1936, 1.

30. Breen to Hays, September 5, 1935, MPAA GCF, Reel 11.

31. Breen to Samuel Goldwyn, May 3, 1935; Breen to Samuel Goldwyn, June 11, 1935, *Barbary Coast* PCAF.

32. Breen to Jack Warner, August 14, 1935, *Frisco Kid* PCAF.

33. Barbara Savage, *Broadcasting Freedom: Radio, War, and the Politics of Race* (Chapel Hill: University of North Carolina Press, 1999).

34. Roi Ottley, "Hectic Harlem: Negroes Applaud Lynching," *New York Amsterdam News,* January 4, 1936.

35. Louis Lautier, "Capitol Spotlight," *Afro-American,* June 20, 1936, 15; Walter White to Eleanor Roosevelt, May 29, 1936; Walter White to Eleanor Roosevelt, June 1, 1936, NAACP LOC Series 1, Reel 26.

36. Roi Ottley praised the film for being as "honest in reaching the kernel of social injustice" as *I Am a Fugitive from a Chain Gang* (1931). Reading the editing and mise-en-scène closely, he argued: "The hideous carnival of a lynching is expertly handled. In swift moving shots … some of the women carry babies and hold them up to see the spectacle of a man burning alive." "The high note" for Ottley was "that these people are actually brought to trial." Although Ottley critiqued the film's silence on race, "the Negro," he stated, "will have no difficulty in identifying

himself with Joe Wilson and appreciat[ing] his bitter experience." "Reviewer Acclaims New Film," *New York Amsterdam News,* June 13, 1936, 8.

37. Even the more conservative *Atlanta Daily World* called the film an "editorial against the evils of mob spirit" and "a steadfast condemnation of lynching which has taken over 6,000 people to death since the Civil War. . . . It has all the usual punch and power backed up by an analogy that touches colored American like it has never been touched before in the cinema." Rig Roberts, "World Scribe Advises Fans to See 'Fury,'" *Atlanta Daily World,* July 22, 1936, 5.

38. Ben J. Davis, "Film Indictment of Lynching," *Daily Worker,* June 9, 1936.

39. Charles Bowen, "On the Air," *Philadelphia Tribune,* March 11, 1937, 15. Archie Seale of the *New York Amsterdam News* also recommended the film because it "shows the colored people the only way to stop lynching." "Around Harlem with Archie Seale," *New York Amsterdam News,* February 13, 1937, 11.

40. "Praise Film Recounting Lynching in Georgia," *Philadelphia Tribune,* July 29, 1937, 2.

41. Wood, *Lynching and Spectacle,* 253.

42. "Praise Film Recounting Lynching in Georgia," *Philadelphia Tribune,* July 29, 1937, 2.

43. Jackie Meares, "On the Air and in It," *Cleveland Call and Post,* July 15, 1937, 5; St. Claire Bourne, "Strand Picture Recommended," *New York Amsterdam News,* July 24, 1937, 16.

44. Wood, *Lynching and Spectacle,* 255.

45. Frances Ball, "Browsing in Brooklyn," *New York Amsterdam News,* July 17, 1937, 10.

46. Ibram Rogers, *The Black Campus Movement: Black Students and The Racial Reconstitution of Higher Education, 1965–1972* (New York: Palgrave Macmillan, 2012), 51; Lillian Johnson, "A Woman Talks," *Afro-American,* November 13, 1937, 9.

47. Floyd Calvin, "The Digest," *Cleveland Call and Post,* January 13, 1938, 8B; Gillespie, "Students Boycott Jim Crow Theatres," *Afro-American,* February 26, 1938, 11.

48. Leonard J. Leff, "*Gone With the Wind* and Hollywood's Racial Politics," *Atlantic Monthly* 284:6 (December 1999), 106. Though the *Chicago Defender*'s Earl Morris told readers to demand that Will Hays ban the film if it used the word "nigger"—even providing Hays's address—epithets were by no means the only point of contention. The Black press reported that during tryouts producers asked Black actors to use the word "nigger." Earl J. Morris, "Race Actors Flayed for 'Gone With the Wind' Parts," *Chicago Defender,* February 11, 1939, 19. Promises to use "darky" sparingly failed to placate some Black commentators. "Opinion," *Afro-American,* February 25, 1939, 4.

49. In her open letter to Will Hays, Minnie Johnson of Washington's U Street Neighborhood Council expressed "fear" that Mitchell's scene showing Black soldiers attempting miscegenous rape would educate white Americans in "vicious propaganda," creating "race antagonism, race prejudice, and great humiliation to a minority group struggling to reach high levels of democracy." "Biased Scenes in New Dixie Film Assailed," *Afro-American,* June 10, 1939, 12. Over two months before the film's premiere, the National Baptist Convention's president and women's auxiliary claimed *GWTW* "defamed" the Black male slave and drafted a public resolution calling it a "disgrace." "Fight Showing of 'Gone With the Wind,'" *Chicago Defender,* September 16, 1939, 20.

50. St. Clair Bourne, "'Gone with Wind' May Cause Strife," *New York Amsterdam News,* December 30, 1939 ,15.

51. Dan Burley, "Gone with the Wind," *New York Amsterdam News,* January 6, 1940, 16.

52. Selznick even attempted to placate the more hostile Black press by involving them in discussions of the film, though only as early as April 1939. "Press Representative Discuss 'Wind,'" *Pittsburgh Courier,* April 8, 1939, 13.

53. Though the film bored Wilkins by retelling slavery's history through southern eyes, he thought it contained nothing Black folks could "work up a good mad over." "In truth, there

is more than a suspicion that someone, somewhere in the long line of production, is taking a few sly pokes at ante-bellum days." Roy Wilkins, "Watchtower," *New York Amsterdam News,* 30, 1939, 7.

54. In 1940, White, worried about the "dangers of . . . the glorification of 'vigilantes' justice' and the taking of the law into their own hands by various groups," in Hollywood films of the decade, asked MPPDA employee Francis Harmon for a list of any cuts the MPPDA had required from *Gone with the Wind.* He told Harmon that he was concerned "about the possible dangers in the circulation of the film." Walter White to Francis Harmon, April 5, 1940, NAACP LOC.

55. Walter White to David O. Selznick, March 26, 1940, NAACP LOC.

56. American Labor Aid called upon labor and liberal organizations, Black and white, to "bring to the attention of their members . . . the real and unvarnished truth" of the Civil War and Reconstruction, a truth that "*Gone with the Wind* distorts . . . and confuses . . . in the minds of the working class." Arthur P. Burch, "Views on Many Questions," *New York Amsterdam News,* January 20, 1940, 14.

57. "Davis Bitterly Attacks Dies, 'Gone with Wind,'" *Afro-American,* April 6, 1940, 23; William Patterson, "Gone with the Wind," *Chicago Defender,* January 6, 1940, 15.

58. The AFL and CIO also connected *Gone with the Wind*'s release to the congressional turn against labor legislation. "*Gone with the Wind* has not appeared on the scene by accident. . . . The picture's theme dovetails completely with the efforts of the reactionaries of the Dies Committee stripe and those who attack labor and progressive legislation to break the growing unity between colored and white workers." "AF of L and CIO Boycott 'Wind,'" *Afro-American,* January 13, 1940, 14.

59. "More Than 100 Urge Boycott of Epic Films," *Chicago Defender,* February 3, 1943. For more on the NNC see Erik S. Gellman, *Death Blow to Jim Crow: The National Negro Congress and the Rise of Militant Civil Rights* (Chapel Hill: University of North Carolina Press, 2012). In Brooklyn, twenty-one civic organizations signed a statement of protest. "21 B'kyln Civic Leaders Decemberry Anti-Negro Film," *Daily Worker,* February 1, 1944. In Chicago, led by William Patterson, pickets met showings at both the Wood and the Oriental theaters. "Chicagoans Picket 'Gone with the Wind,'" *Chicago Defender,* February 3, 1940, 9; "Pickets, Patrons, and Ushers in Washington's Showing of 'Gone with the Wind,'" *Afro-American,* March 9, 1940, 13.

60. In at least one case, arrested picketers leveled charges of police brutality, suggesting that civil rights violations extended from the screen to the protests themselves. "GWTW Pickets Face Trial Tomorrow in Brooklyn Court," *Daily Worker,* February 8, 1940.

61. George Padmore, "Londoners Boycott 'Gone with the Wind,'" *Chicago Defender,* May 18, 1940, 5. This was not the first transnational anti-Hollywood protest by a Black American ex-pat. In his last years of life, Marcus Garvey in London asked the Home Secretary to ban *Song of Freedom* (1936) starring Paul Robeson, claiming that it was, along with *Imitation of Life, Green Pastures* (1936), and other Robeson films such as *Emperor Jones* and *Sanders of the River* (1935), an "exaggeration," part of an international conspiracy "to crush the aspirations of Negroes to higher culture and civilization and to impress them that they are inferior." "Garvey Charges Divine's Role Is 'Blasphemy of Worst Kind,'" *Pittsburgh Courier,* September 19, 1936, 7.

62. Cripps, *Making Movies Black,* 56–60.

63. Though White was against censorship in general, he was remarkably consistent in efforts to restrain *The Birth of a Nation,* throughout the 1940s and 1950s, both picketing the film's showing and calling for its withdrawal. The national NAACP's continued protest of *Birth* operated as a threat, reminding the studios of the organization's strength and interest in film.

With *Birth* they showcased the tactical shrewdness and complexity that many of their film campaigns in Hollywood lacked.

64. Martha Biondi, "The Struggle for Black Equality in New York City, 1945–1955" (PhD diss., Columbia University, 2001), 8; Beth Thompkin Bates, *Pullman Porters and the Rise of Protest Politics in Black America, 1925–1945* (Chapel Hill: University of North Carolina Press, 2001).

65. Walter White to Will Hays, February 4, 1942, NAACP LOC.

66. Walter White to Warner Bros., February 4, 1941, NAACP LOC.

67. Clayton Koppes and Gregory Black, "Blacks, Loyalty, and Motion Picture Propaganda," *Journal of American History* 73:2 (September 1986), 393–396.

68. "I know of no sound reason why Johnson's reputation should be 'redeemed' right now," he stated, alluding to World War II's democratic struggles. Walter White to Lowell Mellett, August 17, 1942.

69. Nelson Poynter to Walter White, August 28, 1942, NAACP LOC. MGM claimed a script had been leaked to the *Daily Worker*. In deference to OWI, MGM avoided the "negro angle" by minimizing scenes involving Stevens's housekeeper, Lydia Hamilton Smith (called Addie in the film and played by Louise Beavers), who in historical fact was Stevens's confidante and perhaps lover. MGM intended to play up their romantic relationship, possibly using it to further condemn Stevens as *The Birth of a Nation* had condemned Austin Stoneman, but the finished film avoided any implication of "intimacy."

70. Walter White to Howard Dietz, November 27, 1942, NAACP LOC.

71. Theodore Bilbo, Tom Connally, and John Rankin were openly racist white members of Congress.

72. "Broadway Theatrical People Ask Scrapping of MGM Film: Says *Tennessee Johnson* Is Negro Hater," *New Journal and Guide*, December 19, 1942, A16.

73. "Film Scored by Noted Actors and Musicians as Harmful to Race Relations and Unity," Release #91, 12.11.42. "Negro Groups Protest Showing of 'Tenn. Johnson,' " *Cleveland Call and Post*, January 16, 1943, 12B.

74. Walter White to Jason Joy, July 28, 1943, NAACP LOC.

75. Walter White to Joseph Hazen, July 10, 1948, NAACP LOC.

76. When the *Herald-Tribune* reviewer suggested that the "days were too depressing for a film about lynching," White, in a letter to the editor, championed the film as "Hollywood facing conditions as they are instead of indulging in . . . trivialities." Walter White, letter to the editor of *New York Herald-Tribune*, May 12, 1943, NAACP LOC.

77. Walter White to Sol Lesser, July 2, 1943, NAACP LOC.

78. Walter White to Preston Sturges, April 22, 1942, NAACP LOC.

79. Miss Crump, memo to staff, August 7, 1942; Miss Crump, memo to Walter White, August 13, 1942; "Protests Film Scene," *New York Amsterdam Star-News*, August 22, 1942, 11.

80. Miss Crump, memo to Walter White, August 13, 1942, NAACP LOC.

81. Julia Baxter was the child of a Louis E. Baxter, a former New York City health inspector, and grew up in a predominantly white environment in Bernardsville, New Jersey. She was the first Black graduate of Douglass College at Rutgers University and in 1938 received her master's degree in English and comparative literature from Columbia University. Jeanette Robinson, "Julia Baxter Bates: Her Legend and Life," obituary on display at Essex County Community College, 2003. Although she dreamed of becoming a high school teacher, she could not get a teaching job except on a segregated basis, even in her hometown, and therefore opted to teach English and American literature to college students at Dillard University in New Orleans. In 1943 she moved to New York and joined the NAACP staff. "New Jersey Black History; Julia Baxter Bates (1917–)," *Bergen County Record*, February 17, 2003, A3.

82. Julia Baxter, "NAACP's Goals and Achievements, 1946–47," January 30, 1947, NAACP LOC. Baxter was also a frequent author for *The Crisis* and was coauthor of the important "Brandeis brief," which contributed to the organization's victory in *Brown v. Board of Education.* Robinson, "Bates," 1.

83. Barbara Ransby, biographer of Ella Baker, notes that in the NAACP, "as in other political organizations, women were indispensable but underappreciated. The association had never elected a woman as its executive secretary, and women were often excluded from the internal inner circle of decision makers. On the other hand, women formed the backbone of many of the most active local branches, as well as of the national staff itself." Barbara Ransby, *Ella Baker and the Black Freedom Movement: A Radical Reconsideration* (Chapel Hill: University of North Carolina Press, 2003), 106.

84. Julia Baxter, memo to Odette Harper, April 16, 1943, NAACP LOC.

85. Julia Baxter, memo to Roy Wilkins on *Music for Millions,* January 10, 1945, NAACP LOC.

86. Ibid.

87. Ibid.

88. Julia Baxter memo to Roy Wilkins, April 10, 1944, NAACP LOC.

89. Roy Wilkins, memo to Miss [Edna] Wasem, May 9, 1947, NAACP LOC. The film came under NAACP review because Archer Winsten of the *New York Post,* another friend of White, publicly criticized Butterfly McQueen's role.

90. Julia Baxter, memo to Roy Wilkins, May 12, 1947, NAACP LOC.

91. Wilkins, memo to David Selznick, May 21, 1947, NAACP LOC.

92. See MPAA General Correspondence File, Roy Wilkins to Paramount Pictures, January 5, 1944, and January 14, 1944. C. L. Evans to Robert Gilliam of Paramount, February 15, 1944. Martin Hayes Bickman to Will Hays, September 25, 1944.

93. Roy Wilkins to William Goetz, February 17, 1944, NAACP LOC.

94. Ibid.

95. Canada Lee protested this characterization on the set, claiming Joe was segregated from other characters and was cast as subservient, even addressing the Nazi captive with a "yes-sir." But scenarist Jo Swerling refused changes, maintaining that Joe's apparent segregation was a matter of his personality. John McManus, "Race Imperialism in 'Lifeboat,' " *PM,* January 18, 1944.

96. Press release dated February 17, 1944, "20th Century-Fox Told 'Lifeboat' Disappointing." Roy Wilkins to William Goetz, February 17, 1944. Joy responded that he felt White would disagree with Wilkins's view and "substantiate . . . that we have made a commendable effort to use Negroes in a normal manner, without attempting to exaggerate or minimize their presence." He cited the fifty Negroes used in Fox pictures. "People should be used [in a role] because of their ability to appropriately enact the role given them . . . not be singled out as Negro, Jew, Methodist, Catholic or any other segregating classification." Jason Joy to Roy Wilkins, March 31, 1944. NAACP LOC.

97. *Pittsburgh Courier*'s Bureau of Public Opinion, "Citizens Advocate a Display of Race Self-Respect," *Pittsburgh Courier,* July 3, 1943, 4.

98. Only a few issues of the *Tribune* from these years are extant, so Davis's review of the film seems to be lost. This quote comes from commentary on the film in Alyce Key's column "Key Notes," *Los Angeles Tribune,* August 17, 1942.

99. Paul Robeson Jr. touches on Morros's relationship to the Black Left, including his ties to NNC president Max Yergan, in *The Undiscovered Paul Robeson: Quest for Freedom, 1939–1976* (Somerset, NJ: Wiley, 2010), 33–34.

100. Tom O'Connor, "Disputed Negro Episode in 'Tales of Manhattan' Film May Lead to

Paul Robeson's Retirement from Movies," *PM's Daily Picture Magazine*, 6–7. Clipping in Papers of the NAACP. See also Manny Farber, "Tales of Manhattan," in *New Republic*, October 12, 1942.

101. Davis-Lomax was indeed one of the chairmen of MOWM's Pacific division. "MOWM Heads Re-Elected," *Afro-American*, July 10, 1943, 7.

102. Almena Davis-Lomax, enclosure in letter to Walter White of September 14, 1942, NAACP LOC.

103. Almena Davis-Lomax to Walter White, September 14, 1942; Walter White to Almena Davis, September 21, 1942, NAACP LOC.

104. Davis-Lomax to Walter White, September 14, 1942, NAACP LOC.

105. Saul Halpert, "Hollywood 'Negro' Disgrace Race," *Daily Worker*, August 16, 1942; "Californians Organize League to Fight Movie Industry Jim-Crow," *Cleveland Call and Post*, September 12, 1942, 1.

106. Peter Suskind, "Stardust," *New Journal and Guide*, October 10, 1942, B21; Wendell Green, "Paul Robeson Discusses 'Tales': Lists Reasons for Accepting Role in Interview," *New Journal and Guide*, October 10, 1942, A17.

107. The NAACP protested several films during postwar years, including a documentary on venereal disease, *Feeling All Right* (1947), and two cartoons, *Lonesome Mouse* (1949) and *Scrub Me Mama with a Boogie Beat* (1949). But the number of protests per year was lower and none concerned major Hollywood films.

108. "Reds in Paris Protest Africa Speaks Picture," *Chicago Defender*, May 16, 1931, 5; " 'Ingagi,' Motion Picture, Gets in Trouble in Chicago," *Chicago Defender*, July 26, 1930, 7.

109. The NAACP, which had previously challenged *Time* (the owner of the March of Time newsreel) for its racism, joined with Associated Film Audiences (a leftist film criticism organ) and the Federal Council of Churches in waging a campaign made up of press releases and open letters openly announcing their disapproval. "NAACP Hits 'March of Time' as Vicious in Political Broadcast: Charles H. Houston Writes," *New Journal and Guide*, September 19, 1936, 4. For St. Claire Bourne, whose *Amsterdam News* review carefully attended to shot structure, the problem was that the film characterized Harlemites as a "group of primitive, ignorant savages, devoid of any knowledge of the civilization surrounding them." St. Claire Bourne, "Harlem 'Black Magic' Film Arouses Storm of Protest," *New York Amsterdam News*, March 27, 1937. Later in 1938, White again protested *Time's* reference to Negroes as "Darkies" in an article about Joe Louis. "NAACP Protests on Epithet by 'Time,' " *New York Amsterdam News*, July 23, 1938, 1.

110. Manny Farber, "The Great White Way," *New Republic*, July 5, 1943. For Archer Winsten quote, see Delores Calvin, "Varied Comments on 'Cabin in the Sky,' " *Atlanta Daily World*, June 30, 1943.

111. William Grant Still, "Charges Music Degrading, William Grant Still Quits All-Negro Film: Noted Composer Admits Disgust," *Atlanta Daily World*, February 16, 1943, 2.

112. Ethel Johnson and Alice Webb to Irving Mills, March 11, 1943, NAACP LOC.

113. The IFRG was originally called the Committee for Unity in Motion Pictures. Leon Hardwick, "MGM to Produce 'Uncle Tom's Cabin,' " *New Journal and Guide*, February 12, 1944.

114. Leon H. Hardwick, "Lena Horne Turns Down Lead in Filming of 'Uncle Tom's Cabin': Lewis Stone to Be Kind Master," *Atlanta Daily World*, February 15, 1944, 2; Fredi Washington, "Headlines and Footlights," *People's Voice*, February 5, 1944.

115. "No Uncle Tom Revival," *Afro-American*, March 18, 1944, 4. Rea stated, "No self-respecting person regards portrayal of the humiliation and degradation of his forbears as entertainment and education." E. B. Rea, "Encores and Echoes," *Afro-American*, January 20, 1945, 8.

116. E. B. Rea, "The 'March of Slaves' Will Be Propaganda," *Afro-American*, February 12, 1944, 8.

117. "No Uncle Tom Revival," *Afro-American*, March 18, 1944, 4.

118. "*Uncle Tom's Cabin* and Unity," *Kansas City Call*, February 11, 1944.

119. Walter White to John Haynes Holmes, October 24, 1945, NAACP LOC.

120. Memorandum to NAACP Branches, November 5, 1945, NAACP LOC.

121. Leon Hardwick, " 'Tom' Plans Are Shelved by MGM," *Atlanta Daily World*, February 20, 1944, 8.

122. "Guild Assails 'Lewd' Play Which Would Star Lena Horne on Broadway: 'Woman' Viewed Vicious Vehicle," *Afro-American*, September 8, 1945, 10; Herman Hill, "Controversy Rages over MGM's 'St. Louis Woman,' " *Pittsburgh Courier*, September 8, 1945, 20. The IFRG was "an educational organization" for "developing interracial understanding and protecting the interests of minority groups as represented through the media." Rex Ingram was chairman and a mix of left-leaning civil leaders and actors made up the board (IFRG Prospectus, undated, NAACP LOC).

123. Fredi Washington, "Fredi Says," *People's Voice*, August 18, 1945, 22.

124. Walter White, *A Man Called White* (Athens: University of Georgia Press, 1995), 338.

125. Walter White, undated letter draft to Arthur Freed, NAACP LOC.

126. Walter White to Countee Cullen, September 4, 1945; Walter White to Countee Cullen, September 19, 1945, NAACP LOC.

127. James Gavin, *Stormy Weather: The Life of Lena Horne* (New York: Atria, 2009), 172.

128. This was not the first or last time Black writers would run afoul of Black activists' racial standards. Angelo Herndon of the Young Communist League used pickets to get Oscar Micheaux to cut scenes from *God's Stepchildren* (1938) that he claimed pitted light-skinned against dark-skinned Blacks. "Motion Picture Withdrawn after Protests in N.Y.," *Cleveland Call and Post*, May 26, 1938, 11. *Beale Street Mama* was part of an IFRG campaign against "inferior," "insulting" low-budget films "dump[ed]" on the Black market by "money-mad" producers from the East and South. "How can we expect . . . better treatment from Hollywood," they asked, as long as these films persist? "IFRG Pickets Close 'Beale Street Mamma [*sic*],' " *Los Angeles Sentinel*, January 23, 1947, 20.

129. Matthew Bernstein, "Nostalgia, Ambivalence, Irony: *Song of the South* and Race Relations in 1946 Atlanta," *Film History* 8:2 (1996), 226–229.

130. "Publishers Protest Walt Disney Film," *New Journal and Guide*, September 9, 1944, C21.

131. Tiny Bradshaw claimed the film, replete with dialect, would make him a "traitor to my race and profession" and "would set my people back 100 years." Leon Hardwick, "Tiny Bradshaw Iggs 'Uncle' Film Role," *New York Amsterdam News*, August 26, 1944, 10A; "Negro Refuses Uncle Tom Role," *Daily Worker*, December 25, 1944; Leon Hardwick, "Bradshaw Won't Speak 'Coon' Language in Disney's Smear," *Afro-American*, August 26, 1944, 8.

132. The critic from *Time* noted that the "tattered ol' Uncle Remus, who cheerfully 'knew his place' . . . is a character bound to enrage all educated negroes, and a number of damyankees" ("New Pictures," *Time*, November 18, 1946). And Bosley Crowther accused Disney of "offense in putting out such a story in this troubled day and age. For no matter how much one argues it's all childish fiction . . . the master-and-slave relation is so lovingly regarded . . . with the Negroes bowing and scraping and singing spirituals in the night, that one might almost imagine that you figure Abe Lincoln made a mistake" (Bosley Crowther, "Spanking Disney," *New York Times*, December 8, 1946, 85).

133. Bernstein, "Nostalgia, Ambivalence, Irony," 221; Cripps, *Making Movies Black*, 192. White wrote Disney as early as 1944, offering to review the script. But Disney preferred that they "get together and talk about the production," a suggestion White, on his way to the Pacific, could

not oblige. Walt Disney to Walter White, July 25, 1944, NAACP LOC. For more on *Song of the South* see Jason Sperb, *Disney's Most Notorious Film: Race, Convergence, and the Hidden Histories of "Song of the South"* (Austin: University of Texas Press, 2013).

134. Walter White, Press release, "NAACP Considers Disney's Uncle Remus 'Dangerous,'" November 27, 1946. White admitted in a memo (January 18, 1947, to Arthur Spingarn, Oliver Harrington, and Gloster Current) that he had not seen the film. NAACP LOC.

135. Walter White, Press release, "Parents Magazine Rapped by NAACP," January 10, 1947, NAACP LOC.

136. "'Song of South' Picketed by San Pedrans," *Los Angeles Sentinel*, March 20, 1947, 5. The quote is attributed to NMU representative Don Wheeldin. "Hollywood Writers Condemn Racial Bias in Motion Pictures," *Los Angeles Sentinel*, March 20, 1947, 20.

137. "Pickets Protest 'Song of South,'" *New York Amsterdam News*, February 8, 1947, 17.

138. Bilboism, a term invented in the postwar years, was the name given to the sensational, racist philosophy espoused by Mississippi senator (and Klan member) Theodore Bilbo, who with open menace and threat opposed Black voting rights and integration following the war. Adam Clayton Powell also joined the protest, making similar appeals to the office of licenses and calling the film "an insult to American minorities, [and] everything that America . . . stands for." Conrad Clark, "Rep Clayton Powell Attacks Film Slurs," *New Journal and Guide*, January 4, 1947, 9.

139. "Brooklyn Movie Chain Ban Sought on 'Song of South,'" *Afro-American*, February 8, 1947, 10.

140. "'Song of South' Picketed," *New York Times*, December 14, 1946, 18.

141. Two women activists who were leading the picket lines, Ruth Mooney and Lynn Earley, were jailed. "Song of the South Pickets Are Jailed," *New York Amsterdam News*, March 1, 1947, 1.

142. "Protest Disney's 'Uncle Remus,'" *Pittsburgh Courier*, August 26, 1944, 13. Faye E. Allen, the first Black woman member of the Los Angeles Board of Education and member of the Mayor's Committee for Civic Unity, assailed the film, as she had the "Little Black Sambo" book she forced from library shelves several years earlier: "Caricatures of the Negro or of any racial group are out of line and unhealthy for the minds of thousands of children." Herman Hill, "'Uncle Remus' Branded Poor Taste for Movies," *Pittsburgh Courier*, September 9, 1944, 13.

143. "Pickets Protest 'Song of South,'" *New York Amsterdam News*, February 8, 1947, 17.

144. "AYD Protests Showing of Disney Film," *Cleveland Call and Post*, January 11, 1947, 11A.

145. Paul Cooke, President, Local 27, American Federation of Teachers, "Song of the South," *Washington Post*, December 28, 1946, 4.

146. "Disney Show Takes Negro Back a Step," *Chicago Defender*, November 30, 1946, 13.

147. "Prisoners Flay Uncle Tom Films," *People's Voice*, February 2, 1946.

148. Alvin Moses, "Nite Life in New York," *Philadelphia Tribune*, October 14, 1947, 12.

149. "'Harrow' Film Misses Boat; Sting Absent," *Afro-American*, October 4, 1947, 6.

150. Harry Keelan, "Voice in the Wilderness," *Afro-American*, October 18, 1947, 4.

151. Lillian Scott, "'Foxes of Harrow' Has Little Appeal as a Movie," *Chicago Defender*, October 4, 1947, 17.

152. White had defused branch boycotts and other exhibitor-level activism in the cases of *Cabin in the Sky* and the non-booking of *The Negro Soldier*. Carolyn Davenport to Walter White, May 3, 1944; A. P. Tureaud, letter to Walter White, July 15, 1943, NAACP LOC.

153. Neil Scott, letter to Walter White, August 1, 1944, NAACP LOC.

154. Roy Wilkins, "The Watchtower," *Los Angeles Sentinel*, June 27, 1946, A7.

155. When White read (in entertainment columns) of new film projects centering on African

Americans or on racial injustice and democracy, like *East River* optioned by MGM, and *Earth and High Heaven* optioned by Samuel Goldwyn, or *St. Louis Woman*, he wrote directly to producers. Walter White to Howard Dietz, August 11, 1945; Walter White to Samuel Goldwyn, March 17, 1947; Walter White to Louis B. Mayer, March 17, 1947, NAACP LOC.

156. For more on White's Negro Bureau, see Thomas Cripps, "'Walter's Thing': The NAACP's Hollywood Bureau of 1946—A Cautionary Tale," *Journal of Popular Film and Television* (Summer 2005), 30–65.

157. Madison Jones to Ray E. Hughes, December 9, 1947, NAACP LOC.

158. The Norfolk branch sponsored *The Burning Cross*, which featured a scene where the KKK tortures a Black man for voting. "Kow-Towing Leaders Flayed by Speaker NAACP Official Tells Norfolk Group," *New Journal and Guide*, April 10, 1948, 5. Upon *Storm Warning*'s premiere, some journalist-activists balked when a North Carolina theater had youth dress up in Klan robes as a publicity stunt. Others used the film content to shame the Jim Crow seating in the movie houses where it showed. But many Black press reviewers praised Warner Bros. for applying its signature hardboiled style to condemnation of the Klan.

159. Also, in Granny's speeches, Roy Wilkins saw "propaganda against social security, maternity and child care, health insurance, old age pension, labor legislation regulating wages and hours of work, health and welfare, etc." Wilkins also took issue with the "central underlying theme, that agitation is wrong, publicity is bad, laws should not be passed to correct conditions, that understanding and good will will eventually correct matters and most dangerous of all—segregation should be accepted and Negroes should 'with dignity' build their own civilization side by side with whites." Wilkins, Memo to Mr. White, August 5, 1948, NAACP LOC.

160. Zanuck accompanied his self-defense with an attack on the organization: "The NAACP has a militant propagandistic attitude in the long fight for civil rights." He fumed at the tone and audacity of their criticisms, claiming that Wilkins's desire to silence Granny's "backward" philosophy would mean censoring the real thinking of many southern Blacks. But the very defensiveness of Zanuck's ten-page letter suggests that the NAACP's criticism had gotten to him. Zanuck was genuinely curious, if also plainly ignorant, about "militant" Negroes and the drama of anti-Black discrimination and wanted to be the first to make a highly successful film treating them. Darryl F. Zanuck to Walter White, September 21, 1948, NAACP LOC.

161. Walter White, form letter to Branches, September 21, 1950, NAACP LOC. The NAACP also issued a commendation, calling *No Way Out* "a masterpiece of film realism in which race hatred in all its despicable ugliness is unmasked to shock the sensitive, torture the complacent, and startle into awareness those blind souls who have never known of the insane violence which prejudice foments" (dictated by telephone, August 22, 1950; NAACP LOC).

162. Henry Lee Moon to Walter White, August 18, 1950; Walter White, telegram to chairman of Board of Motion Picture Censorship, October 20, 1950, NAACP LOC.

163. A local radio program in Chicago even asked White to speak on whether he thought these sorts of pictures did more harm than good. White came out firmly on the side of *No Way Out*'s good for the cause of Black people. White to Sidney Lopez, August 31, 1950; Malcolm Ross to Walter White, July 31, 1950, NAACP LOC.

164. Walter White, "Banning 'No Way Out' Would Be Silly If It Weren't So Stupid," *Chicago Defender*, September 16, 1950, 7.

165. The Black press regularly reported Hollywood's avoidance of interracial scenes in films like *Alaska Highway* (1943), *In This Our Life* (1942), and *Knute Rockne, All American* (1940). After World War II, studio self-censorship of racial tolerance in *It Happened in Springfield* produced protest by the Springfield, Massachusetts, NAACP and a direct public confrontation of MPPDA public relations director Arthur DeBra by Black lawyer and activist Sadie Alexander.

Eugene Zack, "Real Southern Trick," *Chicago Defender*, June 23, 1945, 17; "South Bans Negro Teacher in Movie," *Black Dispatch*, June 16, 1946. Even White earlier recognized censorship as a problem, praising Fox for not censoring *Stormy Weather* after the Detroit riots and questioning Sol Lesser and Warner Bros. about censored prints of *Stage Door Canteen* and *In This Our Life*. Walter White, Cable to Sol Lesser, July 2, 1943; Walter White, Cable to Darryl F. Zanuck, July 2, 1943; Walter White to Joseph Hazen, July 10, 1942, NAACP LOC.

166. Walter White to Eric Johnston, February 19, 1952, NAACP LOC.

167. Constance Baker Motley, memo to Thurgood Marshall regarding *Lost Boundaries*, November 23, 1949. On *The Burning Cross*: Dr. J. M. Tinsley telegram to Madison Jones, October 3, 1947. Madison Jones to Ray E. Hughes, December 9, 1947, NAACP LOC.

168. Thurgood Marshall to Roger Baldwin of the ACLU, July 19, 1944, NAACP LOC.

169. In the late 1940s, Marshall would publicly accuse Hollywood witch-hunters of creating a kind of racial film censorship. Bent on intimidation, Marshall argued that J. Thomas Parnell "investigated writers in Hollywood who . . . dared permit the Negro to appear as regular individuals." "Since the hearings," Marshall claimed to a gathering of the Progressive Citizens of America, "every single instance in which Negroes have appeared in decent light or where a Negro has been called Mr. or Mrs. has been struck out." "Says Negro 'Fall Guy' in Movie 'Red' Probe," *New York Amsterdam News*, December 27, 1947, 2.

170. Walter White, Form letter addressed to "Branch Officer," September 21, 1950, NAACP LOC.

171. "Negro Doughboys Hit Marine's Slur on Air," *Chicago Defender*, January 12, 1946, 6.

172. Though the film also contained blackface sequences, this was not subject to protest.

173. Herman Hill, "Film Studios Pledge Dignified Negro Roles," *Pittsburgh Courier*, July 15, 1944, 13.

174. Earlier White protested the use of the term "darky chorus" to advertise *Belle of the Nineties* (1933). Walter White to Manager of the Paramount Theater, Times Square, October 3, 1934; Dore Schary to Walter White, February 21, 1949, NAACP LOC.

175. Walter White to Louis Lautier, September 19, 1933, NAACP LOC.

176. White noted that the protest, leveled by the Negro Newspaper Publishers Association (an organization that Murphy headed), was "natural" since epithets, though used naturally, were so frequently in *No Way Out*, and "Negroes, like other minorities do not like to have [epithets] used in films. . . . Incidentally," White added, "such epithets are seldom, if ever, used in films depicting the problems and lives of Jews, Italians, Irish, or other minorities." Walter White to Edward Harrison, October 23, 1950, NAACP LOC.

177. Lillian Scott, " 'No Way Out' Hits Bias a Solid Blow," *Afro-American*, August 12, 1950.

178. " 'No Way Out' Hailed as Powerful Drama," *Afro-American*, October 14, 1950, 17.

179. "Pool of London," *Ebony*, October 2, 1951, 61.

180. "Restore Point 4 Funds NAACP Official Urges," *Philadelphia Tribune*, July 18, 1950, 2.

181. Scott also pointed out the civil rights implications of the presence of Freedmen's Bureau founder Oliver Howard in the film. Lillian Scott, "Indians and Intermarriage Get New Treatment in 'Broken Arrow' Film," *Chicago Defender*, July 8, 1950, 14.

182. W. J. Heinman to Henry Lee Moon, July 19, 1951.

183. Marion E. Jackson, " 'Jackie Robinson Story' Is an Absorbing, Dramatic Film," *Atlanta Daily World*, June 30, 1950, 7.

184. Eustace Gay, "Facts and Fancies: THE JACKIE ROBINSON STORY," *Philadelphia Tribune*, May 23, 1950, 4.

185. William Gunn, "Good Lesson for Pirates," *Pittsburgh Courier*, June 3, 1950, 11.

186. Alwin E. White, " 'Jackie Robinson Story' Rated Lukewarm to High," *Atlanta Daily World*, May 26, 1950, 1.

187. Swig, "Amusement Row: 'Jackie Robinson Story' Gets Mixed Reviews," *New York Amsterdam News*, May 20, 1950, 25.

188. Camille Carter to Roy Wilkins, April 12, 1955, NAACP LOC.

189. Herbert Wright, National Coordinator of the Youth Councils, advised Carter to "meet with the manager of the theater and/or members of the film review board of the City of Chicago" but did not join her in the protest. Herbert Wright to Camille Carter, April 21, 1955, NAACP LOC. Despite the lack of national NAACP support, Chicago's NAACP Youth Council protested the film in the press. But the Black press, which confined the protest to the Letters to the Editor section, would not give it the coverage it had previous film protests.

190. The papers of the NAACP clearly document the rise of the Reverend Clarence Dawkins as leader of the Hollywood branch and the new dynamics of leadership, with the Hollywood local using the national NAACP as backup and support, rather than the other way around. In terms of television, the national NAACP had critiqued *Amos 'n' Andy* on the radio, but their full-scale major campaign to have it removed from the air in 1951 demonstrates their greater attention to its televisual iteration. See Thomas Cripps, "Amos 'n' Andy and the Debate over American Racial Integration," in *American History/American Television: Interpreting the Video Past*, ed. John E. O'Connor (New York: Frederick Ungar, 1985). For the national NAACP's critique of early *Amos 'n' Andy* radio programs, see "Amos-Andy Script Draws NAACP Protest," *Philadelphia Tribune*, August 17, 1933, 13.

191. Roy Wilkins, Remarks at MPAA luncheon, Beverly Hills Hotel, October 25, 1957, NAACP LOC.

192. John Morsell to Mr. Jaik Rosenstein, editor and publisher of Hollywood's *Close-Up*, October 29, 1958, NAACP LOC. When rumors of NAACP protest clamored louder than the organization's official stance, Wilkins himself responded. In a letter to *Time* magazine, he noted: "Among Negro Americans there is a division of opinion as to the value of this play. Some regard it as a folk opera, an artistic creation. Others feel that it misrepresents Negro life in America. The fear of these latter is that the public may regard Catfish Row as a typical picture of Negro American life rather than as a period piece depicting merely a segment. Officially the NAACP has taken no position on 'Porgy and Bess.'" This quote evinces Wilkins's film policy in practice—he presents the *various* positions that exist within the Black population rather than choosing, as White often did, one as the organization's stand. John Morsell, letter to *Richmond Times Dispatch*, April 6, 1961, NAACP LOC.

193. In *Cinerama Holiday*, African American New Orleaneans were shown comically "dancing around like monkeys" after a funeral. The offense was the type the national NAACP had stood against providing African Americans comic caricatures in an otherwise "realistic" film. P. L. Prattis, "'Cinerama Holiday' Lacks Quality of First Production," *Pittsburgh Courier*, February 26, 1955, 20. Robert Hairston of the Orange, New Jersey, youth council objected to scenes in *The Snows of Kilimanjaro* where a white man asks a native, "How do you like being the white man's burden?" and where a white woman says of a native child, "Get him out of here. He scares me." Mrs. Freeman, memo to M. Ward, February 2, 1953, NAACP LOC.

194. Milton Hammer, Thomas Hammer, Ruby Dee, Ossie Davis to "friends" thanking them for attending screening of *Gone Are the Days*, September 19, 1963; Adam Clayton Powell to Roy Wilkins inviting him "as my guest" to a preview screening of *Anna Lucasta*, December 8, 1958; "Protest Plan for TV Use of Racist 'Birth of a Nation,'" *Daily Worker*, June 7, 1959.

195. Glouster B. Current, Letter to All Branches in the Metropolitan New York and New Jersey Area Regarding "The Roots," September 6, 1957; Thurgood Marshall to George Staff of Samuel Goldwyn Productions, November 5, 1956, NAACP LOC.

196. Calvin Banks, Memo to Henry Moon, "Reactions to Film 'Voice of the Hurricane,'" June 3, 1964, NAACP LOC.

197. *Hollywood Reporter,* February 2, 1959. Elsewhere she called the film a "fiendish device to injure the pride of colored people in being themselves . . . [and] in their children and . . . to curse every white child with a complex of innate color superiority." "Los Angeles Paper Raps Revival of 'Imitation,'" *Afro-American,* February 14, 1959, 15.

198. As a result of the Oscars protest, Wendell Corey announced that the 1962 ceremony would include a tribute to Black performers. Peterson, still determined, responded by bringing 125 picketers to the red carpet. Police arrested and forcibly removed twelve protesters for trespassing before the ceremony began. Peterson sued the Academy for one million dollars for violation of his civil rights to protest. But the Academy's countersuit, that Peterson had trespassed on private property by treading on the red carpet, held up in court. "Race Relations Bureau in Hollywood Pickets Theatres and Major Studios," *Chicago Defender,* January 27, 1962, 10. Undeterred, Peterson announced plans to protest the 1963 Academy Awards. His protest had a tone of militancy that the local NAACP lacked, promising 500 pickets starting days before the ceremony if the Academy failed to agree to their right to protest. "They roughed up one or two of our boys last year and this year if they try it, they're in for a good fight. . . . We lay the whole responsibility on the Academy, not the police. If they rough us, there will be violence. This is no Martin Luther King movement." "Fear Violence at Oscar Awards over Race Issue," *Chicago Defender,* March 11, 1963, 16.

199. Zanuck himself negotiated with Peterson, but some considered the protest a failure as coordinated activism because Peterson caved to Zanuck's bargain without consulting with CORE. Bob Hunter, "'Longest Day' Not True to D-Day Facts," *Chicago Defender,* October 11, 1962, 21; Dave Hepburn, "In the Wings: What Price Glory!," *New York Amsterdam News,* March 16, 1963, 16.

CONCLUSION

1. Timothy Corrigan, *A Cinema without Walls: Movies and Culture after Vietnam* (New Brunswick, NJ: Rutgers University Press, 1992).

2. Adolph Reed, *Stirrings in the Jug: Black Politics in the Post-Segregation Era* (Minneapolis: University of Minnesota Press, 1999), 8.

3. Thomas Holt, *The Problem of Race in the 21st Century* (Cambridge, MA: Harvard University Press, 2000); Michael Katz, Mark J. Stern, and Jamie J. Fader, "The New African American Inequality," *Journal of American History* 92:1 (June 2005), 75–108.

4. Paul Gilroy, "'After the Love Has Gone': Bio-Politics and Etho-Poetics in the Black Public Sphere," *Public Culture* 1 (Fall 1994), 49–76.

5. Roopali Mukherjee, *The Racial Order of Things: Cultural Imaginaries in the Post-Soul Era* (Minneapolis: University of Minnesota Press, 2006), 87–91.

6. On northern racism during slavery, even within Quaker communities, see Donna McDaniel and Vanessa Julye, *Fit for Freedom, Not for Friendship: Quakers, African Americans, and the Myth of Racial Justice* (Philadelphia: Quaker Press, 2009).

7. Linda Williams, *Playing the Race Card: Melodramas in Black and White from Uncle Tom to O. J. Simpson* (Princeton, NJ: Princeton University Press, 2001), 30.

INDEX

ABOUT THE AUTHOR

ELLEN C. SCOTT is an assistant professor of media history at the Queens College campus of the City University of New York.